WAR AND ENLIGHTENMENT IN RUSSIA

Military Culture in the Age of Catherine II

War and Enlightenment in Russia

Military Culture in the Age of Catherine II

EUGENE MIAKINKOV

UNIVERSITY OF TORONTO PRESS
Toronto Buffalo London

ISBN 978-1-4875-0354-3 (cloth)
ISBN 978-1-4875-1820-2 (EPUB)
ISBN 978-1-4875-1819-6 (PDF)

Library and Archives Canada Cataloguing in Publication

Title: War and enlightenment in Russia : military culture in the age of
    Catherine II / Eugene Miakinkov.
Names: Miakinkov, Eugene, 1984– author.
Description: Includes bibliographical references and index.
Identifiers: Canadiana (print) 20200177869 | Canadiana (ebook) 2020017794X |
    ISBN 9781487503543 cloth) | ISBN 9781487518202 (EPUB) |
    ISBN 9781487518196 (PDF)
Subjects: LCSH: War and society – Russia – History – 18th century. | LCSH:
    Military art and science – Russia – History – 18th century. | LCSH: Russia –
    History, Military – 18th century. | LCSH: Enlightenment – Russia –
    Influence. | LCSH: Catherine II, Empress of Russia, 1729–1796. | LCSH:
    Russia – History – Catherine II, 1762–1796.
Classification: LCC DK171.7 .M53 2020 | DDC 306.2/709470909033–dc23

This book has been published with the help of a grant from the Federation
for the Humanities and Social Sciences, through the Awards to Scholarly
Publications Program, using funds provided by the Social Sciences and
Humanities Research Council of Canada.

University of Toronto Press acknowledges the financial assistance to its
publishing program of the Canada Council for the Arts and the Ontario Arts
Council, an agency of the Government of Ontario.

Canada Council   Conseil des Arts
for the Arts   du Canada

ONTARIO ARTS COUNCIL
CONSEIL DES ARTS DE L'ONTARIO
an Ontario government agency
un organisme du gouvernement de l'Ontario

Funded by the   Financé par le
Government   gouvernement
of Canada   du Canada

Canada

For Hayley

Contents

Figures and Tables

Figures

Tables

Acknowledgments

During one of my daily walks to work, I remember listening to a lecture by the renowned critical feminist Cynthia Enloe, who started her talk by saying, "Here's the hint: always read the preface, first of all it's where all the gossip is!" And second, it tells the story on whose shoulders the author had to stand "to actually produce the book." The "Thank Yous" are not just polite, Enloe continued, they are a road map to how one gets a book published, to how an author makes sense of a larger issue, and they show all the work and people involved in the process. Whatever knowledge we manage to gain is because of other people. Books are children of many parents, and authors require and build on generosity of others.

In the case of this book, the generosity of others helped evolve and refine the final product in at least two significant ways. The project started its life at the University of Alberta. Initially I wanted to explore the emergence of a systematic and conscious examination of the phenomenon of war in Russian thought between 1700 and 1800. Central to my study was supposed to be the question of the role of military thought in shaping the intellectual, political, and cultural foundations of the Russian state. Under the thoughtful guidance of Heather Coleman my approach and questions began to change. I narrowed the scope of the study to Catherine's reign and discovered that I was much more interested in the cultural and intellectual history of the Russian military experience than in the tactics and strategy of the Russian commanders. Heather taught me the art of asking the right questions, and I have learned a great deal from her not only about Russian imperial history but also about being an academic and a historian.

The next evolution of my ideas came from the three anonymous readers of the manuscript at UTP. Their comments made me realize that what I was writing was less about the military culture and more about the Russian Enlightenment, which forced me to reframe the manuscript's aim. I kindly thank the three anonymous readers for their insightful, detailed, and rigorous feedback. I believe that the result is a much better book.

The ideas that found their way into the final manuscript were presented and sharpened at numerous conferences and workshops over the years, including the Association for Slavic, East European, and Eurasian Studies (ASEEES), the British Association for Slavonic and East European Studies (BASEES), the Canadian Association of Slavists (CAS), and the Study Group on Eighteenth-Century Russia. A portion of chapter 2 appeared as "'Your Excellency needs only to wish it': Awards and Promotion Culture in the Army of Catherine II," *The Russian Review* 75 (July 2016): 457–76. I also presented several of my early chapters to the East Europeanist *kruzhok* at the University of Alberta. I am thankful to everyone who participated, especially Victor Taki, Eduard Baidaus, Elena Krevsky, John-Paul Himka, Jelena Pogosjan, David Marples, Franz Szabo, Scott Robertson, and Jeremy Caradonna. At Swansea University, at the seminars in the Department of History and in the Department of Political and Cultural Studies, I benefited from feedback from Luca Trenta, Dion Curry, Bettina Petersohn, Alan Collins, Gerard Clarke, Jonathan Dunnage, Catherine Fletcher, and many others. Matt Wall's question about what my control variable is has now became legendary.

In the past five years, many individuals have read parts of or the whole of the manuscript, and I benefited greatly from their knowledge, comments, and discussions. Leighton James read chapter 3 and suggested that I think of the Russian experience in the wider context. Jordan Claridge and Richard Hall read chapter 6 and made me think about the particulars of the Russian military culture and how it compared to the British one. Gerry Oram read chapter 4 and Robert Bideleux read chapter 5. Michael Sheehan took the time to read and comment on the entire manuscript, pointing out lapses in style and argument and showing me how my work fits into the larger literature about European military culture. Dennis Schmidt provided a critical evaluation of the significance of my larger argument.

Beyond intellectual support and asking the right questions, producing a book takes time, costs money, and requires professional help. Here, I am grateful to many institutions and individuals. Especially I want to thank my editor, Stephen Shapiro, and his team at UTP for their timely help, professionalism, guidance, and advice. Whatever faults remain are my own. This book benefited greatly from financial support from the Canadian Federation for the Humanities and Social

Sciences, especially from an award by Scholarly Publications Program. The final manuscript of the book was completed during a half-year sabbatical in 2018 at Swansea University. The research has been generously funded by the University of Alberta and by the Social Science and Humanities Research Council of Canada (SSHRC). Not only has the funding enabled me to go on numerous research trips to Moscow, but in 2012 the Michael Smith Foreign Study Supplement provided me with a host supervisor, Elena Marassinova, a senior fellow of the Russian History Institute at the Russian Academy of Science, my host institution in Moscow. Professor Marassinova, an expert on the eighteenth-century Russian nobility, encouraged me to think in new ways about the Russian experience in the eighteenth century and introduced me to many of her Russian colleagues.

In Russia, the Russian State Military History Archive could have been an intimidating experience for a new researcher, but the staff – and Kirill Tatarnikov especially – were patient, accommodating, and helpful in answering my questions and inquiries. The staff at the department of military literature in the Russian State Library showed a great interest in my project and made numerous suggestions about available literature. The staff at the Russian State Archive of Old Acts has been equally accommodating.

Finally, my family and friends have provided continuous support and encouragement. My children Hugo and Adele have spent the first years of their life with their father living part-time in the eighteenth century. I want to thank my wife, Hayley, in particular. She contributed more to this book than she imagines, she cheered me on when the going got tough, and over the years became an expert in Russian history in her own right. I am thankful for her patience and good humour, and it is a great pleasure to dedicate this book to her.

Note on Translation, Spelling, and Dates

All translations from Russian are the author's own, unless specified otherwise. The Library of Congress transliteration system was used to render Russian words into English. Where Russian words are used in plural, a "y" instead of an "s" has been added (e.g. *soldaty* in place of *soldats*). The dates on all documents are given as listed in original sources.

Abbreviations

PSZ   *Polnoe Sobranie Zakonov Rossiiskoi Imperii*
RGADA   *Rossiiskii Gosudarstvennyi Arkhiv Drevnikh Aktov*
RGB OR *Rossiskaia Gosudarstvennaia Biblioteka, Otdel Rukopisei*
RGVIA   *Rossiiskii Gosudarstvennyi Voenno-Istoricheskii Arkhiv*

WAR AND ENLIGHTENMENT IN RUSSIA

Military Culture in the Age of Catherine II

The Enlightenment, the Army, and the State

In 1795, a short historical play by an anonymous author was quietly published by a press in Saint Petersburg. The play, *Zelmira and Smelon or the Storm of Izmail,* used the love affair between a Russian officer and the daughter of a Turkish military commander to recount the events of December 1790, when the Russian army finally took the Turkish fortress of Izmail in a desperate and bloody assault. Rich in drama and personalities, the siege has long attracted the attention of historians and contemporaries. Our mysterious author was none other than General Pavel Potemkin (1743–1796), nephew of Prince Grigorii Potemkin, the renowned favourite of the Russian Empress, Catherine the Great. The lesser-known nephew had participated in the inglorious siege and had experienced first-hand the horrors of the battle for the walls of Izmail. We do not know how long it took Potemkin to finish the play, why he wrote it, or why he published it anonymously five years after the event. For him it may have served in part as a therapeutic exercise, a way to work through a traumatic experience. Potemkin was probably trying to come to terms with a disturbing military moment in his life that clashed with the world of the Enlightenment he inhabited. He wanted to share his thoughts about the nature of war with the broader society, and a play was a fashionable way to do that.

In a classic case of blaming the victim, Potemkin worked through his feelings of anger, shame, and frustration as he tried to reconcile the massacre of 30,000 civilians with the values of Russian military culture. In his play, after the Russian forces at last captured the fortress, the Turkish commander begged him to "spare the blood of the innocent." To these pleas, the play's main protagonist, the Russian officer Smelon, angrily retorts, "Your stubbornness has ruined us and the city; You! you are to blame for all of this." The Turkish commander replies that by resisting the Russians to the last soldier, "I was performing duty for my fatherland," the same duty Potemkin and other Russian officers had been performing for Russia.[1] This duty helped justify the uglier acts of war, for it meant that the Turks, not the Russians, were to blame for the massacre. It was much easier to blame Turkish stubbornness than to acknowledge the breakdown in Russian discipline or even the quiet acquiescence of the Russian officers that resulted in the deaths of women, children, and disarmed Turkish prisoners.

Through the eyes of a captured Turkish pasha, Potemkin painted the picture of the price the Russian military paid for Izmail:

> We gazed upon dark marvels, never seen before;
> We gazed, by horror stricken,
> How blood in rivers flowed from heaps of conquered soldiers,
> How death devoured life in vicious cycle;
> All that fills the human heart with abhorrence [...]
> It was as if nature made a groaning sound;
> The air howled from screams, from stench it thickened.
> We clashed, and slashed on piles of lifeless bodies.

This passage describes acts of vulgar cruelty, yet it does so in humanistic, Enlightenment, and philosophical language. Through the pasha, Potemkin was bemoaning the abyss of evil into which the war had taken both the Turkish and the Russian soldiers:

> Our stubbornness helped to hold our shields with hope.
> Your every step had to be washed with blood [...]
> But apparently God wanted to make your bravery famous.[2]

Similarly, surveying the city after the siege, and observing the aftermath of the Russian massacre, Smelon cries out:

> A horrible sight! A miserable condition!
> We try to render them all assistance,
> That in the hour of despair one can only give,
> Oh! How many people are condemned to suffer in their lives![3]

In Smelon's gaze we feel the tension between the Enlightenment sensibility and the actual outcome of war. Potemkin yearned to resolve this tension between what he saw that day and the values of a military culture informed by heroism, professionalism, and humanism. Potemkin sympathized with the enemy he had conquered that day, and by incorporating the view from the other side of the parapet – that of the Turkish commander and his daughter – he was expressing his dismay at the nature of war.

With its wider obligatory themes of personal sacrifice and duty to defend the fatherland, and with its paeans to Catherine,[4] the play was part of a larger Enlightenment discourse among the Russian military relating to war, its conduct, and its consequences. As he recounted the past siege, Paul Potemkin showed himself to be part of something new – part of a group of people who were contributing to new military practices and a new military ethos, one that took root in Russia during the reign of Catherine II. The generals who had fought for Peter the Great had not written lyrical poems about their military experiences. Nor did Christoph Münnich, who founded the Cadet Corps in 1730s, nor did Stepan Apraksin, the Russian commander during the Seven Years' War in the 1750s. Neither of these men had revealed their thoughts on the conduct or nature of war in the same intimate way that Potemkin had done, or try to reconcile their profession with the harm it inflicted on the world around them. While it is easy to overestimate the impact of the Enlightenment on warfare, *something* was changing in military culture at the end of the eighteenth century.

Only recently has this change begun to command the curiosity of historians. Intermittent work over the past thirty years has started to bridge the gap between Enlightenment practices and the military sphere. For example, research about eighteenth-century France has revealed that army leaders shared the language and ideals associated with the Enlightenment. The officers were largely secularist, and practical in outlook; they welcomed change and wanted to solve problems in the same way that engineers tinkered with their machines.[5] More generally, for the European military, the Enlightenment simultaneously had an effect on tactical thought and "inspired a kind of controlled revolution from above," one that was reflected in new physical, political, and ethical constraints in warfare.[6] In the process, ideals of the larger Enlightenment rooted in reason, professionalism, merit, mutual self-respect, sensibility, and pursuit of knowledge entered the military.

The Enlightenment emphasized reforms that would elevate societies above superstition, cruelty, and ignorance; it called for rational analysis of social policy, of institutions, and of politics. Some historians of the Enlightenment, such as Peter Gay, thought that war was a foreign agenda for this movement, but Armstrong Starkey and other scholars disagree. Anyone could be part of the Enlightenment provided that they professed its values and played an active part in their society, took an interest in shaping it, and took responsibility for its welfare, its coherence, and its continuity. It was in this sense that the military participated in the Enlightenment and that the Enlightenment influenced military culture.[7] The military soon realized that the catechizing spirit of the Enlightenment could be placed at the service of war and began to apply that spirit to problems specific to the military – to officers, soldiers, and the army as an institution. The broader military community of the Enlightenment lamented that war "was ruled by 'arbitrary traditions,' 'blind prejudices,' 'disorder and confusion.'"[8] The Enlightenment wanted apply a system to this chaos, to study it, to map it, so that war could be better understood, soldiers could be better trained, and officers could be better educated. Finally, the relationship between the Enlightenment and war was deeply dialectical. The Enlightenment shaped the thinking about and the practice of war, and conversely, the practice of war in the eighteenth century – especially the Seven Years' War – informed Enlightenment thought.[9]

My interpretation of the intersection of the Enlightenment and war in Russia has been influenced by Christy Pichichero's recent book, *The Military Enlightenment*, which provides a frame of reference for thinking conceptually about military culture in the eighteenth century. Taking inspiration from Madeleine Dobie's contention that the second half of the eighteenth century saw "the appearance of the first true meta-discourse on the aims and effects of war,"[10] Pichichero labelled this meta-discourse the Military Enlightenment. The Military Enlightenment was an intellectual and cultural movement that systematically contemplated the nature and conduct of war, pondered what martial characteristics were desirable, explored the relationship between the military and civilian spheres, and assessed the effects and costs of war for states and for individual soldiers. As such, the Military Enlightenment had two impulses or strands, which usually but not always reinforced each other.[11] The first was the commitment to uphold rational, moral methods in military activity, *esprit philosophique*, as they affected war aims and strategy, honour and merit, discipline and professionalism. But the Military Enlightenment also went beyond the philosophical questions – it was interested in affecting practical change in military institutions, in the mentality of the officer corps, and in how war was practised. This second strand, *technicalism*, involved seeking greater technical proficiency as well as the deployment of the scientific method in pursuit of improvements to planning, engineering, logistics, schematization, and quantification. Thus, the subjects covered by the writers of the Military Enlightenment included sodiers' uniforms, their training, tactics and weapons, the behaviour of officers, and the role of religion in war, as well as military education and the very meaning of professionalism.[12]

The Enlightenment inspired military writers and reformers to advocate alternatives to harsh modes of discipline and punishment and to provide models and mechanisms for techniques that worked on a psychological level. These men wanted to put down the lash and explore psychology, indoctrination, and positive reinforcement as means to motive soldiers and discourage desertion. They wanted to make officers more qualified and to strengthen soldiers' confidence in their leaders. In their efforts to extract new resources from conscripts and officers alike, and to improve morale and commitment, Enlightenment military writers and reformers looked beyond the physical body and sought new sources of energy in the realm of the mind. In the process, the Enlightenment sharpened the boundaries of military culture, helped officers find a new sense of purpose in their profession in a rapidly changing world, and began to define a *military* identity for soldiers and officers in addition to their peasant or noble identities.[13] All of this is evident in military manuals of the time with regard to attitudes toward the military, individual soldiers, and war in general. To capitalize on these new trends was arguably even more important for the Russian military than for Western forces, for Catherine's soldiers served for a quarter of a century and the Russian military had to meet challenges on a scale very different from that of smaller European monarchies.

In this book, I contribute to the exploration of the Military Enlightenment by shifting the focus from Western Europe to Russia. While I build on existing insights from Pichichero and others, this works attempts to go beyond them. The overarching argument here is that the Enlightenment had an important, deep, and lasting impact on Russian military culture. This is a new argument. The conventional wisdom among historians writing about Russia and the Enlightenment has been to ignore the interaction between war as a cultural practice and the Enlightenment as an intellectual movement. This relationship has not been explored previously either in Russian or in English scholarship, which is true for both older and newer works about the Russian Enlightenment.[14] While there is a sizeable literature about the Enlightenment's impact in Russia on administration, economy, government, manners, literature, and theatre, the analytical framework that would enable us to provide an account of this impact on the military does not exist. By situating itself at the point of convergence of War and Society and Enlightenment studies, this book begins to address this gap.

While focusing on the military, the argument also has significantly wider implications. First, it challenges the narratives of Russian *samobytnost'*, or cultural and intellectual independence from the West that underscored nineteenth-century debates between Slavophiles and

Westernizers and that continues to shape debates about Russian identity today. Second, the book challenges the traditional picture of the Russian military. Instead of being successful because of its backwardness or non-Western practices, Catherine's military was successful because it mobilized and instrumentalized elements of the European Enlightenment.[15] Third, this work addresses the larger question of militarization in Russian history. While Catherine's reign was not a sponsor of ardent militarism, the practices that were nurtured by the Military Enlightenment laid the foundations for militarism in Russia.

Each chapter examines a specific way in which the Enlightenment influenced military culture, be it through the creation of a military proto-intelligentsia, through patronage and education, or through concepts of merit, ideas about the military profession, thinking about soldiers, or personal behaviour. How did members of the military – and here we are talking invariably about noble Russian officers – reconcile the Enlightenment ideas of "equality and moral worth of all humans" with the Russian reality, a reality based on strict hierarchy, absolute respect for authority, and subordination to seniority and everyday brutality of military life? Did the writings of Catherine's generals have a place within the broader Enlightenment discourse? Did the Russian military participate in the wider public sphere? Did the Military Enlightenment further separate the military culture from that of the nobility, and if so, what were some of its values and how were they expressed?

Before attempting to answer these questions, we need to consider what military culture *is* and why it is a useful analytical concept. Investigating military culture offers an opportunity to approach the Enlightenment in Russia from a "de-centred perspective – neither from below, nor from above, but from the side," that is, from where thought and culture, war and bureaucracy, soldiers and officers, institutions and individuals were commingled.[16] This will indicate another way in which the Enlightenment entered Russia and how the military was influenced by the broader Enlightenment discourse just as were writers, poets, philosophers, and social and political reformers.[17]

Over the past twenty years, historians and sociologists both in Russia and in the West have carried out a multifaceted treatment of the term "military culture." It has been described as comprising both formal and non-formal cultures, each of which incorporates material and spiritual components, including established value systems, religious-ideological imperatives, and symbolic elements. It includes the political culture of the army, its administrative culture, its disciplinary culture, and its military-technical and General Staff culture, as well as the culture of relations *within* the military.[18] To this, we can add "language, mentality, ethics, the philosophy of military men, as well as physical culture."[19] Recently, scholars have refined the term by adding masculinity, total- ity, regulation of the body, sacramentality, and the ability to influence the culture of society at large. In theorizing military culture I have also been influenced by Isabel Hull and Laurence Cole. Hull's work exam- ined the influence of German military culture on German practices in war. Borrowing concepts from cultural anthropology and the sub- field of organizational culture, particularly from the works of Clyde Kluckhohn and Edgar H. Schein, Hull defined military culture "as a way of understanding why an army acts as it does in war."[20] Hull was interested in institutional extremism, or in explaining why the German army resorted to extreme violence in its conduct of war; Cole asked to what extent military culture "permeated the Austrian society" in the late nineteenth century and what the consequences of this were. Thus, Cole used military culture "to describe the impact and meaning of mil- itary symbols, ideals, and behaviour in a society as a whole."[21] Taking inspiration from Hull and Cole, this study is interested in the ideas, aspirations, values, and behaviour that shaped Russian officers' atti- tudes toward war and the profession of arms. With this goal in mind, I use military culture as a unifying term for a variety of processes that helped the military define its own distinct system of beliefs in the last forty years of the eighteenth century.

My guides for the world of eighteenth-century military culture have been cultural historians and practitioners of the war-and-society strands of military history. From Robert Darnton and Clifford Geertz I have learned how to approach an unfamiliar system of meaning and come to terms with the proverb that the past is indeed a foreign country.[22] Yurii Lotman and Marc Raeff taught me to think of the Russian nobility as an incredibly complex and heterogeneous social and cultural group with its own interests and agendas, which consistently escape reduc- tionism.[23] Lotman especially helped me see the nobles of Catherine's period as individuals and to think of the eighteenth century as a pivotal time in Russian history or, as he called it "the century of fracture [*vek pereloma*]."[24] Richard Wortman taught me the importance of ceremony, symbols, and rituals.[25] Rafe Blaufarb turned my attention to the letters of recommendation, and from David Bell I learned how to conceptual- ize war in cultural and intellectual terms.[26] Military historians Jeremy Black and Azar Gat challenged me to ask questions beyond the narrow purview of the drums-and-trumpets school of military history.[27]

This project makes use of a wide variety of sources, including previ- ously untapped materials from the chancelleries of Catherine's military commanders, such as letters of recommendation, and secret surveillance reports from the Russian State Military History Archive (RGVIA) and the Russian State Archive of Old Acts (RGADA) in Moscow. In addition to archival sources, this study draws on a broad array of printed materials. Memoirs and diaries serve as a window onto the early years of military officers, one that allows us to understand their intellectual and cultural upbringing and their cultural journey. Finally, military manuals present another set of overlooked materials. I have collected more than twenty military manuals that were written in Russia during Catherine's reign; they are analysed here for the first time. By combining memoirs and private correspondence with institutional sources such as letters of recommendation and military manuals, this study seeks to engage Russian military culture on a personal rather than bureaucratic level and to shed light on the lived experiences of people who were part of that culture. Where appropriate, I try to draw comparisons with the West to put Russian developments into perspective.

The Enlightenment and the Military in Russia

Russia's engagement with the Enlightenment commenced only in the second half of the eighteenth century, largely coinciding with the reign of Catherine II. The Enlightenment in Russia saw the circulation of ideas that challenged established beliefs about relations between serfs and nobles, questioned the authority of the Orthodox Church, and tested traditional institutions and forms of government. Reason was celebrated as a tool for devising the most rational approach to maximizing the efficiency of the state, the resources of the country, and the happiness and well-being of the people. In this new political and intellectual milieu, opposition to the new empress coalesced around many issues, the most prominent of which are usually considered to have been debates about whether the power of the autocrat should be limited and the question of serfdom. However, what is often forgotten is that there was a third major issue that remained prominent in the minds of Catherine's critics, the issue of war. Even the passionate attack on serfdom in *Journey from St Petersburg to Moscow* by the famous radical thinker Aleksandr Radishchev was "much less immediately significant than denunciation of war" in the context of its publication in 1790, at the height of the bitter conflict with Turkey.[28] The progressive elements of Russian society influenced by the Enlightenment criticized the empress and her wars on moral, political, and economic grounds. Debates about war and the military were therefore firmly part of the larger Russian Enlightenment. Despite this, the task of applying the Enlightenment lens to military culture is complicated by the fact that the Enlightenment was not a homogeneous process – there were many enlightenments across Europe, the Russian Enlightenment being just one of them.[29] Furthermore, the impact of Western intellectual and cultural influences in Russia changed over time. If at the beginning of the century Peter the Great reduced Western ideas to matters of technical and military knowledge that had immediate practical benefit, then during Catherine's reign there emerged a greater sensitivity to moral issues that transcended the earlier narrow, utilitarian ones.[30]

The Russian Enlightenment had several European sources, for Russia was in a position to pick and choose her technological, philosophical, scientific, and artistic ideas from Denmark, Italy, France, Prussia, France, and Austria. French art, conversation, dress, and manners may have dominated Russian cultural life, but the strongest philosophical influence was exercised probably not by the French *philosophes* but by the German cameralists.[31] Germany was closer geographically and had a similar social and economic outlook; that said, the German intellectual universe appealed to the elites of eighteenth-century Russia mainly because it emphasized Christian doctrine and submission to authority, both of which resonated with the autocratic regime. This stood in contrast to more the individualistic impulses of French and Scottish thinkers such as John Locke, Adam Smith, David Hume, Montesquieu, and Rousseau.[32]

Over the past decades, historians have offered various interpretations of the Enlightenment in the Russian context. Some saw the Russian Enlightenment as something akin to an implementation of a cameralist program of reforms. If this was the case for Catherine, then the Enlightenment to her represented a means to maximize the state's power and the government's efficiency and to improve the welfare of her people.[33] This statist view, however, comes dangerously close to dismissing the Enlightenment in Russia as a practice in rhetoric, which would be to overlook the role, values, and aspirations of the educated society.[34]

As research into the Enlightenment in Russia advanced, scholars began to show how this movement transcended the narrow bounds of cameralist philosophy and how it was rooted in ideas that penetrated the consciousness of the elite, how the Enlightenment constituted a search for public good, a duty to fellow men and women. This involved the flow of ideas among the Russian nobility about participating in intellectual and cultural life and using secular, rational, and scientific knowledge to solve problems ranging from government administration to economic reform. [35] I propose to extend this circulation of ideas to the military sphere. This book shows how the broader currency of Enlightenment ideas was strongly reflected in military culture, in which the paternalism of the officers, conceptions of merit, proposals for a more rational organization of the military, and emphasis on education and professionalism were couched in language that was closely aligned with the values of the French *philosophes*.

Reflecting the strides made in previous years, more recently a major effort has been made to bring together the Enlightenment and the rich and powerful heritage of the Orthodox religion. Gary Hamburg has illuminated how the Enlightenment in Russia had its origins in Orthodox religion and its teachings – in other words, how the Enlightenment in Russia blended the Orthodox emphasis on submission to authority with the Western Enlightenment's search for rationality and reason.[36] The Orthodox value system and teachings concerning virtue and human dignity aligned well with similar ideas of the Western Enlightenment, which made it easier for Russians to accept many strands of European thought. In the military, for example, this was reflected in officers who emphasized scientific and professional education while simultaneously theorizing about the importance of religion for their profession. In Russia, Hamburg argued, the Enlightenment was both spiritual and intellectual and there was a stronger continuity in values between the seventeenth and eighteenth centuries than we have previously appreciated. This explains why the secular Western Enlightenment did not contradict Russian doctrines about obedience to authority or Russia's own religious heritage.[37]

Approaches to the study of the Enlightenment in Russia have changed over the years, from asking how Enlightenment ideas migrated beyond the Dniester to how they were practised. Elise Wirtschafter, for example, contends that the Russian Enlightenment was "too diverse and too diffuse a phenomenon" for a precise definition.[38] She is much more interested in what might be termed a "lived Enlightenment." No longer is the focus on tracing how European Enlightenment ideas found their way into Russia; instead there has been a shift to unearthing how Russians practised the Enlightenment in their daily lives, how they lived their lives according to the principles of the Enlightenment as they saw them in the context of the Russian autocracy, serfdom, and Orthodox religion.

I build my understanding of the Enlightenment in Russia on these competing and complimentary approaches. I see the Russian Enlightenment as rooted in education, the rule of law, and humanistic impulses with an admixture of religion and the cameralism of the well-ordered police state. I am interested as much in the transmission of Enlightenment ideas into military culture as in the practice of the

1 Catherine II by Richard Brompton, 1782.
Courtesy of Wikimedia.

Enlightenment by the military. I also take inspiration from recent scholarship about the Enlightenment that sees it as a process full of strains
and problems and without a clear ontological end.[39] Instead of thinking
of the Enlightenment as a set of values, I propose to think of it as set of
tensions, not all of which could be or were resolved.

In the context of Russian military culture, these tensions reared their
heads in many places. Prince Potemkin was an ardent defender of merit
yet he simultaneously presided over an extensive patronage network
of family members and favourites. The military welcomed Muslim
conscripts into the army even while launching inflammatory rhetoric
against the Muslim infidel before going into battle. And the aspiration
of military writers to make war more humane or to regulate how it
was conducted evaporated in the smoke of Izmail. By taking the lived
Enlightenment approach, this study focuses on the experiences of people, their successes and frustrations, rather than institutions and policies.

For military culture, Catherine's reign was a time of transition. The Enlightenment provided the intellectual energy to further professionalize the military, encouraged uncomfortable questions about the condition of peasant recruits, and focused attention on the link between noble status and military calling. Military service meant more than fighting battles; it also involved a commitment to limit waste in resources, an emphasis on secular, scientific education, the abandonment of cruelty to soldiers, and recognition of performance based on merit rather than status.[40] All of this provided a framework for understanding how the Enlightenment simultaneously helped the Russian Imperial Army confront the military challenges of the Napoleonic Wars and made some of its officers susceptible to the very ideas they were supposed to be fighting to destroy.

The Russian Enlightenment found cultural and intellectual nourishment in the "legislatrix persona" of Catherine II.[41] Having risen to the Russian throne in 1762, at the age of thirty-three, she reflected the spirit of the movement that aspired to challenge the arbitrariness of the daily lives of her subjects through laws, edicts, and instructions.[42] Reason and logic would replace the uncertainty and randomness of government actions. However, what distinguished the Russian brand of Enlightenment under Catherine from other Western European enlightenments was that she strove to establish the terms of the conversation around the "ethical activity of shaping individual behaviour" rather than around a discussion about changing the political structure or social relations that maintained the empire.[43] Catherine was more a philosopher than a revolutionary at heart, and her main object was not to change the autocracy but to make autocracy more rational and responsive to the needs of Russia and its people, and to reform the people to be better subjects of the Russian autocracy. The Enlightenment in Russia was therefore filtered through a prism of initiatives undertaken by the new empress, initiatives that included the expansion of education, the creation of a legislative commission to codify Russian laws, the emancipation of the nobility from compulsory state service, and sponsorship of an incipient public sphere. The last third of the eighteenth century was an age of intellectual and political development that engulfed all of Russian society, and the military were swept up in the broader cultural efflorescence of the times.

The impact of the Enlightenment on Russia's military culture must be viewed in the context of the emancipation of the Russian nobility. Perhaps in the spirit of the Enlightenment, but more likely from a desire to placate the noble estate after she had come to power through a coup d'état, in 1762 Catherine upheld her deceased husband's emancipation manifesto to the nobility.[44] This meant she could now redirect the mental and creative energies of the most educated estate in Russia into the running of the empire at the local level. The manifesto marked a psychological and cultural evolution in the mentality of the Russian nobility in two ways. First, the nobility was finally given the power of choice: nobles could serve in the military or in civil administration, or they could retire to their estates. Second, the release from compulsory service, which for most nobles meant military service, meant that the noble could think of himself not only as a warrior, but also as a learned gentlemen – a shift that had been under way in Europe since the Renaissance.[45] Indeed, as Catherine's reign progressed the two would become conflated and reinforced. To be a warrior often meant to be a learned gentleman.

In 1775, Catherine promulgated the reform of local administration, which laid the groundwork for the empire's administration until the Great Reforms of 1864.[46] After Catherine's reforms in local administration, the newly established Boards of Local Welfare set up their own printing presses, and for the first time in Russian history, the countryside was able to read locally printed edicts, and local news, prose, and poetry, some of it written by women.[47] By the end of Catherine's reign, even in the quiet provincial towns, nobles had erected assembly halls and were attending clubs and participating in social life.

The next major reform came a decade later. The Charter to the Nobility, promulgated in 1785, defined nobles' rights and further reinforced the corporate identity of the nobility as an estate.[48] The charter also solidified the noble estate by outlining its rights and privileges for the first time in Russian history. No longer could a noble lose his life, rank, or property simply for displeasing the monarch; instead, a formal trial by his equals was required. The Charter to the Towns was promulgated the same year. This new piece of legislation decentralized administration, gave local authorities more powers, and devolved some of the responsibilities of the central government to the provinces.[49] For the first time, nobles found themselves occupying elective and salaried posts in the provinces with responsibilities for local affairs and courts. Catherine would have to rely on the nobility to carry out her reforms, and the charters were part of the larger strategy of the Russian state to begin to treat nobles as partners.[50] Thus, during Catherine's reign the Russian nobility, most of whom wore a military uniform, enjoyed the cultural and intellectual freedoms, as well as the social confidence, that their Muscovite and Petrine predecessors had not possessed. The new relationship between the state and the nobles should thus be seen as one of interdependence rather than simple vertical subordination.[51]

Out of this interdependence, a social space developed in which military culture had room to define itself and to develop under the aegis of the Enlightenment. The new laws and decrees began to recast the identity of the Russian nobility, their relationship to the monarchy, and their place in Russian society. Many of the nobles served in the military, and they injected this new orientation into their regiments and armies. All of this, grounded as it was in a codified legal framework, allowed space for Russian officers to think about the meaning of their new rights, as well as to contemplate their responsibilities not only to the sovereign but to their own profession, their soldiers, and to the Russian people more generally.

Building on the momentum of the manifesto that emancipated the nobility in 1762, in 1766 Catherine called for the assembly of the Legislative Commission to codify and update Russian laws, the first such gathering since 1649. To guide the commission's proceedings, the empress wrote her *Great Instruction* of some 655 articles, which took her eighteen months to complete. Most of the articles were copied verbatim from Enlightenment thinkers such as Montesquieu or Italian reformers such as Beccaria, and the final document was considered radical enough to be banned in France.[52] Catherine's instruction to the Legislative Commission firmly put many ideas of the European Enlightenment – especially the notions associated with the well-ordered police state – into circulation in Russia. As a consequence of this experiment, which was widely publicized, debating and writing about the betterment of society became a respectable, indeed aspirational, pursuit among the Russian nobility, and this laid the foundations for an emerging professionalism.[53] Furthermore, the instruction set the tone for the writers and reformers of her reign, in that it declared that society should be based on rational laws and that those laws should use the carrot rather than the stick and provide correctives to past patterns of social and economic behaviour, rather than mete out punishment for transgressions.[54] The commission's debates could not have gone unnoticed by the military, especially when so many serving officers participated in its deliberations. For instance, General Aleksandr Bibikov was one of the six people Catherine asked to read a draft of her famous instruction before it was published, and he provided insightful feedback to the empress.[55]

The publication of treatises by Western authors, and their theoretical discussions about rules governing societies, and the publication of Catherine's instruction, all encouraged the military to embrace prominent currents of the Russian Enlightenment. Inspired by the empress, at least some officers took up their quills to write military instructions of their own that aimed to do for their regiments what Catherine's instruction aimed to do for the empire. The military soon had a pro-liferation of detailed instructions and manuals that discussed how to govern officers' and soldiers' behaviour in peace as well as in war.[56] Military writings increasingly deliberated on the qualities of officers, styles of leadership, and mechanisms for integrating recruits into mil-itary culture; they also outlined various logistical and tactical models, offered thoughts about regulating relations between soldiers and civil-ians, and addressed many other aspects of the military profession.

As Catherine's reign unfolded, these home-cooked manuals, as Christopher Duffy called them, multiplied. The tone of Russian military manuals had changed since the days of Peter the Great, when officers and soldiers could to be hanged, mutilated, or beaten for the slight-est infraction; more benign approaches were now being advocated by military writers. In these writings of Catherine's era we find the many strands of the Russian Enlightenment, especially a commitment to what Gary Hamburg called "spiritual illumination" and "ethically grounded rationality."[57] Catherine's general concern for her subjects' welfare was reflected in military writings that began to put the soldier and his well-being at the centre of the army, if only out of utilitarian concerns (rather than humanitarian ones). Education and calls for pro-fessionalism grew louder in tandem, and here we can begin to discern a separation in values and attitudes between a military professional and a noble, a separation that before this period was often difficult to detect.

Institutionalization of the Enlightenment and of Westernization in Russian cultural life was initiated by the founding of the Naval Academy in 1715, the Academy of Sciences in 1726, the Cadet Corps in 1731, the University of Moscow in 1755, and the Academy of Arts in 1757. Catherine continued this tradition by setting out to use education to create "a new type of people" – to transform the Russian nobility into dutiful, rational, modern, enlightened subjects. Catherine's grandiose ideas about social engineering found expression in her efforts in the 1760s and 1770s to create and encourage a system of national educa-tion throughout the Russian Empire, but time soon showed that it was much easier to author instructions and edicts than to overcome lazy students, thieving administrators, and cruel teachers.[58] Nonetheless, the Smolnyi Institute for Noble Maidens was founded in 1764 and the Russian Academy of Letters opened its doors in 1787. The impact of Western, especially cameralist ideas continued and was amplified by the influence of German tutors and schoolmasters, including in the Cadet Corps, which prepared many nobles for military service. Cadet education emphasized among the future military elite the importance of scientific knowledge, the virtues of military service, obedience to and respect for the sovereign, the development of a community of military professionals, and the study of languages.[59] When these men grew up and began to write their own military manuals and thereby shape military culture, they perpetuated Enlightenment ideas they had encountered during their schooling. The impulse for national education extended to the military as well, where officers took the cue from their empress and began to create a "new type of officer" and to lay the foundations for the nineteenth-century military professional.

In this new era, study of the French and German languages meant that the Russian nobility was no longer shielded from contemporary European literature about politics and philosophy. Furthermore, the adoption of foreign languages by the Russian nobles meant that now they could read and collect books about the privileges and responsibilities of European nobility. In their encounter with Western luminaries, the Russian nobles discovered concepts of personal self-worth, honour, liberty, dignity, and national consciousness.[60] For instance, the Russian encounter with concept of honour meant that starting in the eighteenth century, *valeur*, *honneur*, and *service* became as important to the identity of the Russian military as they were for the Western ones.[61] Many military men were actively involved in this encounter and helped disseminate Western ideas in Russia. For example, General Pavel Potemkin published a translation of Rousseau's *Discourse on the Origin and Basis of Inequality among Men*.[62] Also imported from the West was the concept of noble ethos, which connected one's life to duty to the nation and to society. Even before the eighteenth century, noble ethos had become mixed with military ethos, which varied across the nobilities of Europe. The Hungarian nobility's military ethos, for example, was "put to the service of what they understood to be the ancient Hungarian constitution."[63] This gave their military values purpose and set the Hungarian military culture apart from that of other European militaries. In Russia, there was no ancient constitution to shape military ethos, but there was a long tradition of state service. Cossack, Baltic German, Serbian, and Russian authors of diaries, memoirs, and military instructions did not reveal significant differences in their military ethos, bur rather a convergence and intensification of the commitment to tradition.

Many of the concepts that precipitated a change in the mentality of the Russian nobility were to some extent imported from the West, and Catherine stimulated this development with her edicts. In one of her decrees, she wrote that nobles should no longer sign themselves as slaves when submitting a petition to the empress, but instead sign themselves as subjects. Western ethos was combined with an injection of the self-critical and reflective Enlightenment tradition that had developed against the backdrop of the American and French revolutions; this would lead to a serious commitment among at least some of Russia's elite to propose changes not only in ethical behaviour and in how Russians signed petitions, but also in the realm of government and politics. Some historians have asked whether the Western-style noble ethos and Catherine's reforms created a tension between nobles' loyalty to the state and their estate or *soslovie*.[64] It was no coincidence that starting with Catherine's reign, leading intellectuals began to question the foundations of the autocratic order and whether serfdom in Russia could be morally justified.[65] All of this meant that throughout the second half of the eighteenth century the Russian nobility, many of whom served in the military, "gained a sense of purpose, of a humanly significant commitment that transcended the immediate task in hand," and began to think of themselves as subjects of an empire rather than as personal slaves of the Tsardom.[66]

The public sphere is the final piece in the mosaic of the Russian Enlightenment that we need to consider. One product of Catherine's reformist zeal was that starting with her reign we can begin to detect the embryonic public sphere in the womb of the Russian autocracy.[67] In 1765 the first public, voluntary association in Russian history, the Free Economic Society, was founded, which gives weight to the general consensus that Catherine was interested in building a civil society in Russia, even if she imagined it as being in service to the state.[68] Furthermore, Catherine funded and encouraged satirical journals of all sorts, modelled after English and German weeklies – for some of these she actually ghost-wrote articles. In this way, she and her government created space for public criticism that had been unknown in previous periods in Russian history.

Coterminous with the general spirit of political reforms and internal changes was the relaxation in censorship and publication laws.[69] In 1768 Catherine founded the Translation Society, which published 112 translations. In 1771, Russia's first private publishing house opened its doors, and in 1783 Catherine issued an edict that allowed private individuals to own and operate printing presses without any interference from the government. As some historians have noted, this was part of a process of inventing a public sphere "from above."[70] As we shall see, the military was also part of this larger cultural milieu, and military writers took the opportunity to participate in this public sphere from above. Some began to publish their own military essays, and others began to translate and comment on European works. For example, a Cossack captain in the artillery critiqued serfdom and wrote social commentary in his introductions to translations of German and French Enlightenment authors.[71]

The proliferation of public presses and the growth in literacy and education among the Russian nobility ensured the publication of original and translated military texts that a few generations earlier would have developed no further than handwritten notes in dusty drawers.

In conclusion, in the last forty years of the eighteenth century, Russia felt the full impact of Catherine's seismic initiatives. Her impulses in education, her creation of the famous Legislative Commission and her attendant instruction, her careful management and nurturing of the public sphere, and her emancipation of the nobility together left a lasting impression on Russian society and culture. It was in this intellectual and cultural world that the Russian military existed, and it was this world that exerted influence on, inspired, and nurtured the minds of Russian officers. From humble colonels commanding their regiments on distant frontiers, to field marshals in their luxurious headquarters, they drew their most lasting inspiration and took their cues from the larger world of Catherine's policies. All of these ideas were absorbed by the military as part of the Military Enlightenment. High-ranking officers had a chance to share their critiques directly with the empress about her legislative projects; others translated and published popular Western treatises. Countless others read works by Western military writers and were well-versed in philosophy, economics, the sciences, law, and government. Thus the military emerged from the eighteenth century carrying within it and indeed reflecting the legacy of the Enlightenment in Russia.

An Army of Success and Contradiction

In 1788, Prince Charles-Joseph de Ligne (1735–1814), a foreigner serving in the Russian army, wrote to a friend from a military camp outside the fortress of Ochakov: "Here in my tent on the shores of the Black Sea, on the hottest of nights which prevents me from sleeping, I go over in my mind the extraordinary things which are passing daily before my eyes."[72] The Russian army of the eighteenth century was an extraordinary institution – violent, massive, and crude, simultaneously innovative and disciplined, successful but full of contradiction and disorder. No wonder the sleepless Ligne was in awe of what he saw and struggling to make sense of it. In little more than a hundred years, this army had shattered Sweden as a military power, pushed back the boundaries of the Ottoman Empire, successfully challenged the Prussian armies of Frederick the Great, and twice defeated the Polish uprisings that led to the disappearance of that country from the map of Europe; by the end of the century it was clearing the Italian peninsula of French revolutionary armies. As one success followed another, Catherine famously remarked that Russian arms were not victorious only where they were not employed. The Russian military successes of the eighteenth century were unprecedented and indeed amounted to a "golden age."

Why was the Russian military so successful in that era? There are institutional and military explanations. Some historians have explained this golden age as a product of growing and improving bureaucratic and fiscal mechanisms, underpinned by "institutional modernization."[73] Taking a long-term view, it was Peter the Great's ability to build on Muscovite bureaucracy and the government's ability to turn the abundant human and material resources of the Russian Empire "into practical power" that heralded the age of Russian conquests in the eighteenth century.[74] Not all agree, though, that the modernization of institutions and their sophistication lay beneath the floorboards of Russian military success. Some argued instead that Russia's military was so powerful because it reinforced and exploited existing socio-economic relationships rooted in serfdom, recruitment levees, and the nobility.[75] Instead of finding the origins of Russian military success in fiscal policy, historian Janet Hartley, for instance, saw it in the increasing control of human and economic resources. Instead of innovating in banking or fiscal administration, the state found a way to devolve the costs of war onto the population.[76] For example, the soul tax levied on individual male peasants of working age increased from 4 to 10 million roubles between 1725 and 1796, while the rents collected from serfs owned by the state over the same period grew from 700,000 to 14 million roubles. Combined with demographic growth, this enabled the Russian autocrats to spend lives and coins on war.[77]

While some historians have sought explanations for Russian military success in the corridors of institutional and political power, others have explained it in terms of military and strategic ascendancy. In Eastern Europe, non-military factors enabled the "use of new military techniques" that strengthened the Russian Imperial Armies.[78] Others have explained Russian military success in terms of a coherent grand strategy that called for cautious infiltration of neighbouring regions by military campaigns, deployment of military forces to specific regions, and the management of a client system of states that encompassed parts of central and northern Europe.[79] This strategy placed new garrisons on the edges of the imperial borders, facilitated communications, and shortened marching distances into enemy lands.[80] As a result, there was a kind of symbiosis between the conquests of new lands and subsequent military successes. Annexed regions and vassalized territories provided stronger lines of defence, worked as springboards for new offensives, and fed new pools of conscripts and taxes into the military.[81] In other words, new conquests made the Russian military stronger, and the stronger Russian military made new conquests.

Others have emphasized the impact of reforms and innovations on military practice as explanations for the Russian army's geopolitical successes.[82] Instead deploying infantry in the conventional way – in neatly packed lines – Russian generals used more imaginative formations such as squares, columns, and irregular troops, such as sharpshooter units. Catherine's armies were also extremely skilful in use of artillery. This flexibility and experimentation was in part a response to the irregular forces the Russian army confronted on the steppes and along the frontiers, an experience many Western armies did not share.[83]

Finally, Soviet historians offered a Marxist interpretation of Russian military success in the eighteenth century. In their view, at least three factors underpinned Russian victories. Developments in industry in eighteenth-century Russia, including in metallurgy, helped make the military materially self-sufficient. Equally important were the brutal recruitment drives among the enserfed populations that supplied the tsarist armies with reliable cannon fodder. But the aggressive tactics followed by Russian commanders were the main reason for Russian military success during the Age of Enlightenment – Russian generals were willing to sacrifice their recruits in battle.[84] Following to some extent their Soviet predecessors, today's Russian historians often explain their country's eighteenth-century military success in terms of the unique qualities of the Russian military (*samobytnost'*) rooted in Russian culture and society. These attributes ranged from how individual soldiers were trained to the willingness of Russian commanders to reject linear tactics, which quashed the individual initiative even of the best-trained recruits and officers.[85]

Historians have provided thought-provoking accounts of the Russian military ascendancy in the eighteenth century. But they do not agree on how it came about, and none of them locate this ascendancy at the intersection of the Enlightenment and military culture. There are those who think that Russian military success in the eighteenth century hinged on particular military initiatives rooted in tactics, technology, and leadership; then there are those who link these initiatives to larger forces of political will and the bureaucracy's greater ability to extract more material and human resources from the bowels of Russia. Blending these two approaches, William Fuller summarized it best when he wrote that in the eighteenth century, military strategy was related to realistic, achievable goals and to the practical questions of "geography, logistics, and climate." Building on these considerations, the state promoted talented military individuals into positions of power, which enabled the development of innovative tactics and made it possible to exploit operational opportunities in the field. Most of these opportunities rested on the shattered backs of Russian peasant-soldiers, who were devoured by endless campaigns, enemy fortresses, hostile environments, and above all by terrible pestilence and disease.[86]

These are powerful and convincing explanations; however, they are incomplete if we do not consider factors such as the size and recruitment practices of the Russian army, its multi-ethnic character, its tactics and logistical system, and its officers and General Staff. It is terribly difficult to determine the exact size of the Russian Imperial Army in the eighteenth century, but by all accounts it was gigantic. It also grew very quickly. At the beginning of the century, during the Great Northern War in the course of which Russia replaced Sweden as the new hegemon in northeastern Europe, the Russian army, cavalry, artillery, and garrison forces numbered 180,585.[87] After Peter's death, by 1774, the infantry alone were greater in size than the entire Russian military had been just two generations earlier.[88] By 1796, the final year of Catherine's reign, her army towered over the European continent, with 522,000 men, at least on paper.[89] By contrast, the Prussian army was about 194,000 strong in 1786, and the British army passed the 100,000 mark during the Seven Years' War, in the 1750s.[90] Only the Hapsburg army, with 315,000 men by 1788, approached Russia's in size.[91] Ironically, the Russian army may have been enormous by European standards, but it rarely if ever impacted the lives of the Russian Empire's inhabitants, because its forces were largely stationed on the borders with Sweden, Turkey, and Poland.[92]

How did Catherine's government amass and sustain such a colossus? The foundations of the modern Russian army are usually traced back to the policy of military conscription, introduced in 1705, which over the century that followed launched seventy-three levies that combed the vast countryside.[93] While there were many conscription systems throughout eighteenth-century Europe, ranging from the British "press-gangs" to the cantonal system in the German lands, the Russian approach was very different from those of other European states in at least two ways.[94] First, in the rest of Europe, armies relied on volunteers and mercenaries, and even in militaristic Prussia, where a form of conscription had been introduced in the 1730s, recruiters had to resort to tricking prospective recruits into joining the military or to outright kidnapping them when persuasion failed.[95] In Russia, recruitment officers never turned to such tactics because the quotas were filled by noble landlords and village communities. The second major difference was that while other European states, such as England or France, had more foreign soldiers than natives under their colours, the Russian conscript armies consisted largely of Russian peasants; some historians contend that as a result, unlike other eighteenth-century armies, the Russian army was a *national* army.[96]

In 1766 the government published its new conscription regulation, which systematized the conscription of all the *soslovia* or castes of Russian society. Under the new recruitment regulation, no one escaped the invasive levees. Merchants, servants on noble estates, taxpayers, state peasants, serf peasants, church peasants, Old Believers, foreigners and Russians working in the admiralty, and peasants working in private enterprises, if aged seventeen to thirty-five, all were subject to recruitment. Peasants and artisans working in industrial centres could arrange for a replacement if they had 120 roubles – an enormous sum at the time. After a levy was announced, regimental recruitment officers would descend on Russian villages and towns over the next two months. Before Catherine came to the throne, military service was for life, but she deigned to reduce it to twenty-five years, which in effect changed very little for most conscripts. (For the Cossacks, and other ethnic groups such as the Baltic Germans, the service was fifteen years.) In 1795 the average age of a fit veteran was just over forty-eight, which made them around twenty-three when recruited.[97] As a result of this process, unlike in other European armies, Russian soldiers became completely alienated from the civilian world by the end of their service, and even those who survived the gruelling quarter-century ordeal often chose to end their days in a garrison rather than their home villages. Being torn from the civilian world for such a long time made Russian soldiers a more perfect target for practitioners of the Military Enlightenment, who set out to accelerate their departure from the peasant culture and its values.[98]

When representatives from a regiment arrived, the villagers would work out a deal with their noble overlord regarding how to select conscripts for the levy. The village council usually designated those peasants for conscription who had committed a crime, failed to pay their taxes, or were accused of theft or laziness. The villages typically saw conscription as an opportunity to rid themselves of unproductive troublemakers.[99] The troublemakers, in turn, anticipating their imminent conscription, would try to resist the draft through self-mutilation, by cutting off their toes and fingers, which would prevent them from marching or firing a musket. Others took potions to cause temporary illness when the army representatives arrived.[100] Soldiers' children constituted a separate caste and were expected to follow in their fathers' footsteps. Many of these youths were able to escape military service, as the state found it a struggle to keep track of them; even so, this was one more way that the army replenished its ranks.[101] For all its flaws and corruption, and despite the opportunities for substitution and desertion, the Russian Empire's conscription system was so effective that it exhausted its capacity only toward the beginning of the nineteenth century.

The first step in joining this military world was the taking of the oath. As General Iogan von Meiendorf (1706–1776), a Baltic German who served in the Russian army all his life, wrote in 1772, "the military oath is the premier and most important union of a soldier with his regiment and with his government."[102] Taking that oath tied the soldiers and officers closer to the institution of Russian autocracy, both legally and psychologically, for every warrior was required to sign an oath of allegiance. The following oath of service was signed by Ensign Fedor Toskisovskii in January 1763:

> As below named I promise and swear before Almighty God on his Holy Bible that I want and must serve, diligently and honestly, her Imperial Majesty, my gracious and great monarch, Empress Catherine Alekseevna, the Russian autocrat, and her imperial highness' son Tsarevich, Grand Duke Paul Petrovich, the lawful heir of the Russian throne; not to spare my stomach until the last drop of my blood ... and try to promote in the best way everything that concerns Her Imperial Highness or her government ... I shall keep all of the military secrets that come to my knowledge ... I promise not to act in contradiction to my oath and thus conduct myself as an agreeable and dependable slave and subject of Her Imperial Highness.[103]

These oaths varied subtly in their phrasing, but many of their points coalesced around clear rhetorical blocks. References to God, Catherine, and Paul, to giving blood, to preparedness to sacrifice one's stomach, the promise to keep military secrets, and physical and moral submission to the sovereign were common to all of them. Their language amounted to a covenant that welcomed new members to service for the Russian royal house and that bound them to the throne. Those soldiers who refused to take the oath or who later renounced it were excluded from military service and exiled.[104] There was also a whole ritual, almost religious in its solemnity, surrounding this important step of entrance into the military culture. "Put the left hand on the Bible," instructed the *Military Statute*, "and the right hand up in the air with two fingers raised. And soldiers need only to raise their right hand, and repeat after the reader of the oath, and at the end to kiss the Bible. This oath is made to the General Staff in the military chancellery, or to Staff, Ober, and Unter-Officers and other soldiers in front of the regiment or a battalion, with flying colours."[105] The ritual of taking a military oath was one of the most symbolic parts of military culture, and not only in the Russian military – other European countries had their own oaths. Taking it signified joining a culture with its own values, laws, and regulations, a culture that by design was distinct from the civilian one.

The Russian military was not only national and Christian but also multi-ethnic and multi-confessional. That the Russian military strove to build a unified culture out of a patchwork of national groups was an important aspect of the Military Enlightenment in Russia. An example of the flexibility of the Russian military culture and of the application of the Enlightenment framework was the incorporation of the Cossack Host, the Hetmanate, into the imperial military world. The Cossacks were runaway peasants who had settled in southern Ukraine along the major rivers. During Catherine's reign the Cossack Host was absorbed into the Russian Empire and the Cossacks were granted special privileges, such as shorter military service, in return for their allegiance to the Russian Empress and for their commitment to protect the empire's southern frontiers from Turkish raiders.[106] In the 1760s the Russian Governor General of Little Russia, modern-day Ukraine, set out to improve the efficiency of the Cossacks as a military force. Using laws as his weapon of choice, the governor general forbade Cossacks from becoming peasants. He also placed them under the jurisdiction of the Russian military laws, while introducing measures to protect Cossacks from abuses by their officers. He borrowed ideas from reforms then being carried out in the Russian military, and demanded equal performance from the Cossacks.[107] Even the distinct Cossack military ranks were incorporated into the Table of Ranks and aligned with the Imperial Army.[108] As Zenon Kohut concluded, "[all of] this constituted another step in the introduction of the Russian military practices into the Hetmanate."[109] By enforcing new legal codes, new responsibilities, and new training based on the Russian model, and by aligning Cossack military ranks with the Russian ones, the Russian military culture slowly but steadily eroded the distinct Cossack military heritage.

The Cossacks were not unique. During Catherine's reign, the military began to organize regiments along ethnic lines, incorporating tribal hierarchies into the Russian military; it even paid the newly minted Bashkir and Kalmyk officers for their service.[110] Officers and soldiers were recruited from all the inhabitants of the Russian Empire. Recruits from the Baltic regions were Protestants or Lutherans; Tatars, Bashkirs, and Kalmyks were Muslim or even Buddhist. In the 1780s one Russian field marshal even experimented with a Jewish regiment, but conscription of Jews began only in the nineteenth century.[111] Most of these ethnic groups were stationed in garrisons along the imperial frontiers and were used as irregular troops. As the century wore on and the empire expanded, many Russian regiments began to take in more non-Russian soldiers. There were even cases of Muslims, and recruits from other confessions, converting to Orthodoxy.[112] The ethnic and religious consciousness of Russian soldiers in the eighteenth century is difficult to assess because the sources are sparse, but it seems that the presence of Muslim and non-Orthodox soldiers and officers was not seen as problematic.[113] The army was clearly aware of its multi-ethnic character, and in the spirit of the Military Enlightenment, its manuals reflected a benign approach toward religion and ethnic diversity. Historians have suggested that in this multi-ethnic environment the Imperial Army may have served as an early vehicle for the assimilation of various peoples and tribes into the Russian Empire, but more research needs to be done on this subject. That said, the heaviest burden of soldiership still fell on the shoulders of Orthodox soldiers from Great Russia.[114] The challenge for the military was how to promote Orthodoxy as a motivational tool, and use religious hatred to stir the hearts of soldiers before battle, while at the same time making the military a place where conscripts of various faiths could do meaningful service for the Russian Empire.

The size of Russian armies would have no effect and its vast numbers would have no meaning if the military did not develop a system for quickly delivering its soldiers and equipment to flashpoints across the empire. Warfare in Eastern Europe and southern Russia presented a logistical challenge well into the twentieth century. The combination of vast distances, difficult terrain, volatile weather, and meagre rations generated intense strain on both the soldiers and the means of transportation, in an age when railways were the stuff of science fiction. Many times during wars and conflicts, logistics determined Russian military success more than strategy, tactics, or the skills of individual commanders. In 1737 the Russians had to retreat from their newly conquered lands in southern Ukraine and the Crimea not because of military defeat, but because the army had exhausted its means of subsistence. Russian control of the Black Sea slipped away with the breakdown in army logistics.[115] Even more jarring was the extent to which supply shortfalls determined the conduct of Russian operations in the Seven Years' War (1756–63).[116] Russian armies had to retreat four times during that war not because they were pressured by the Prussians, but because they could not sustain themselves in the field. The failure of Russian logistics was the real miracle of the House of Brandenburg.[117] The operations of the Russian armies against the Ottoman Empire during Catherine's first Russo-Turkish War (1768–74) were likewise beholden to logistics. The Russians finally crossed the mighty Danube in 1771 but were forced to retreat to the eastern bank when they failed to establish supply bases.

These experiences taught Russian generals to develop a system of advance depots and to train their soldiers to be swift and well-organized marchers. Low population density on the steppe meant that stores had to be established for upcoming campaigns in advance or supplies had to be taken along. By Catherine's time, the military was turning Ukraine into the breadbasket of the Russian army and establishing a network of forward grain depots along the major river routes in anticipation of future campaigns.[118]

To overcome massive logistical challenges, marches were carefully planned. Every 10 kilometres, infantry would take off their heavy backpacks and rest. The first break was to last an hour, after which the soldiers would move out again. After 20 kilometres, they rested for an hour or more, and after 30 kilometres, if such a distance was covered, twenty minutes were allowed for catching a breath, before camp was set up. This relatively simple system had the potential to achieve remarkable results. In 1769, the Russians under General Aleksandr Suvorov marched from Minsk to Lokshinze (near Brest, in modern Poland) in twelve days. The march was done in twelve stages, and on average the soldiers covered 35 kilometres a day. During the Second Russo-Turkish War (1787–92), Suvorov's troops covered 50 kilometres in twenty-eight hours from Barlada to Adzhud.[119] One of the most famous marches took place in September 1789, when, according to one historian, the Russian forces marched 103 kilometres in thirty-six hours, an impressive feat in pre-Napoleonic times.[120]

Most of the supplies were transported in carts, each loaded with about 400 kilograms of provisions. One cart was required to keep two soldiers in the field for a few days.[121] Soldiers who tried to steal from the supply carts were to be hanged.[122] Also, cavalrymen were released for foraging missions every week. These missions usually lasted one or two days, and care was taken not to abuse local civilians. When it was learned that some soldiers were not paying for their provisions, the army insisted that they settle their arrears with the villagers immediately.[123] Taking anything but fodder could lead to a court marshal, but that probably did little to stop soldiers from looting or abusing local populations.[124] Whatever the foragers brought back complemented the Russian kitchen. It was a spartan life, but apparently the diet was good enough to attract the attention of Western observers. For example,

France's most famous military reformer and a father of the Military Enlightenment, Marshal Maurice de Saxe, recommended to the French army in 1730s that "the Russian biscuit, called Soukari, is the best of all because it does not crumble; it is square and the size of a hazelnut. Fewer wagons are needed to carry it than bread."[125]

As the logistical system evolved, the Russian Army was able to march faster and farther and to extinguish rebellions in newly conquered territories more quickly, thus further cementing the central government's control. As the speed of the armed forces increased, along with the distances they could travel, the Russian armies marched deeper into Baltic, Polish, Ukrainian, and Ottoman lands on systematic and consecutive campaigns. This allowed the Russian state to conquer and hold new territories. Thus from the tiny grain of logistical support grew the political power of the Russian Empire.

As the armies moved around the vast empire, how did the military billet hundreds of thousands of soldiers, artillerymen, and cavalry? The task of locating proper housing for the marching soldiers fell to the *Generalquartermeisters*, who were attached to each regiment and who rode ahead of their troops to find proper billets. Russia did not have enough barracks to house its armies every winter, when the campaigning season came to the end, so the burden of quartering soldiers fell on the civilian population. This problem was especially acute in southern regions. For example, in 1763 there were only 30,000 households in Ukraine to quarter the Russian army of 20,000 soldiers, which meant that every three households had to quarter as many as to two Russian soldiers.[126] The practice seems to have been to place the men in barns rather than actual homesteads. This was done to reduce friction between the army and the local population and to avoid criminal incidents. Before leaving towns, officers made sure that everything their men had stolen from civilians was either given back or paid for.[127] Before leaving their civilian hosts, colonels had to collect signatures from the peasants as testimony that their soldiers had not stolen or caused their families any harm. However, these best practices were often undermined and circumvented, and those peasants who refused to sign release forms were threatened, bribed, or plied with alcohol until they signed.[128]

Since Russian soldiers and officers could not always count on the central government to provide them with the necessary supplies, a unique military institution came into existence. When the government failed to supply new equipment, or deliveries were delayed, the soldiers turned to the *artel'*. Created at the beginning of the eighteenth century by Peter the Great, *artel'* were cooperatives that pooled the communal resources of soldiers as a means to cope with late salary payments and irregular deliveries of ammunition, as well as uniforms. Above all, *artel'* funds were used to purchase food. Each company of about a hundred soldiers had several *arteli* of up to ten members, and each member contributed up to half his pay to his *artel'*. The day-to-day running of the *artel'* was usually entrusted to experienced and reliable veteran soldiers. Considering that military service lasted for up to a quarter of a century, some *arteli* accumulated significant sums of money. While the *artel'* as an organizational form in the eighteenth century remains to be fully explored, some historians have pointed out that it was the military parallel of the village peasant commune. This raises interesting questions about the social forces that shaped the Russian army, as well as the relationship between noble officers and their serf soldiers.[129]

Regimental commanders often relied on *arteli* for assistance when the regiment failed to receive necessary funds for equipment or provisions. A foreign officer serving in Russia during Catherine's reign remembered how the government on one occasion did not send his regiment money for salaries or food for eleven months. This Frenchman was forced to borrow as much as 5,000 roubles from twenty *arteli* in his regiment – an enormous sum for the time. He claimed that he paid it back in full when the funds from Saint Petersburg arrived. However, there were many occasions when Russian officers borrowed *artel'* money and gambled it away without ever paying it back.[130] This organization was a unique and important part of the Russian eighteenth-century army, one that created a symbiotic relationship between officers, who often were short of funds, and soldiers, who as *artel'* members were in a position to be credible lenders to their social superiors. Through their *arteli*, Russian soldiers actually possessed property (unlike their Western counterparts), and this may have helped reduce desertion in the ranks.[131]

Russian tactics departed significantly from those of Western European armies. The deployment of Russian troops into lines was rare in Eastern Europe and was used mostly against Polish forces. The neatly arranged lines popularized by Frederick the Great may have worked well against similar European armies, but they were less effective on the steppes of southern Russia, where the army had to defend itself against the Turkish and Tatar irregulars. Linear deployments would easily have been encircled and annihilated by the fast-moving cavalry of the Ottomans and their allies.[132] Russian commanders preferred to organize their soldiers into massive squares, which was an effective way to reinforce the centre line and eliminate the danger of a flank attack. The infantry usually consisted of *Jaegers*, who were trained as sharpshooters and who covered the flanks and softened the enemy targets, and grenadiers, who carried out the main bayonet attack. Russian commanders also experimented with columns even before the French Revolution, when this arrangement was popularized. Western armies relied on firepower, maximized by linear deployments; in the East, the Russian armies were known for their desperate but effective bayonet charges.[133]

Commanding this military effort was the eighteenth-century Russian officer. He has been the subject of many plays, satires, and novels that have tried to capture the essence of this elusive and complex historical actor, yet he escapes easy description. Despite the 1762 proclamation that emancipated the Russian nobility from compulsory state service, the number of officers during Catherine's reign expanded by more than 4,000, from 8,295 to 12,478.[134] To put these Russian numbers in perspective, in France in 1775 there was one officer for every four soldiers, whereas in Catherine's Russia in 1796 there was an officer for every forty-one soldiers.[135] Similarly, France suffered from an excess of 1,200 generals before the revolution, whereas Russia had only 158 of them in 1792.[136] The officer corps was made up almost exclusively of nobles. Between 1755 and 1758, 83.4 per cent of Russian imperial officers belonged to the nobility, which was a higher percentage than in the Prussian and Habsburg armies.[137] That so many nobles remained in military service had to do with the cultural and social but also economic realities of Russian life. Military rank carried social status, was an important part of the noble identity, and above all provided a source of income for many lesser gentry.[138] The estimated male noble population in 1782 was around 108,000. That meant that more than one in ten Russian male nobles had served as officers at some point. This made for a steady dissemination of military values, military education, and military culture. By 1796, the year Catherine died, the number of nobles in uniform must have been much greater, because by then, 35 per cent of Russian nobles were in some kind of state service.[139]

The century started with a large number of foreigners occupying high military posts in the Russian Empire; but by the 1790s, their ranks had begun to thin out. Even so, there were many Baltic Germans, Cossacks, French, Prussian, Austrian, and even English officers in the Russian army in the eighteenth century, and resentment of them was ongoing.[140] By the time Catherine came to power, only 59 per cent of staff officers were Russian. The lives of all these gentlemen revolved around the infamous Table of Ranks that had been introduced by Peter the Great at the beginning of the century. The Table of Ranks had fourteen grades, ranging from Ensign, grade fourteen, to General Field Marshal, grade one. One's position on the table determined one's status, office, title, and privileges. For instance, any non-noble who achieved the lowest grade on the table gained personal nobility, and if he achieved grade eight and became a major, he was granted hereditary nobility. When Catherine came to power, she assuaged the nobility by making the promotion to the lowest grade on the table automatic after seven years' service. Promotion beyond that depended on length of service but also on merit, as was the case with armies in Western Europe. In France, again as an example, starting in 1750, families that had three generations of officers were given ennoblement, and in the Habsburg Empire, all officers after thirty years of unblemished service were ennobled from 1757 onwards.[141]

By the end of the eighteenth century, officers were also some of the best-educated people in the Russian Empire. Most officers of the 1780s and 1790s generation were literate, more than one third were fluent in a foreign language, and more than one in ten had knowledge of at least one branch of science.[142] The ethos of this group conformed to the broader ethos of the nobility, which formed around ideas of service to the state, either as civilians or in the military, but also around the Enlightenment principles of humanism, education, and rationality.[143] During Catherine's reign, many of these officers began to participate in the Military Enlightenment. The military ethos continued to evolve beyond simple service to the state as officers began to exhibit a sense of association with one another in addition to their loyalty to the Crown, and wrote with pride about their responsibility to defend the Orthodox faith, the Russian people, and Russian lands. Traditional values were being commingled with the Enlightenment emphasis on knowledge, reason, and search for the common good. Some historians suggest that the dominance of the military ethos among the nobility may have dampened the development of other groups and classes of people who were informed by non-military ideals. In other words, it is possible that the military elbowed out the bureaucratic class of civil servants. For instance, toward the end of the eighteenth century, 85 per cent of senior public administrators came directly from the military, and these men injected their experiences, ideas, and values into the civilian bureaucracy. This may have had a negative effect on the development of legal consciousness in Imperial Russia.[144]

In the context of the eighteenth century, then, Russian officers were a significant group of educated, often wealthy, and sometimes politically active individuals who had sworn to protect and serve the Russian autocracy. They were members of the cosmopolitan European elite, consuming Western Enlightenment and Western cuisine with the same appetite. Yet it was these same Russian officers who, contradicting their oath, brought Catherine to power in 1762 during her coup against her husband, Peter III. And it was these Russian officers again who would murder Catherine's son, Paul I, in 1801. Despite these palace revolutions, we should be careful not to see the officer class as a challenger to the state's authority or as some sort of Praetorian Guard. Russian officers did not question the righteousness of the Russian autocracy or the existing social order, at least not yet. It is more helpful to see eighteenth-century officers as playing an important intellectual and cultural role in the life of the empire, with important consequences after Catherine's death.[145]

The officers in the Russian Imperial Army belonged to two kinds of regiments, each of which carried with it a different culture and different privileges, postings, and promotions. The two types were the guard regiments, in the capital, and the regular line regiments, stationed in Russian frontier towns and garrisons. The guard regiments were initially created around the villages of Preobrazhenskii and Semenovskii by Peter the Great at the beginning of the eighteenth century as his play toys. Over time, these two regiments distinguished themselves through their steadfastness in the Great Northern War (1720–1721), during which their officers often died alongside their soldiers in the legendary battles of Narva in 1700 and Poltava in 1709. Peter the Great was so proud of his Preobrazhenskii Regiment that he named himself its colonel, establishing a tradition that all subsequent Russian autocrats would follow. Peter had established these units as training incubators for future officers, who upon transfer to the army would be placed in positions of leadership and command. These elite regiments were staffed almost exclusively by the offspring of the Russian gentry. All members of the Guard Regiments had to start at the very bottom of the Table of Ranks and rise through the grades. That said, the guardsmen enjoyed better pay, access to better medical services, superior food and accommodations, and above all seniority among their army counterparts. The major privilege enjoyed by guardsmen, be they officers or soldiers, was that upon transfer to the army they were eligible for an automatic promotion of up to two military ranks. Thus a lowly ensign in the Guards could become a senior lieutenant in the army overnight.[146] Equally important for the Guards was their role in protecting imperial palaces, which lent them enormous political significance.[147] In the eighteenth century almost all of the Russian monarchs ascended the throne or descended from it through political coups in which Guard Regiments played a key role.[148] Over the eighteenth century, the Guard Regiments became severely bloated with noble youths whose families had enlisted them at birth. By the time these young men reached adolescence they were already sergeants, and the Guard Regiments quickly exceeded their established numbers.[149] The Petrine ideal of the Guards serving as a shining example of valour and professionalism for other officers became corrupted, and during Catherine's reign the Guards never saw active military service.

How was the largest army in Europe managed and commanded? In the eighteenth century, the Russian Imperial Army did not yet have a General Staff in the modern sense. The origins of the General Staff in Russia are usually traced back to early in Catherine's reign, when the military and the young empress set out to address weaknesses and shortcomings that had come to light during the Seven Years' War. When the General Staff was established in 1763, it had only forty officers.[150] At that point, it was merely a helping hand for commanders in the field, in a sense that it was subordinated to them, rather than the other way around. As an organization it existed only in embryo, and its institutional powers were weak. Forceful and powerful individuals in the field often took the reins of intellectual and cultural leadership, ignoring the staff officers tucked away in their Saint Petersburg offices. What precluded the General Staff from reaching its potential during Catherine's reign were influential and jealous commanders, such as Petr Rumiantsev, who viewed the General Staff as challengers to their own power and authority.[151]

The responsibilities of the General Staff were limited to quartering the troops during winter, organizing logistics for army movements, and providing road reconnaissance. They taught officers how to make and read maps, collected statistical and topographical data, and wrote descriptions of battles. It was outside their purview to develop detailed war plans, devise military strategy, produce theoretical works, or organize the material base for the Russian military.[152] As one contemporary concluded, the work of the Russian General Staff in the eighteenth century was far behind that of their French and Austrian counterparts.[153] To address these shortcomings, Catherine invited Frederick the Great's former *Generalquartermeister*, Friedrich Wilhelm Bauer, to shape and improve the Russian General Staff, but he had only a limited impact on the powers and responsibilities of its members. Bauer did, however, bring with him two important ideas from Prussia: that the General Staff needed to have an independent existence as an office separate from the armies in the field, and that staff officers required special training and knowledge in order to become members. Both ideas were hallmarks of the Military Enlightenment, in that they ensured that the General Staff remained an independent department instead of being absorbed by some other government office. After 1772 the General Staff became a department within the War College, a ministry of the central government.[154] It seems that Russian contemporaries gave little thought to the General Staff, did not understand the need for it, and probably did not foresee the role it would play as the eighteenth century drew to a close.

Such was the state of the vast and powerful Russian military machine as it rumbled to meet the challenges of Sweden, Prussia, Turkey, Poland, and revolutionary France in the eighteenth century. Building on this experience, the Russian victory over Napoleon's Grande Armée displayed the resilience and potency of military organization modelled after eighteenth-century traditions "over the armies built on modern principles."[155] Russia fielded the largest army in the eighteenth century, and while its soldiers dressed in European fashion and were equipped with modern weapons, beneath the uniforms the Russian army was very different from its Western counterparts. While European states recruited their soldiers, Russia conscripted them. While in Western Europe, volunteers or mercenaries filled the ranks and soldiers served only during wars or campaigns, after which they were demobilized, in Russia soldiers effectively served for life, prompting some observers to write that Russia had one of the first national armies in Europe. Unlike other European armies, save for the Habsburgs, the Russian Imperial Army was also a multi-ethnic and multi-confessional society, which created both challenges and opportunities for the government. With the Cossacks, for example, the Russian emperors and empresses acquired a reliable military caste. While the government tried to supply its hundreds of thousands of troops with money, food, and equipment, delays were inevitable, and the socio-economic institution that stepped into the gap was the *artel'*, another uniquely Russian creation. Also, military logistics had to adjust to the geographical conditions, which were different from those of other European countries. Since Russian armies had long distances to travel whichever way they went, they had to develop a system that would sustain them if living off the land was impossible, such as in the southern regions. Russian tactics also broke with the prevailing standards of the day, eschewing linear deployments. While other European countries were strengthening and relying on their General Staffs, Russian commanders in the field continued to hold considerable sway over technical and strategic questions in wartime. Perhaps slow communications and the boundless distances between the General Staff and Russian commanders prevented the former from serving as an effective, coordinating brain of the military.

The Russian military in the eighteenth century was laced with contradictions and tensions, but also full of opportunities and drama. It was where Russian culture met, appropriated, rejected, and modified

Western intellectual influences and practices. It was a school for some of the most prominent politicians and writers of Catherine's era and indeed of the nineteenth century. The army fired up the national consciousness within the Russian Empire and made for a frightening apparition beyond its borders.[156] Russia had the largest army in Europe, but it was only as strong as its logistics, and Russian strategy was more often than not a handmaiden of supply arrangements. Russian peasants were destitute, yet they owned property worth thousands of roubles through *arteli*. While officers lorded over their soldiers, sometimes they had to borrow money from them, which must have altered the vertical relationship between the estates and introduced a degree of moderation. The imperial government nurtured its elite regiments, but they became a tool of political intrigue rather than a proficient fighting force. While Russia had a national army, it also had a strong tradition of multi-ethnic and multi-religious tolerance. On the one hand, the Russian military was fighting infidel Turks, on the other, it was tolerant of Muslim soldiers in its ranks. While the officers had an ethos of service to the sovereign, they often participated in coups. What follows is a story of how and to what extent the Military Enlightenment penetrated this giant from the East, how the Military Enlightenment exerted its force on it, and how it slowly saturated the minds of those who served it.

With the above in mind, the first chapter traces paths to military culture through patronage and education, both of which were at the heart of what I call the military proto-intelligentsia. By considering how young nobles were introduced to the military and by documenting their education, the chapter shows the values and traditions of Catherine's military and the slow influence of the Enlightenment on its culture. The chapter argues that patronage provided a venue for getting noticed through informal introductions, mentoring, and recommendations, and supplied young officers with stints of practical service. It was through patronage that some of the most notable and capable men rose to the top of the military. Along with patronage, the chapter argues, military education introduced aspiring officers to a new identity, to specialized professional knowledge, and to traditions of hierarchy, subordination, and hard work. Customs and values cultivated through patronage and education coalesced around the discourse of the Enlightenment, which fostered the emergence of a military proto-intelligentsia.

An important aspect of the Enlightenment was the fight for recognition based on merit instead of social status. Contemporary European writers, satirists, and *philosophes* expended much ink on decrying and mocking the privileges of elites. How did merit become an instrument of the Military Enlightenment in Russia, and what impact did it have on seniority and favouritism? This is the focus of chapter 2, which shows that despite occasional nods to favouritism, the machinery of merit kept steadily humming in the background, and that the tensions between merit and seniority did much to shape Russian military culture.

Chapters 3 and 4 shift to military writers, or as Pichichero has called them, *militaires philosophes*.[157] Chapter 3 analyses military manuals, essays, and instructions, not so much for their military content as for what they reveal about the culture that produced them. Catherine's reign was the first time in Russian history when there appeared a critical mass of domestically produced military literature. Before that time, most works about war were imported from abroad or translated from foreign languages. Chapter 3 shows how this first generation of Russian military essays, manuals, and instructions was influenced by the Enlightenment and how many of the values and proposals of Russian military culture were aligned with the larger pan-European Military Enlightenment rather than truly autochthonous. These early Russian military authors were a community of individuals who wrote, thought, discussed, and often critiqued the military and its culture, and all of this intellectual activity existed in parallel with official military decrees and regulations. Collectively, the writings of this group expressed both the aspirations of educated professionals and the realities of military life. Some of the manuals were actually accepted by the government; others were used on a regular basis in various parts of the army. In the process, the military began increasingly to participate in the wider public sphere. The public sphere was an intellectual and cultural space outside the court and the bureaucracy; it was something that was not directly controlled by the government, yet in dialogue with it; it was something that had developed under its own momentum; it was non-clandestine and collective in its activities. Participation in this public sphere by the military gave the ideas of the *militaires philosophes* both validity and wider circulation. Chapter 4 continues to examine military texts but shifts its focus to how the Enlightenment influenced the ideas about and attitudes toward soldiers. The Enlightenment helped Russian military writers theorize the peasant as a military man and gave the writers a road map for developing his psychological and physical transformation to serve the purposes of war.

Building on the ideas of Richard Wortman and Iurii Lotman, chapter 5 connects the performance of the Russian military culture during Catherine's reign to the Enlightenment emphasis on individualism. The chapter shows how the military marshalled Enlightenment individualism and linked it to the practices of power. The sanctioning of individuality allowed the values of military culture to be symbolically reinforced by the military elite. Here, individual semiotic performances were central to the diffusion and promotion of the Military Enlightenment. I focus on the performance of military culture by three of its most extraordinary representatives, Petr Rumiantsev, Grigorii Potemkin, and of course Aleksandr Suvorov.

Chapter 6 uses the tragic siege of Izmail, an event that sent shockwaves throughout Europe, as a case study to focus and crystallize the themes of the previous chapters. I use the siege as a "cultural site," to borrow William Sewell's phrase.[158] Izmail was not only a contest of arms between the Turks and the Russians but also a cultural arena, a social space where values, anxieties, ambitions, and identities came into focus. Based on published and unpublished sources, both Russian and Western, the Izmail chapter demonstrates how merit was observed, documented, and rewarded; how symbolic behaviour was harnessed for military purposes and to what effect; how the siege served as inspiration for military writing and the solidification of Russian military culture; how it clashed with Enlightenment sensibilities; and how war refused to be constrained by the ethical, physical, and political consideration of the Age of Reason.[159] It was a watershed moment in the political and military history of Catherine's reign, and it was not by accident that Russia's first National Anthem was composed to commemorate the victory at Izmail.

In Chapter 7, the book concludes with the clash between the Military Enlightenment as it evolved during Catherine's reign, with its own traditions, values, and intellectual independence, and the new military culture introduced by Emperor Paul I (r. 1796–1801), Catherine's son. A staunch admirer of Prussian militarism, Paul tried to Prussianize the Russian military. The moment of tension came when it was discovered that some officers actively resisted this process, sometimes by highly symbolic means, such as wearing dressing gowns instead of new uniforms. The clash of the two cultures resulted in exile, surveillance, and reprimands. In the end, Paul not so much destroyed Catherine's military enlightenment as modified it, and in doing so reaffirmed its existence in the early nineteenth century and beyond, when other writers and reformers picked up its threads.

Chapter One

Between Patronage and Education: The Enlightenment and the Military Proto-Intelligentsia in Catherine's Russia

Joining a regiment for the first time and swearing the military oath was an emotional and cultural milestone for many young men in Catherine's Russia. One of them, nineteen-year-old Mikhail Petrov, remembered the day he took his military oath and stood under a regimental standard as one of the happiest in his life. "The time of the beginning of my service in the Smolensk Regiment remained for me memorable ... as pleasant and holy," he wrote. He reminisced how

> for the first time, there glistened and sounded on my young shoulders a soulful desire and the magnificent adornment of a nobleman – a military weapon, entrusted to me by the Fatherland for its protection. There, under the standards, I uttered the oath of a warrior, requiring one to sacrifice one's tranquility, blood and life in defence of the Tsar's throne, the Fatherland, and the Holy faith.[1]

The ritual of taking the military oath had a profound effect on the young Petrov, both psychologically and politically, for it also signalled the beginning of cultural and social identification with the military. Moreover, the occasion when he received his first officer rank was one of the most important in his life. When a young nobleman or even a soldier received a commission, he stepped over a line that separated him from the most privileged group of people in the empire. In that one step he changed his position in society – becoming an officer was more important than receiving any subsequent promotions, more important than even being promoted to the highest of military ranks. For in socio-legal terms, there was little difference between an ensign and a field marshal.[2] After the oath of allegiance a cadet or a soldier became a warrior and a member of military culture. By embracing sacrifice, autocracy, the fatherland, and faith, Petrov was joining a much broader group of people whose cultural and intellectual position remained ambiguous and whose world and values were rapidly changing.

One cannot really talk about the existence of a military intelligentsia in the context of eighteenth-century Russia because it began to emerge as a formal social group only in the first half of the nineteenth century. That being said, a small but growing number of nobles began to systematically examine the phenomenon of war in the specifically Russian context, having been exposed to a new form of military education, and they shared their thoughts with the broader public as well as with their comrades-in-arms. I label this ambiguous and porous group, which existed in the intellectual and cultural space between the ancient regime and modernity, as the military proto-intelligentsia. That term does not mean the same as "military professionals," who have existed in Russia since the founding of the Kievan Rus. Military professionals are concerned with the professional obligations of conducting military actions such as campaigns or wars, which demand special training, and they are united by corporate values. The purpose of the military proto-intelligentsia is to manage the military, and this is linked to the creation, diffusion and communication of military culture.[3] This chapter examines two strategies of this process in the context of the Enlightenment.

This chapter begins by arguing that patronage did not undermine the Military Enlightenment. Patronage was not just an archaic noble practice that sustained incompetence and prioritized social status; it also provided an opportunity to participate in military culture. It was through patronage that some of the most capable men rose to the top of the army. The second part of the chapter examines military education in Catherine's Russia and shows how youths were introduced to a new identity and new customs, as well as to specialized professional knowledge and the traditions of hierarchy, subordination, and hard work. It was here that the influences of the Enlightenment began to leave their intellectual mark on the new generation of warriors. It was here too that the interplay between Enlightenment aspirations and the military became most visible. Instead of examining patronage and education as points of tension, this chapter shows how they were mutually supportive. Patronage networks served as conduits that delivered promising material to military culture, which education then shaped in accordance with the ideas and customs of the Enlightenment. Traditions and values cultivated through patronage and education coalesced to define Russian military culture during Catherine's reign and led to the growth of a military proto-intelligentsia, which coincided with the broader Russian Enlightenment project to create "a new type of people."

Our sources for the early years of the military proto-intelligentsia are limited.[4] The records of service, the so-called *posluzhnye spiski*, are often incomplete and provide only the barest of personal information. Many of the available personal accounts focus on what the authors considered their career highlights, often glossing over what struck them as trivial details of their youth. For example, Aleksei Ermolov, the future hero of the Napoleonic Wars, wrote in his memoirs that "At the age of 22, I became a lieutenant colonel in the reign of Catherine."[5] How did he become an officer to begin with? Who was behind his rapid promotion? Where and how had he received his education? All of these questions remain unanswered. Similarly, Nikolai Protasev, another nobleman from Catherine's reign, offers no details about how he became an officer, and even Ivan Gudovich, a Russian field marshal renowned for his conquests in the Caucasus, states on the first page of his memoirs that no one would be interested in his early years; thus he begins his reminiscences at a point when he is already in military service.[6] By what path he got there is something he does not tell us. Similarly, Iakov de Sanglen writes in his memoirs that "to talk about one's youth would only satisfy one's self-esteem, but for the reader it would produce no interest."[7] Inevitably, the authors of memoirs and diaries selected details they considered important, ordered and juxtaposed various events to make better sense of them, and framed their stories in such a way as to bring out what was most meaningful for them.[8] It is while looking between the lines that we encounter the Enlightenment's influence on the Russian military.

Patronage in the Russian Military

Enrolment into the military often hinged on strong patronage networks. Large families and formal client networks have disappeared from modern Western societies, making it more difficult to understand the function and the importance of these relationships in the eighteenth century.[9] In early-modern societies, patronage networks were deeply embedded in military culture and often made or broke the careers of aspiring officers. Patronage involved more than just casual relationships from which benefits were sometimes extracted. It was a vast political system based on personal relationships between benefactors and followers, between clients and their patrons. In this system several parties had something to offer one another, in both the material and the symbolic sense. Clients provided patrons with more than political support, information, or money; they also offered respect, poems and artistic works celebrating their deeds, gestures of submission, symbolic gifts, and so on. In return the patrons offered their hospitality, recommendations, jobs, and protection. By this process patrons were able to convert their social status and wealth into political power and influence.[10] For clients this patronage meant access to education and mentorship and other sociocultural resources. Patronage networks were outside the control of the government and were deeply embedded in Russian culture by the time Catherine came to power. Patronage helped cultivate a cultural elite within the military while nurturing a sphere of influence that operated outside the laws and regulations of the War College or the empress. In 1762, the same year she came to power, Catherine was already writing that "it is not unknown to us that people younger than 15 have been entered into the guards," and she ordered that the old Elizabethian law forbidding this practice be reinforced.[11] The same year, she also asked several high-ranking military officers to review the Russian army and offer suggestions for reform. General Fedor Bauer, one of the authors of the subsequent report, candidly stated that patronage networks were undermining discipline and subordination in the army.[12] The government was clearly aware of the problem and saw a need to reverse this noble practice, but it seems that it could not or did not want to break the patronage networks and enforce Catherine's edict. In 1780 Catherine was still receiving reports that the army was overburdened with supernumerary officers, the hopeful protégés of various powerful patrons.[13] The Russian regiments were bursting at the seams with officers, and the situation in the West was no less severe. The French army of the same era, for example, was also suffering from an extreme excess of officers, who numbered 35,000, fewer than one third of whom were fully employed. Most of them spent at least four months of each year away from their regiments.[14]

The situation in Russia was not unique, and the eighteenth century saw efforts across Europe to overcome the practice whereby money and social status determined one's access to the military. In the Habsburg Empire, for example, the government instituted measures to ensure that poor but capable officers had a chance to succeed in the military profession and passed tough legislation to curb some of the abuses associated with favouritism and the purchasing of ranks. Officers could now only purchase a rank that was one above their current station. However, enforcing such edicts was another matter.[15] In the French army, the purchasing of ranks persisted until the revolution. The army sold military positions, especially to captains and colonels, to raise money for the state treasury.[16] In England, sales of commissions were notorious in the second half of the eighteenth century, and Lord Barrington, the war minister, tried to regulate them. He forbade commissions to be awarded to anyone younger than sixteen, and officers who were discovered to be below that age were "immediately dismissed from service."[17] Clearly, then, Catherine's efforts were neither unique nor particularly surprising. They reflected the general European practices influenced by the Military Enlightenment that had begun to emerge in the second half of the eighteenth century.

Patronage networks encompassed powerful familial ties at the pinnacle of the Russian nobility as well as weak and sometimes broken ties among the country gentry. Noble fathers, uncles, and brothers-in-law, and also mothers, enrolled their sons in the best regiments, lobbied hard to arrange staff positions for them, and expected swift promotions. Prince Petr Volkonskii left a candid and detailed account of a strong patronage network that smoothly raised him to officership in the Guards. Born in 1776, Volkonskii was enrolled as a sergeant in the Preobrazhenskii Guards on the day of his baptism.[18] As Volkonskii clarified in the first pages of his memoir, only those nobles "who had a chance" could take advantage of the opportunity of early enrolment, especially when it came to the empire's most prestigious regiments. In his case this chance was presented by his uncle, Prince Dmitrii Volkonskii, an officer in the Preobrazhenskii Guards, who lobbied on his nephew's behalf. After formal enrolment, young Petr Volkonskii was given a leave of absence until the end of his studies, after which he would be expected to return to the regiment.[19]

Most families would have been ecstatic at the prospect of their son serving in the Preobrazhenskii Guards, yet Volkonskii's candidacy was pushed further still. His own father was an officer in the Cavalry Guards and wanted to transfer his son to them, and to that end, he turned to his close friend, Ivan Mekhelson, the famous vanquisher of the Pugachev Rebellion and a major in that regiment. Young Petr Volkonskii thus became a royal cavalryman.[20] In 1792, when he turned sixteen, his uncle once again intervened by mobilizing an extensive network of family and friends. The uncle was related to General Nikolai Saltykov, the brother of the Field Marshal Ivan Saltykov and of Sergei Saltykov, who in the 1750s had been an imperial favourite. Another helpful connection was General Aleksandr Rimskii-Korsakov, a relative of Catherine's lover. With such a patronage network at his back, Petr Volkonskii was destined to serve in the Russian army's oldest and the most prestigious regiments, and at the age of eighteen, he became a junior lieutenant and adjutant in the Semenovskii Regiment.[21] These were fitting beginnings for a boy who would one day become a field marshal and an imperial minister.

Volkonskii's case is probably an extreme example of how a small minority of the Russian nobility entered military culture. That being said, Petr Volkonskii was not an exception. Nikolai Tregubov was also a guardsman in the Semenovskii Regiment during the reign of Catherine II. In Tregubov's case it was the efforts of his benefactor Count Andrei Tolstoi (1721–1803), the great-grandfather of Leo Tolstoi, that saw him transferred from an army regiment to the Guards.[22] Mikhail Zagriazhskii followed a similar path when he was enrolled in the military. One of his relatives was married to the daughter of Field Marshal Kirill Razumovskii, the last Hetman of the Cossack Host in Ukraine. Another family friend was Aleksandr Mamonov, the favourite and lover of the empress. In due course these helpful connections produced results.[23] Fedor Pecherin also relied on family connections, but his education no doubt played a role as well. Born in 1773, he graduated from Moscow University in 1791 and a year later enrolled in the army. With a letter of introduction in hand from his father, Pecherin went to see a family friend, Major-General Igor Markov. Markov and Pecherin's father had once been pages at the court, and now Markov was a major in the Preobrazhenskii Guards. He agreed to enrol his old acquaintance's son in the supply and provisions department as a junior officer. Pecherin's immediate superior was another family friend.[24] Lev Engelgardt was similarly elevated to the Preobrazhenskii Guards on the wings of a patronage network. Engelgardt came from a distinguished and well-connected family, originally from Courland, that had served the kings of Poland.[25] Relying on his father's connections, the eleven-year-old Engelgardt was enrolled as a cadet in the Belarusian Hussar Regiment, which was commanded by his uncle. His uncle was the nephew of Prince Potemkin, the powerful favourite of the empress, and young Engelgardt was soon transferred to the elite Preobrazhenskii Guards. In 1783, at the age of seventeen, Engelgardt was made one of Potemkin's adjutants.[26]

Illia Glukhov and his older brother also benefited from a well-oiled family patronage network. It was the passing visit of an uncle – that familiar figure in patronage networks – that placed the boys on the path toward the military. As Glukhov wrote, Uncle Nikolai was a captain in the elite Semenovskii Guards and took them under his wing with "fatherly care."[27] He withdrew the boys from Moscow University and brought them with him to Saint Petersburg to enrol them in the Artillery and Engineering Noble Cadet Corps. While Glukhov and his brother waited to be enrolled, the good uncle stepped in once again and gave his nephews enough money for food to last the whole year; he also purchased uniforms for the boys and even left them an extra sum for miscellaneous expenses, making them probably some of the most comfortable students in the capital.

Eighteenth-century Russia held a relatively static view of the social order and lacked strong legal traditions. The resulting legal insecurity meant that eighteenth-century Russians made extensive use of personal relationships, which often cut across institutions, ranks, geography, and social status. In this environment, patronage networks flourished because they were informal, they involved no legal contract between parties, and there were no laws to codify, control, or restrict them.[28] This was especially true in the military. Writing in the 1770s, Grigorii Vinskii (1757–1818) wrote that "even though the military calling has an outward appearance of strictness, in reality there hardly exists any other social estate with greater autonomy."[29] The military space allowed choices of action and behaviour; within that space, the ideas and values of the Enlightenment could take root, or be adapted or modified, and traditions and practices could be tested. Military patronage networks created a space that was central to the Enlightenment and that drew promising young talent to itself. Volkonskii, the future field marshal, Tregubov, the future senator, Zagriazhskii, a typical representative of the Russian middle nobility, Pecherin, the future Collegiate Councillor, and Engelgardt and Glukhov, the future generals, all were enabled by their benefactors to participate in and contribute to the Enlightenment in Russia as military men.

Patronage was also important for Adrian Denisov, the future Hetman of the Cossack army. Denisov was born in 1763 into a noble and well-connected Don Cossack family. By the time he was seventeen his father was taking him to military meetings and to court, clearly with the intent of introducing his son to the world of politics and military service, and by the age of twenty Denisov and his brother were both enrolled in their uncle's regiment.[30] As scions of an important Cossack family, the young Denisovs were often courted by Potemkin, who invited them to dinners and even to a General Staff meeting at his headquarters, no doubt out of courtesy to their father.[31]

In 1787, the Second Turkish War was brewing, and Denisov's first assignment was to recruit and equip 1,400 men for a Cossack regiment. Denisov was sent "enough cloth, hides and belts for the whole regiment," as well as 120 Don Cossacks for training new recruits, but among them was not a single officer. The years of shadowing his father were about to pay off. Denisov searched for scribes among his men, and after finding a few capable soldiers he organized a chancellery that would be responsible for examining recruits and selecting those fit for service. "After creating a registry," continued Denisov, "I divided the regiment into hundreds, chose two elders per hundred troops, and wrote up instructions outlining everybody's duties."[32] In Denisov, as with so many other beneficiaries of patronage networks, we see the ratiocination of the Military Enlightenment in action. Denisov immediately imposed a clear organizational structure on his regiment, applied the tools of literacy to serve military needs, instituted health inspections and training of new soldiers, and even found time to try his hand at military writing, producing an instruction.

By early 1788 the regiment was kitted out, drilled, and ready for service, but at that point Denisov's patronage network broke down. He was ordered to transfer the regiment to another officer, while being excluded from its ranks. To add insult to injury, by order of Prince Potemkin – the same Potemkin who earlier had flattered him with dinner invitations – Denisov was summoned to join the army as a volunteer.[33] What happened to bring about such a reversal in the young man's fortunes? The cause was Potemkin's displeasure with Adrian's uncle, the Cossack Hetman, and his displeasure extended to the entire Denisov clan. For patrons like Potemkin, patronage in the military was also a tool of social control – a way to extract loyalty, to punish political dissent, and to put pressure on powerful fathers and uncles who held sway over many parts of the Russian military. But as often happened, here too old acquaintances of Denisov's father, Prince Iuri Dolgorukov (1740–1830) and General Ivan Gorich (1740–1788), promised to intervene on his behalf with the prince.

When one patronage network failed to produce results, clients resorted to another. Dolgorukov and Gorich must have influenced Potemkin, because Denisov was eventually invited to Potemkin's headquarters, where he was formally told that his serene highness wished him to take over the very same regiment he had helped create.[34] At the age of twenty-five, Denisov became a regimental commander. His family connections had done much to bring him into the orbit of Potemkin, whose patronage made it possible for him to participate in the Military Enlightenment; then the same connections worked against him to undercut his military career; then he was saved by old friends of his father, themselves senior army officers.

Sometimes the task of preparing children for the military culture fell to mothers. The most famous example of this matriarchal power was probably Princess Ekaterina Vorontsov-Dashkov (1743–1810), a close friend of the empress. Her husband was killed in the opening campaigns in Poland against the Confederation of Bar in 1768, which left Ekaterina in charge of preparing their son, Pavel (1763–1807) for a military career. She did this with obsessive persistence. When Pavel finished his studies in Europe, his mother began to exploit her good relations with Potemkin and her friendship with the empress to find a good place for him in the army.[35] At the age of seven Pavel was made an ensign in the Cavalry Guards Regiment, the same one in which Petr Volkonskii was to serve as a junior lieutenant, and the empress promised to gradually promote Pavel through the ranks while he was studying abroad. This practice was another reflection of the interaction between the Enlightenment and the military: Dashkov's studies were rewarded with military rank, and his knowledge was recognized as just as important as participation in battle.[36] Despite her decrees, Catherine was hardly reluctant to help friends or dispense patronage.

Sergei Mosolov was another young man who advanced through his mother's connections. Born in 1750, his father was a retired artillery captain who died when his son was ten. Mosolov remembered that on his deathbed, his father blessed him with his old military marching icons. It was probably this ritual that marked Mosolov for a military career and began his mental preparation for military service, a preparation that was continued by his mother.[37] To enrol her son in a regiment, his mother mobilized family connections and took Sergei to Moscow. There she met with an old acquaintance, Countess Praskoviia Saltykov, the wife of Field Marshal Petr Saltykov. Their friendship dated back to the days when their husbands had served together in the Seven Years' War. Mosolov clearly did not belong to the high nobility so as to qualify him for a place in a Guards regiment; thus, Saltykov kindly agreed to enrol the boy as a musketeer in the Arkhangelgorodskii Regiment, where his older brother was already serving.[38]

Two years later, when Mosolov's mother came to visit him in his new regiment, he was already fully immersed in the military culture.[39] The sixteen-year-old, musket-swinging, uniformed Mosolov was whisked away by his mother, who took him on yet another career-building trip to Moscow. There, wearing his impressive uniform and new epaulets, Sergei thanked both Field Marshal Saltykov and his wife. Mosolov was now on a steady path to becoming a professional soldier: he belonged to a good regiment, and he could always count on the help of his older brother, who was again reminded not to leave his younger sibling in want.[40] It was a rather unremarkable beginning for the future general, participant in the Siege of Izmail, and critic of Russian military practices. Thanks to patronage, the Russian military had taken in another officer who would participate in the Military Enlightenment.

So far we have examined strong patronage networks. But what happened when patronage networks failed or when familial connections did not exist? The cases of Aleksandr Pishchevich and Ivan Migrin illustrate that even for the Russian nobility of the old regime, the path toward the military was often long and arduous. Pishchevich was born in 1764 to Serbian parents who had immigrated to Russia during the exodus of the 1750s, during the reign of Empress Elizabeth.[41] Pishchevich senior retired as a colonel and in 1782 went to Saint Petersburg to feverishly search for a regiment for his son. Artillery was the father's first choice, so the retired colonel went directly to Prince Orlov, Catherine's favourite, to ask him to find his son a place in an artillery regiment.[42] Orlov declined this request, explaining that since Pishchevich's son was not trained in artillery, the enrolment of someone from a different branch would offend artillery officers already on the waiting list. Disappointed, the father went to General Fedor Bauer (1734–1783), the author of the 1762 memorandum to Catherine about army reform, to see if his son could join the General Staff. Bauer's answer was similar to Orlov's. There was already a long line of people waiting for a place. These were excuses offered to a man with a weak patronage network. When these paths were blocked, the father decided to enrol his son in a Guards regiment, just like the parents of the great nobility. With this in mind he made a request to see Prince Potemkin himself, but predictably his request was denied. All of these rejections fostered deep bitterness in Pishchevich's father toward Orlov, Bauer, and Potemkin. When it became evident that his patronage networks had failed, he decided to enrol the young man into any regiment that would take him.[43]

The father now turned to an old acquaintance and the anonymous author of the Izmail play, Pavel Potemkin. Potemkin agreed to enter Pishchevich in the Saint Petersburg Dragoons, which he commanded, and promised that within a few months Pishchevich would be made a quartermaster, and after that a senior adjutant. Six months later, Potemkin sent Pishchevich a letter informing him that his son had finally been accepted in the Saint Petersburg Dragoons, but instead of making him an adjutant or a quartermaster, the boy was enrolled as a regular junior officer. This was probably one blow too many for Pishchevich senior, who sent his son to stay with his maternal, Croatian uncle, who assumed the burden of preparing the young man for military service and whose character brought together Enlightenment values and the qualities of a military professional.[44]

What happened when there was no father with military connections, and no kind uncle to rely on? Ivan Migrin, a nobleman and a Black Sea Cossack, left a fascinating account of his journey toward becoming an officer in the Russian army in the late eighteenth century. Migrin was born in 1770 into a military family and by the age of eighteen was gainfully employed in the local administration, where he steeled himself to settle down to an unexceptional life as a provincial clerk.[45] A chance encounter just before the Second Turkish War began in 1788 changed Migrin's life forever. He struck up a friendship with an army medic, who "began to convince me to come with him, promising to help me enter a regiment where after a year of service I would attain the rank of ensign and come home as a military officer," wrote Migrin. Eventually he succumbed to the smell of gunpowder and the glitter of the military uniform, and secretly left to join the army without saying anything to his parents or his employers in the local administration.[46] But when he arrived in Moldavia, it was clear that the army did not need any more officers. By this point, the young soldier of fortune was almost penniless and starving. "My situation was most difficult," wrote Migrin, "one can even say, desperate. Far away from my homeland, without any connections, without money and even bread, I did not know what to do with myself." But another chance encounter with another stranger saved Migrin again.

Migrin was evidently still well dressed when Anton Golovatyi, the head of the Cossack infantry in Potemkin's army, noticed him and asked who he was and what was he doing here. "I explained to him," remembered Migrin, "that I was a nobleman, had come to foreign lands, that I had neither money nor food, was almost dying from hunger, and wished to enter military service." After discovering that he was literate and well-educated, and that he had once worked as a secretary in a land court, Golovatyi enrolled Migrin in the army as secretary to an alcoholic colonel. One of Migrin's assignments was to make a careful inventory of the regiment's ammunition, food, and other supplies. Satisfied with his competence, Golovatyi promoted Migrin to junior lieutenant. "This is an officer rank," recounted Migrin, "and should have required the approval of the highest authority – but back then it was simpler – just by the appointment of Golovatyi I became an officer."[47] Migrin's new benefactor quickly noticed his skills as an administrator, and he put them to use during the war against the Turks. The Russian army needed officers who could not only lead soldiers into battle but also maintain an inventory of everything from musket balls to grams of wheat, organize voluminous correspondence between regiments and headquarters, draft reports, and fill in copious forms – in other words, people who could maintain and expand the rationally organized, bureaucratic system of modern military power.

Far from of being a corrosive socio-economic practice, patronage brought individuals into the orbit of military culture. It was up to them whether they chose to stay there, but fathers, mothers, and the ubiquitous uncles all tried to open doors and create opportunities for meaningful engagement with the military. They introduced youths to military culture by sharing stories about wars and campaigns, by glorifying Russian military heroes, and through introductions to their superiors. Patronage also gave the military a degree of independence. Migrin wrote about the relative autonomy senior officers enjoyed when it came to handing out promotions, and Vinskii reflected on the freedom within the military culture more generally. During this time of relative freedom in the military, which reflected the broader contours of the Enlightenment, professionalism and education began to join patronage in shaping Russian military culture.

Educating the Military Proto-Intelligentsia

Until the 1770s, private tutors were the main source of enlightenment for most young nobles, because of the scarcity of educational institutions and the limited number of students they could accommodate.[48] After that, educational opportunities in Russia, especially for military service, expanded, and this fostered a generation of individuals who, besides being introduced to a specific set of military values, sciences, and texts, acquired a broader sense of what it meant to be a modern officer. There were three ways in which the children of the nobility were exposed to the Military Enlightenment.[49] The families occupying the top pantheon of the nobility relied exclusively on tutors, most of them foreigners. The middle nobility turned to a combination of private tutoring and boarding schools, as well as to the cadet corps schools, of which there were three. The lesser country gentry often placed their children's preparation in the hands of a regimental commander in a garrison school.

Princes Petr Volkonskii and Pavel Dashkov undoubtedly belonged to the first group. Volkonskii remembered how he was educated "in the house of my parents who always tried to find the best tutors and, within their means, never spared any expense for this purpose."[50] Volkonskii did not go into any other details of his intellectual preparation for military service, but he wrote about how his education was often supplemented by actual service in the army. By the time he was fifteen, Volkonskii's studies were over, and his diligent father decided to introduce his son "to real service" by enrolling him in a series of regiments. There the young man could observe the drills, watch the training, and listen to military discussions. Being a member of the military during the Enlightenment required more than just the wearing of a uniform and having swagger – it involved the pursuit of specialized knowledge and participation in military life.

Sergei Tuchkov, the future lieutenant-general and senator, left a detailed record of home-schooled military education. When he was three, Tuchkov was taught the alphabet and the catechism, and when he was four, the whole family moved to Saint Petersburg.[51] "Here my father and my mother began to ponder – should I be enrolled in the Noble Cadet Corps, some other institution, or be home schooled?" wrote Tuchkov. The parents decided on the latter, and in the meantime their son was enlisted in an artillery regiment and granted leave for home schooling. It was not the quality of instruction in the corps that decided Tuchkov's education, but family sentiment. "One had to be enrolled there [in the cadet corps] for eighteen years in order to receive commission," he explained. "Such prolonged separation in my youthful age from the family seemed too much for my mother, and that is why it was decided to educate me at home."[52]

When the family moved again, the father hired a local priest and an officer to teach his five-year-old son how to read and write Russian. "Both of them had not the slightest ability to make their scarce knowledge either relatable or interesting," remembered the student.[53] After two years of such riveting education, Tuchkov was enrolled in a school run by a Protestant pastor, and after two more years, once it was decided that Tuchkov would become an artillery officer, the father set out to find a permanent tutor for his son. The family soon learned that it was a challenge to find someone who could prepare the young man to pass the military exams, which were necessary to join the artillery branch as an officer.[54] To gain a commission, aspiring officers had to pass exams related to the branch of military service in which they wanted to serve. The examinations for the army were taken at either the Noble Cadet Corps or the Engineering Cadet Corps. The rank of the graduate depended on how well he did on the exams, which included subjects such as languages, mathematics, history, and geography. For example, in the Noble Cadet Corps there were seven exams, and successful completion of all seven earned the graduate the rank of lieutenant. If the candidate passed five out of the seven, he graduated as a junior lieutenant, and if he passed only two out of seven, he graduated as an ensign.[55] The role of education, the importance of practical and scientific knowledge, and the awarding of rank based on merit all reflected the incipient spirit of the Enlightenment in the military, and Tuchkov need an instructor who could help him succeed in that world.

Eventually the family hired a Dutch tutor, who agreed to all the conditions. The only problem was that he did not speak a word of Russian and, as Tuchkov wrote, was "slightly mad." It turned out that the Dutchman was a member of a secret society and a fanatical alchemist.

"Since he had no knowledge of chemistry," observed Tuchkov face-tiously, "all of his experiments were a total failure, but he never gave up."[56] Meanwhile, Tuchkov's father maintained a large office in their house, in which he kept many of his engineering projects, graphs, and drawings, and which served as a natural meeting place for his friends and subordinates. Tuchkov senior persuaded some of his frequent guests to teach his son arithmetic, geometry, fortification, artillery, and drawing.[57] Armed with this knowledge, at the age of seventeen the home-schooled Sergei Tuchkov passed the military exams and was made a lieutenant in the artillery.[58]

Immediately below this privileged group of home-tutored young officers we find Lev Engelgardt and Adrian Denisov, who belonged to the middle nobility. Like Tuchkov, Engelgardt was raised by his grand-mother until he was five. "My physical education was in line with the teachings of Rousseau, even though my grandmother had not only never read this author, but barely knew Russian grammar," remembered Engelgardt. He confessed that he barely learned anything during that time and was the most spoiled of grandsons.[59] When he was nine, his education began in earnest. Engelgardt was taught Russian grammar by a local priest; it took him almost two years to master it.[60] A year later his father hired a retired lieutenant, who taught him Russian writing, basic arithmetic, and the German language. A Jesuit priest was hired to give him lessons in French. When the efforts of the two instructors showed no results, Engelgardt began to study with his sister and her French governess. The following year he was enrolled in a boarding school, where he stayed for another year, terrorized by a despotic German headmaster. The students studied a smattering of subjects, including the catechism, grammar, history, geography, and mythology, all without the slightest explanation by their instructors. One redeeming feature of this school, in Engelgardt's eyes, was the almost military discipline the place maintained. The students were beaten without mercy and were made to kneel for three or four hours for the pettiest infraction. "Such splendid education left many students maimed," remembered Engelgardt sardonically, "however, it seems that I needed this to change my lazy nature."[61] By the time he left the school, Engelgardt excelled in arithmetic and geometry and was a good dancer and fencer. He had also acquired fluency in French, which was admittedly easy to do, because speaking Russian in the school was forbidden.[62] Fluency in European languages gave Engelgardt access to more foreign literature, fencing and dance provided him with the polish required for polite society, and his scientific knowledge reflected the aspirations of the Enlightenment for rational and professional study of and participation in war.

When Engelgardt's father was promoted to vice-governor of Mogilev, he sent his son to the school of General Semen Zorich, a wealthy Serbian émigré who had founded an impressive military academy, another product of the Military Enlightenment in Russia. The school had space for 300 pupils, and its graduates were given officer commissions in the army. "Many of these officers came out with much knowledge, especially in mathematics," wrote Engelgardt.[63] After a year at Zorich's school, he spent a short time studying practical geometry with one of his father's friends, at which point his formal studies were over at the age of fourteen. However, Engelgardt continued to advance his military education while serving with the army. In his spare time he read recent treatises on tactics and fortification, as well as books about military science. Many of them came from the library of his acquaintance, Prince Pavel Dashkov. Affluent young Russian officers kept libraries of military works, and their comrades-in-arms eagerly pursued military knowledge long after their headmasters asked whether they had done their homework.

At the age of twenty Engelgardt received first-hand military training from a relative. His brother-in-law, who was a brigadier-general, explained to him the perils of his position – of becoming an officer without being familiar with the customs of military service. He reminded Engelgardt that if he became a colonel and a regimental commander without having acquired this familiarity, he would not be respected by his peers and, even worse, he would be despised by his subordinates.[64] These informal conversations between relatives exhibited corporate consciousness among serving members of the Russian military as well as the influence of the Enlightenment on military culture. Engelgardt's brother-in-law invited him to join his regiment; Engelgardt readily agreed and "went to live a camp life."[65] He embraced the service of a line officer, which included guard duties, drill instruction, and standing on pickets. By the time his brother-in-law's regiment was ready to leave the camp, Engelgardt could proudly declare in his diary that "I could now be sent to any regiment and without shame hold on to my rank."[66] The once spoiled grandson had been fully introduced to military culture.

Engelgardt was not the only one who left behind the comforts of a noble lifestyle to learn the customs of military service first-hand. Pishchevich voluntarily enrolled in the Macedonian regiment of his uncle to accustom himself to what it meant to serve in the army. He wanted to compliment his cadet education with practical skills, so he spent his free time reading and conversing with his uncle about military sciences, of which the latter happened to understand a great deal. While living with his uncle, Pishchevich often joined regimental drills, "which supplied me with good practice for my future service".[67] The Macedonian regiment was drilled and educated according to the instruction of General Stepan Rzhevskii, whose military manual and ideas we will examine in later chapters.[68] The budding growth of military professionalism and a military identity manifested themselves in the memoirs of Catherine's officers, even if these notions were, for now, displayed by only a few members of the military proto-intelligentsia.

Dedicated study and even practical stints in service were an important part of Russian military culture during Catherine's reign as well as a realization of Enlightenment notions of professionalism. To borrow Harold Perkin's explanation, professionalism is based on the "exclusion of the unqualified." In other words part of the process of professionalization has to do with claiming expertise "beyond the common sense" in a particular field of study or a job.[69] The officers in Catherine's Russia were clearly engaged in claiming expertise in the art and science of war with numerous references to their experience and knowledge, which they used to develop criteria for excluding those people who did not fit in. In this regard, Senator Nikolai Tregubov, writing about his own early days in Catherine's army, commented that it was impossible to prepare for military service by reading books alone: "To really get to know it, one must be present with the ranks at exercises and do guard duty."[70] An officer not only had to know how to socialize with his superiors and how to find his way around a ballroom, but also had to show himself to be proficient in drill, as well as knowledgeable in weapons, fortifications, tactics, and other subjects of military craft. Above all, he had to strive to be respected by his subordinates and peers. Engelgardt's brother-in-law clearly valued merit, esteem, and knowledge, and viewed all three as part of military identity and service. Engelgardt and Pishchevich volunteered in their relatives' regiments to learn these values and to experience the realities of service, and in the spirit of the Enlightenment, they attempted to read the most recent literature on the subject. Even the scions of the powerful elite like the Volkonskiis were preoccupied with imparting some military training to their sons, which reflected how notions about what constituted an officer, as well as attitudes toward military service, were tilting in the direction of professional, specialized knowledge. The realization was growing that noble status had to be complemented by leadership skills and experience.

Adrian Denisov's early education resembled that of many of his peers. He studied the alphabet until he was seven, but he confessed he did not entirely master it and could barely write by the age of twelve, when his education was continued by an able officer in his father's suite.[71] When the family moved to Saint Petersburg, Denisov attended a boarding school and found he had an aptitude for arithmetic, and once he had finished studying "cubes and squares," he asked his father to let him begin studying geometry. When he was seventeen, the future leader of Cossack armies summed up his education as a smidgen of several subjects, most of which he knew only superficially: some knowledge of the French language (though not written French), arithmetic, some knowledge of geography and religious history, and fluency in Russian, which he could both read and write.[72] After his son finished formal studies, Denisov senior continued to advance his son's education, asking his friends in Saint Petersburg to send him their books. "My parent, after taking me away from the boarding school, never ceased to concern himself with my education, never left me out of his sight, and ensured that I spent my free time reading and writing," he recalled.[73] By the second half of the eighteenth century, the expectations of an easy-going life were giving way to the realities of the growing technical requirements of war. Volkonskii, Pishchevich, Engelgardt, Denisov, and their contemporaries were part of a generation of officers who belonged to the world of the Military Enlightenment and who had begun to value professionalization as an end in itself. They were the generation that read military works and sometimes even wrote some of their own. It was this generation that helped make Russian military culture more self-aware and that laid the foundations for the military proto-intelligentsia in Imperial Russia. Their knowledge and assumptions about their profession radiated across the army, first in ripples and later in waves.

But setting aside the army of personal tutors, the most lasting influence of the Enlightenment on Russian military culture was exerted within the walls of the cadet corps schools. Families that could not afford to hire instructors for their sons or pay for boarding school, but that still wanted them to embark on a military career, sent their children to the three government-run military academies, the Noble Cadet Corps, the Artillery and Engineering Noble Cadet Corps, and the military school run by General Zorich, which eventually became the Third Noble Cadet Corps. Over the course of the eighteenth century, these institutions graduated more than 5,000 officers.[74] Among the earlier generation of graduates were the military and government reformers of Catherine's reign. General Petr Panin, the conqueror of the city of Bender in southern Ukraine and the nemesis of the Pugachev Rebellion; Prince Aleksandr Prozorovskii, the father of the Russian light cavalry; General Petr Melissino, the master of Russian artillery in the eighteenth century; Count Nikolai Panin, Catherine's first foreign minister; and field marshals Petr Rumiantsev and Aleksandr Suvorov – all participated in the Russian Enlightenment and all traced their education back to the Noble Cadet Corps.

A few of the 5,000 graduates left detailed accounts of their years as students. Our best guides to the cadet world of the Russian Enlightenment are Sergei Glinka (1774–1847), the renowned historian, and Petr Poletika (1778–1849), the future diplomat and senator. Both were educated in the First Noble Cadet Corps, which was a unique institution in Imperial Russia. In 1765 the cadet corps was brought under the purview of Ivan Betskoi (1704–1795), the founder of the Russian national school system and a proponent of the Enlightenment world view. Betskoi was the moving spirit behind Catherine's program to create "a new type of people" in Russia, and it is not surprising that he set out to reform the school and update its statute. Catherine herself often visited the cadets, especially while her illegitimate son, Count Aleksei Bobrinskii, was a student there.[75] The Noble Cadet Corps prepared students for the civil service and the military, and specialization began at the age of fifteen. The cadets were divided into five age groups, each separated by three years. This meant that in theory the boys entered the Cadet Corps at the age of five and were about twenty-one when they graduated as junior officers.[76] The first age group, five to nine, were in the care of governesses, the second and third age groups, nine to twelve and twelve to fifteen respectively, were under the supervision of inspectors, and the final two age groups, fifteen to eighteen and eighteen to twenty-one, were taught by officers.[77] The corps offered a careful blend of classical humanist education and specialized military subjects. The school was enclosed by walls that were meant to protect its inhabits from the corrupting influences of the world beyond. The habits, thoughts, and nature of the cadets had to remain pure so that one day they could become the imaginary perfect citizens that Catherine and Betskoi longed for.[78] This restriction of contact between future officers and the world at large was also widely practised in Western Europe, such as at the Theresianische Militärakademie in Vienna, for example, but as we shall see below, instead of creating "a new type of people," this isolation would drive some cadets to depression and suicide.[79]

The Noble Cadet Corps was more than a military training school; it was also a purveyor of new Enlightenment culture and ideas within the military. According to Glinka, the first Russian theatre was founded in the Cadet Corps, as well as the Society for the Lovers of Russian Literature.[80] The Cadet Corps had its own printing press, and its library was one of the best in Russia, boasting more than 10,000 volumes, including many Western titles.[81] The walls of the library were plastered with various graphs and scientific tables, which made it difficult for even the most lackadaisical students to walk through it without absorbing at least some knowledge.[82] On the table in the recreation hall, books about history, geography, and languages were left for the students to read in their spare time, and the walls were decorated with maps. During the French Revolution, a new table appeared that had all of the contemporary European newspapers for the students to read at their own leisure.[83] In the middle of the hall stood a statue of Mars, the Roman god of war, but it was not the same Mars who had presided over the destruction of Troy and who thrived on bloodshed. The cadets' Mars was a creature of the Enlightenment. On one side of the pedestal, the students could read these lines from a poem by Frederick II: "And in the smallest of your soldiers, endeavour to see your children, / For they love their pastors, not their tyrants"; and on the other side, by the same author, "If you want to pass under a triumphal arch, / Campaign like Fabius, and like Hannibal march." The statue of Mars taught the cadets to see soldiers as their children, to fight tyranny in the army, to take inspiration from the ancient world, and to emulate the wisdom of the great commanders. In all this, Mars made the young cadets feel that they were a part of a larger military tradition and set the standard for their participation in it. Next to Mars nestled busts of renowned classical generals. At the other end of the great hall was a model of a Vauban fortress. Above the fortress hung a handsomely illustrated collection of French fairy tales, most likely as bait to attract children to examine the fortress.[84]

The cadets had access to some of the best educators in the empire, spoke foreign languages, and read foreign books. Perhaps most unprecedented was the unrestricted access to European newspapers during a time of great revolutionary turmoil beyond Russia's borders. The curriculum was vigorous: the cadets covered nineteen general subjects and three specialized topics and participated in nine extracurricular activities. In addition to games and exercises, during long winter nights the boys would form reading circles. Physical education was equally important. Glinka recounted numerous daily physical exercises and even claimed that the posture and deportment that was taught during dance lessons had military utility. "The bearing on the dance floor prepared our bearing at the front," he wrote.[85] Fresh air, hygiene, dental care, and a balanced diet went hand in hand with academic studies. Explication was favoured over simple rote learning, and emphasis was placed on developing the creative and even artistic talents of the students; the latter included drawing and sculpting.[86] The image that springs from the pages of cadets' memoirs is that of a cultural and intellectual centre under the close watch of the government; even so, many reports complained that the results of the cadet education were still not satisfactory enough.[87] Yet it was precisely this cultural and intellectual milieu that produced heroes of the Napoleonic Wars and the progenitors of the Decembrists.

In rewriting the Noble Cadet Corps statute, Betskoi was participating in the project to create a new type of officer for the Russian military, and he had chosen the tools of the Enlightenment to do it.[88] Following the latest pedagogical ideas, corporal punishment was forbidden, for it was seen as counterproductive. Instead, kindness, explanation, and reason were used to show the cadets their errors.[89] Betskoi instructed the academic staff to take care "to discover the inclinations of the students, to learn what gifts have they been endowed with by nature."[90] The Cadet Corps had two churches, and its priests were to be chosen among the most educated.[91] Keeping servants was strictly forbidden.[92] At the age of eighteen, the cadets were made to understand that their future depended on their studies, their behaviour, and their attitudes.[93] The Cadet Corps would not help its students find placements in the army or in the government service upon graduation. Betskoi wanted the cadets to find their place in the world "not based on patronage, but on their individual abilities, and especially their temperament and behaviour." However, the cadets were given priority over other applicants whenever an opening appeared in the branch of service they wanted to pursue.[94]

In his notes to the empress, which were appended to the new Cadet Corps Statute, Betskoi set out his vision for the Russian military estate, which Catherine wholeheartedly embraced. Writing about the previous purpose of the Cadet Corps, Betskoi stated that "in the past the only goal of this corps was to produce diligent officers. Your Imperial Highness wishes that now the institution produces skilled officers and knowledgeable citizens, who would be useful to the fatherland ... in other words, with new education to give us a new way of life, and to create a new type of people."[95] Starting in the 1760s, there was a gradual change in the cultural and intellectual orientation of the military – diligence alone was no longer the defining quality of officership. Officers who served under Catherine were to be knowledgeable and useful citizens of the fatherland – part of the new generation, a new type of people who would promote a new way of thinking about war and military practice. Betskoi pointed out to Catherine that "today every officer, it appears, is only suited to fight during battle ... He knows nothing of the strength, power, or revenues of the government he is fighting for."[96] In

Betskoi's mind, this state of affairs in the military was unacceptable, and he set out to inject political and economic considerations into the practice of war.

Throughout his report to Catherine, Betskoi confidently quoted both classical works and contemporary writers to support his program for educating new, enlightened officers. From Cardinal Richelieu, Betskoi had learned that teaching staff were more difficult to find than money to open military academies.[97] So he took the time to personally select all the instructors. Besides abandoning physical punishment, the teaching staff had to throw out the window educational conventions of the past. From Michel de Montaigne, Betskoi had grasped that active learning starts with listening, hence the emphasis was on critical thinking rather than memorization.[98] Betskoi wanted the teaching staff to approach their pupils with love and care and to teach them more "through conversation and discussions" than through formal classroom lessons.[99] Knowledge was to be acquired through listening, observation, and participation in educational activities. Betskoi insisted that metaphysics and passive learning "be banned from this institution once and for all." Instead, the cadets needed to learn about the individual's relationship to society, about the demands of the various ranks, statuses, and places in which they might find themselves, and about how to relate to parents, subordinates, and superiors. Through kindness and persuasion, the teaching staff would guide the cadets to discover subjects they thought would be useful for them.[100] Discipline in the Cadet Corps was to be governed by a manual inspired by the ideas of Montesquieu. [101]

Persuaded by his correspondence with Antonio Ribeiro Sanches (1699–1783), the renowned medical practitioner, Betskoi declared that "cleanliness was the best medicine [for] ailments," and the cadets were taught the importance of good personal hygiene and nutrition.[102] Suetonius's works on Caesar taught Betskoi that only those who learn how to submit themselves to higher authority are then capable of governing.[103] One day the cadets would be thrust into positions of leadership and responsibility, but before then they had to learn how to submit themselves to their instructors and to the authority of the Enlightenment. Quoting Vegetius at length, Betskoi described the training regimen for young Roman warriors, which stimulated his own prescription for the training of the cadets.[104] Locke inspired Betskoi to emphasize economics in the education of the cadets, with regard to both their professional duties and their personal finances.[105] From Charles de Saint-Evremond, Betskoi learned the importance of a diversified education for practitioners of the military craft.[106] No longer would cadets learn only how to fight battles: in the coming decades, as Russian officers, they would need to be not just warriors but also economists, managers, and judges.[107]

Legal training had a special place in Betskoi's universe of military education, reflecting the Enlightenment world view. Here Betskoi relied on the ideas of the seventeenth-century German jurist and legal scholar Samuel von Pufendorf.[108] Betskoi wrote that Russia needed a new type of an officer. "In the past, officers knew no more than how to teach musket drills to soldiers," and not a single one of them was ready to participate in the military judiciary. Betskoi set out to apply the principles developed by Pufendorf to encourage officers to read military laws, statutes, and articles; this would turn them into competent auditors of military justice.[109] He called for a judiciary office in the Cadet Corps to resolve various issues and to introduce students to the importance of the legal process. Falling back on one of his favourite examples, the ancient Romans, Betskoi wrote: "We know that children of Roman senators went with their father to the Senate to listen to the current affairs and to hear the debates about them. By this practice, they naturally observed the functioning of justice ... Their presence witnessed court cases, and procedures for rewards and punishments," which were based on clear and discernible laws.[110]

What kind of a military creature would emerge from the cadet corps doors by the end of his education? Who was Betskoi's ideal, enlightened officer?

> When the cadets, upon leaving the corps, have learned to obey authority, knowing all the details and all the facets of the military calling, have learned how to delegate and to maintain cavalry or infantry units entrusted to them, learned how to compose a letter, a report, or an appeal in their own language and in a foreign one, learned not only the general duties of fellow citizens, but the actual laws of their fatherland, learned how to behave not only with their superiors but with people in general, have acquired the solid knowledge of Geography, Politics, Ethics, Arithmetic, Geometry and other mathematical sciences; when they have obtained awareness of History and the desire to read books about the deeds of famous military commanders, about how to keep records of revenues and expenses in their regiment or their corps; when they have understood the mechanical movement of a clock or a mill, how to build a fortress or a redoubt, how to construct a bark or pontoon bridge, how to make a river lock, how to pick a site for a military camp, etc.; when the basis for all of this intelligence establishes itself in the memory and the gentle hearts of youth more from examples and models, rather than from reading books:

then we can consider this education to be sufficient, and not demand further excellence in knowledge.[111]

Mastery of all of these practical skills, a broader awareness of legal imperatives, and the intellectual motivation to pursue further professional development were all essential to the creation of an enlightened officer, who could then pass on this knowledge and "educate the soldiers."[112] Betskoi's Noble Cadet Corps Statute and his appended rationale for it are among the documents that demonstrate most fully the influence of the Enlightenment on the Russian military. To perpetuate the influence of his ideas in the Cadet Corps when his own position at the court began to wane, Betskoi appointed Count Fedor Anhalt (1732–1794), a distant relative of Catherine, as the new director in 1786. As memoirs suggest, Anhalt turned out to be an even greater force for the dissemination of the Enlightenment among the cadets than Betskoi was.

The atmosphere of the Noble Cadet Corps in the late eighteenth century was laced with Western ideals of personal virtue and the ascendency of reason. It was this world that Sergei Glinka entered in 1785. In the excellent library, the cadets read many children's books in French, such as Joachim Heinrich Campe's *Robinson Crusoe*, a reworking of Daniel Defoe's famous novel by the same title. Glinka remembered the impression these readings made on him, especially how they instilled the importance of hard work, knowledge, and the individual's ability to conquer nature if guided by the "light of rationality."[113] As he grew older, Glinka was also exposed to the weightier teachings of Newton, Voltaire, and Rousseau. He would recall an episode when a priest's lesson about the catechism was interrupted by one of the corps' francophone inspectors. The man had brought with him Voltaire's political novel, *Zadig*, and now he challenged the priest to read a chapter from the book to show the students how the French *philosophe* presented the path of providence.[114] As if challenging religious dogmas was not enough, when the cadets were reading classical works the old Anhalt would often say he was impressed by the Spartans' courage but dismayed at their treatment of the helots. "The Spartans wanted to be heroes," he would tell them, "but in their slaves they forgot their people. True heroism is inseparable from love of humanity."[115] Glinka related numerous instances when Enlightenment notions were grafted onto the Russian military. At one point, Betskoi declared to the future military proto-intelligentsia that "he who boasts about his status, boasts about achievements of others." The students were taught that they would be judged based on their own achievements and personal deeds, not on their lineage or their status at birth. Betskoi strove to introduce notions of merit and egalitarianism among the young cadets, hoping they would carry these with them into the military once they had graduated.[116] This critical engagement with the writings of the *philosophes*, which challenged the political practices of the ancient Greeks, and this concomitant emphasis on personal merit and achievement, left their mark on Glinka and many of his peers. Enlightenment ideas confronted these future military officers with dilemmas they did not know how to address. It was left to the students to find ways to be heroes in an empire in which most Russians were enserfed.

The philosophical and classical readings were blended with military education. For instance, Glinka remembered an essay by one of the instructors, Nikolai LeClerc (1726–1798), a rather famous French educator and a great propagator of the Enlightenment in Russia.[117] In LeClerc's essay *The Duties of a Military Man*, Glinka found especially memorable the line about how the power of the armed forces must always be guided by the sovereignty of reason. "The power of arms safeguards the fatherland," LeClerc wrote, "only when it is guided by reason."[118] This was a perfect symbiosis of Enlightenment rationality and military policy. This rich diet of the Enlightenment thought and classical texts found its way into the memoirs of Glinka and other cadets, which often allude to the importance of laws, equality, respect, justice, and a world in which "the rich do not resent the poor."[119] During Catherine's reign, this emphasis on laws, humility, mutual respect, and the "light of rationality" was transferred to the military, whose officers began to rethink their attitudes toward their profession, toward one another, and toward the "helot" Russian soldiers.

Petr Poletika remembered his time as a cadet with less fondness than Glinka: by the end of his studies he was struggling with depression. Unable to afford to educate their children at home, his parents were compelled to petition education institutions to accept their sons as pupils. Petr and his older brothers were eventually accepted into the Noble Cadet Corps, and in 1782 the four-year-old Petr was brought to Saint Petersburg to enrol there.[120] Poletika's rather negative assessment of the Cadet Corps may have had something to do with the fact that his older brother was once viciously beaten by other cadets for his arrogance. Apparently, the young man could recite almost all of Rousseau's *Emile* from memory.[121] Poletika remembered the harsh treatment meted out by the governesses while he was a student in the first group and that he almost died from what he called "education fever." When he was transferred to the second age group, the French governesses were replaced by French tutors, who were rude and poorly educated, as well as cruel toward their charges. Despite all this, Poletika later wrote: "I cannot complain regarding myself during this stage of my education." Echoing Engelgardt's comments about the discipline imposed on him during his education, Poletika concluded that "to tell the truth, it was beneficial for me."[122] The consensus among the officers was that Enlightenment was built upon discipline, especially in the boys' early years, which were so crucial to preparing them for military service.

Like other cadets of the time, Poletika fell under the influence of Anhalt, the new director. According to the cadets, the old count dedicated to the corps "his unbounded attention and, one could even say, fatherly care."[123] In German-speaking Central Europe, the early expression of the Enlightenment concept of *Bildung*, the emphasis on education through self-cultivation, began to shape military education. In the 1770s the famous military educator Count Friedrich Wilhelm Ernst Graf zu Schaumburg-Lippe-Bückeburg (1724–1777) taught his pupils that an officer must acquire knowledge beyond his routine duties. Understanding of war and the meaning of the military profession could be achieved only through appreciation of how they related to other fields, disciplines, and branches of knowledge.[124] Even though Russia did not have the German tradition of *Bildung*, Anhalt began to introduce this Enlightenment concept into Russian military culture through his influential post at the Nobel Cadet Corps. The most creative part of the new director's approach to education was the "talking wall."[125] The walls of the garden were painted with astronomical drawings and moralistic expressions extracted from different books.[126] It was as if the very walls that separated the cadets form the outside world were imparting knowledge to them. Poletika recalled a similar custom practised under Anhalt: the cadets had to write their thoughts about what they had read throughout the week on special blackboards, and every Sunday there was a public reading of everything that had accumulated throughout the week in the presence of the director. Writing about the Talking Wall, Poletika concluded that "useful, even though superficial information of different kind[s] always struck one's eye, so that even those pupils who were less disposed towards learning than others, unwittingly accumulated at least some knowledge." Eventually Anhalt published a small pocketbook, titled *La Muraille Parlante* or *The Talking Wall*, comprised of all the sayings and wisdoms that once adorned the garden walls of the Noble Cadet Corps. Poletika proudly kept this book in his library even as an adult.[127] The generation of officers who wrote those sayings without doubt also purchased Anhalt's little book and carried many of the Enlightenment ideas they encountered in the corps with them beyond its walls. The words of wisdom that Anhalt and Betskoi imparted to their students were becoming part of the new military identity.

By the time Poletika reached the fourth age group, his studies had acquired a markedly military air: his dull grey tunic had given way to military green, and military discipline, including military exercises, had been introduced to the curriculum.[128] In 1794, Count Anhalt died and was replaced by Mikhail Kutuzov, the future vanquisher of Napoleon.[129] In these last years, Poletika was completely consumed with the desire to graduate and leave the Cadet Corps. "During my lonely walks in the cadet yard I could think of nothing else." The corps had begun to feel like a prison.[130] When the liberation finally came, it was from a most unlikely source. On 6 November 1796, Catherine II died of a heart attack, and a few days later, with the crown barely on his head, her son Paul, the new emperor, was already inspecting the classrooms of military schools. On one occasion, Paul dropped in during an evening class at the Nobel Cadet Corps and found the students, including Poletika, studying drawing. The emperor inspected the students' blueprints and ordered that the five top pupils be released immediately for service. Paul was looking for young officers with technical knowledge and proficiency in cartography, statistics, geography, and other relevant sciences to join the newly expanded General Staff. "Even though I was among the best students in the class, I almost got excluded from this group of graduates due to the fact that I was not distinguished in my drawings," wrote Poletika. He was saved by Kutuzov, who intervened on his behalf and wrote a special recommendation letter to the emperor.[131]

The education in the Noble Artillery and Engineering Cadet Corps did not yield to the Nobel Cadet Corps in the scope of subjects it covered or in the influence of the Enlightenment. Its director for much of Catherine's reign was Petr Melissino (1726–1797), the first General of Artillery in Imperial Russia, the brother of the director of Moscow University, and an admirer of Betskoi. In his memoirs, Illia Glukhov described an impressive curriculum designed to prepare cadets for a demanding and highly technical military career. During the Glukhov brothers' first year in the corps, they were taught geometry and algebra, Russian grammar and syntax, geography, and the German language, besides taking drawing and dance lessons. In the second year, the program of studies intensified, with history now added to the list of courses. The following year saw artillery and fortification introduced into the curriculum, along with the French language. When the time came, Uncle Nikolai visited from the army to watch his nephews take their examinations in person. "He found that we were good students," wrote Ilia Glukhov with satisfaction.[132] The school's director saw potential in Glukhov and advised him to concentrate on the study of fortifications – cadet Glukhov was to be groomed as a fortress engineer. On graduation, he was sent to the Davydovskaia fortress in Finland to report on the progress of the work being done there.[133]

Aleksandr Pishchevich was also destined to graduate from the Artillery and Engineering Cadet Corps. When he was ten years old, his stern father hired a French tutor, and at the age of thirteen, in 1777, when the Glukhov brothers were in their senior year, Pishchevich left home to become an artilleryman. [134] Pishchevich confessed that algebra lessons left him bored and indifferent. But he was an avid reader of history and geography, boasting that by the age of fifteen he "was already familiar with all the great military leaders." Pishchevich's favourite commander was Prince Eugene of Savoy.[135] It was a telling sign of the influence of the pan-European military culture that the young man's hero was a famous Habsburg military commander from the age of Louis XIV. The memoirs of cadets during Catherine's reign reveal the lived experiences of the Military Enlightenment. In the Noble Cadet Corps the taboo against formal education for the nobility was losing its grip, and lifelong learning was being normalized. Anhalt used to remind his students that it is better to be an old student than to be old and ignorant.[136] Glinka, Poletika, Glukov, Pishchevich, and many of their peers accepted the importance of merit, education, and rational thought, but also of respect for the law and humility in one's dealings with others. The cadets were taught that the armed forces must be guided at all times by the sovereignty of reason. On the surface, the experiences encountered by these "ancient cadets," as Glinka referred to himself, were in many ways in tension with one another and with the Russian historical experience, but they all highlighted the numerous intersections between the Enlightenment and the military. Glinka's brother Fedor left us perhaps the most prescient verdict. "Separated by their wall from the civilian world," he wrote in his memoirs, "the pupils of science and theory were left behind this wall without venturing outside for about a decade, taking with them from their exile feelings of sensitivity, kindness, often so fool hearted that it was amusing, and an inclination for romantic day dreaming."[137] By the 1820s, the generation of eighteenth-century military proto-intelligentsia that had been influenced by the Enlightenment would turn from romantic into political daydreamers and challenge the very order they had taken an oath to defend.[138]

At the very bottom of the military-educational pyramid were families that lacked the means to send their sons to a Cadet Corps let alone hire private tutors. Future officers who could not afford to acquire their education elsewhere often ended up in garrison schools. Relatively little is known about these institutions in the eighteenth century beyond the official edicts concerning their founding. The garrison schools were established in 1721 by Peter the Great, who declared that every garrison regiment had to operate its own school. By the beginning of Catherine's reign, there were 108 such schools, which taught around 9,000 students; by the end of the century that number had grown to 12,000. By Beskrovnyi's calculation, 40 per cent of educated Russians of that time had been taught at garrison schools.[139] Unlike in the Noble Cadet Corps, education in garrison schools ended at the age of fifteen, at which time the students were appointed to whatever position required their specific skills and knowledge. These schools were designed to prepare lower-ranking officers as well as specialists in carpentry, medicine, bookkeeping, and secretarial work. Their curricula varied, but generally, the students were taught arithmetic, how to read and write in Russian, and various facets of military work such as exercises and manoeuvres. While the schools were designed mainly to educate soldiers' children, starting in 1774 they began accepting the sons of the nobility as well, one of whom was Sergei Mosolov.[140]

Mosolov's father was a retired artillery captain who had a sound knowledge of fortifications, astronomy, mathematics, and the German language, and as Mosolov remembered from his childhood, their country house was a cultured destination for many dignitaries.[141] After the father passed way, Mosolov's mother gave him all of his father's military books along with his handwritten notes and told him stories about his father's military career.[142] This was clearly an attempt to pass on knowledge and to introduce the boy to the values, heritage, and customs of the military. Through her patronage network, Mosolov's widowed mother managed to send her son to a garrison school, where he too felt the long reach of the Military Enlightenment.

Mosolov's memoir offers a rare glimpse into the world of an eighteenth-century garrison school. The commander of his regiment, Colonel Neronov, gathered all the young nobles in his headquarters and founded a Gymnasium. Eventually a large hall was built to house the school, which was divided in two parts: one for the children of nobles, the other for the children of regular soldiers. Mosolov wrote that there were about seventy young nobles and almost as many other children in the Gymnasium. Even more impressive was the egalitarian tuition system that Neronov introduced into his regimental school – the colonel paid for poorer pupils out of his own pocket.[143] Colonel Neronov was clearly an enthusiastic supporter of the Military

Enlightenment and brought books, scientific instruments, and a teacher from Moscow who taught the students mathematics, the Russian language, rhetoric, and later arithmetic, geometry, trigonometry, algebra, history, and religion. "I do not know whether it was Providence or fear of the headmaster," remembered Mosolov, "but I surpassed my peers in both academic studies and in discharging my military duties." For his excellent performance during the exams, which were held in the presence of the colonel and all the staff officers, Mosolov was promoted to the rank of sergeant. Furthermore, the headmaster made him the tutor for those students who were struggling with their studies.[144] As in the Cadet Corps, military preparation was not neglected either. The students practised guard duty, marching, and musket handling, so the intellectual Enlightenment was fused with military training. It seems that Colonel Neronov was not unique and that he was participating in a widespread practice. The memoirist Grigorii Vinskii (1752–1819), for example, related how in 1770 he became a student in the school of the Izmailovskii Regiment, established by General Aleksandr Bibikov, one of the six initial readers of Catherine's *Great Instruction*, which provided young nobles with a military education.[145] The regiment was becoming more than just a military unit; it was now also a place where knowledge was received, values were inculcated, and the Enlightenment was perpetuated.

After Catherine ascended the Russian throne, education continued to grow in social and practical importance, especially in the context of military culture.[146] Whether with a tutor or in a boarding school, in a Cadet Corps or in a garrison school, young minds were introduced to the basic principles of military culture – strict hierarchy, promotion based on merit, and unconditional subordination to one's superior.[147] But they were also introduced to the Enlightenment notions of self-worth, to the importance of humility, to law, and to participation in the economic and political life of the empire. All of this played an important role in the formation of values and identity of the military proto-intelligentsia. By the last third of the eighteenth century, aspiring Russian officers required knowledge, experience, and education – and not just social graces – in order to participate meaningfully in military life. Future officers still studied dancing and fencing, but these were now supplemented with military education in the context of the Enlightenment.

An examination of the military proto-intelligentsia through the prisms of patronage networks and education reveals how military culture intersected with the Enlightenment and was reinforced and perpetuated by it in the late eighteenth century. The narratives that have survived point to the fact that during the reign of Catherine II, patronage and education served to broaden and reinforce participation in the Military Enlightenment. The generation that entered the military during Catherine's reign embraced the culture of merit, possessed specialized military education, and accepted military identity and professionalism. This generation also increasingly expected commitment to these values from others – their peers, their seniors, and their subordinates – and later began to express and promote their ideas in the wider public sphere. It was this generation that would create flourishing pockets of intellectual curiusity about war "amidst the sea of Philistines," as Armstrong Starkey put it.[148] Catherine and her government were aware that patronage could have an adverse effect on the military, yet even here, family networks simultaneously reinforced the military proto-intelligentsia and perpetuated a set of practices. Indeed, patronage often ensured that young people riding the wave of personal connections had the opportunity to receive the best military education, had access to the best military knowledge through books, tutors, and family friends, and had a chance to encounter real military service in the regiments.

The experiences of home-schooled warriors, cadets, and garrison school students varied, but on a deeper level, they reveal the strong influence of the Enlightenment. Perhaps the best example was Betskoi's proposal, which was saturated with references to Enlightenment thinkers and with applications of their ideas to the military. This was the result of a process that had begun earlier in the century with the education reforms of Peter the Great, which at first encountered resistance. As a result of the increasingly complex demands of early-modern warfare, resistance to education had been replaced by acceptance by mid-century, and finally by active pursuit of it by the time Catherine came to power in 1762.[149] As Marc Raeff has summed it up, "the obligation to serve also implied the obligation to be educated."[150] This new obligation, in turn, was changing the face of military service as well as redefining the expectations of the military profession and the landscape of Russian military culture. Knowledge, persistence, initiative, hard work, and professionalism were often determining factors for young men from undistinguished backgrounds. Knowledge of languages, legal processes, and arithmetic was seen as vital. Frequent mentions of exams, supplementary readings, and voluntary field service show the extent to which the customs and values of military culture were embraced by its members. Glukhov's uncle came to watch the boys take their examinations in person.[151] Engelgardt's brother-in-law encouraged him to learn what it was like to serve at the front.

Pishchevich's uncle taught and drilled him in his regiment. Around this time, war was beginning to shift from being the preserve of amateur adventurers toward being a field of concentrated study by dedicated professionals. In this, Russia largely followed European trends.[152] Gradually, under the aegis of the Enlightenment, polite and professional behaviour was becoming the new fashion in the Russian military, and questions of honour and rewards based on merit progressively gained greater importance.[153]

Chapter Two

Favourites and Professionals: Merit, Seniority, and Advancement in Catherine's Military

The Enlightenment was famous for its critique of undeserved privilege and its commitment to the idea of merit.[1] In the military, too, merit became the subject of considerable attention and analysis. Military writers were debating the criteria for advancement, emphasizing the recognition of ability, and pondering charismatic leadership and military managerment long before twentieth-century military sociologists followed suit.[2] In the context of the Military Enlightenment, merit was more than just a recognition of ability; it involved wider issues of professionalism, the relations between officers and the state, and the reciprocity, equity, and justice that governed this relationship.[3] Debates about merit were one means by which the eighteenth-century military "operationalized" the Enlightenment by turning thought into reality. Merit was no longer about status but about practical benefits to the military. It was about maximizing efficiency, raising self-esteem, nurturing professionalism, and rewarding performance based on personal achievement. If honour, rooted in medieval chivalric practices, created competition among the nobles, then merit, as it was promoted during the Military Enlightenment, "supported combat effectiveness, recruitment, and retention."[4] In pre-revolutionary France, for instance, officers embraced the spirit of equality or "equal competition to meet objective qualification," and merit and talent played an important role in this.[5] Similarly, in Habsburg Austria, Maria Theresa turned to merit *to make military service more appealing.*[6] And in Britain of George III, merit and experience played a more important role in military promotions and rewards than is usually recognized.[7] What about Russia? Did Catherine's military embrace this crucial tenet of the Military Enlightenment, and if so, to what extent?

From the start of Catherine's reign, when her favourites such as the Orlov brothers were promoted to high military ranks, to its last days, when her young, handsome lover, Count Valerian Zubov, led an incursion into Persia, merit seems at first glance to have been peripheral in military culture. For example, Varvara Bakunina, who accompanied her husband on that fateful expedition against Persia, complained that only one officer was ever promoted due to merit. Except in his case, rewards were given only to the favourites of Count Zubov, "who, it should be pointed out, did not deserve them at all."[8] Diaries and memoirs point to an almost total disregard for merit in the army, in which, it seems, favouritism and patronage ruled the fortunes of officers and soldiers. Aleksandr Lanzheron wrote that generals promoted their hairdressers and cooks to sergeants, who later became officers and adjutants. He accused the famous Suvorov of appointing 600 staff-officers in two years, and wrote that Suvorov's favourites openly sold ranks. Prince Grigorii Potemkin, Catherine's most illustrious favourite, apparently promoted officers for their good dancing skills.[9] Diaries and memoirs paint a picture of a military that blatantly circumvented merit and refused to embrace meritocratic practices. In this chapter, I challenge this narrative. While many studies have focused on the role of patronage and favouritism in Catherine's military, I argue that this ignores the importance of professionalism and of a variety of other values that began to emerge during Catherine's reign. Advancement in the military, with a few exceptions, remains a largely unexplored topic.[10] There were many instances of favouritism, and patronage networks played an important role in promotions and rewards, yet merit was equally significant and played an equally important role. Merit, as a modern concept, and patronage and favouritism, as remnants of earlier periods, were not mutually exclusive. In this sense, the Military Enlightenment of Catherine's reign was a transitional period before a true military professional class emerged in the nineteenth century.

This chapter asks how advancement based on ability was practised and shows that despite occasional nods to favouritism, the machinery of merit kept steadily humming in the background. The practice of recognizing ability was less about the triumph of a meritocratic order in Catherine's Russia and more about how the subscription of some people to the principles of merit demonstrated the influence of the Enlightenment on the Russian military culture. In fact, Catherine's reign left behind copious amounts of evidence that point to the gradual development of a meritocracy and the articulation of merit in the military culture. To gain access to this development, this chapter examines various forms of recommendations – especially personal letters of recommendation called *atestaty* – that reached the desks of Catherine's military commanders. Letters of recommendation allow us to document merit and to evaluate the language used to describe, assess, reward, and convey it. Such letters are an important legacy of the Russian Enlightenment because they speak to the shared values of military culture during Catherine's reign, to how individual performance was evaluated, and to how it was recorded and analysed.

The Machinery of Promotion

The idea that promotion in the military should be based on merit and ability began to be articulated by Peter I in his 1716 manual *Military Statute*, which the Russian military used until the beginning of the nineteenth century.[11] Peter summarized his views regarding promotion and merit in his decree of 1 January 1719 in three points. First, even the children of nobles had to serve in the ranks in order to become officers. Second, promotion had to be sequential, one rank at time. Third, new officers would be commissioned as vacancies became available based on assessments of ballots with two or three candidates at a time. Furthermore, no officer was to be promoted to the next rank unless he had the necessary qualifications, nor could a rank be inherited. Peter went on to legislate his idea of meritocracy in the famous Table of Ranks in 1722, and thus the dual system of promotion based on seniority or *vysluga* and merit òr *zasluga* was born.[12] From that point on, whenever a vacancy opened, candidates with the required number of years of service were automatically considered, and the decision was based on their qualifications and ability.[13]

Throughout Catherine's reign, the army, and the officer ranks, continued to grow to meet the new international challenges of her expanding empire. A quick quantitative analysis of available data in Table 1 reveals that while the absolute number of senior officers continued to grow during Catherine's reign, the proportions within the seniority pyramid remained remarkably stable. For example, while the number of major-generals increased by a factor of two between 1762 and 1792, they still constituted roughly 63 per cent of general officers. Similarly, the data from the General Staff rolls reveal that on average these men served for thirty years before being promoted to the general's rank. That being said, years of service were counted from the time the young men began their studies. As we saw in the previous chapter, that age could range from as young as four to as old as eighteen, depending on when the children were officially enrolled in a regiment. There were, of course, a few exceptions to this pyramid of promotions; for example, Count Kiril Razumovskii (1728–1803) became a field marshal after

Table 1 Increase in the number of senior officers during the reign of Catherine II[14]

Ranks	Years					
	1762		1774		1792	
Field marshals	3	4%	4	4%	2	1%
Full generals	8	10%	10	11%	14	9%
Lieutenant-generals	18	23%	19	20%	41	26%
Major-generals	48	62%	61	65%	101	64%
Total	77	100%	94	100%	158	100%

only seven years of service, and Major-Generals Mirian and Shemben served for seven and three years respectively before becoming generals. But they were most likely foreigners and received their rank based on their previous experience abroad. On the other side of the scale was Fridrikh Numsen, who took fifty-six years of service to reach the rank of lieutenant-general. He entered Russian service in 1733 and was promoted to his final rank by Catherine in 1789.[15] If we ignore these obvious outliers associated with favouritism and foreign transfer, it appears that to become a senior officer in Catherine's army was a long and arduous journey. But we know relatively little about how the machinery of promotions worked, where it succeeded, and where it failed. This chapter will attempt to reconstruct the practices, means, and deliberations used for earning rewards in Catherine's military, and contextualize them within the Military Enlightenment.

The promotion process during Catherine's reign was quite formal. It usually began with an officer asking for a promotion in a *chelobitnaia*, or petition; in this, in several numbered paragraphs, the applicant provided information about his service, described his skills, and explained why he was asking for a promotion. The applicant then secured a letter of recommendation or *atestat* – preferably several such letters – from his superiors, which detailed the candidate's best qualities, his acts of bravery, his leadership characteristics, and how long he had been known to the referee. Even the humblest of soldiers sometimes managed to arrange a recommendation from a general or a prince.[16] The next step was to request the record of service history (*posluzhnoi* or *formuliarnyi spisok*), which resembled a detailed curriculum vitae and documented the length of service in each rank, education, age, and whether one had ever been court-martialled. When the package was ready, it was sent to a higher authority, such as to the chancellery of Prince Potemkin. The package was usually accompanied by a cover letter, called a *raport*, written by the regimental commander, which summarized the contents of the package and what was being asked.[17] If the candidate was pro-moted to the next rank or earned an award, or when he retired, he received an official "patent" with the royal stamp.[18]

Building on the Table of Ranks, and on the idea that "the Muscovite service principle was now openly expressed in terms of merit rather than lineage," the machinery for determining promotion in the military began to come together at the end of the 1760s and the beginning of the 1770s.[19] It was outlined in official military manuals such as the *Military Statute*, the *Military Article*, and (crucially) *Instructions of the Infantry Regiment to the Colonel*, which went through several editions during Catherine's reign and was authored by an impressive collection of experienced generals from the War College.[20] In addition to the official government regulations, a score of private military manuals reinforced the ideas of merit, ability, and professionalism. In the spirit of the Enlightenment, these documents outlined and codified the legal framework for achieving merit in Catherine's military. Non-nobles at the beginning of Catherine's reign typically had to serve for at least twelve years before becoming eligible for a promotion to ensign, which was the lowest officer rank. By 1766 the twelve-year rule had been relaxed, and children of soldiers and priests needed to serve only eight years before petitioning for an officer's commission, while university graduates and foreigners could do so after only four years of service. For nobles, three years was the minimum length of service required before joining the officer ranks, and as we saw in the previous chapter, time spent in private studies or cadet schools could count in those calculations. During Catherine's reign, Guards officers still came exclusively from the nobility, but most rank-and-file guards-men were commoners.[21]

However, such laws were "honoured more in the breach than in the observance."[22] The almost continuous wars during Catherine's reign ensured a steady attrition of officers and rendered some of the rules untenable. Catherine's commanders in the field often circumvented official regulations and promoted the most fitting candidates with little regard to ceremony and bureaucratic red tape. Sometimes the twelve-year rule was forgotten and commoners were promoted to the rank of ensign. This practice was called promotion *zauriad*.[23] It referred to people performing the duties of an officer without legally having an officer's rank. It came about due to the high demand for officers during the wars against the Turks, for which there were not enough noblemen to plug the holes in the officer corps.[24] Clearly, for many Russian com-manders bravery and ability in the field weighed more heavily than adhering to the instructions of the War College, whose responsibility it was to enforce the military regulations.[25] Merit and ability, and not birth and seniority, often guided the decisions of field commanders.

The government and the empress herself often took a keen interest in rewards, promotions, and merit. In her personal notebook from the early 1760s, Catherine wrote that he "who does not give importance to merit does not have it. He who does not seek merit and who does not discover it, is unworthy and incapable of ruling."[26] In 1773, a year before the end of the First Russo-Turkish War, Catherine asked Prince Aleksandr Viazemskii (1727–1793), the conscientious Secretary-General of the Senate, to send her his notes about military officers and civil administrators, along with comments about their ranks, how long they had served, who had recommended them, and for what promotion. The secretary-general may have been following in the footsteps of Marshal Christoph von Münnich (1683–1767), who in 1737 sent a similar note to Empress Anna that classified all the generals of the Russian army, assessing their merit in terms of temperament and natural talent as well as experience and skills.[27] Viazemskii sent the empress his notes but apologized that they were eight years old. Catherine was probably looking for patterns and qualities that had served as promotion triggers after the end of the Seven Years' War in 1762. Upon submitting his list to the empress, Viazemskii added that he did not make any comments about those whose merit and dignity were not familiar to him, so that he "would not have a guilty conscience afterwards." Clearly, Viazemskii took the idea of merit very seriously. As far as the standards by which people should be promoted, the general-secretary wrote: "I think those who have remained in their current rank since 1763 and have been deemed worthy and shunned vice, should be transferred from the Vth rank to the IVth rank."[28] In other words, in Viazemskii's eyes only those with a record of eleven years of uninterrupted and unblemished service qualified for a promotion. It is clear that Catherine was trying to establish some basis for the rewards and promotions that would come at the end of the war, and that she and her government were soliciting advice and information for this purpose. And indeed two years later, after the successful completion of the war, there followed an orgy of promotions and awards, based in part on Viazemskii's recommendations.

A similar attempt to evaluate merit came after the Second Russo-Turkish War (1789–1792), when a rough note, probably in the hand of Count Aleksandr Bezborodko (1747–1799), Catherine's workaholic secretary and foreign policy adviser, was sent to the War College. The note requested from the War College lists of generals, brigadiers, and colonels along with descriptions of their service: where, which units, and "when they had distinguished themselves." The lists had to be approved by the Senate and then delivered to Catherine herself.[29] Furthermore, in the upcoming celebration to mark the Russian victory over the Turks, Catherine was presented with a memorandum on how to best dispense royal favour "to the people in general, and to the army in particular." The document consisted of five points for Catherine's consideration. The empress was encouraged to reward the navy and the army in a similar manner, to avoid any jealousies. The document, like many of its kind, was noteworthy for its rhetorical nods to the "loyalty," "bravery," "manliness," and "dedication" of the imperial troops. It prescribed rewards for every act of bravery in great detail. For example, for the capture of a regimental or battalion standard, Bezborodko recommended rewarding soldiers with twenty roubles. For capturing enemy insignias, soldiers were to be given two roubles.[30]

The machinery for evaluating merit originated with Peter I and by the 1760s had come under the organizational and rationalizational influences of the Enlightenment and the careful eyes of Catherine's government. Every military act was carefully recorded, investigated, reported, and weighted. All awards had to correspond to the act's worth. Expansion of the army did not disturb proportionality or standards for promotion. The ideas and the criteria for evaluating merit were developed in government regulations, reinforced by the top managers in the bureaucracy, and sustained by personal attention from the empress.

Recommendations and Petitions

In the 1790s, Prince Nikolai Repnin sent one of his favourites, a major, to Count Aleksandr Suvorov, a rising star in Catherine's army, with a recommendation letter calling for his promotion to colonel. Suvorov met the major with extreme courtesy but at the same time tried to test his worthiness, his wit, and his ability to think on the spot. Suvorov was trying to see if the major was one of the "don't-knowers" (*nemoguznaiki*), a word of his own invention that he used to describe people who were unable to stand up to the onslaught of his bizarre questions. Suvorov tried hard but could not fault the major as a *don't-knower*. When asked, for example, how many stars were in the sky or how many fish were in the sea, the major steadily supplied astronomically large numbers. Finally, Suvorov asked, "What is the difference between Prince Repnin and me?" The question was a difficult and sensitive one, but the major did not lose his nerve and replied: "The difference is that Prince Repnin wants to promote me to colonel, but he cannot, and Your Excellency need only to wish it." Suvorov was satisfied with this witty reply, and the major received his promotion.[31]

On the surface, this anecdote makes military promotion in Catherine's Russia look capricious and arbitrary. But on closer reading, it tells us something about how a practitioner of the Military Enlightenment evaluated and tested ability and what merit meant to him. What the colonel unwittingly participated in was essentially an interview. He demonstrated knowledge and ability in answering questions under pressure from a very eccentric superior instead of saying "I don't know." The colonel was a favourite, but that is not why Suvorov approved his promotion. Beyond the anecdotal evidence, how was information about individual merit fed into the bureaucracy? And what sort of information was it? The most important way that information about merit and rewards reached the state bureaucracy was through letters of recommendation, which came in two main forms: battle reports directly from the field, and individual letters of recommendation called *atestati*.

Usually battle reports were sent by the commanding generals directly to the empress, and there rarely was a better way to recommend a soldier than by mentioning his name in a document that would be read by the sovereign herself. There are many examples of battle reports that were sent to the empress upon successful conclusion of combat. A good place to start is the dispatches sent by Count Petr Rumiantsev (1725–1796) during the First Russo-Turkish War (1768–1774). Battle reports gave detailed descriptions of military engagements and usually concluded with a list of names deserving the monarch's recognition for their personal contribution to victory. After a major battle, these lists could be quite long. In the summer of 1770, after a major Russian victory engineered by Rumiantsev at Riabaia Mogila, a burial ground in present-day Romania, Catherine received a full report of what had taken place that day. Rumiantsev painted the action in vividly intense language that described for the empress, blow by blow, how her army had defeated the Turks. Near the end of the letter, he wrote: "I cannot remain silent before Your Imperial Majesty about the witnessed praise [*zasvidetel'stvovannoi khvaly*] from individual commanders, for Major-General[s] Podgorichani, Potemkin and Tekelli, Hussar Colonels Chorbe, Satin, Lieutenant-Colonels Elchaninov, Pishchevich, Fabritsian, Majors Vuich, Misuiriv and Zorich, Captains Gangablov, Chalinovich, Bantysh, Trebinskii and Pulevich, Lieutenants Shutovich, Vukotich, who was wounded [...]" A few names from old Russian noble families and that of his quartermaster-general also made the list.[32] Considering that this was a major battle that involved close to 40,000 Russian troops, the list of recommendations was thin indeed. Other commanders were more generous. In 1792, General Ivan Gudovich presented the War College with a list of people who had distinguished themselves during the siege of Anapa, a fortress on the Black Sea coast. Out of about 20,000 troops under his command, he recommended close to 200 for promotion to the next rank.[33]

Rumiantsev expressed very clear ideas about the role of merit, ideas that aligned with the broader world of the Military Enlightenment. The count recommended an advancement system based on "earned merit." He summarized his view thus: "those who only dispense their service as they should, deserve their regular pay, and nothing more."[34] Doing one's duty did not merit any special reward. Rumiantsev was very restrained when it came to dispensing rewards and praise. Even to earn a promotion in the lower rungs of the Table of Ranks was not easy. As Aleksandr Turgenev wrote, "Zadunaiskii [Rumiantsev's victory title] gave out the patents for the rank of captain with great selectiveness and it was not easy to receive them."[35] Lev Engelgardt, who campaigned with Rumiantsev, added that promotions and medals were rare in Rumiantsev's army, but at least every decoration was distributed according to merit and "every award was received with utmost satisfaction."[36]

In another letter, this one about a Russian victory around the River Larga in modern-day Moldova, Rumiantsev wrote: "In the end I also must not remain silent before your Majesty about praise, because rewards are in order first of all to the Corps commanders Lieutenant-Generals Plemiannikov and Prince Repnin, and the Quartermaster-General Bour. Their example and courage served all their subordinates as a model." Rumiantsev continued with his list from the top, all the way down to the most junior of officers and even foreign volunteers in the Russian service. In total, ninety-five people were cited for rewards.[37] Humble soldiers were rewarded too, and 3,000 roubles were parcelled out to deserving individuals. As well, the spoils taken at the Turkish camp went to the soldiers as a reward for their brave actions.[38]

As Rumiantsev's star continued to rise, so did the tally of his victories and the number of recommendations he made. In 1774 he was again writing to the empress, from the other side of the Danube, about the Battle of Bazardzhik. "It is my duty, Most Gracious Empress, in this case to give fair credit to the diligence and enterprise of Lieutenant-General Kamenskii with which he has distinguished himself, [and] who, according to prisoner reports, managed to forestall the numerous enemy with his quick manoeuvre." In his letter, Rumiantsev also incorporated recommendations sent to him by other generals, who singled out individual colonels for distinction.[39] Rewards and promotions were grounded in observation and witness reports. Rumiantsev's subordinates submitted their recommendations to him in just the same way that the field marshal submitted his own to the empress.

Promotions and rewards served symbolic and even Machiavellian functions. In one letter to Catherine concerning the Cossacks, Rumiantsev neatly summarized this other purpose of awards and his reasons for giving them out. In the summer 1769, at the beginning of the war with the Porte, Rumiantsev decided to reward the brave actions of some of the Cossack forces under his command. "The brave deeds described in the attached letter by the Zaporozhian Cossacks were worthy, it seemed to me, of a reward, which I granted to them in the name of your imperial majesty," he explained to his empress. "I wanted to present this reward to them, and to all others, as an example of how magnanimously your imperial majesty rewards [her subjects] for courage and true bravery ... to motivate them and others into similar action."[40] Awards served as symbolic gestures to inspire confidence and loyalty and as a motivation for further exertions.

Rumiantsev's battlefield dispatches were only a part of the larger picture of the promotion culture. Catherine also received recommendations through more private channels, in which the ubiquitous Prince Potemkin often took centre stage, but here too merit played an important role, as did ability. Unlike Rumiantsev, who was never a court favourite and who was never especially close to Catherine and her inner circle, Grigorii Potemkin was an advisor of the empress and probably her husband.[41]

During the heat of the Second Russo-Turkish War (1787–1792), Potemkin dispatched several short notes from his headquarters at Iassi, in eastern Romania, with recommendations to Catherine that illustrate that he deliberated carefully on people's abilities and merit when it came to important posts. In February 1790 he wrote to the empress recommending Lieutenant-General Krechetnikov for the task of supervising the recruitment levy in present-day Ukraine. "For the recruitment of people into existing regiments and for the formation of new regiments, so that it would be done successfully and without taxing the population too much, there must be a commander there who could cut out the abuses that harm military service and the oppression of people, and bring everything to good order," he wrote.[42] In Potemkin's opinion, Krechetnikov had the qualities needed, so he recommended him for this challenging job. Potemkin probably also calculated that this post would give Krechetnikov ample opportunity to earn awards and promotions. On 17 April, Potemkin fired off another note of recommendation to Catherine, this time to replace a retiring governor with Major-General Levanidov. "He is quite a worthy man for this kind of job, and considering the proposal for the formation of forces in that region, he will be useful there with great effect for he has excellent skills for such a purpose."[43] Potemkin was masterful at matching "skills" with "purpose" and at identifying meritorious individuals to carry out difficult military and political tasks, but at the same time, he hesitated to recommend an officer if he was unfamiliar with his service record.[44] Both Rumiantsev and Potemkin were leading representatives of the Military Enlightenment in Russia and saw advancement in terms of individual ability to perform military tasks, rather than status.

Battle reports and similar letters were sent directly to the empress. In addition to these, there was a steady flow of individual letters of recommendation, or *atestati*, which overwhelmed the slow bureaucracy of the War College. Many officers who were not singled out in commander's reports describing breathtaking battles resorted to asking their superiors to write individual letters recommending them for an award or a promotion. Some officers felt they had been overlooked and were seeking to address that injustice. They ranged from powerful generals to obscure provincial officers and men in lower ranks. Colonel Nikolai Kozhyn wrote an *atestat* for one of his captains. "Captain Mansurov has been under my command since May 1774 and during the villain Pugachev's rebellion he was sent to find rebels and to put down the Bashkir revolt," wrote Kozhyn. The captain was "diligent and hard working" in his search for rebels, and in many situations showed himself to be "especially industrious." Furthermore, he had been wounded while carrying out his duties. Later, he was sent out to drive the Kirghiz rebels from a fortress on the steppe, and defeated them, inflicting heavy casualties and taking many of the Kirghiz rebels prisoner. "During all the time that he was under my command, he conducted himself with integrity, to which I give him this attestation," concluded the colonel.[45] The bases for evaluating the captain's merit were clear. In the space of six crucial months of an eventful year, Mansurov had put down the Baskhirs, captured the Kirghiz rebels, and been wounded.

On 20 April 1778, Prince Aleksandr Prozorovskii (1733–1809) wrote a recommendation letter for one of his colonels, a man by the name of Repninskoi. Repninskoi and his regiment had been placed under Prozorovskii's command in 1774. For four years the prince observed the colonel's performance. During this time Repninskoi had ample opportunity to prove himself to his commander. In 1774, Repninskoi and his regiment crushed a strong detachment of Turkish soldiers. The following year the colonel was transferred to take up command of the Kinburn detachment. With the forces that had been entrusted to him, Repninskoi "demonstrated his considerable experience in the military craft." In two years, between 1775 and 1777, through his tireless efforts, Repninskoi had shaped his detachment into a formidable force and "[had] finally discovered his full abilities as an independent commander, and is both trustworthy and commendable." The prince concluded, "I have been observing all this with great satisfaction, and in this I give him credit as a capable officer, and think him worthy of any great distinction."[46] Prozorovskii's letter demonstrated merit implicitly by referring to personal improvement. Repninskoi had not always possessed the qualities of an independent commander, but over four years he had "finally discovered" them.

In 1775, Prince Potemkin received a letter about Lieutenant Klebek that began with these words: "This deserving officer asked me for a recommendation to your Excellency; and in light of his reasoning about his fine qualities, good behaviour, and his labouring in the current rank for nine years, I could not deny him his fair request."[47] The examples of Captain Mansurov, Colonel Repninskoi, and Lieutenant Klebek show how more senior officers evaluated the skills and the courage of their subordinates as well as their dedication and leadership qualities. To give just praise was considered a professional duty, one that governed the relationship between superiors and subordinates, which was based on reciprocity, equity, and justice. Prince Prozorovskii and Colonel Kozhyn were proud of the accomplishments of their subordinates and declared as much in their letters. In doing so, they embraced the idea of merit in the context of the wider ideal of the Enlightenment.

Not all recommendation letters were as detailed or as magnanimous as those above, nor did they all carry the same weight. Some were very short, sometimes just stating the dates of service, reflecting the relatively unknown status of the candidate.[48] Others concentrated on one particular trait such as good behaviour – hardly a rationale for significant reward.[49] Still others recommended officers for promptly bringing discipline to the troops and keeping regiments in good order.[50] Some recommendation letters named several people simultaneously.[51] In 1790, Colonel Selunskii sent a report to Potemkin asking him to consider for promotion some of his lower-ranking officers. The three men had diligently carried out all of the tasks they had been assigned by Selunskii. "With respect to their continuous labours, I humbly ask not to leave them behind in promotions," wrote the colonel.[52] What all recommendations had in common was an effort to provide an objective evaluation of the ability and personal skills of the candidates based on observable and verifiable criteria.

It was not only front-line officers who received letters of recommendation: fortress commanders, supply officers, military doctors, and even military translators all asked for and received recommendations from their superiors. Many of these people toiled away humbly in remote posts and barely entered the historical record. They never had an opportunity to fight in the great campaigns of their time, but they still thought they deserved promotions and recognition. In their minds, their work was as essential as that of battlefield officers even if it was less glamorous. Their efforts did not go unnoticed by the machinery of merit. In December 1777, Major-General Iakovin wrote a long letter to Potemkin recommending a *Praviantmeister* (provisions officer) by the name of Grikhvostov to the next rank. "I cannot, your Highness, but recommend him into your good graces," wrote General Iakovin. "Even though the order to supply the troops of the line came too late, and even though he did not receive money from the chancellery to do it, he still somehow managed to deliver all the provisions and supplies on time." What Grikhvostov had done, according to Iakovin, was charm the local population to such an extent that the locals agreed not only to supply the necessary provisions but also to help deliver them to their destinations. Iakovin did not describe the methods by which Grikhvostov managed to inspire the local population to such magnanimity, but we can safely assume that it was done either by threat of force or by promises that the peasants and merchants would be paid back in full with interest. Either way, *Praviantmeister* Grikhvostov was unstoppable in dispensing his duties. "I give him full credit for this," wrote the general, "for in doing so he greatly helped me out in reinforcing the line, and if he did not manage to attract the suppliers with his kind actions, the delivery of supplies would have been quite small indeed, and consequently there would have been a great need in everything." Grikhvostov's prompt actions, he summarized, had helped avert starvation among the front-line troops.

Furthermore, Iakovin pointed out that Grikhvostov had already received recommendations from the governor of Kazan province, Prince Okercheskii, which he attached to his own letter. The prince also testified to the almost magical abilities of Grikhvostov. For example, even during the Pugachev Rebellion (1773–1775), the largest peasant uprising in Russian history, Grikhvostov proved himself up to the task of supplying the army. Moreover, in addition to feeding the passing troops, he managed to supply three nearby provinces simultaneously, including Kazan. And the praise did not stop there. "In addition to feeding the local population, which back then was experiencing a great scarcity of bread, he managed to put aside for them enough supplies so they could plant it as a crop themselves." The *Proviantmaister* had successfully carried out every task that had been thrust upon his shoulders, "but he still has not received any awards," Iakovin pointed out. At the end of the letter, the general confessed to Potemkin that he needed Grikhvostov and was afraid he might leave his service or that his efforts might begin to slacken if he was not rewarded. "I summon the courage to ask that Your Highness seek the *Oberproviantmaister* rank for him," the letter concluded.[53] This was a compelling recommendation: the general was making a strong case for his subordinate, based on the latter's merit and ability.

The long wars with the Turks and the annexation of the Crimea, with its large Tatar population, meant that reliable translators were in strong demand. They too received recommendation letters. The case of Khalik Badirov is a good example. Badirov wanted a promotion to the next rank, and in the fall of 1781 he wrote a long and detailed petition stating his case. Attached to the petition were seven recommendation letters, one of them written in Tatar by a local chief, which Badirov translated into Russian. Major-General Fedor Faritsanz wrote the longest of these letters, in which he attested that Badirov had always been loyal to the Russian cause even when it had required him to go against the wishes of his khan during the rebellion of the Kuban people, and that Badirov had many times been used as a courier on dangerous missions. In all this he had remained a true servant of Her Imperial Highness. His loyalty and service to the military, therefore, should be rewarded with the promotion he requested.[54] It appears that Khalik Badirov had chosen the right side to fight on, and joined the Russian cause and abandoned the doomed rebellion by his kin at the opportune time. Now he felt the time had come to collect his compensation. In his case the claim was based on loyalty as much as merit, and he found seven people to testify to that loyalty.

The deeds of medical personnel also did not go unnoticed. In 1792, General Iosif de Ribas wrote a recommendation letter for his private physician, Major Viktor Podzhio. Ribas reflected on two years of Podzhio's work and based his recommendation on personal observation and on reports from other witnesses. Ribas wrote that when the Russian Black Sea Fleet was anchored near the Ochakov fortress in June 1790, his physician had established a hospital where he tended to the sailors of the fleet before it left for the Danube. By the time the siege of Ochakov had ended, Podzhio was already near Izmail, the site of the next major battle. "From the beginning of the siege of the city of Izmail, he was employed to take care of the wounded on the batteries, that were located on the island opposite of the city, where he, during uninterrupted cannonades, often put himself in danger," wrote Ribas. Moreover, on 11 December, alongside the sailors, the good doctor had been involved in the storming of Izmail, and the following day, after the city was taken, he opened another field hospital to treat soldiers and sailors wounded during the siege. "Despite difficulty and lack of medical resources," noted Ribas, "his alacrity and skill benefited the patients with great success, as I have been told by the ships' captains." By January 1791, Podzhio was working in another field hospital he had opened in the port city of Galats. Despite the total absence of other medical personnel or subordinates, and the usual shortage of medicines, Podzhio did all he could to "cater to the welfare of the sick." On 31 January the indefatigable doctor was on the scene of another siege, this one near the island of Brailov. In August he was back in Galats, where he set up three field hospitals to treat 1,700 people. Finally, he was by de Ribas's side when Turkish prisoners of war began to arrive, "many of who[m] enjoyed his great care."[55] Podzhio's Herculean labours clearly merited recognition.

All who served the military effort – translators, provisions officers, doctors – were eligible for an equitable evaluation of their merit. Letters of recommendation reveal how rewarding personal achievement was more than a matter of honour – it was also a professional obligation of superiors. The practice of observing, evaluating, and recording merit was important for justifying nobles' privileges, but it also indicates how the Enlightenment was influencing the military. Merit was necessary as a means to encourage professionalism among the officer corps, to maximize the performance of the lower ranks, and to make the military a desirable place of service. It was part of what Daniel Roche called the subjection of officers' and soldiers' behaviour "to rational controls and evaluation."[56] Letters of recommendation showcase the mentality of Catherine's military, its values, how it evaluated service, and what qualities and deeds were viewed as deserving an award. More senior officers based their recommendations on concrete personal characteristics grounded in observed behaviours. Aleksandr Viazemskii, the Procurator-General of the Senate, refused to comment on the merit of those he was not familiar with, thus setting a high professional standard. Prince Aleksandr Prozorovskii referred to the military craft and the importance of discovering one's abilities. General Iakovin described several occasions when Grikhvostov distinguished himself under his command, clearly demonstrating a pattern of excellence. Ribas wrote in his recommendation letter that he had witnessed his doctor's efforts on the front lines first-hand; he also referred to other witnesses to support the doctor. Nowhere in all of this was social status mentioned; instead the letters were based on personal accomplishments and achievements over a specific period of time. In the context of the Military Enlightenment, there was an understanding that if hard work went unrewarded, morale and dedication would gradually decline, thus undermining the military culture.

When recommendation letters failed to produce results, there was a final recourse: petitions, pleas, and sometimes even begging. This process usually started with a document called a *chelobitnaia* or petition. The *chelobitnaia* had a standard form comprised of several points, which were to be filled out in a predetermined manner.[57] It began with a brief description of service as a justification for petitioning, followed by the description of an injustice incurred, and concluded with a request or a plea to a higher authority to rectify the injustice. A good example of such a document was the petition filed by Major Ivan Astefev, a Baltic German, in the early 1790s. [58] Astefev detailed his long service and thorough education and questioned the government's decision to promote his peers (whom he listed by name) while holding him back.

Many officers wrote to influential commanders such as Rumiantsev and Potemkin. In August 1775, Potemkin received a letter from Brigadier Andrei Meduz. "Passing over in silence the fact that many junior and less capable colleagues had been promoted from quartermaster ranks to the highest ranks ahead of me, I will only report on my service record starting with when I became a colonel," wrote Meduz.[59] Meduz's was one voice of embitterment and frustration among many. Even when officers had the qualifications for a promotion and the seniority to receive it, there sometimes was no place to put them, however princely their status.[60] For example, Prince Aleksandr Prozorovskii wrote in 1763 that the military commission was examining cases of promotion according to seniority, where he, along with other two colonels, should have been promoted to the rank of major-general. However, the commission decided against it because it would create too many supernumerary (*sverkh komplekta*) major-generals. Upon hearing this decision, Prozorovskii and his comrades immediately submitted their requests to resign from military service, given that more junior officers had already received the rank they sought. The prince's resignation, however, was declined because of a technicality, and afterwards Prozorovskii was persuaded to remain in service. Moreover, his request to resign made the empress indignant. "I saw the anger of Her Highness, because her gracious treatment of my persona turned cold," lamented the prince.[61] Catherine, evidently, stayed well-informed about requests to leave the military and took a personal interest in retaining capable officers in her armies. Prozorovskii remained in service and eventually achieved the rank of field marshal in 1807. Sometimes there were simply no open spots for new candidates, no matter how qualified they were. But even when there was a long queue of qualified candidates for an opening, as historian Nikolai Glinoetzkii observed in his nineteenth-century study, "merit was used for promotion into the supernumerary in the case vacancies were unavailable."[62]

Informed by the larger world of the Enlightenment in which they lived, a world in which arbitrary decisions were increasingly being shoehorned into specific frameworks, military petitioners had a keen sense of their legal rights and due process, and they based their petitions on legal precedent and military law. This was an attempt, no doubt, to intimidate their superiors and challenge the status quo. In 1768, Aleksandr Leontiev sent his petition to Catherine. He was a retired colonel working in the civil service, but he now wanted to return to the army. As if to remind the empress, he slyly concluded his request with a short legal observation: "In the name of the blessed memory that is worthy of eternal glory, Sovereign Emperor Peter the Great's Ukaz from 11 November 1724, ordered that those who are transferring from civil service into the army should transfer with the highest rank achieved in the civil service."[63] He received no answer, and in 1771 he wrote another petition, and still another in 1774, in which he repeated his main concerns and requests. Leontiev once again hammered in his point about his right to promotion according to Peter's decree, "according to which those from civil service who want to transfer to the army should be awarded same rank of seniority from the day of their promotion in the civil service." He also took the opportunity to vent his frustrations "against the promotion of those junior to me to the rank of a Major-General." Above all he felt wronged that despite his unblemished and zealous thirty years of service, men of less seniority were getting promotions and high salaries.[64] In December 1792, Major Ivan Kiraver also made reference to customs of service, but he did not go into detail about which specific laws, regulations, or documents he was referring to. He began by stating that he knew that the "attention of Her Imperial Highness extends to all the servants and offers each rewards commensurate with their merit."[65] These letters reveal a growing expectation in the military that not only status, seniority, and connections but also ability played a role in decisions of the military to promote individuals. Moreover, such decisions were demonstratively based on clear and objective performance targets. All members of the military had equal and legitimate claims to merit, based on observation and analysis.

The narratives found in petitions had to do with the pursuit of advancement. Together, they illuminate the nature of Catherinian military culture, in which officers had recourse and leverage. When pressuring the authorities for their just rewards, petitioners referred to military law as well as customs of service, cited powerful patrons, and made thinly veiled threats to leave service if their requests were not fulfilled. Dmitrii Repalovskii wrote to Potemkin in 1774 or 1775, after he had not received any answer from the War College, that "in view of the above I have taken this last recourse, to bother Your Serenity about equating me with my peers by promoting me to the rank of a lieutenant with seniority. This grace of Your Serenity would encourage me to continue further my diligent service to her Imperial Highness!"[66] Whether they came from a prince or from an obscure junior officer, threats to leave service had to be taken seriously, especially after 1762, when the Russian nobility was no longer required to serve the state. In a way, the government machinery had no choice but to respond to the pleas and petitions of officers by embracing the ideal of the Military Enlightenment that rewards must be commensurate with the merit the recipients displayed. Otherwise, many capable officers might retire to their estates, or resent their continued service, or just do the bare minimum. The government thus had to play a difficult balancing act between promoting people with ability and paying homage to people with seniority.

Seniority or Ability?

Clearly, there were two competing principles whereby achievement and worth were measured in Russian military culture. On the one hand, there was merit, backed by the strong influence of the Enlightenment. Professionalism, efficiency, strong leadership, the drive to acquire more knowledge – all of these depended on the observance of merit. It would have been dangerous to completely throw away the principle of personal merit, even though as a concept it was a subjective calculation at best. Superiors could write splendid recommendations in their letters of reference in exchange for bribes or having felt pressure from patronage networks. Merit was in the eye of the beholder, and the functioning of a meritocracy depended on the honesty and good faith of superiors in their evaluations and recommendations. As such, meritocracy was a system easily subverted and vulnerable to intrigues and favouritism. On the other hand, there was the rigid practice of promotion according to seniority. In 1780s France, military committees were convinced that "seniority was the best way to safeguard equality and prevent birth, wealth, and influence from usurping promotions due to merit," and in the Habsburg armies promotion by seniority was likewise seen as a potent tool for fighting favouritism.[67] Promotion by seniority worked like clockwork, but it completely overlooked merit, ability, and intelligence. It was completely objective and independent of personal influences and evaluations, but it also overlooked less tangible factors that were equally important.

Balancing the two systems posed a philosophical dilemma deeply entrenched in the military culture that Catherine had inherited from the times of Peter the Great.[68] Even though he had insisted on orderly promotion according to merit, Peter had to balance his need for qualified personnel with the demands of the elites.[69] Catherine similarly compromised, and the Russian army began to practise promotion according to "seniority and merit," whereby especially distinguished officers and soldiers could be recommended for promotion outside the seniority framework (*vne ocheredi*).[70] The same year Catherine came to power, she reiterated an edict from the days of her predecessor Empress Elizabeth. It concerned promotions in the civil, naval, and military services. Catherine made it clear that promotions from then on were to be made according to seniority and merit (*po starshenstvu i zaslugam*), thus reinforcing consideration of both concepts in evaluations of worthiness. The edict also described a scenario in which someone was recommended for promotion due to seniority but otherwise did not deserve it. In such cases, it had to be explained exactly why the candidate could not be promoted due to seniority alone.[71]

The gradual acceptance of the importance of merit over seniority by Catherine's government began to reach the military through new military manuals. In the winter of 1764, two years after Catherine came to power, the War College published *Instruction to a Colonel of an Infantry Regiment*.[72] One of the factors it emphasized in the promotion process was merit, so that "senior and deserving people were not offended." In addition to this, the colonel should never write letters of recommendation for those who were unworthy and incapable.[73] The document also reminded the colonel that "the functioning and vigour of the whole service depend[ed] on him." That is, the colonel was placed in the very centre of the promotion mechanism. All junior officers and non-commissioned officers such as sub-ensigns, sergeants, and corporals could be rewarded and promoted at the colonel's own discretion, but even here the colonel had to make sure that people of superior ability and talent were not subordinated to their inferiors. The *Instruction* warned its readers "to strictly observe that the unworthy would not be chosen over the worthy ones." It was not enough just to rely on the recommendations of the company's commander, warned the *Instruction*. The colonel had to discover for himself the merit of each candidate and find out on his own whether he was worthy of promotion. The manuals reinforced merit over lineage or years of service in the military when promotions were being considered. From the references to "worthiness," "care," "ability," and other rhetoric of merit, it is clear that the government sought to shape the Russian military as a meritocracy and was instructing its officers to use sound judgment in its enforcement.

Similar deliberations and procedures were extended to the promotions of the colonels themselves and to the bestowing of imperial orders, which took place in the War College, in committees for various awards, and even in the correspondence between the sovereign and her advisers. The promotions committee at the War College examined service records and the validity of promotion requests, and consulted the reference letters that candidates received from their superiors. In the case of a Hussar Lieutenant-Colonel Leshievich from 1771, one letter was written by *Generalquartermeister* Vokhovskii, another by Major-General Zorich, and a third by Major-General Shcherbinin. All three attested to the bravery, good leadership skills, and unwavering service to the empire by Leshievich. In its final report, the committee resolved to recommend Leshievich for promotion to full colonel.[74] Similarly, each imperial order had its own commission (*kavalerskaia duma*) comprised of past recipients of the award, which deliberated the worthiness of nominated candidates. For example, the commission for the Order of St George included Suvorov and Potemkin, and their deliberations show the importance such commissions attached to letters of recommendation and how it cross-referenced them with reports from commanders-in-chief.[75] This was part of the broader drive to implement a rational and methodical framework for evaluating merit by the military bureaucracy in the context of the Enlightenment.

Another example of the inner workings of the machinery of merit was a nomination list for the Order of St Vladimir sent to the War College by Lieutenant-General Mikhail Potemkin (1744–1791), a distant relative of Prince Potemkin and the head of the *Krigs-komissariat* or supply services in the summer of 1785. As Potemkin explained, according to the charter of the Order of St Vladimir, the Senate, the War College, and the College of Foreign Affairs were supposed to send Catherine lists of people nominated for the above award, along with special forms, as well as notes documenting their conduct. This was done once a year, on 8 September. All such documents were to be signed off by the candidates' superiors. "In this regard I have the honour to present the War College with a list of names from the army supply services from which you can examine everyone's efforts on individual basis." Deliberations for rewards were grounded in discussions based on the very long paper trails of each individual candidate. At the end of the letter Potemkin subtly reminded the War College that "in the supply department, care [*racheniem*] and diligence that bring considerable profit to the treasury is something that is not immediately obvious, and can be seen only through the comparison of numbers with the previous years. I am not going to burden you with such details because the War College already knows how it is, and that is why these people should be worthy of promotions."[76] Mikhail Potemkin himself received a nod from the War College, in the form of the Order of St Vladimir, for his efforts to balance the books, which actually created a surplus in his department and saved money for the treasury.[77] Being a Potemkin and close to the inner circle of the empress no doubt also helped.

Another example of the process of recognizing merit once again comes from the private notes that Potemkin sent Catherine. They offer insight concerning the tension between seniority and ability. On 23 January 1790, Potemkin wrote to Catherine "that since Senator Aleksei Shcherbatov, who is one of the Lieutenant-Generals employed in civil service, is senior to Lieutenant-General Krechetnikov, will it not please Your Imperial Highness, due to the former's long service in that rank to graciously promote him to Actual Privy Councillor. As far as the general officers in civil service are concerned, who have seniority equal to those in the military, taking into account the hardships of war, the civil servants have the same right to promotion as the people from the army." Potemkin went on to explain his position to Catherine: "Army officers often have a chance to fill in a vacancy after their brothers-in-arms, with whom they share misfortunes in danger and death, are killed or wounded, and cannot consequently be part of preferential promotion."[78]

Finally, there was the case of Aleksandr Suvorov. There is hardly better case study, or one that demonstrates the struggle between merit and seniority more thoroughly, than Suvorov's career. Aleksandr Suvorov (1730–1800) came from the minor Russian nobility, which benefited from the reign of Peter the Great. Suvorov's appearance did not dispose observers to think that one day he would become a great military leader. Short, with small sloping shoulders, wiry, and sickly, Suvorov had more in common with Prince Eugene of Savoy than with tall, portly giants like Potemkin and Rumiantsev. His life coincided with six major wars, which brought him to the pinnacle of military fame by the end of the century.[79] He became a field marshal at the age of sixty-four and eventually a *generalissimo*, a rare and unprecedented rank he shared with Joseph Stalin. His bumpy road to fame serves as a powerful lens for examining the promotion culture in Catherine's army and the meaning of merit in the context of the Military Enlightenment. It is also a career that has been very well documented, which allows for a greater scope of exposition and analysis.[80]

In their private correspondence in 1787, Prince Potemkin wrote to Catherine about Suvorov, pondering how to reward him for his successes. "Truth be told: here is a man, who serves with his sweat and blood. I will welcome the opportunity, when God gives me a chance to recommend him."[81] And indeed God gave Potemkin just such a chance. A week after the bloody and closely fought Battle of Kinburn, which took place in October 1787, Potemkin was writing to Catherine: "The efforts and bravery of Aleksandr Vasilevich must receive their fair credit. He, being wounded, did not leave the battlefield to the very end, and in doing so saved everyone."[82] Taking the hint that Potemkin meant for Suvorov to be rewarded for his actions at the Kinburn Peninsula on the Black Sea, Catherine wrote back to her "dear friend" and shared her thoughts on how to reward the brave general. Her letter brought to the fore the clash between respecting traditions and seniority and the promotion of the Enlightenment ideals of merit in the military:

> It came to my mind, why not send Suvorov a ribbon of St. Andrew, but then there is another consideration, namely that Prince Iuri Dolgorukov, Kamenskii, Miller, and others who are senior to him – do not have one. I am even more hesitant to send the Large [cross] of St. George. And so, I cannot make up my mind, and am writing to you asking for your friendly advice.[83]

The Order of St George had been established in 1769 by Catherine herself as the highest military honour in the Russian Empire. It had four classes, the first being the highest.[84] More than 10,000 people have recieved this prestigious award over the 250 years of its existence, but only twenty-three of them have received the first-class award, Prince Grigorii Potemkin and Prince Mikhail Kutuzov being the most famous.[85] Suvorov had already won the Order of St George, Second Class, for his deeds at the Battle of Turtukai in the summer of 1773.[86] To grant him the first class of the award would single Suvorov out as the empire's premier military man, and this would upset myriad powerful noble families whose members included field marshals: the Dolgorukovs, the Repnins, the Saltykovs, and many others. Besides, at that time, Suvorov had yet to command armies, lead campaigns, or win a war. The same consideration governed the awarding of the Order of St Andrew, the highest award for chivalry established by Peter the Great, the Russian equivalent of the Hapsburgs' Order of the Golden Fleece. The empress was clearly vacillating between the two very concepts she herself had decreed that the army respect – seniority and merit – and in the end she decided to defer to the counsel of Potemkin, who had a better view of the situation at the front.

The following month Potemkin replied with a letter that bore the full stamp of the energy and conviction he was known for. "Before I share my thoughts with you, I will describe in detail his heroism," he began. He vividly illustrated how for two days Suvorov had hidden his forces in the Kinburn fortress and forbidden anyone to come out; how he and his men had endured a severe bombardment by the Turkish fleet for more than a day without firing a single shot back; how the enemy had finally judged that the fortress was either empty or undermanned and decided to land its forces; how only after the entire enemy force of more than 5,000 had disembarked had Suvorov opened the gates and his soldiers poured out in a desperate counter-attack; how the Russians had been driven back seven times; how Suvorov's presence on the front line had held his soldiers in place; how he had been wounded with a musket ball; how he had suffered a concussion from grapeshot and still had not left his place; and how he finally had driven the Turks back into the Black Sea. After interrogating the surviving Turkish prisoners, Greeks, and others who had observed the battle from the nearby fortress of Ochakov, Potemkin calculated that out of 5,000 troops that had been sent against Suvorov, only 800 were left alive. Such vicious fighting and such a shattering defeat had forced the rest of the Turkish fleet to retreat. "The General, having already earned all possible distinctions, in his sixtieth year still serves with the vehemence [*goriachnostiiu*] of a twenty-year-old, who still needs to make a reputation," concluded Potemkin. As far as rewarding Suvorov, Potemkin thought the general was worthy of the Cross of St Andrew:

> I await Your justice to reward this deserving and honourable old man. Who has deserved to be singled out more than he?! I do not want to make any comparisons, for a mention of names may embarrass the dignity of St. Andrew: but there are many who have neither faith, nor loyalty. There are many who lack dedication to service, or bravery. It is an honour for the order to be awarded to those who deserve it [*Nagrazhdenie ordenom dostoinogo – ordenu chest'*]. I shall start with myself – give him mine ... The importance of his service is clear to me.[87]

Like Napoleon a decade later, Potemkin was prepared to take one of the medals off his own chest and give it to one of his deserving soldiers. He passionately endorsed the concept of merit over seniority, and it was a matter of honour to reward his subordinate justly. However much pressure he felt from the nobility and from the seniority framework, Potemkin supported the type of advancement he believed was in the best interests of the army. In doing so, he reinforced the larger project of the Military Enlightenment in Russia.

Suvorov's career is a good illustration of how the meritocracy functioned and how it generated conflict between seniority and ability. The ideal of merit filtered down through the ranks, and it was not just the most senior officers who were rewarded for their ability. Suvorov himself once wanted to promote a humble soldier, Stepan Novikov, to the rank of commissioned officer after the latter saved his life in battle. But the shy man refused this honour, explaining that he was illiterate and instead preferred a monetary reward, which was duly granted to him. Plainly, the nobles no longer had the monopoly on battlefield heroism. "There are heroes in the lower ranks as well," Suvorov wrote in his battle report in 1771. [88]

The same month that Potemkin was writing to Catherine about how to reward Suvorov, in a parallel correspondence, he was writing to Suvorov about how to reward his subordinates, while reinforcing the idea of impartiality and justice. The letter remains one of the best examples we have of how awards were distributed among the lower ranks. After apologizing for not being able to come visit the hero of Kinburn in person, the prince wrote:

> Rest assured that I make it a matter of honour to be just; and of course I will never put you in such a position as to make you feel sorry to be under my command. I have promoted Generals Rek and Commandant Tuntselman on your recommendation. Be assured that their wishes will be satisfied. From the crosses that have been sent, I left one for Lombard, on whose behalf I asked Her Highness ... One I designate for Colonel Orlov; the remaining four I ask you, my dear friend, to give to the most deserving and to send me their names. By God, summon all your powers of justice and judgement. Golden crosses will be sent to the two Don [Cossack] Colonels. Also designate, to whom I could send them in the Navy. With the exception of one, the nineteen silver medals are for the lower ranks, who distinguished themselves in battle. Divide them by six among the infantry, the cavalry, and the Cossacks; and give one to the artillery man who sank the enemy ship. I think it would not be a bad idea for you to collect several soldiers, or ask entire regiments, and see who the soldiers think should be honoured with medals.[89]

Several interesting points and ideas are expressed in this letter that tie together many aspects of the reward and promotion mechanisms in Catherine's armies. First, the sinews of patronage are made quite clear to Suvorov. One of the awards was "designated for Colonel Orlov," a member of the Orlov clan of imperial favourites, and one silver medal was to be given to an unknown beneficiary. At the same time, Potemkin reassured the general that the clients of his own patronage network, Rek and Tuntselman, had been recommended for awards. Distribution of the rest of the rewards was left to Suvorov's discretion, which shows both trust from above and remarkable room for personal initiative and judgment from below. That being said, Potemkin could not resist providing some guidelines to Suvorov. He displayed his political tact by asking Suvorov to distribute the awards as much as possible equally among all the branches of the military: the infantry, the cavalry, the Cossack forces, and even the navy. Curiously, he implored Suvorov to use his "powers of justice and judgment" when distributing the awards. Finally, the last sentence of Potemkin's letter is perhaps the most intriguing: soldiers were to be consulted to see who in their opinion deserved to be rewarded. It hints that merit in the lower ranks was self-regulated and self-administered, and indeed, the officers were happy to comply with this system of selecting among themselves the deserving candidates for rewards and promotions.

Catherine too showed an interest in how merit was distributed in the lower ranks. After the successful capture of the Polish capital of Warsaw by Russian troops, bringing an end to the Polish uprising of 1794, the empress took immediate care not to leave her soldiers in want of awards and promotions. On 1 January 1795, she penned a letter to Field Marshal Rumiantsev, who had commanded the campaign. She wanted to distribute awards according to the established meaning of merit, which she herself had done so much to shape during her long reign. Catherine began by writing that it was important for the high command to recognize the efforts and bravery of everyone, "from the most junior to the most senior people who serve us."[90] The empress made it clear in her letter that the awards should go only to those who actually took part in battles and sieges – she mentioned this twice – rather than to everyone recorded in regimental registers, some of whom may have been away or may not have participated at all. She then asked Rumiantsev to prepare a report about soldiers and officers who had earned a special distinction. Only at the end of the letter did the empress turned to Rumiantsev himself, thanking him for taking command of the campaign.[91] The special attention to rewarding soldiers in Potemkin's letter, Suvorov's attempt to elevate the lowly Novikov, and Catherine's instructions to Rumiantsev all indicate sincere attempts to accurately evaluate individual efforts. Officers were looking for merit in all corners of the military organization. They wanted to embrace the rational, impartial, deliberative methods aimed at promoting efficiency and encouraging the development of personal abilities. If the Enlightenment wanted to create a world based on reason, logic, and merit, then the Military Enlightenment wanted to do the same for the military world.

Receiving Awards and Promotions

What did all these deliberations amount to? For example, was Rumiantsev recognized for his military success in crushing the Turks and crossing the Danube? And what about all of those officers he recommended to the empress in his battle reports? And how was Suvorov rewarded? What reward did Catherine end up giving him for the victory at Kinburn?

To begin with Rumiantsev, he was rewarded generously. The three crushing defeats, following so closely one after another, that he inflicted on the Turks in 1770 earned him the rank of field marshal. In early August 1770, the president of the War College, Zakhar Chernyshev (1722–1784), wrote to Rumiantsev: "Her Imperial Highness most graciously deigned to promote you into her general-field marshals for [your] loyal and assiduous efforts and for [your] bravery in commanding her forces."[92] And at the end of the month the new field marshal received a personal letter from Catherine. Just as Rumiantsev wanted to justly reward his subordinates, Catherine wrote that she must do justice unto him. In justifying his promotion, she referred to his intelligence, his bravery, his not inconsiderable military art, and his ability to defeat "the countless hordes of unsettled bastards" not through greater numbers but through greater skill. Catherine concluded her letter by writing that the officers Rumiantsev had recommended would also receive just rewards.[93]

By 1774, after the victory in the First Russo-Turkish War, the final list of award recipients had been compiled. Each reward that descended from the royal favour was prefaced with a clear description of what had been done to deserve it. The rewards were simultaneously symbolic, material, and personal. Field Marshal Prince Golitsyn was listed first, reflecting his seniority. For his successful command of the First Army and for clearing the Turks out of modern-day Moldova, Golitsyn received a sword encrusted with diamonds and, as a special mark of royal favour, a silver dining set.

Rumiantsev was junior to Golitsyn, yet he was rewarded the most for his efforts during the war. The moving spirit behind the Russian victory received a diploma (*pokhval'naia gramota*) that detailed his services during the war; then, after negotiating a peace treaty with the Ottoman representatives, he was awarded the special title of Trans-Danubian or Zadunaiskii, which was to be added to his name after a hyphen. "For his capable military leadership," continued the document, Rumiantsev was to receive "a diamond-studded baton. For courageous actions, a diamond-studded sword." Other marks of distinction heaped upon him were equally symbolic. For his victories he was given a laurel wreath, and for the conclusion of the peace, an olive branch. And as a confirmation of his abilities, the field marshal received from the empress the Order of St Andrew encrusted with diamonds and a special medal celebrating his achievement that had been minted to set an example for future generations. Then followed the usual dispensation of serfs from conquered lands, of whom Rumiantsev gained 5,000 in the recently conquered Belorussia. In addition to that, he was granted 100,000 roubles from the treasury for the construction of a palace, paintings to decorate it, and another silver dining set. Rumiantsev's victories had contributed the most to the Russian triumph, and the rewards he received reflected their importance.[94]

After the two army commanders received their rewards, the machinery of promotion turned to their subordinates. General Count Panin, for his efforts to subdue the Pugachev Rebellion, received a diamond-studded sword, a Cross of St Andrew encrusted with diamonds, and 60,000 roubles "for the betterment of home economy." General Prince Dolgorukov received virtually identical laurels.[95]

Only five paragraphs later did Catherine begin to mention her favourites, the Orlovs and the Potemkins. Alexei Orlov received the coveted extension to his name – Chesmenskii – for his naval victory at Chesma, which annihilated the Turkish fleet in 1770. He also received the by now familiar diamond-studded sword, a silver table set, and 60,000 roubles for his household. In her letter, Catherine carefully detailed his bravery as justification for his awards. General Grigorii Potemkin was elevated to count "for his kind counsel concerning the peace negotiations," as well as yet another diamond sword for his "brave and persistent services in the past war." In addition to all this, Potemkin received a portrait of Her Imperial Highness as a special mark of Catherine's personal gratitude. His nephew Pavel Potemkin, as well as Suvorov and Fedor Orlov, all received pensions, diamond swords, or awards of some sort. Numerous officers from lower ranks were granted promotions to the next rank.[96]

Catherine's earlier correspondence with Potemkin about Suvorov led to yet another award. Potemkin's forceful letter to Catherine on behalf of Suvorov after the Battle of Kinburn and his symbolic gesture of sharing his awards with Suvorov had hit their mark. "Discerning from your letters the details of Aleksandr Suvorov's service, I have decided to send him the Order of St Andrew, for faith and loyalty," wrote the empress. Catherine carefully weighed how to reward Suvorov, and in the end the reward he received was based not simply on seniority (some powerful generals and field marshals were senior to him), or on favouritism, but on objective criteria in the context of his achievements. Suvorov was a brilliant soldier and his victories were important, but his exploits were not of the same scale as Rumiantsev's, for example, who had broken the back of the Ottoman military in the Danube region. Yet the empress still singled out Suvorov for the highly coveted award, which she thought reflected his performance and his contribution to the Russian war effort.[97]

Twenty years later the Russian and Turkish empires clashed once again, and after the Russian victory and the conclusion of peace in 1793 the military once again enjoyed an explosion of monarchical favour. But this time it was clear that new heroes were replacing the old masters of the 1770s. By this time, the sixty-eight-year-old Rumiantsev wielded only a shadow of his former power.[98] He was still the nominal commander of the Second Ukrainian Army, so he received another diamond-studded sword, but this time not much else. Grigorii Potemkin had died in 1791, yet in death he received more than some among the living.[99] Catherine ordered the production of a diploma detailing his services to the Russian monarchy during the war, starting with the command of the Russian army and navy in the Black Sea and ending with a detailed list of all the fortresses he had taken and all the battles he had won. This document was to be kept in the city of Kherson, in a church he had founded in 1778, where he was buried. Catherine also ordered that a marble statue of Potemkin be erected in the city, that his portrait be hung in the armoury, and that a medal be minted in his honour. Even in death Potemkin's merit was upheld and rewarded.

The next in line to receive imperial favour was Suvorov, who by now had been raised to a count and who had received the addition of Rymnikskii to his name, in honour of his victory over the Turks in the Battle of Rymnik in 1789.[100] The paragraph began by singling him out from the crowd of other officers. Using the language of merit, it read, "General Count Suvorov, so famously distinguished for his earned merit and his deeds [*stol' znamenitymi zaslugami i delami otlichivshemu-sia*], is given a diploma detailing all of his feats of bravery." Moreover, as evidence of the empress's highest trust and respect, Suvorov finally received the Order of St George, First Class, which he had not qualified for earlier, and was encouraged to recommend others "who[m] he considers to have distinguished themselves in military knowledge and bravery" for this award. Clearly, at this point he had risen above those more senior to him. As further evidence of monarchical favour, Suvorov received a ring covered in diamonds. After all the senior officers had been ticked off the list, there followed further lists of names and rewards stretching for thirty pages, extending down all the way to humble majors and even captains.[101]

Huge numbers of awards and promotions immediately followed wars and campaigns, and all the while, the military bureaucracy kept slowly but steadily documenting merit and parcelling out rewards.[102] Once again, Suvorov provides an instructive example. After he took the Polish capital of Warsaw in a bloody assault, Catherine could no longer keep a marshal's baton from his hands. According to legend, Suvorov informed Catherine about the conquest of Warsaw with "Hurrah, Warsaw is ours!," and the witty empress indulged the general by writing back an equally short and dramatic reply: "Hurrah, Field Marshal!" This signalled the empress's decision to finally give Suvorov the highest military rank. Suvorov's promotion outraged more senior generals, providing another example of tension between the Enlightenment framework of distinction and the more traditional framework of seniority. In January 1795, Prince Aleksandr Vorontsov wrote to his brother in London about the gossip that Suvorov's promotion had generated in Saint Petersburg: "The promotion of Suvorov has aggrieved generals senior to him. Count Saltykov, Prince Repnin, Prozorovskii, Prince Dolgorukov, have all asked to be relieved from service. Count Saltykov, due to his more aggressive stance, has already been dismissed."[103] But Catherine at this point did not care whether she was offending other powerful officers and their noble clans. Suvorov's work was militarily decisive, politically important, and with the drama of the siege, sensational.[104] The eyes of many young officers were on Suvorov. Had the government failed to reward the hero of the hour, and caved to the pressures of seniority, it might have demoralized the officer corps as a whole and undermined the military culture in general. Younger officers might lose heart and weaken their commitment if they felt that the empress and her government valued seniority more than merit. If Suvorov did not receive a just reward for conquering a major European city, what hope for recognition could the rest of the officers have? Suvorov's career points to the incipient triumph of the Military Enlightenment.

Suvorov's career was like a meteor that slammed into Russian military culture. It did not, however, overshadow the reality that much more junior officers than generals and field marshals were privy to the rationalizing, documenting, and analysing forces of the Military Enlightenment. In March 1792, Lieutenant-Colonel Appolon Dashkov

(1753–1808) received a letter from the War College informing him that he was to be awarded the Order of St George. The letter followed the familiar style, thoroughly describing the candidate's conduct in meritocratic language. It began with the usual avalanche of carefully selected adjectives to describe the personal character of Dashkov during the recent war; this was followed by a more detailed catalogue of events. Dashkov had distinguished himself at the Battle of Machin in 1791, in modern-day Romania, with his "dedicated service, brave and courageous feats." He had commanded two battalions during the battle and had acted "with exemplary quickness [*otlichnoiu rastoropnostiiu*] and skill, using field artillery to repulse an enemy horde and cause great harm to their batteries." Moreover, the brave Lieutenant-Colonel Dashkov had been able to repulse another attack and capture nearby hills, "from which you rushed directly at the enemy camp." The letter ended on a reassuring note, as was the custom: "We are convinced that after receiving from Us this sign of approval you will continue your service, which was worthy of Our Monarchical reverence."[105] Such letters reveal the workings of the machinery of merit behind the scenes of battle. They tell us how the military collected, organized, and processed information. In this case, Dashkov's conduct in the heat of battle had most likely been observed by his peers and superiors, recorded in letters and reports, sent off to the War College, and analysed by the bureaucracy. His conduct was then weighed against that of other contenders for a similar distinction. Finally, the contenders were ranked, and it was decided that Dashkov deserved the Cross of St George, Fourth Class.

By the end of Catherine's reign, members of the military had grown used to the Enlightenment idea of meritocracy and dared to hope that their performances would be recognized under the broader system of advancement. They expected to receive rewards based on their ability and performance as set out in the observations of witnesses, evaluations by their superiors, and recommendations by their commanders. After participating alongside Colonel Dashkov in the Battle of Machine, Lev Engelgardt wrote: "All my acquaintances congratulated me on the occasion that I managed to demonstrate my readiness for service in front of the whole army, so to speak, and were confident that, since I was vital in securing this victory, I would get splendidly rewarded." He explained:

> Usually, everybody went to the chancellery of Prince Repnin, to speak to its head, Lieutenant-Colonel Pankratev, and to seek his help to be well recommended; I have never liked to drag myself around chancelleries and seek patronage from their heads. I knew that the commander-in-chief was my witness, I knew that the commander of the center of the army while

recommending his Major-Adjutant and others who were present with him, testified to a fair presentation for awards of other commanders; and I was mentioned as one of them. Because of all this I did not want to be bothered, thinking that if I have deserved something, I shall receive it, but to beg for it I considered below me.[106]

It was more than nobleman's pride. It is clear that Engelgardt, having been subjected for more than thirty years to the practices of merit shaped by the Military Enlightenment, trusted the system's equity, fairness, and justice, all of these rooted in the empirical observation of performance. Those who remembered serving in Catherine's armies would look back on that era with nostalgia, as a world ruled not by favouritism but by the Enlightenment, with its a rational evaluation of talents of abilities. "Catherine! Look what a difference!," wrote Major-General Vasilii Viazemskii a decade after the empress's death. "You saw the potential in ensigns and raised them to the rank appropriate to their talents; when they reached a level they could not surpass, you knew how to keep them in their place, and thus you did good for them and for the fatherland."[107] Recognizing ability and holding on to those who possessed it was seen as part of a rational state policy for strengthening the nation's defence.

In conclusion, references to merit in military texts, recommendation letters, petitions, battle reports, and government deliberations illustrate that more often than not it was not enough for "an Excellency to wish it," as the colonel had stated to Suvorov at the beginning of this chapter. That is not to say that excellent cooks, graceful dancers, and handsome favourites were not promoted unfairly.[108] Rather it is to say that merit was an instrument of the Military Enlightenment in Catherine's Russia, which means we must qualify the traditional picture of the military experience during that period. As Jay Smith had argued about France in the 1760s, "to make the army a more efficient institution, the king, the war minister, and the generals had to take greater care in cultivating and rewarding true merit."[109] The idea of a "career open to talent" did not originate with the French Revolution; rather, it had been developed under the *ancien régime* by aristocratic reformers of the Military Enlightenment. The concept of merit that was espoused after the revolution did not rest on talent alone, as the myth suggests, but was combined with education, patronage networks, and even social standing, and owed more to the Enlightenment than to the revolution of 1789.[110] Advancement based on merit was part of the Enlightenment drive to challenge traditional yet inefficient and even self-serving practices within the military.[111] This was also true in Catherine's Russia, where official military manuals and private military writings all emphasized the importance of developing and reinforcing the idea of merit. Catherine's senior advisers, such as Bezborodko and Viazemskii, understood the importance of advancement based on rational analysis of individual ability. The latter even refused to comment on the merit of those he was not familiar with, thus displaying a strong embrace of professional standards. From their correspondence and their military writings, it is clear that Catherine's top military commanders such as Potemkin, Suvorov, and Rumiantsev all subscribed to the ethos of merit as well. Naturally, merit was not, and could not have been, the only determinant of promotions and rewards, and patronage networks, seniority, and availability of openings were important; but so was personal distinction. Furthermore, the letters of recommendation reveal references not to social status but rather to years in service or particular qualities such as hard work, intelligence, and initiative.

Of course, there was always the danger that more senior figures could be bribed or pressured to write letters for undeserving or little-known candidates, or simply write them as a favour. Such infractions, however, were mitigated by a system of checks. Thus such letters were required to include a clear and detailed description of what the particular candidate had done over a specific period of time, with precise dates and locations, all of which could be checked against official reports. Recommendations were often based on several sources that included several witnesses. All of this represented an attempt by the bureaucracy to weed out hollow stories of heroism and to unmask incompetence. Finally, the merit of the candidate could be cross-referenced because he usually had to produce several letters from different superiors to prove a pattern of leadership, skill, and hard work.[112] The evidence left by the trail of documents seems to suggest that Russian military culture in the late eighteenth century was attempting, sometimes struggling, to establish a very modern system of rational management of army resources and professionalism, inspired by Enlightenment preoccupations with efficiency and reason similar to what was found in other European armies.[113] The government, Catherine herself, and other upholders of the Military Enlightenment understood the importance of not alienating talent and created the means to recognize it.[114] Equally important, this enforcement of merit was controlled and carefully monitored from above by the empress personally. It was a tough balancing act that managed for the most part to keep the talent happy and the powerful nobility satisfied, while perpetuating the Military Enlightenment in Russia.

Chapter Three

"We must distinguish the military establishment from other callings": Writers and Ideas of the Russian Military Enlightenment

In 1788, three years before he was committed to an insane asylum, Fedor Dmitriev-Mamonov published a military essay titled *Rules, According to which any Officer Can Fulfill His Military Service with Total Satisfaction*. That work was part of the expanding literature on the military in Catherine's Russia. Mamonov was born in 1727 and retired in the late 1770s as a brigadier. In his retirement Mamonov collected coins and other articles of antiquity in his house in Moscow, hoping to establish a public museum. But it seems that few people came. After the empress began to receive reports of Mamonov's strange behaviour, especially his cruelty toward his serfs, she launched an investigation, as the result of which Brigadier Mamonov was found to be mentally unstable.[1] Before he was sent to a convent and then to a village, where he would be watched over by a state-appointed guardian, Mamonov left an important literary legacy for Russian military culture. The opening page of his *Rules* read:

> I think it is quite true when I maintain, that every officer, by observing his exact duties can liberate himself from any censure. But since this is not the only goal of my proposed undertaking, I wish, for those who would want to use this friendly instruction, especially for those who were not graced by nature with the best of upbringings, to offer some guidance on which they could base their behaviour, that would enable them to solicit praise from worthy persons and to be capable of achieving significant military ranks, which should be the goal and ambition of any true soldier.[2]

Mamonov identified his audience, outlined what the goals and values of young officers should be, promised his readers liberation from professional contempt, and offered a guide to overcoming inherent social disadvantages and to gaining swift promotion. His decision to write the book reflected the Enlightenment's interest in self-improvement. Mamonov was just one representative of the military proto-intelligentsia, and one of many authors who began to bring military subjects to the expanding public and publishing space of late eighteenth-century Russia.

Throughout the seventeenth century only 483 books were published in Russia, but during Catherine's thirty-four-year reign alone that number grew to more than 8,000.[3] In recent years, research has probed ever deeper into the development of a public sphere in Imperial Russia. Religion, the Freemasons, and various intermediary bodies such as the Free Economic Society, founded during Catherine's reign, all energized the development of this space in the eighteenth century.[4] This chapter shows how the military contributed to that process. By the time Catherine came to power there were dedicated military presses that published everything from translations of Italian opera librettos to professional military texts.[5] Military publications joined the growing stream of literature about science, religion, statecraft, and various other subjects of the Russian Enlightenment. For example, between 1763 and 1766 the Russian reading public could peruse *Infantry Statute* (1763), *Military Statute for Cavalry Exercises* (1763), *Instructions of the Infantry Regiment to the Colonel* (1764), *Instructions of the Cavalry Regiment to the Colonel* (1764), *On Training of the Jager Corps* (1765), *Additional chapters for the General Statute about Military Service* (1765), and *Garrison Statute* (1766).[6] Between 1725 and 1800, at least eighteen military and war-related works were translated into Russian, most of them during Catherine's reign. Good examples are Anton Leopold von Oelsnitz's *Exercises for Officers* (1777), translated from German; and Anglezi's *Advice of a Military Man to his Son* (1787) and Frederick II's *Secret Instructions* (1791), both translated from French.[7] And in 1777, Catherine, with Potemkin's encouragement, ordered the reprinting of old Muscovite military texts from 1607 and 1621.[8]

This chapter examines around twenty military works by officers from Catherine's reign. What distinguished Russia from Western countries was that its military authors belonged to various ethnic backgrounds. Baltic Germans, Russians, and Cossacks all wrote military manuals. In the process they began to give shape to a unified military culture that would develop in the nineteenth century. Their texts demonstrate the subtle influence of the Enlightenment on Russian military culture and its values in at least four ways. Eighteenth-century military authors like Mamonov constructed an ideal officer type based on the principles of the Enlightenment; they critiqued military culture; and they began to separate the military culture and those who wanted to be a part of it from the larger civilian world. Some began to connect war to broader politics; others started expressing national consciousness. These writers saw themselves as "actors in the history of progress," and they applied *esprit philosophique* to the military profession.[9] In this way, the Enlightenment influenced the Russian military culture and the Russian military participated in the Enlightenment.

The Ideal of an Enlightened Officer

One of the first people to write a private manual in Catherine's reign was Aleksandr Suvorov. Suvorov's father, who rose to become the governor of Moscow, was a military intellectual in his own right and carefully home-schooled his son. The young Aleksandr Suvorov became a connoisseur of ancient Greek and Roman literature and an ardent admirer of Julius Caesar, while being a student and follower of Rumiantsev, even though he was once court-martialled by him.[10] Suvorov's career reached its apex in 1799 when he was chosen as a compromise candidate to lead the allied Austro-Russian armies in Italy and Switzerland during the wars of the French Revolution.

Long before Suvorov became a national hero and a commander of armies, he brought order and discipline to his first regiment, in the northern Ladoga region in 1763. How did the young colonel navigate the chaos of military administration that confronted him there? What practices did he consider ideal for his regiment and its officers? And how did he impose this ideal? He decided to write a manual called *Regimental Administration*. Recent work has shown that Suvorov's ideas were less original than many Russian historians have claimed. His manual was influenced by various official military instructions produced by the War College and even by Western literature, such as the Prussian infantry manual from 1743.[11] Motivated by the Enlightenment's emphasis on rationalism, efficiency, and education, and relying on the wider world of military texts, Suvorov began to impose order on the turmoil that reigned in the army. His manual painstakingly outlined everyone's duties and prescribed daily routines for all, from the new recruit to the new officer. For Suvorov, becoming an officer began with education, and here, mentorship by seniors was crucial.

> The only distinction that an illiterate nobleman has from others in a regiment is that he is punished not with a stick but with a fuchtel [flat side of a sword] ... He is not promoted to a higher rank until he learns to read and write in satisfactory Russian. At the same time a literate nobleman with good references, once he has been assigned by the regiment[al]

commander to a detachment, is taken by the detachment commander under his personal care.[12]

Suvorov developed a powerful mechanism for integrating young nobles into military culture. By pairing new officers with experienced staff, he gave the former the chance to observe the bearing and customs of the world they had just entered. During this time, young officers remained under the close supervision of their superiors. They had to learn military regulations, and their knowledge was later tested by commanders. The mentor was to order his charge to "copy excerpts from *Regimental Administration* and check his knowledge of it, and keep this nobleman under his close supervision, teaching him gradually and kindly, with the help of a sergeant," wrote the young Suvorov.[13] Through observation and tests, senior officers transferred their knowledge and customs to the younger generation of servicemen. Suvorov insisted that even young nobles start at the bottom rungs of the military ladder and advance only when they had mastered their tasks sequentially. This demonstrated the remarkable persistence of the ethos of Peter the Great:[14]

> If a nobleman...has been promoted to the rank of an ensign or a sergeant, or has been assigned to a regiment in these ranks, without having enough knowledge and training, and is found not sufficiently competent...as happens to people with non-military background, this person is obliged to undergo full schooling in the regiment.[15]

The young noble had to serve as a private before his superiors deemed his knowledge of the military worthy of a higher rank. From the early years of Catherine's reign, her officers stressed the importance of meritocracy, a meaningful approach to learning, individualism, and fraternity. Under the influence of the Enlightenment, Suvorov was turning young, often illiterate nobles with no previous experience in the military into officers. To inculcate pride and self-esteem, he constantly drummed the beat of professionalism and self-worth.[16]

Suvorov finished his *Regimental Administration* with a popular Enlightenment metaphor comparing the regiment to a human body: "only the accomplished agreement of all the parts within the regiment gives it unwavering strength, and the watchful observation of necessary military rules serves as a soul enlightening a body." As soon as "the firm order of the regiment falls apart, it becomes like a soulless carcass."[17] For Suvorov, the military was more than a random collection of people or a bureaucratic institution; it was a living thing that required its own order and rules, which animated it and gave it purpose, and to that end, he demanded ongoing audits of military expertise and professionalism. His manual became popularly known as the *Suzdal Regulations* after the name of the regiment, and it remains a powerful statement about eighteenth-century military culture in Russia. Suvorov's ideas were not necessarily autochthonous, and he was not the only one who set out to command a regiment on Enlightenment principles. The point here is that his efforts marked the beginning of an age during which members of the Russian military culture regularly wrote manuals.

Another private military manual, this one from 1770, was *Customs of Military Service in the Sumskii Hussar Regiment*, by Colonel Timofei Tutolmin, who had fought alongside Rumiantsev in the first Russo-Turkish War and later became the vice-governor of the Tver province.[18] As in many other military writings from Catherine's era, we encounter in this manual numerous first-person appeals by the author to the readers. The narrative is more personalized, and the military is discussed as part of the public sphere.[19] Besides offering an account of daily life in a hussar regiment, Tutolmin describes in detail the training of corporals and junior officers. Incredibly, in Tutolmin's regiment, senior officers had to personally examine at least one corporal every day. During these tests, officers went point by point through the list of duties of their subordinates, testing their knowledge, and if there was evidence that the latter did not have sufficient understanding of their station, they were reprimanded. Officers also had to keep notes on the abilities of each subordinate they tested.[20] The values that officers such as Suvorov and Tutolmin put forward in their first forays into the world of military writing touched on several universal principles of the Enlightenment, which were continuously reiterated by their peers: the importance of education, professionalism, and meritocracy, of knowledge of military skills, and, finally, of coordination and internal cohesion *within* the military.

The work to define the qualities of the Enlightenment officer continued throughout Catherine's reign. By the 1770s, military manuals had become more detailed and were addressing more sophisticated issues, and many more writers were contributing to the debates about the nature of the military service, its customs, and the training and identity of officers. One of these writers was Mamonov, whom we met at the beginning of this chapter. In 1770, Mamonov composed *Epistle from a General to his Men*. The *Epistle* was a military manual written entirely in verse. As a piece of poetry it was wanting, but as an example of a military instruction it remains undoubtedly unique. In a systematic and methodical way, Mamonov created a holistic narrative covering almost all the aspects of leadership, logistics, uniforms, tactics, sieges, and communications. What made Mamonov's work so different from the numerous odes about war and military victories by Mikhail Lomonosov, Gavril Derzhavin, and others was that he was writing a military manual, not a poem. No stone was left unturned in a supreme effort to produce an ideal type of the Russian officer, outlining his duties, the customs he should follow, and even the mentality he should possess.[21]

If Suvorov concerned himself with turning young nobles into officers, then Mamonov taught officers how to *think* about war, about their profession, and about their soldiers. If Suvorov was describing how to turn nobles into officers, Mamonov was beginning to assign them qualities and responsibilities to define their role in the military:

> What other valid purpose a junior officer would serve?
> He always must present an example of highest honour.
> Like the older brother is ashamed of being worthless,
> A junior officer should be a decent model to follow.[22]

Leadership by example was at the heart of many Russian manuals in the late eighteenth century; the emphasis was on the ability of individuals to shape the customs, behaviours, and manners of their subordinates. It was up to them to spread the gospel of the Military Enlightenment.

Mamonov also explained the nature of war as a simple binary between good and evil:

> Two kinds of war exist; one war is offensive,
> Another kind is one's defence with only fighting back.
> One country will always have justice on its side,
> Whereas another is guided by avarice and harmful pride.[23]

He warned that it was not up to soldiers to philosophize about the reasons for war, hinting that the military should stay out of politics. Officers and soldiers should obey orders and limit their discussions to war and other professional topics:

> To dwell on these parables is still not for the army,
> Our only task is to go fight, and win.[24]

An officer's intellectual place was in the sphere of his military competence, not in highbrow debates about the nature and causes of wars. One of the most interesting parts of the *Epistle* is where Mamonov begins to meditate on the life of the Russian soldier, using powerfully graphic language. Soldiers crying out in pain and begging passers-by to kill them were familiar scenes of eighteenth-century warfare, but such images clashed with the polite and highly aestheticized world of the Enlightenment:

> You hear countless horses' strident neighing,
> Sounds of vociferous command, and moaning of the wounded.
> Sometimes the wounded beg with all their soul,
> To terminate the lives in which they suffer so...
> The entire battlefield is covered with lifeless bodies,
> Between the corpses flow rivers of blood and brains.[25]

The carnage was meant to convey a set of ideas to the officers about the fate of soldiers, and about their own responsibilities, but also about the meaning of war. In the above macabre scene, both officers and soldiers were reduced to ornaments on the field of battle. They had given their lives for "the fatherland, the faith, and for the legacy of their fathers and grand-fathers."[26]

Rhetorically, Mamonov's style was driven by the ideas and values expressed in the wider public sphere about the military. The language was designed to expose young officers who danced at balls, played billiards at their uncles' headquarters, and showed up to examine their soldiers only during parades, to the real hardships of military service. For these gentlemen, the difficulties of daily life in the military flowed unknown past them. Mamonov wanted to bring the two worlds together. At least three times he reproached his readers for being unaware of the hardships faced by regular soldiers:

> You cannot comprehend from the tranquility of your place,
> What labour, great and tough a soldier has to face.
> The soldier has, like you, his soul alive and heart.
> You are asleep; he moves ahead, his road is being hard.[27]

Mamonov clearly wanted his officers to understand and appreciate the hardships faced by Russian soldiers, and this would become one of the themes in the larger discourse of military culture. The reference to heart and soul was not accidental either. The focus on knowledge of the human heart had been popularized by the French Marshal Maurice de Saxe in *My Reveries on the Art of War* and was an important aspect of the Military Enlightenment and the birth of military psychology. By the human heart Saxe meant the amalgamation of "emotion, psychology, physical reflexes and instincts." In proposing that officers focus on the human heart and compassion, Saxe was advancing "a new framework for military leadership," wrote Pichichero, and officers like Mamonov worked to introduce this Enlightenment framework to Russia.[28]

The influence of the Enlightenment on Russian military culture started at the regimental level, where young colonels experimented with instructions for their officers and soldiers, but by the 1780s it was visible among the senior leadership as well. Potemkin was certainly aware of the challenges the Russian army faced when he became the head of the War College in 1784. Influenced by the Enlightenment emphasis on humanism, merit, and education, in his many notes and instructions the prince attempted to address the key failings of the military he was now heading.[29] For example, in 1788 Suvorov received an instruction from Potemkin that succinctly outlined his vision of a perfectly functioning regiment according to the Enlightenment ideal, and ordered Suvorov to make it a reality:

> I demand that people [be] taught with patience and with clear explanations that would lead to their improvement. Regimental commanders have a duty to test junior and middle ranking officers themselves to determine the extent of their knowledge; they are forbidden to punish soldiers with beatings, but need to encourage the lazy ones with a stick, and nothing more; distinguish diligent and well-behaved soldiers, which will give birth to laudable ambition, and with it, to courage. In addition to that, in free time read from the *Military Articles* to remind soldiers what they owe to their service; during Saturdays do not miss an opportunity to bring them to prayer.[30]

Potemkin's instruction neatly summarized major tenets of Russian military culture. The role of officers was to educate soldiers about the nature of the military world rather than to instruct them in simple drills – and Potemkin wanted to see results, hence the reference to tests and improvements. The brutal discipline of the instructions from the Petrine period, which sometimes descended to the methods of the Inquisition, was replaced by using "nothing more" than a stick. Good conduct was observed, recorded, and rewarded. Soldiers were indoctrinated through the reading of military manuals, to reinforce their new purpose and responsibilities. Finally, religion was neatly woven into the busy schedule of Russian soldiers, probably to inspire them and unburden their conscience. "It is with such predilection that a regimental commander can distinguish himself, for I will look favourably upon

this, and not at the harmful panache that is burdensome for the soldier's body," concluded Potemkin.[31] Two years later the prince sent a
similar note to Colonel Iosif de Ribas.[32]

Mamonov returned to the military publishing scene in 1788 with
his *Rules*, which asked an important existential question: what were
some of the criteria for achieving personal satisfaction in military service? His book aspired to teach what junior officers needed to know
in order to succeed in the military world.[33] Returning to the theme of
merit, Mamonov wrote that he saw many officers who deserved to be
promoted but had been passed over for people who were inferior to
them in ability, because the latter had three qualities the former lacked:
a pleasant temperament, social graces, and knowledge of the sciences.[34]
To explain how to develop these qualities was one of Mamonov's goals.
Keeping good company and reading Enlightenment literature should
occupy the free hours of young noble warriors. Spending time in the
houses of respectable families was very important to Mamonov. Such
houses served as the primary incubators of military culture, with their
collections of books, art, and mechanical objects and their learned conversation. But to get invited to such places one first had to follow the
prescriptions laid out earlier. Crude, simple people and their uncouth
habits were rarely tolerated at such gatherings.[35]

Mamonov saved his most important point for last. "My last advice is
for the young man never to forget the word of God; for whoever forgets
about God, God in turn forgets about them."[36] As Gary Hamburg has
argued, the Enlightenment in Russia was less anti-religious than in the
West and had a strong spiritual component, which was reflected in the
military culture. This helps explain how calls to read more books about
science could sit comfortably with advice for more religious devotion.
Those who were ignorant of the Lord's teachings would do damage to
the traditions of honest military service. Mamonov's officer was both a
professional soldier and a Christian. To be a full member of the military
culture one had to be pious, educated, and appropriately socialized.
Mamonov's *Rules* was more than a collection of rules to be followed;
it was also an eloquent guide for navigating military life during the
Enlightenment.

The last major intellectual contribution to military culture of
Catherine's Russia was also a work of military psychology and was
made by Aleksandr Suvorov just before his exile in 1795. Suvorov's brief
but famous manual *Science of Victory* has a rich and interesting history
and has become the most celebrated artefact of the eighteenth-century
Russian army.[37] The manual was as eccentric as its author, and Suvorov's
adages such as "Shoot rarely, but deadly, with the bayonet stab firmly,"

"Train hard, fight easy," and "The musket ball is a fool, the bayonet is a fine chap!" have become part of the Russian military lexicon.[38] Contemporaries called his manual *Talk with Soldiers in Their Tongue*. In *Science of Victory*, Suvorov established a paradigm that would influence the progress and evolution of Russian military theory for the next hundred years and beyond. In the nineteenth century and the early twentieth, Suvorov's work became a rallying cry for military nationalists and influenced the thinking of Russian imperial military pedagogues, and even some of the Bolshevik revolutionaries and Soviet generals.[39]

The manual focused on the training soldiers, but Suvorov did not forget to summarize what he saw as the core values of Russian officers. Suvorov demanded that soldiers know his manual by heart, and he finished *Science of Victory* with a list of tenets the troops had to cry out in chorus after a public reading of the text: "Subordination, Exercise, Obedience, Education, Discipline, Military Order, Cleanliness, Health, Neatness, Sobriety, Courage, Bravery, Victory! Glory! Glory! Glory!"[40] Suvorov wrote a note to a friend in which he reflected on the personal qualities he thought an officer should possess in addition to these military values: he "is extremely brave but not vehement, he is quick in reasoning, yields to authority with no humiliation, and commands without practicing excessive authority. He is victorious without vanity, ambitious without haughtiness, appreciative without arrogance, firm without stubbornness, modest without pretence."[41] These, then, were the ideal personal qualities of the Russian officer in the Age of Enlightenment.

An influential representative of the Military Enlightenment was the British military writer Henry Lloyd (1718–1783). Lloyd was a military adventurer who fought in the Russian army in 1773–74 against the Turks and then sailed to North America to participate in the American War of Independence. In his writings, Lloyd was the earliest proponent of what can be called the scientific approach to the study of war. According to Azar Gat, he was the first to theorize "the moral qualities of the troops into a systematic study by applying the mechanistic-hedonistic psychology of the Enlightenment to the military field." Lloyd was particularly interested in the emotions and motivations of soldiers, and he wrote at length about the pleasures and pains of military life, such as women, religion, glory, honour, envy, pride, shame, and music. When they understood the causes of pain and pleasure in their soldiers, officers could "control and manipulate the human material at their disposal."[42] It is not clear whether Suvorov or other Russian military writers read Lloyd's work, but undoubtedly they understood this dimension of military psychology and wanted to teach their audience the sublime art of how to become the masters of soldiers during war.

By the 1790s the outer shell of the ideal officer was beginning to be more clearly defined in Russian military culture, in many ways inspired by the broader currents of the Enlightenment. However, one crucial facet of that shell was missing – how did military culture accommodate officers who chose to retire? Deliberating on the ideals and tenets of his predecessors, in 1793 Lieutenant-Colonel Grigorii Rzhevskii presented a powerful condemnation of early retirement from military service. In his *Essay of Lieutenant-Colonel Rzhevskii*, he reflected on the military values and lifestyle that could not be practised in retirement and showed what happened to a member of the military culture once he had left the military world for civilian life. In his narrative, Rzhevskii upheld the principle of utility, of being useful, that was so important to the Enlightenment frame of mind.

Rzhevskii was born in 1763, a year after Catherine II came to the throne, and at the age of ten was enrolled in the elite Semenovskii Guards. In 1790 he participated in the Russo-Swedish war, retiring as a captain in 1792, at the age of twenty-nine; but six months later he returned to military service. Like many officers of his time, Rzhevskii was a patron of theatre and a lover of literature, who tried his hand at writing novels and poetry. But as some literary critics had noted, his literary career was hopeless. His poems and plays did not "reflect even an inkling of talent: everything he wrote is void of content and carries within it a stamp of poor taste."[43] Rzhevskii was better at writing military manuals than poetry. In the opening pages of his *Essay*, he confessed: "I inwardly cursed the minute I decided to retire from service."[44] It took the patronage of Prince Iurii Dolgorukov, a general and the future governor of Moscow, to arrange his return to the army. The happiest day of Rzhevskii's life had been the day he was taken back into the military by the magnanimous monarch so that he could eradicate that dark spot of idleness from his consciousness and serve his fatherland once again.[45]

Rzhevskii returned to military service because he felt there was not enough opportunity for him to serve his country from his estate and to distinguish himself. After all, "to strive to distinguish oneself by knowledge and merit is one's dignity and obligation," he wrote, neither of which ostensibly could be fulfilled in civilian life.[46] His longing for service, his disappointment with the idle life, and the little respect he received in his new social position as a civilian made his existence unbearable. He wrote this emotional appeal to his readers: "Oh you, my young comrades! Your hearts, inclined to freedom from superiors compel you to resign from service early, whereas only now you are at your prime time to start serving the fatherland with dignity and loyalty."[47] He implored the new generation of officers not to repeat his mistake, for they would regret it. Rzhevskii tried to show that the respect officers enjoyed from their noble and non-noble subordinates vanished the minute they tendered their resignation and traded their uniform for civilian clothes. Speaking to the wider military community, Rzhevskii concluded:

> let our will and thoughts be limited to the silent compliance with military obedience; let us adorn our souls with military heroes, inspiring discipline; let us fill our hearts not with the swagger of a military uniform, but with courage and manliness for defeating the enemies of the fatherland; and finally, to achieve these noble qualities, let us tie ourselves with an unbreakable knot of friendship and concord.[48]

This was a powerful call for fraternity and connection based on shared values among members of the military culture. Like Mamonov, Rzhevskii encouraged professional preoccupation with the military world and pointed out that real soldiering was more than just the wearing of a uniform – it entailed dedication to a lifestyle that came from the heart. Rzhevskii's essay neatly summarized the benefits of serving in the military – respect from civilians, opportunity for personal growth and honour, and a chance to actively serve the greater good of the Russian state and society. Out of the noble ethos by the late eighteenth century there had emerged a military ethos, a set of values and mores that was reflected in the military essays of officers who served in the Russian military. Influenced by wider Enlightenment thinking, military writers began to construct an ideal type of a modern officer. They argued that to be considered a true son of the fatherland and a member of the military it was not enough to be noble, to exercise one's rights, or to follow the law. It was also important to possess virtue, and for officers that meant fulfilling their duties to their profession and to their soldiers. Officers who made no contribution to the betterment of their regiments, who contemplated retirement, who did not seek technical military knowledge, and who did not embrace professionalism and merit, could not claim military status and were not the true defenders of the fatherland.[49]

Critiquing Military Culture

The 1770s were fertile years for military writing. The long wars with Poland and the Ottoman Empire had fostered reflection, soul-searching, and even critique among the Russian military. One influential person of that time was Count Petr Rumiantsev, who was then at the peak of his military career and political power. In the 1770s he wrote two military manuals. The first of these, written in 1770 and called *Customs of Military Service* (*Obriad Sluzhby*), was a detailed military text that governed the day-to-day activities of his army. *Customs of Military Service* instructed soldiers about everything from marching formations to how to set up pickets at camp. In the course of all this, Rumiantsev was actually critiquing existing practices and pointing out gaps in *Military Statute*, *Military Articles*, and other official regulations. In many of its sections, his manual expressed Enlightenment humanity as well as concerns about hygiene, treatment of soldiers, and respect for civilians.[50] Rumiantsev's manual was so effective that in 1776 the War College recommended that the entire army adopt it, which gained his ideas intellectual currency in the military as a whole.[51]

The Enlightenment influence on Russian military culture was extended by Baltic Germans living in western parts of the Russian Empire. One of them was Baron Reingold Iogan von Meiendorf, vice-governor of the city of Riga, the capital of modern-day Latvia, and a lieutenant-general in the Russian army. In 1772 Meiendorf distilled the results of more than thirty years' active service in his Russian homeland.[52] In *Experience of Some Reflections about the Military*, he emphasized the professional qualities of officers, the need for them to be politically aware, and the uniqueness of the military calling. In doing so, he also offered a critique of military traditions. He challenged the medieval aristocratic notion that only people of noble birth were qualified for the military. "Often [young officers] have the same thoughts and opinions as Mascarille portrayed by Molière, saying that 'a man of noble birth knows everything and does not require studying,'" Meiendorf wrote.[53] Mascarille was a character in a seventeenth-century play, *The Blunderer*, by Jean-Baptiste Poquelin, whose pen name was Molière. The character Mascarille, whose name suggests "masquerade," was the archetypical boastful soldier. Meiendorf's reference was clear to the educated public, and his critique of the military culture was biting.

Meiendorf's ideal officer was the opposite of Mascarille. He was patient, hard-working, and insightful and possessed both practical military knowledge and sound judgment. He was precise, wise, and experienced in many arts and sciences. He was a man of the Enlightenment. All of these qualities were crucial because, as Meiendorf bluntly put it, an officer, especially a colonel, "will have to inculcate into state service two thousand unenlightened and for the most part callous people for good work, the security of the entire society and national pride." He would have to tame their appetites, teach them the customs of military service, and turn them into obedient and respectful members of the military culture. It seemed a daunting task indeed, and Meiendorf hoped his *Reflections* would serve as a kind of guide to young Mascarilles to help them steer away from some of the hidden reefs of being a Russian officer.[54] After all, flawed officers produced equally flawed regiments, or as Meiendorf put it, "if the original is filled with defects, then its copies will be no less defective."[55]

Another notable work of the period came from the pen of young Stepan Rzhevskii, whose writing reflected the influence of the Enlightenment and who offered a critique of the Russian military. At the time he wrote his first manual, *Instruction about How to Conduct Training in Military Camp for Infantry and Cavalry*, in 1774, he was a humble major serving in the Saint Petersburg Legion. Rzhevskii identified his audience as "staff and ober-officers," presented them with a critique of military culture, shared his observations about military movements, and above all urged his readers to apply his observations.[56] Though his text is drily technical, embedded in it are illuminating insights about military culture that are worth digging out.

Rzhevskii's criticism developed the theme of professionalism, which was shared among all the military writers of Catherine's age. He accused many senior officers of amateurism: "Many regimental commanders think only superficially without going into the delicate details."[57] Rzhevskii was frustrated with the military even as a young man, and he demanded that all officers be able to demonstrate their knowledge of the military profession in practice.[58] For example, when discussing troop movements, he reflected on parades, uniforms, and the pageantry associated with the army: "I make the following conclusion that anything that only brings beauty to the ranks is impractical, unnecessary, and therefore superfluous." He added that "the service requires movements not only of beauty but also practicality."[59] This was one of the first grumbles against the glitter of parades, which would continue to rise after Catherine's death.

Rzhevskii contrasted the superficiality of parades with Enlightment calls for timing and precision, as in the following example:

> I would love the type of colonel ... who based the movement of his regiment and reinforced it in such a way that he could find out without fault that from this to that place it would take him a certain amount of time, that his ... regiment take this many minutes and so many steps, and finally after sizing up the place where he would contest his enemy, say: I will reach this knoll with my regiment in ten minutes, deploy the column within 200 steps of the enemy in 2 minutes, and quickly tear into the enemy in 2 minutes.[60]

All the elements of rational, methodical, disciplined thinking about war were present here: calls for precision, for timetables, for the rapid deployment of troops, and for commanding officers who were knowledgeable about geography and tactics. All of these qualities grew from systematic practice and the study of professional literature. Amateur approaches to war were giving way to inculcated professionalism.

In his conclusion, Major Rzhevskii addressed a community of "gentlemen-officers" who together with the author exemplified military participation in the wider public sphere.[61] The *Instruction* hoped to encourage single-minded commitment to military service and described the qualities of a perfect officer: "supreme desire for service and diligence in military craft, unquenchable and boundless subordination, strictness and politeness among all the ranks, holy reverence for the name of the St. Petersburg Legion, friendship and marvellous understanding among each other."[62] By the 1770s there was a professional audience of readers and practitioners of the military craft, who joined Rzhevskii in promoting the "marvellous understanding" within the military, but also in critiquing the military culture.

The same year Rzhevskii wrote his instruction, twenty-year-old Count Andrei Viazemskii wrote his *Military Note*. Like his peers, Viazemskii participated in the larger public sphere and was influenced by the progenitors of Europe's Military Enlightenment. He claimed knowledge of the military world through the many works he had read by foreign authors about war, military science, and military thought. Having become a self-taught expert, he must have wanted to share his own thoughts on the matter, as many young men do when they think they can make a difference. "I, knowing my limitations, would not even endeavour such an enterprise if I was not motivated by reading the best works in the field and deliberating on this subject," he wrote.[63] For a wider audience, he outlined and critiqued many aspects of the Russian military and offered his solutions to the problems he perceived.

He criticized the recruitment of peasants and backed his allegations with personal experience. "I myself was a witness to this, for two people were sent to my regiment that were completely deaf and could not even hear a cannon being fired."[64] He criticized soldiers' medical care, which he said turned minor problems into "severe illness."[65] He criticized training regulations, specifically the *Colonel's Instruction*, which required teaching recruits everything they needed to become soldiers in five weeks. Viazemskii thought this was unreasonable. In Britain, for example, the initial phase of training could take up to a few months.[66] He complained that the principal methods of instruction and training continued to be based on thorough beatings, remarking with sarcasm that "soldiers were taught without mercy."[67] He criticized soldiers' and officers' uniforms, arguing that they did more harm than good. And he criticized officer pay, which was too low for the financial burdens they were expected to carry, once again giving examples from his own observations and experience.[68] Viazemskii's work was part recommendation, part critique of Russian military practices and Russian military culture. The critical spirit of the Enlightenment had entered the military culture and was being made public through books and notes by young officers such as Rzhevskii and Viazemskii.

The 1780s saw earlier authors returning to the scene with new material, ideas, and critiques. By 1782 Stepan Rzhevskii had become a general, and that year he composed *Various Notes about Army Service*, in which, with twelve succinct points, he laid down a formidable indictment of the Russian military in Catherine's reign. The following were his most biting critique:

V. Resentment amongst honest and deserving officers for promotion of favourites or devious and nimble parasites ruined all desire for military service and shattered all patriotism.

VII. Ease of retirement departs the young man from military service; for he, following the natural desire of the human heart and the predilection of the former towards independence, does not see any obstacles for it.

XV. Can one expect valour from such a perverted military where, the first order of business is to depart from service, where the officer is brought to despair, where he, from immense and enforced panache, is bankrupted; where a soldier, shedding bitter tears, crunches his dried bread, cursing military service and his commanders, only looking around for a road and opportunity to desert?

XVI. It confuses me that there exists no important or necessary enterprise or craft, which does not require its student to pass a rigid examination if he wishes to become its apprentice or master. Is military science so seemingly easy, that advancement within it can be affected without any discrimination, as if the uniform imbues officers with knowledge, and a personal order creates a general?[69]

This was a remarkable document for several reasons. In many ways Rzhevskii was presenting Russian military culture as an intellectual, cultural, and social project to be taken up, shaped, and developed by his peers. His was a challenge to the whole community. Rzhevskii confirmed that tensions between merit, favouritism, and seniority persisted. He commented negatively on Peter III's manifesto, which freed the nobility from obligatory state service, for this had drained the military of capable officers. He addressed the miserable situation in the ranks and the lack of proper training and education for officers. Rzhevskii did not provide answers or recommendation; rather, he asked questions and pointed out problems. He was talking to other military participants in the public sphere, and in that regard his work was a rallying cry. General Rzhevskii wanted things to change, and he wanted and expected others to read his *Notes* and to contribute to the discussions that had been going on since the 1760s.

In 1788, Mamonov published his *Rules*. In his view, low-ranking military men such as retainers, valets, and other subordinates killed virtue, diligence, intelligence, and merit. He offered an antidote to the virus of manservants and underlings (*lakei*) from which young men could protect themselves by looking professional. He wrote that the first quality that meets one's eye is "the external appearance"; this was not a mark of eighteenth-century noble vanity, but rather a statement of professionalism. Mamonov thought that proper military dress showed that an individual belonged to a larger culture, that he belonged to a particular group governed by codes and rules that distinguished itself from all other groups. An officer should never dress out of style, Mamonov warned. Otherwise such young men would be thought of as self-indulgent or ill-mannered. But Mamonov also warned that an officer should never over-dress to impress women, as many young officers tended to do. "In all honesty one can call them brainless Adonises," he quipped.[70] Too much emphasis on the uniform distracted from professionalism; too little reflected negatively on the officer's professional qualities. In retrospect, Mamonov had written not necessarily a military manual or a rule book, but a critique and program to turn "the brainless Adonises" into military professionals.

Meiendorf challenged the notion that the nobility alone were suited for military service, hinting that status at birth was not sufficient to justify a monopoly on the military profession. Viazemskii presented a series of criticisms, ranging from lack of health services to poor training. Rzhevskii chastised officers publicly for being only superficially familiar with the technical aspects of military service; he then decried "devious parasites," unchecked departure from the military, and the lack of formal exams to test officers' knowledge. Mamonov called many of the Russian officers simply brainless. These writers and many others were creating a cultural tradition and an intellectual space within the public sphere where the military could critique established methods, disagree with official policies and regulations, and offer suggestions and sometimes even implement them.

Separation between Civilian and Military Worlds

A prominent discourse of the Military Enlightenment revolved around the idea that the military was separate from the civilian world.[71] In Russia this idea began to take shape in the 1770s, when Meiendorf, in his *Reflections*, began to set apart the military from civilian society. He was one of the first to do so. While civilian society goes about its business, the church prays for the souls of sinners, and the government enacts laws, "a soldier does not think of anything but protecting the faith, defending the government [and] its people [and] enforcing the government's laws." In other words, the military as a whole toiled for "the general good of society."[72] The functions of the military were fundamentally different from those of civilian, religious, and governmental institutions. Officers had to learn the values of self-sacrifice and respect, and to learn to cooperate with civilian society while not being part of it. Building on this idea, Meiendorf argued that "with this actual and existing law of separation, we must distinguish the military establishment from other callings."[73] Belonging to the nobility did not necessarily mean belonging to the military culture. His words reflected a growing awareness in Catherine's Russia that the military was a separate world, one whose identity was built on a set of values and goals that were different from those of the civilian world.[74] He shared this point of view with his contemporaries, such as Count Semen Vorontsov.

Before he became famous as the Russian ambassador to London, in 1774, as a thirty-year-old colonel, Semen Vorontsov (1744–1832) wrote *Instructions to Company Commanders* for his regiment. In it he stated that the lot of a military man was hectic, difficult, and dangerous, compared to that of the civil servant; but at the same time it offered greater honour and glory. Vorontsov made a clear distinction between civilians and the military. Officers and soldiers "defend their fellow citizens from enemies, defend the fatherland and the holy church from enslavement by heathens, and in so doing win the appreciation of the Autocrat, the thanks of the people, and the gratitude and prayers of the churchmen."[75] By the late eighteenth century, the military was defining its cultural boundaries and differentiating itself from other callings and institutions.

Senior commanders soon joined the voices of junior officers. Rumiantsev's second military work was *Thoughts of Count Petr Rumiantsev about the Military*, which he wrote in three days at the request of the empress in 1777. It was arguably Rumiantsev's longest-lasting and most philosophical contribution to Russian military culture. The opening page of this overlooked work read:

> The military institution, which is different from all others, has become simultaneously indispensable to all states, according to some European views; however, due to the inequalities in a physical and moral sense, they could not have been in either quantity nor quality similar to one another, and as governments have discovered that the army is a burden on all other components of the state, they are now striving to employ all means to improve the connections among them, an endeavour in which some countries have done better than the rest.[76]

Rumiantsev reaffirmed in his writing that the military was different from other institutions – it was governed by its own laws and customs and had its own culture. He also underscored its premier importance to "all states."

In the process of drawing the boundaries of military culture, its members began looking for visual and material symbols of distinction, something that could mark them apart in the larger social and cultural milieu. Inevitably their eyes turned to the uniform. The uniform held a particular sway over young men: it epitomized the military calling and served as a powerful symbol of the military as an institution distinct from the civilian world.[77] Andrei Bolotov (1738–1833), who belonged to an earlier generation, recounted in his memoirs the full effect that donning his first uniform had on him.

> One way or another, for me the call of a soldier was the highest honour, and once they tailored me a small uniform, and found a corporal's trim, I did not know what to do with myself from joy. Thus I entered military service, even though I was ten years of age, but already I began to think about the military and in my free time entertained myself with such things that were relevant to it.[78]

The uniform had a psychological and emotional impact in that it drew young nobles into military culture. As Engelgardt wrote, already as a young boy he was impressed by the symbolic trappings of military culture: "I still remember my childhood joy and excitement, when I was dressed in hussar uniform; the most thrilling for me was the sabre with sabretache."[79] The new uniform generated similar excitement in the young Sergei Mosolov. "When they dressed me in the uniform of a soldier," he wrote in his memoir, "it made me so happy, that now I cannot even explain it."[80] Mikhail Petrov likewise recalled how "the arrival of our father's brothers for home leave, one in the red uniform of an infantry officer and the other in the fine hussar attire, delighted us about our future fate."[81] All of these boys fell under the spell of the military uniform and the values and aspirations it presented.

For military writers like Rumiantsev, the uniform was meant to serve as a mark of pride for those who were in military service and were part of its culture, as well as a sign of distinction after a long and diligent military career. Rumiantsev too contributed to the discussion of what it meant to belong to the military culture. He wrote that wearing a uniform was not a right but an earned privilege. "Therefore," he wrote in his *Thoughts*, for "those who in the fine years of their youth, forsaking the natural burden of their responsibilities and following their whims, left military service ... the wearing of the uniform is disrespectful and should not be allowed."[82] Unlike the War College, which maintained in its instructions that anyone who at one point had served in the military had the right and indeed the obligation to wear their uniform, Rumiantsev wanted the uniform to reflect the identity of the military community in a narrower sense. Lack of differentiation between active servicemen and dandies who had served for a few years only to earn their epaulets was offensive to the community of professional officers.

Some argued that the uniform was a necessary means for separating professional soldiers from civilian interlopers; others called for an end to ornamentation; still others suggested the introduction of standard, universal uniforms across the entire military, anticipating nineteenth-century trends. Referring to the custom in some units of dressing according to the individual whims of their commanders, Mamonov wrote in his *Rules* in 1788 that he supported the standardization of uniforms across the military.[83] This was another attempt to underscore the differences between the military culture, whose members wore specialized dress, and civilian society, whose members did not. Mamonov clearly wanted to keep the two separate, and what better way than through clothing? He maintained that "it is not commendable when an officer of high standing voluntarily sheds the uniform." Military men should not change their suits like card players, for their identity was vested in their uniform. If it was up to Mamonov, he would stop such practices.[84]

Mamonov and Rumiantsev were not the only ones who connected the uniform to military culture. In the 1780s even the busy Prince Potemkin wrote a short piece about uniforms and equipment, which he addressed to Catherine, at her request. Potemkin noted that Russian military culture was growing more independent from that of the West, or rather, the military elite had stopped looking to the West for inspiration. He began his analysis with a history of the military uniform dating back several hundred years:

At the time of the introduction of regular military service, many foreign officers were admitted into Russia. They brought with them the military formalities of that time, and our military men, not knowing the real importance of body armour, considered everything sacred, if not even mysterious. It seemed to them that regular military service consisted of [armoured] plates, hats, flaps, cuffs ... and the like. Busying themselves with this nonsense, they did not know until now the most important things.[85]

Potemkin was suggesting that following European customs had led to the introduction of many unnecessary and absurd items to Russian military equipment, including to uniforms. Describing for Catherine how weaponry had evolved and how the nature of war had changed over the centuries, he concluded that the Russian uniform – the visual manifestation of imperial power on the field of battle – should change and adapt as well. Catherine evidently liked Potemkin's arguments and instructed him to carry out his program of clothing the entire army in new, simplified uniforms, which became known as "Potemkin's Uniforms."[86]

War, Politics, and National Consciousness

Finally, an important part of the Military Enlightenment was the discourse that related military practice to politics and nationality. As Mark Wishon points out, under the influence of Montesquieu's *Spirit of Laws*, among other works, the use of language in military writings began to reveal how its authors created stereotypes and assigned national traits rooted in military experience. For many countries in Western Europe, including Britain, the eighteenth century was a formative period for national identity, which was "forged through intense and continued conflict."[87] In a similar way the fusion of war with Enlightenment culture stimulated the growth of national consciousness in Catherinian Russia. Reading about other European militaries and their traditions forced the Russian military to ask questions about their own identity. Moreover, military victories did much to articulate the sense of Russian-ness. In the same way that Frederick's victories "helped to overcome the long-standing German inferiority complex regarding the French,"[88] Russian successes over European and Turkish foes helped Russians to define their own national character and critically consider the wider European political landscape.

In 1747 the King of Prussia wrote in his *Instruction to the Generals* that "one should know one's enemies, their alliances, their resources, and the nature of their country in order to plan a campaign."[89] In the case of Russia, this meant insisting on officers being aware of the international political situation and connecting the military profession to government policies. The ideal officer had to know more than simply how to command his regiment; he also had to be familiar with European politics in general, and with the politics of the country where he served in particular. In his correspondence with General Nikita Panin, Rumiantsev underscored the need for military men to be fully developed political animals. As Christopher Duffy wrote, Rumiantsev viewed war in an almost Clausewitzian terms. The embryonic notion that a military conflict was just one piece of the political calculus and that it did not constitute an end in itself was evident in Russian military culture as early as 1771, when Rumiantsev wrote to Panin: "A man who simply looks at what lies immediately before his eyes will be unable to see what advantages may derive from the perception of the less obvious attendant circumstances. I could easily go astray if I left myself in ignorance of the political side of affairs, for this lays down the guidelines for the military aspect."[90] In Rumiantsev's mind the link between the "political side" and the "military aspect" of war was paramount. A year later, Meiendorf wrote that an officer dispenses only half of his service "if his understanding and his knowledge does not touch upon political rules."[91] Both men may have been influenced by the writings of Frederick the Great, whom they read and admired.

Out of all this there soon emerged an argument for allowing the military profession to have political independence and to have input into how wars were fought. Although Simon Dixon correctly concluded that in eighteenth-century Russia no profession "developed a sense of autonomy," the military profession was one case where plans and arguments for such autonomy began to emerge.[92] In his *Thoughts*, Rumiantsev went further than anyone else in asserting the political autonomy of the military and of its senior officers. He wanted the military to be self-regulating, with minimum government involvement. The sovereign, Rumiantsev thought, should not meddle in or be occupied with the inner workings of the military. Instead, she should have a dedicated body of appointed professionals who managed the military, sent recommendations for promotions, and provided general military advice.[93]

In general there is a gap in our understanding of Catherine as a "military commander-in-chief," but it seems that she largely followed Rumiantsev's model.[94] She restricted herself to delegating responsibilities, requesting advice directly from her commanders in the field, or sending them instructions based on advice from the high-ranking military men such as Rumiantsev, Saltykov, and Repnin, and above all

Potemkin, the president of the War College and the commander of the Russian forces in southern Russia. During the Second Russo-Turkish War, Catherine gave Potemkin the authority and the initiative to make decisions and solve problems, which she promised to support. "As much as you can, you will make full use of your intelligence to extirpate evil and to overcome all possible obstacles," she wrote to him in 1787. "And for my part, I shall not miss a single opportunity to lend help where it may be required."[95] And true to her word, when the president of the War College asked his empress for help, she responded. A few months later Potemkin asked the empress to "raise no fewer than 60 thousand recruits," to which Catherine duly replied, "My friend, a recruitment levy has been ordered."[96] She read battle descriptions, wrote back congratulatory notes, rewarded people her senior commander advised her to reward, and acted on requests and suggestions of the War College. It seems that Catherine co-managed the military effort with her chief lieutenants rather than assuming exclusive command of the military and the war effort, and according to a recent study, her leadership in war was more successful than that of her predecessors.[97] Her ability and willingness to step out of the sphere of military culture played a vital role in its development. In many ways, the military was beginning to be in dialogue with the empress, offering her advice, trying to address various shortcomings, and participating in the discussion about the use of national resources for war, as well as its political goals. Many junior officers went unheard and probably unread by Catherine, but at least with Rumiantsev and Potemkin, the ideas they proposed were implemented. Thus the military took advantage of the political climate of the late eighteenth century, which saw the development of a political dialogue between autocrats and their subjects, to shape the military culture and its prerogatives.[98]

By the end of the century the community of senior officers felt comfortable enough to produce war plans for the government even when they had not been formally solicited. Less famous than *Science of Victory* was Suvorov's 1795 war plan against the Ottoman Empire, written with Admiral Iosif de Ribas and other officers. If *Science of Victory* was written for soldiers, then this war plan was composed for the sovereign and her cabinet. It is not clear whether the plan had been developed at the request of Catherine or whether, knowing her desire to expand southwards and build on the work of Potemkin, the officers presented it as their own initiative. The military played on the ambitions of the empress and began to relate the practice of war to larger political objectives. The officers wanted to insert themselves into the larger discussion about the use of the military, displayed awareness of international politics, and related that awareness to their profession. In the war plan, Suvorov and his comrades painted a bold and detailed vision of war against the Porte, with 100,000 Russian soldiers and sailors who in three campaigns would conquer nothing less than the city of Constantinople. The plan was distinguished by its careful review of previous experience of military actions in the Black Sea region, methodical calculations of sieges of regional fortresses, commentary on the political and diplomatic situation in Europe, and attention to time and logistics. "The time is more precious than anything, and we must learn to save it; our previous victories were often hollow because we lacked this insight," wrote Suvorov.[99] The empress and her advisers dismissed the plan, but this probably was beside the point. All Suvorov wanted to do with this document was influence Catherine's strategic considerations in the region, where he was now the commander-in-chief. He wanted to demonstrate the feasibility of such a campaign, the strength and resilience of the Russian army, and the ambition and imagination of the officers of Her Imperial Majesty. Between the 1760s and the 1790s, Russian military writings evolved from considering the necessary qualities for a successful officer to deliberating on the political awareness of the military and the need for its autonomy; in this, they refleccted the wider aspirations of the military culture of Catherine's Russia.

While discussing the military as an autonomous institution and placing war in the larger political context, some writers began to ask a new set of questions. To what extent should Russia follow Western military practices? How were the Russian military and its soldiers different from their European counterparts? And what should the military's policy be for recruiting foreigners? One of the first young officers to reflect on the connection between military practices and a country's character was Viazemskii. After reading the rich Enlightenment literature, he concluded that Russia was different from Europe. Probably influenced by Rousseau, who wrote in *The Social Contract* that laws must be "modified in each country to meet local conditions and suit the character of the people concerned," Viazemskii wrote that those military laws and practices that proved beneficial in France might not necessarily do so in the Russian Empire.[100] The young officer attempted to extract only those ideas from all the military works he had read that he thought would benefit "our state."[101] Similarly, writing about artillery in 1777, Ivan Volyntsov synthesized foreign works and saw it as his mission, as an instructor, to write down his ideas for the Russian audience.[102] Reading the works of the European Military Enlightenment compelled Russian officers to confront their own national consciousness.

In his *Thoughts*, Rumiantsev revealed even more the extent to which the national consciousness was taking shape in the military culture. "Since we, due to the extensive territory, mixed and for the most part wicked neighbours, and the sectarian and customary differences of our inhabitants, are least comparable with other states, we should expand as much as it is beneficial and advantageous for us and imitate others only to the extent that it suits our needs."[103]

Russia had a different political and social composition than the rest of Europe and thus could not wholeheartedly adopt the Western way of war, or its military customs. He was signalling to the empress that the military no longer had to "imitate" European military institutions and adopt their customs. In Rumiantsev's writings we hear a voice that represented a community with its own ideas about its role and importance in the wider society. By the 1770s, Russian military culture was acquiring a degree of self-awareness that reflected its new confidence.

But Rumiantsev did not stop there. He was also concerned about the influx of foreigners into the Russian army, a worry shared by many of his contemporaries; also, he wanted to promote merit. Foreigners, especially from Poland, "gathered the ranks from Princes" and then sought transfer into the upper echelons of the Russian military. This meant that their employment reflected favouritism instead of ability.[104] Such recruits from abroad were undermining merit, professionalism, and the morale of the larger community of Russian officers. Rumiantsev clearly connected the influx of foreigners to the lack of intellectual capital at home – capital that he wanted to develop: "Due to the shortage of trained professionals of the middle-rank and of tradesmen required for the army, and in view of considerable difficulties in attracting foreign specialists and the high costs of their up-keep, it is essential to ... establish educational institutions in the fashion of military schools, art schools and vocational schools, in major and other key cities all over the country."[105] He wanted to break the intellectual and cultural dependence on foreign militaries and encourage the growth of local talent. He was one of the first military writers to assert national distinctions between Russia and the West, and among the first to think about Russian military culture in national terms, but he would not be the last.

Around 1793, General Aleksandr Samoilov composed a note with his thoughts on the state of the military after Potemkin's death, focusing especially on reforms in the lower ranks. Addressing Her Imperial Highness, he wrote that soldiers "are dropping like flies due to the great disturbance they experience in their lives transitioning from peasantry into the military. This, one time, preoccupied the thoughts of the deceased Prince, who concerned himself a great deal with the lower ranks, and whose way of thinking breathed national character into Your soldiers."[106] It is not clear what Samoilov meant by the "national character" that Potemkin had impressed on Catherine's soldiers and what the consequences of his efforts had been. Clearly, though, the notion that Russian soldiers had a national character was taking root in the military culture.

The last word, as often happened, belonged to Suvorov. By the end of the century, Viazemskii's and Rumiantsev's restrained remarks about Western militaries had been amplified by the French Revolution. A striking feature of Suvorov's *Science of Victory* was the degree of xenophobia it expressed. Listing Russia's enemies, Suvorov wrote unflatteringly: "There are also the atheist, wind-bag, maddened, Frenchies."[107] By contrast, Russian soldiers were religious, down-to-earth, and quite sane. He then moved on to the Germans: "Beware of hospitals! German drugs are from far away, expired, useless and dangerous. The Russian soldier is not used to them!"[108] Suvorov's undisguised contempt for foreigners was part of an emerging national consciousness in eighteenth-century Russia, but it was also a characteristic of the Enlightenment influence on Russian military culture during Catherine's reign. The writings of the Russian military proto-intelligentsia point to how they saw Russia as different from many Western kingdoms and empires; those same writers perceived the Russian soldier, if not the Russian officer, as fundamentally different from his European counterparts. Viazemskii and his contemporaries no longer saw a need to follow the West. Perhaps because of this, military writers wanted to curtail the practice of hiring European soldiers of fortune. Rumiantsev and others probably saw their presence as reflecting poorly on the Russian military and as an embarrassment to the country as a whole.

By the 1760s, writings about war were reaching a critical mass and making a distinct contribution to the Russian Military Enlightenment. Military writers delineated personal qualities and norms of behaviour, provided an alternative narrative to official regulations, and attempted to construct a new identity for members of the military culture. They made numerous statements about enforcing meritocracy and wove religion into military culture. The authors wrote about professionalism and discipline and in the process devised means for integrating young officers into the military world. Above all, their texts sought to raise the military vocation to new levels of autonomy and respect, while also subjecting the military to serious reflection, study, and even occasional critique. Under the influence of the spirit of the Enlightenment, military culture continued to evolve during Catherine's reign and increasingly stepped into the emerging public sphere.

Circumstantial evidence indicates that the texts that have survived represent only a fraction of the total intellectual output of military culture during that time. It seems that by Catherine's reign, writing and engaging in professional discussions was a common practice among Russian officers.[109] As the historian S.N. Liutov wrote, much of the writing "existed in hand-written form and [was] used in the part of the military that [was] commanded by, or in which served, their authors. These works were an organic part of the immense, growing military literature of the second half of the eighteenth century."[110] Many of these handwritten manuscripts did not survive. We can say, however, that this immense literary activity led to military participation in the public sphere and that these works were read, debated, and applied in various parts of the Russian army. Writing about his early life, Aleksandr Pishchevich remembered how Stepan Rzhevskii's *Nastavleniia* was used in his uncle's regiment, and Lev Engelgardt reminisced about how during long winters he and his fellow officers read military texts that had been collected by one of their comrades.[111] No doubt these communal readings led to many animated discussions; they may have even prompted some readers to turn themselves into writers, as was the case with young Andrei Viazemskii. In doing so the young *militaires philosophes* were establishing the firm footing for Enlightenment practices within the Russian military.

Furthermore, military authors sought to distinguish the military from the civilian sphere, while at the same time writing its concerns into the broader agenda of the Enlightenment. Meiendorf called for the military establishment to "distinguish [itself] from other callings," and Rumiantsev wrote that "the military institution is different from all others." They wanted members of the military to wear uniforms, to talk and behave in a certain way, and to possess a different identity than their civilian counterparts. The military culture saw itself as a separate entity from the civilian world, yet simultaneously connected to it, even subservient to it, through the notions of service to country, defence of its religion, loyalty to its people, and protection of its government. Military manuals reflected the larger intellectual world of the Enlightenment and expressed that the military was not a static monolith but a cultural space that was developing a tradition in which private views were publicly expressed, dialogues were established, and ideas were exchanged in a horizontal as well as vertical fashion. This space created opportunities for criticism – from Mamonov about uniforms, from Rumiantsev about foreigners, and from Rzhevskii about everything else. Military texts also served as a platform for an incipient national consciousness, expressing cultural anxiety about Western Europe. As Hans Rogger argued, the eighteenth century was a time of a growing search for national identity, a search that found its way into military writings.[112] Unlike Peter the Great, who imported foreign customs wholesale, Viazemskii wanted to use only those foreign ideas that benefited the Russian state, discarding the rest. Similarly, Rumiantsev wanted to "imitate others only to the extent that it suits our needs." And Suvorov, it seems, dismissed French and Prussian military practices altogether. Connected to the expressions of national consciousness within the military was the story of how its members were trying to create a unified imperial military culture that transcended ethnic and religious differences. As Geoffrey Hoskins argued, the military "became the principal social base for an imperial Russian consciousness."[113] Everyone was aware that Russia, as Rumiantsev eloquently put it, "was least comparable with other states." Russia was a multi-ethnic empire with Cossack, Baltic German, Russian, Kalmyk, Polish, and Serbian officers all serving in the military. Many of them, at some point in their lives, became military writers. The values and aspirations they expressed were remarkably similar. By writing instructions, essays, and manuals, by creating ideal types, by trying to rationalize military service, the texts were trying to create a shared culture for the Russia's military.

Imperial, Soviet, and contemporary Russian scholarship has persistently described the Russian military and its culture in terms of *samobytnost'*, what in German historical tradition is often called a *Sonderweg*, a special path, thus underscoring the uniqueness of the Russian army, its military thought, and its traditions, values, and goals.[114] However, the ideas expressed in military texts indicate how congruent Russian military culture and thought were with broader developments in the European Military Enlightenment.[115] The Russian military proto-intelligentsia increasingly recognized the need to relate military practice to its social, cultural, and political background and submitted the military profession to systematic and rational analysis. The ideas and aspirations of the emerging *militaires philosophes* laid down a web of interconnected values, of systems of personal, social, and intellectual significance that were expected to be practised and embraced by members of that culture. The next chapter will show how these practices and ideas were applied to Russian soldiers.

Chapter Four

"Always remember that he is not a peasant, but a soldier": The Enlightenment and the Shaping of Russian Soldiers

Contemporaries wrote that General Mikhail Kamenskii possessed "the ferocity of a tiger. He was seen biting soldiers during manoeuvres and tearing out their flesh with his teeth."[1] Kamenskii was an extreme case, and even if such methods of coercion were effective, they were crude and could not be replicated indefinitely. In addition, such corporal punishments were forbidden when it came to the officer class.[2] Indeed, it is difficult to believe that brute force would have sufficed to establish and preserve control and subordination across the complex military structure that was the multi-ethnic Russian army. Nor would such methods have succeeded in disseminating the ideas and values of military culture in the context of the large and eclectic armies of Catherine's Russia. There must have been other forces beyond coercion at play. Recent works have challenged the traditional picture of soldiers' experience in eighteenth-century Europe. The various ways in which soldiers could have escaped the military, especially in a vast and thinly populated country like Russia, meant that the military could not have been a "straightforward coercive enterprise." Attitudes toward soldiers were changing, and soldiers of the old regime stayed in the army because they wanted to.[3] This change to how soldiers were treated and trained was in large part precipitated by influence of the Age of Reason. Traditional approaches to military life were accompanied by mechanisms that went beyond physical intimidation and oppression, mechanisms that arose from the framework of the Military Enlightenment. This chapter asks to what extent these approaches were also reflected in Russian military culture.

Challenging John Keep, Richard Pipes, and others, Janet Hartley has recently argued against the existence of a "garrison state" in Russia during the reign of Catherine II and her immediate successors.[4] Russia was not, in fact, a militarized state; only the nobility and various servitors in the borderlands possessed any real military *mentalité*. For example, according to available data only 1.2 per cent of the Russian Empire's population was in the army by the end of the eighteenth century.[5] Most Russians in Catherine's vast empire had little contact with the military, and some probably had never seen a soldier or a sailor in their lives.[6] Soldiers were separated from the civilian world for at least twenty-five years, those who survived their service did not return to their original communities, and military habits did not seep into village life. The militarization of Russia had to wait for the collapse of the Romanov dynasty. On the contrary, in the eighteenth century it was *village* habits that entered the *military* along with the recruits.[7] The challenge for military culture, therefore, was how to stop this from happening and how to militarize the Russian peasant and imbue him with the proper martial spirit.

In her pioneering work about the lower ranks in the Russian army of the nineteenth century, Elise Wirtschafter saw the Russian soldier "as an autonomous actor on the stage of history" rather than a passive victim of a vast military machinery.[8] Russia in the late eighteenth century was a very different place from many parts of Western Europe, and unlike in the West, most soldiers had been conscripted into the army rather than freely enlisting. This chapter argues that the Enlightenment influenced how Russian military thinkers theorized about peasant recruits and laid the psychological, religious, emotional, and physical foundations for the "wonder-hero" Russian soldier. It shows the extent of the Enlightenment influence on how peasants were transformed into soldiers, on how they were drilled and taken care of, and on the roles played by religion and indoctrination in this process. The military's changing attitude toward soldiers was another example of the Enlightenment's lasting and important mark on Russian military culture. That so many soldiers did remain under the colours of Catherine's army was at least in part due to its military culture, which simultaneously tried to improve their lives and to help create them as rational, if not necessarily autonomous, historical actors.

Transformation into Soldiers

Despite new possibilities that were open to them as soldiers, peasant recruits saw military service as a burden, and it fell on the shoulders of the military culture to change their minds.[9] For instance, *Instruction to the Colonel* from the early 1760s explained how to bring new recruits into military culture and how to make them embrace their new military identity and its associated values:

> During the readings of *Military Articles* ... explain to them [the recruits] their power and their contents, especially ... the nature of soldier's service and the necessary uninhibited bravery, and that no hardships and fear can

dent the courage of Russian soldiers ... Teach such a newcomer the names of the generals, names of regimental staff and senior officers, and especially of his company officers, so he without timidity and with confidence may approach them and talk to them if there is a need for it, and so that he may always remember that he is not a peasant, but a soldier, the calling and rank of which give him an advantage over all his previous stations.[10]

The *Military Articles*, which the *Instruction* cites, served as the basis for the Russian military code, and woven into its fabric were threads of the Enlightenment. This document instructed officers to explain to the soldiers the advantages of their new calling instead of just ordering them to accept it. It also wanted soldiers to internalize their new identity. Its narrative suggested a more humane approach to treating soldiers: officers were to read to and interact with new recruits, who would thus feel more comfortable talking to their superiors if there was an issue.

Both *Instruction to the Colonel* and the *Military Articles* placed checks on abuses of power by officers and outlined venues for recourse that their subordinates could use. The Russian military culture wanted to create layers of belonging, identity, and commitment, and to that end at least some minimal legal protections were extended even to humble soldiers. For example, "Nobody from the officers dares to beat or harm people under their command, without an important and verifiable cause," stated one of the articles. "Those who will not heed this stipulation will be court-martialled; and those who are often found [inflicting] this abuse will be bereft of their rank; for he has abused the powers of his office." Furthermore, the articles reminded officers that "command of officers over their men does not extend beyond what is necessary for the well-being of His Highness and His government; and what does not relate to the services to His highness soldiers have no obligation of doing." This too was read out loud to the soldiers. For example, in 1788 Potemkin wrote to Lieutenant-General Nashchokin in anger: "I am letting you know that 60 hussars were found in the suite of Major-General Neranchin, and all were taken back as per my order. I have decreed to enforce this with most rigor, and if it turns out that I discover soldiers or irregulars in your suite, then for each I shall demand from you 10 recruits, or maybe more. I already know," warned Potemkin, "that you have two soldier-artisans – for God's sake do not drive me to offend you."[11] Such outbursts revealed the frustrations of senior officials but also attempts to enforce professionalism, to forbid the use of soldiers as personal lackeys, and to show that the government was aware of abuses and was prepared to punish the guilty. Another system for checking abuses was the practice whereby every soldier had the legal right to submit a petition – *chelobitnaia* – regarding his problems and injustices.[12] Enforcing such practices was a challenge, but clearly, the military was embracing the Enlightenment emphasis on humanity, legal procedure, and professionalism.

When new recruits arrived, officers explained their new legal status to them by reading and interpreting the *Military Articles*; they then engaged them in small talk to gauge their abilities, making note of the slackers and encouraging men with potential. The next step was to pass the wide-eyed and inexperienced arrivals into the hands of older soldiers, who showed them proper military behaviour and introduced them to the mundane details of military life – how to put on marching boots, how to dress in the complicated uniform, and how to look like military men in general. The goal was to eradicate what the military perceived as devious peasant habits – shiftiness, grimacing, scratching during conversations – and replace them with military values of restraint and self-discipline.[13] From the day recruits arrived in their regiments, military manuals worked to affect a break between the two worlds, the two identities, and the two modes of behaviour – that of a village peasant, and that of a military man.

In the second half of the eighteenth century, as a means to bring about and maintain this break, military writers carefully articulated the themes of subordination, professionalism, training, and punishment. Here again Suvorov's voice was the earliest and the loudest. In his *Suzdal Regulations* he began to provide concrete mechanisms for turning exhausted and often violent Russian peasants into professional soldiers. The enforcement of subordination was an important part of this transformation. Addressing company commanders, Suvorov wrote, "the bedrock of military governance is derived from subordination, which has to be religiously observed."[14] No subordinate was allowed to argue about, question, or even discuss military orders emanating from his superiors. Suvorov's methods broke down the rebellious and often stubborn spirit of recruits and brought them into the brotherhood of soldiering. The principal agent of this process was the captain, who had to know his subordinates by name, be aware of the capabilities of each soldier in his outfit, and keep an eye out for men with potential. In addition to that,

> in case it turns out that a new recruit has a vice, like a weakness for drinking, or any other wicked conduct inappropriate for an honest soldier, he [the captain] would try to deter the soldier from it by admonishment and moderate punishment. A striving soldier should rather benefit from moderate military punishment in combination with clear and precise

assessment of his misconduct, than from cruelty which would drive him into despair.[15]

Subscribing to the broader trends of Enlightenment humanitarianism, Suvorov maintained that mindless tyranny had no place in turning recruits into soldiers. He made his officers responsible for the well-being and performance of their men, and he insisted that officers take time to ascertain the abilities, qualities, and vices of their soldiers, so as to define expectations and solidify cultural norms between the people in the ranks and their commanders. Through this discovery process between noble officers and peasant recruits, professional bonds and identities would develop and military culture would be fixed and transmitted.

Once in the military, soldiers were carefully watched to ensure that they maintained their new identity. For example, when soldiers were quartered among the civilian population in winter, Suvorov made his officers examine their accommodations a week after they had settled in – each soldier's dwelling was to be inspected individually. Officers were to pay attention to "how and where [the soldier] keeps [his military things] and his provisions, if he keeps himself in cleanliness, if he listens to the instructed prayers in the regiment, if he keeps well with his hosts."[16] Moreover, during these visits officers were expected to interact with each of their soldiers. This was to be more than casual small talk, explained Suvorov – it was an exercise to discover whether the men were slipping away from the orbit of military culture. A short talk with a quartered soldier would reveal "if he had taken on peasant language, looks, mentality and scheming, and if these detract from military countenance." Suvorov used this simple test to discover whether the quartered troops, all of them former peasants, were beginning to regress to their previous mental, visual, and linguistic state. It was the officer's job to defend the boundaries of military culture and the soldier's job to remain within them. If any soldiers were found to have lapsed into their former peasant identities, their immediate superiors were to be punished and the soldiers were to be taken under the personal supervision of the company commander.[17]

In 1770, in his *Epistle*, Mamonov took the theme of subordination a step further – according to Mamonov his soldiers were his "children" and they, in turn, were to regard him as their "real father," a benevolent parent who thought only of their well-being. At night the men could sleep because the general was awake, thinking of how to care and provide for his family.[18] Mamonov continued to cement the symbiotic relationship between the officer/father and his soldiers/children by explaining to the latter that it was a general's job to keep his men healthy as well as free of hunger and thirst:

> Believe me, my beloved children,
> My happiness is in having you all fit,
> And to provide you food and nourishment,
> My mind and memory must always be on it.[19]

The idea that the relationship between officers and soldiers resembled a contract was gaining acceptance in Western Europe by the first half of the eighteenth century.[20] Mamonov was probably channelling the French *philosophe* Claude Helvetius (1715–1771) in his military writings. Helvetius thought that society should be built on social contracts and that laws should govern social relations "whereby the individual relinquishes part of his innate freedom for the sake of his own safety and the universal good."[21] As long as soldiers followed orders, their officers would protect and take care of them. The price soldiers paid for a sound sleep was discipline and subordination. Mamonov returned to the theme of merit and seniority, connecting it to obedience and respect for authority. He wrote that only "idiots fear their superiors" and that orders were to be respected, not dreaded.[22] Mamonov warned soldiers and reminded officers about the military law, no doubt referring to the *Military Articles*. When soldiers disobeyed their orders, this broke the contract between the two groups. As long as this social contract was maintained, together they could scale any mountain, ford any river, overcome any obstacle. In this way, soldiers were placed at the centre of Russian military culture.

Once they were recruited into the army, villagers were no longer peasants but soldiers. Their new identity came with a new sense of respectability, which meant they no longer had to follow the conventions they had absorbed during their civilian life. For example, as Iogan von Meiendorf wrote, if a soldier spotted an officer coming his way, he was to use his left hand "to remove his hat, he should look straight into the eyes of the officer coming his way, and avoiding any kneeling gestures, simply pass him by." Similarly, no soldier should prostrate himself on the ground before his superiors, not only because it caused damage to the uniform but also because "this kind of action is demeaning and unbecoming for the soldier."[23] Meiendorf was making a highly symbolic statement intended to redefine soldiers' behaviour and change the relationship between subordinates and superiors. Meiendorf wanted a disciplined interaction by trained professionals to replace the ancient custom where a slave had to kneel before his master. In military culture, soldiers were no longer serfs and their officers were not their owners.[24] What Meiendorf wanted to implement in the Russian army reflected the larger Enlightenment re-examination of human behaviour and personal dignity more generally. In Habsburg Austria, for example, Emperor Joseph II's highly publicized edict proclaimed that "no one, no matter who he might be, who wished to petition for something or to submit anything, shall kneel down, because this is not a fitting form of behaviour from one human being to another."[25]

Joining Meiendorf, Vorontsov added to the narrative about transforming recruits into soldiers, and clearly built on the work of his peers and of the broader Military Enlightenment. In his *Instruction* (1774), Vorontsov saw the potential of Russian soldiers and suggested to his fellow officers the ways to realize it. "Before developing the mind and cognition relevant to soldiering," wrote the count, "they [soldiers] must first be explained everything that has to do with their body." Vorontsov demanded cleanliness and neatness from soldiers and explained why: "The former preserves their health and the latter gives them the appearance both pleasant and noble."[26] He set out in great detail how the physical transformation of soldiers was to take place. They had to wash their faces, eyes, and hands, rinse their mouths and comb their hair once a day. Twice a week they had to clip their fingernails. Once a week they had to wash their feet and twice a month clip their toenails. When soldiers were quartered during winter they had to go to the steam bath once a week, and during summer campaigns they had to take regular swims in rivers and springs.[27] In this way the rugged and coarse peasant material was to be transformed into a clean and polished instrument of Russian military power. Cleanliness was a practical necessity to preserve the lives of new recruits, and a neat appearance lent credibility and respect to the image of soldiering. Clean, shiny uniforms, groomed hair, and shaved faces projected an image of understated power and respectability, which was especially important to the civilian population. Perhaps Vorontsov thought that by changing men's physical habits – by altering how they looked, walked, and talked – he could alter their mentality as well.

Building on regulations, the military culture in the late eighteenth century began to show increasing interest in the Russian soldier, and military writers turned their thoughts to those humble recruits who were to be transformed from peasants into military professionals. The writings from Catherine's reign do not present a romanticized image of the Russian soldier (unlike those from the nineteenth century).[28] Writers of Catherine's time dealt with the subject on its own terms, wrestling with and sometimes accepting imperfections and shortcomings. Each manual or instruction added a new layer to the process of developing a healthy relationship between recruits and their officers. Suvorov thought to moderate punishment. Mamonov embossed a family metaphor onto the military. Meiendorf emphasized the importance of developing self-respect in soldiers. Vorontsov described how officers could affect the physical and mental transformation of soldiers through a simple routine, and their role in that process. Officers were teachers, fathers, and disciplinarians. Discipline was both a military virtue and an educational necessity, yet a balance had be struck between blind and sadistic punishment and enlightened reprimand.

Drilling and Caring for Soldiers

The military's approach to drilling and taking care of soldiers was part of the larger Enlightenment influence on Russia that found its way into many aspects of Russian society and culture. For instance, since about the 1750s, while officers were writing military instructions for their regiments, a group of powerful Russian landowners were working to redefine and implement a new relationship with their peasants. "Their goal," wrote Edgar Melton, "was to establish and maintain an administrative and economic order on their estates that would promote the moral and economic welfare of their peasants." Melton referred to this practice of enforcing the framework of the "well-ordered police state" as enlightened seigneurialism.[29] Much like the enlightened seigneurs in the countryside, the military proto-intelligentsia extended the ideal of the "well-ordered police state" to their regiments, working to promote the physical and emotional well-being of their troops. During Catherine's reign, manuals gradually abandoned the severe punishments of Petrine Russia in favour of encouraging more humane treatment of soldiers. Suvorov, for example, thought that to be effective, a military exercise had to take on the character of a game.[30] He insisted that military "exercise [be] made into a fun activity for all."[31] He realized that the monotony and harshness of regular drill would plant the seeds of aversion to military service, so he tried to turn drills into entertainment. Using the rifle as a metaphor for military service, Semen Vorontsov summarized his views on training in his *Instruction*: "It is perverse and detrimental when a soldier hates his musket, and ... does not see his musket as anything but an instrument of his torment."[32] Exercises, discipline, and marches, while absolutely necessary, had to be for a reason, and drills had to be explained, not just taught.

Some authors began to critique established training practices and suggested new ideas. Andrei Viazemskii thought that the five weeks of training that recruits usually received was laughably inadequate to truly transform them into soldiers. He proposed extending training to six months and creating special battalions dedicated to training and drilling, "where the soldiers could be educated in peace." He recommended that these special battalions be staffed with distinguished and experienced older officers who, because of their age or their wounds, could no longer assume active positions in the field.[33] Viazemskii wanted to create a dedicated social space where new arrivals could be taught about their new world and its rules, where they could interact with and learn from their officers, where they could internalize the values of military culture, and where they could be drilled "in peace."

New training practices were linked to the increased attention given to care for soldiers. In 1788, in his *Rules*, Mamonov emphasized the importance of public displays of affection for subordinates. He recommended that instead of carousing with women and losing fortunes in smoke-filled gambling dens, young officers should spend more time with their soldiers. He called for young officers to show kindness and magnanimity toward their subordinates every chance they got. This way the young officer "[would] win their respect and their hearts."[34] Politeness and good deeds fostered an emotional and psychological bond between an officer and his men that was necessary for subordination and mutual respect. Social proximity helped erase cultural and mental boundaries. Even the giant figure of Potemkin stepped into the conversation. Writing from his increasingly powerful political position, Potemkin addressed the burden of soldiership through numerous instructions, threats, and notes. His writings reflected how the Enlightenment was influencing Russian military culture and how deeply he subscribed to its broader values. For example, in 1789 he wrote to General Krechetnikov to ensure that officers used faculties of persuasion and advice rather than brute force during training. "Above all I demand patience and clarity in explaining the means of performing better service when educating soldiers," wrote Potemkin.[35]

By the 1780s, it was no longer enough for officers to simply order their soldiers to perform drills. Their responsibilities had evolved, and they were expected to explicate the need for and utility of various drills and exercises. Sociologists have shown that unexpected transfer to an unfamiliar institutional environment without adequate explanation of the rationale for it often produces traumatic effects.[36] Eighteenth-century military writers transposed this insight onto the military, where recruits were already experiencing physical and mental stress from their journeys to the regiment and from the separation from their families. It was the officers' job to explain why they had been ordered to march instead of walk, to talk using new jargon, and to learn new rules and laws. This approach was embraced by some of the most famous Russian officers, including Mikhail Kutuzov. The future prince, field marshal, and vanquisher of Napoleon made a contribution to eighteenth-century military culture when he wrote, or most likely dictated, *Notes on Infantry Service* in 1786.[37] Kutuzov demanded that officers explain the reasons for each drill and manoeuvre. In the process he alleviated some of the stress among the recruits while transforming officers from tyrants into patient pedagogues.

Kutuzov continued to develop a favourite theme of Enlightenment authors: rational concern for soldiers' health. "Since caring for soldiers is the first sign of kindness and strength of any military Corps, I designate this to be the most important of subjects and the first concern of the battalion-commanders," read the first lines of his *Notes*. Showing sensitivity to human nature, Kutuzov wrote that "a soldier cannot be left unprepared for his duty, and cannot feel anything but faithfulness and readiness to carry out service required from him." A soldier's "faithfulness and readiness" could be achieved only by ensuring that he received everything that was due to him in supplies and money, insisted Kutuzov. He warned "gentlemen-battalion commanders" that this had significance for the military as a whole, for if a soldier was robbed of his due in food, clothes, medical supplies, or money it could lead "to the destruction of his health, sometimes even life, and can consequently cause irreparable harm to military service."[38] Kutuzov had probably read or at least heard of Stepan Rzhevskii's *Note on Military Service* and was trying to address in his corps some of the challenges the latter had placed on the doorstep of the Russian military culture.

Contemporaries often commented on how Potemkin tried to alleviate the stress of the transition from peasant to military life for incoming recruits and how he admonished officers for not taking care of their soldiers. In 1782 he wrote to Major-General Talyzin to organize apartments in Kharkov for new recruits, "and to keep them there for as long as it is needed to get them restful and instruct them in the matters of service. For this, your excellency, has the duty to observe that officers take benevolent care of their recruits, move away from employing excessive strictness, and are never too bored to explain in the comprehensive way the customs of military service."[39] In 1788 he wrote to Prince Nassau: "I strongly hope that you will not miss anything towards the improvement of health and maintaining of good order in service by reducing unnecessary burdens. To achieve this, terminate excessive beatings, instead of which a better method is to clearly explain to people what they need to know."[40] Appealing to human reason, Potemkin tried to limit excessive punishments, encouraged officers to take more interest in their men, and tried to curb the practice of officers using soldiers for their private businesses or works, which robbed the army and the state of valuable manpower. Writing to Colonel Selinov in 1788, he ordered him "to collect his regiment and to announce out loud to everyone the following: that I have taken the regiment under my command, and that I see as my first duty to satisfy the people in everything they are owed. To gentlemen-officers announce that they should deal with their soldiers with kindness and every restraint, labour for their benefit ... and behave with them as I do, for I love them as my children."[41]

Potemkin wanted to redefine the relationship between generals and soldiers. In this, he was following in the footsteps of European Enlightenment military thinkers, who had been promoting a new relationship between soldiers and officers since the 1720s. Spanish General Santa Cruz de Marcenado advised generals in 1728 to visit the field hospital, hand out money, and "talk to the wounded officers and soldiers, investigate ... most honestly and humanely how the men are treated, and whether no care is omitted."[42] Frederick II wrote that officers should "appear friendly to the soldiers," "speak to them on the march," and "visit them while cooking."[43] No longer could officers, however much their seniority removed them from the social milieu of the rank-and-file, concern themselves solely with leading their troops into battle. Increasingly it was expected that in addition to combat leadership, part of an officer's job was the moral and psychological care of his men.

If in the 1760s military writers relied on drill and discipline as the source of unit cohesion and obedience, by the end of the century they were beginning to explore alternatives to that model. They began to ask questions about loyalty and human nature. Iron discipline could weld recruits into a line but "it could not instil loyalty."[44] In order for soldiers to be obedient and effective, they had to fear their officers more than their enemy, wrote Fredrick the Great in his 1763 *Cavalry Instruction* and in his 1768 *Political Testament*;[45] Russian military writers began to disagree. By the end of the eighteenth century, military writings were giving increasing voice to practices aimed at improving service in the ranks. These narratives were applying the rationalizing and humanitarian spirit of the Enlightenment to the military establishment to combat wastage and extract greater resources from the human capital at the army's disposal. Through this process, the Enlightenment helped strengthen the military's potential. Suvorov pondered how to turn drills into games to make training more effective and soldiers less resentful. Vorontsov and Viazemskii both warned against harsh punishments and proposed a sensible training regimen. Kutuzov wrote about making soldiers follow orders but also explaining the customs of their new military life. Mamonov wanted his officers to spend more time with soldiers than with women. By the 1790s, ideas and attitudes toward soldiers that had been inspired by the Enlightenment and that were proposed by colonels and military essayists in the 1760s and 1770s were firmly entrenched in conversations at the highest levels of Russian military culture. Potemkin, the commander-in-chief, saw the Russian soldier in the same light as did his lesser-known peers: the soldiers were his children, they had to be treated with humanity, and the throne valued and honoured their profession. This mentality, the values that Potemkin reflected in his letters, helped curb at least some of the tyranny in the army.[46]

Religion and the Military Enlightenment

Maurice de Saxe, a major figure of the European Military Enlightenment, wrote in his *Reveries* in the 1730s that "the man who devotes himself to war should regard it as a religious order into which he enters."[47] In Catherine's Russia, Saxe's followers put his ideas into practice. Russian military culture used religious rituals as an extension of drills and transformative processes to condition peasant recruits. Religion provided comfort to new soldiers; it was also a powerful tool for the military to justify its customs and practices. For the officers, religion played an additional role. Orthodox religion allowed "socially aware and morally self-conscious" officers to justify and reconcile the realities of military life with the principles of the European Enlightenment. In Catherine's time, Russia's educated people had no opportunity to enact programs of social or political reform; all they could do, according to Wirtschafter, was assimilate "the moralistic dimension of the Enlightenment."[48] From religion, the military took the idea of God-given hierarchy and natural order that explained the harsh and sometimes arbitrary world around them. At the same time, religion supported the strong moralistic impulses that many officers received through their encounter with the Enlightenment. This intellectual encounter was projected onto the military world.

Soldiers were compelled to attend church service whether they wanted to or not. According to the *Colonel's Instruction*, published by the War College in 1768, "all officers should enter the church with their men and stay there until the services are over; and so that officers or soldiers would not attempt to leave beforehand, place at church door an officer with a halberd." Bored or distracted members of the congregation were forbidden to leave. The same instruction explained that if a soldier happened to be of a different confession, he should be sent along with an officer of his confession, if such was to be found, to pray according to his own religious customs. Recent research into the religious policy of Imperial Russia shows that the state not only recognized various religions but also, to a degree, protected them. As Paul Werth has argued, this was seen as good business for Russian statecraft. For the multi-ethnic Russian Empire, sensitivity to religion functioned as a method of governance and management.[49] The state's sensitivity to confessional multiplicity extended to the army, which understood the importance of religion to military culture.[50] For example, the first article of the *Military Articles* was about Christian faith:

> While all people in general and every Christian with no exception ought to live in accordance with the Christian laws and be honest without maintaining a hypocritical fear of God, soldiers and military men especially must respect these laws earnestly and follow them sincerely. By the will of God they are often placed in a situation where every hour of their service to the Emperor is fraught with deadly danger to their lives, and because every blessing, conquest and well-being originates from the one and only God almighty, the genuine source of all good, the righteous Giver of victory, they must pray only to Him and have all their faith in Him.[51]

The military culture appropriated Christian virtues as a means to reinforce and perpetuate its own values and its position within Russian culture as a whole. God himself would be responsible for Russian victories, because every conquest originated with the will of the Almighty, and Russian soldiers needed to know that.

The *Military Statute* similarly assigned religion a prominent role in military culture and in war. Besides praying three times a day, all military men had to say a silent prayer twice a day, in the morning and before bedtime – so instructed the statute. It was the job of officers to teach their men how to pray, and even those who were illiterate and who could not memorize all the prayers still had to know the Lord's Prayer. Every day at nine in the morning a priest was to serve the liturgy in every regiment.[52] Furthermore, prayer services should take place on Sundays and on the eve of great holidays. There was to be a drum roll before each prayer, a clear attempt to mix the military with the religious.[53] The Russian army was a religious army, and Russian military culture was drenched in religiosity, which lent it a set of values around which its members could coalesce.

Religion worked as a binding social mechanism, much like the military oath, and much like Mamonov's contract between fathers and sons.

Officers were to ensure that each soldier attended one of three daily prayers at least once and that everyone in the regiment went at least once a year to confession and to the Eucharist.[54] Similarly, the blessing of new regimental standards had a religious component that involved a priest, a prayer, and a military oath.[55] Participating in religious ceremonies was mandatory for everyone in military culture. At first glance, the intersection of the Enlightenment and religion in Russian military culture seems confusing. Enlightenment scepticism and belief in science represented a powerful attack on organized religion and superstition. However, as Gary Hamburg has argued, the Enlightenment in Russia was both cultural and spiritual, and this created intellectual conditions in the military such that religion and Enlightenment rationalism were not mutually exclusive.[56]

Military instructions embedded religion in Russian military culture, and individual writers in Catherine's Russia developed its role even further. Suvorov, for example, was known for bombarding his soldiers and officers with religious propaganda in his orders, his speeches, and his military instructions. He composed a canon of nine songs; he even crafted a wooden cross for the Church of St Peter and Paul in Ladoga when he was a young colonel. However, there is no context to indicate how rare it was for an officer to do so.[57] Being a great churchgoer, an aspiring monk, and somewhat superstitious, Suvorov began emphasizing the importance of religious service on his soldiers and officers in his *Suzdal Regulations* in the early 1760s. His "church parade" was a ritual that entailed eight separate steps. Soldiers had to enter the church on the right and exit on the left. Each officer had to line up his men before the church door and command that they remove their head gear before entering. All hats and helmets were to be placed in one corner of the church instead of being held under the arm.[58] This was an exercise in obedience and respect for the Orthodox Church as an institution but also a way to discipline each new recruit's mind and behaviour.[59]

Everyone in Suvorov's regiment had to know at least the following: a prayer to Jesus Christ, the Lord's Prayer, the Hail Mary, and the Nicene Creed ("I believe in one God ..."). Soldiers and officers had to memorize these, and every day in the morning and at night, pray with these to the Almighty. Suvorov made his men recite all of them "out loud and from memory."[60] But he did not stop there:

> During important holidays, officers take their men to church at noon. On Sundays and big holidays he [officer] takes his regiment to church for the mass and brings them back, all in full church attire ... If considered necessary he takes the regiment to the evening mass as well. During Lent each member of the regiment fasts for a week.[61]

When not being drilled or inspected in their lodgings, soldiers were observed during religious services. Religion was another tool in the hands of the military culture to instil integration and cohesion and also to surveille and control new recruits.

As Bruce Menning wrote, Suvorov recognized and reinforced religious and patriotic sentiments and tried to awaken them in his recruits to strengthen "common identity and loyalty to shared values."[62] Geoffrey Best remarked that Suvorov took religion to such "a heady pitch" that it almost served as a brainwashing mechanism.[63] Borrowing the messianic message from the first page of the *Military Articles*, Suvorov wrote to his soldiers in *Science of Victory* in 1796: "Pray to God! He delivers us victory. Wonder-heroes! God is our general!"[64] Russian soldiers sacrificed themselves for "the Mother of God, the Empress, and for the Holy Kingdom!"[65] By the end of the century, one soldier related, every regiment in Suvorov's army had a church tent where a regimental priest presided over services. Suvorov himself went to some of these to pray every Sunday.[66]

Rumiantsev, too, touched upon religion in his *Customs of Military Service*. His manual had a special section titled "Prayer" that outlined the religious service. At nine o'clock in the morning everyone had to gather on the parade ground. Weapons were to be left behind, and only swords were to be worn, probably to reinforce the idea of belonging to the military rather than to civilian society. The men formed a circle, and while the priest chanted his usual prayers, the listeners had to stay on one knee. Furthermore, on holidays, on Sundays, or when it was ordered, brigades could construct their own churches, which were to be placed in the middle of camp.[67] Between memorizing prayers, forming prayer circles, participating in church parades, and going for confession, one has to wonder when soldiers found the time to drill.

By the 1770s the concept of divine leadership was being further entrenched in Russian military culture. Suvorov and Rumiantsev were far from the only writers attempting to fuse piety with military service.[68] In the preface to his translation of General Meiendorf's work, Iakov Khoroshkevich wrote that now "enlightened with Godliness [soldiers] no longer fear infidel tribes that pervert the law and piety," but feel the power of God, "who guides their hands in battle."[69] Meiendorf also commingled religion with the Enlightenment optimism. "No matter how much his soul is darkened ... every human being has natural qualities, and enters on the path of enlightenment, if only he can be given true and real conviction." It should not be impossible for an insightful and enterprising colonel "to imbed thoughts about God into the soldier, to explain to him about His kindness and his sacrifices, about punishment and rewards coming from Him, and about the soul and eternity."[70] Once religion was introduced, the military had the power to shape a soldier's identity, his world view, and the meaning of his new life. This was to be accompanied by constant reminders about the importance of military service for igniting in the deepest recesses of soldiers' thoughts feelings of pride in their profession.[71]

If an officer had to sometimes double as a missionary, it was for the greater good of the military culture. Teaching soldiers religion would mean that even during war they would not become so heartless as to kill wounded enemy soldiers or harm civilians. Moreover, unless soldiers were fully introduced to religion, they could not and should not be allowed to take the military oath. For how, Meiendorf asked rhetorically, can one bring a person to the military oath if he is unenlightened and does not possess reason or consciousness? Potemkin likewise saw pride in the military profession in religious terms and wanted to reinforce it in his soldiers. "Being a soldier is an honest calling, which applies to the lower ranks," Potemkin wrote to Lieutenant-General Igelstrom in 1784. He considered it offensive when soldiers deserted because that broke their military oath, which was "a sin before God."[72] The military oath was seen as a personal covenant that bound together the soldier, the military, the sovereign, and God. If soldiers were introduced to religion, the thinking went, they would be less likely to desert. For Meiendorf and Potemkin and their peers, religion was one method by which to enlighten Russian peasant recruits, and for the latter, following religious customs was a prerequisite to membership in the military culture.[73]

The religious declarations of Russian military writers were not hollow statements of Orthodox piety. Religious narratives of war that emerged from military culture were part of the Russian Military Enlightenment and were deployed for real military purposes ranging from the motivation and indoctrination of soldiers to explaining the reasons for a particular war. General Petr Panin's *Instructions* to his army from 1770 was one example of how religious rhetoric was deployed before battle.[74] Panin had served in the Russian army since 1736, when he was fifteen years old. He was a veteran of the Seven Years' War, the suppressor of the Pugachev Rebellion, and one of the most experienced generals in Catherine's army. In the summer of 1770 his army was participating in the war against the Ottoman Porte in southern Ukraine. Panin summarized Russia's position against the Turks in religious terms and explained what Russian soldiers should rely on in battle:

> We should rely: first of all on Christ the Saviour who redeemed us with his blood, and in whose name we fight against the enemy of his Holy name, the church and the Christian faith, who will of course in all instances lead us onwards, and those sacrificing their stomach for Him, will earn their

coronets in heavenly kingdom ... Each one of us will advance fearlessly on this foe and enemy of Christ the Saviour.[75]

Reinforcing the theme of divine leadership, Panin wrote that his army was advancing into battle under the banner of Christendom. Those who survive "will be the makers of victories and fame; but those who will be sacrificed will receive eternal peace in His heavenly Kingdom."[76] Panin did not forget to remind his army that

this murderous, barbarous foe and the scourge of the Christian race ... does not give it any mercy, but kills it for the sake of acquiring for every Christian head a monetary reward established by his commanders, and for the general promise of heaven for the murder of Christians.[77]

If his instruction at times read more like a sermon than a military manual, it was because Panin intended it to do so. Panin imposed a clear narrative on the upcoming and evidently bloody battle: he created the main characters, set the scene, and set the plot in motion. The Russian soldiers were the principal heroes fighting the Muslim antagonists. The Turks were not Russia's personal enemy but the enemy of Christ, and the Russian soldiers were fighting for something greater than themselves. Panin used the language of religious struggle – like the Crusaders of days of old, the Russian armies would be guided by the hand of God against the infidels. Declaring that being beheaded was the only thing Russians could expect from the Turks, Panin wanted his army to hate its enemy. The Russian army, of course, would not participate in such barbaric customs as cutting off the heads of their enemies; Russian soldiers were rational professionals, not fanatical henchmen. Panin gave his soldiers a choice between a desperate fight to the death or a victory achieved through calm subordination and methodical discipline. In his narrative, Russian soldiers who died would go to heaven, and on earth they would be remembered as heroes. If they survived, they could expect rewards and fame. To make sure his ideas were disseminated and that the indoctrination could take hold, Panin's instruction was distributed and read out to the whole army. The general demanded that "not only ... all ranks and positions carried out, observed and enforced, but also read this entire instruction before the regiments, companies, and commands, and carefully explained it to all ranks, and especially to the lower ones."[78]

Military writers in Catherine's Russia viewed religion as indispensable to military culture. Many of them were genuinely religious men, but that was beside the point. Religion to them served a practical purpose. Besides being an organized collection of beliefs and a source of comfort, it served as a method for moral teaching, and for transforming peasants into soldiers as well as servants of the state. In the context of the Military Enlightenment, religion was a tool for reaching into the soldier's soul and for making it receptive to the military values of self-sacrifice, humility, and respect for authority. The surviving evidence, at least in part, indicates that by the end of the eighteenth century the zealous religious indoctrination had had the desired effect of motivating the soldiers and making them accept their fate.[79] In many ways, then, religion played an important part in indoctrination, which was also clearly outlined in the military manuals.

Indoctrination

In the 1760s, indoctrination centred on passive and vertical practices such as reading out loud parts of official military manuals to soldiers. In his *Suzdal Regulation* in 1765, Suvorov stated:

> At the encampment, each Sunday and during holidays before the liturgy, [the officer] orders that the following chapters and listings be read in front of the regiment for three or four hours: one or two chapters from *Military Articles*; one chapter from the 1763 *Regimental Regulations* ... and one chapter from the *Suzdal Regulations*.[80]

For several hours every week even those recruits who could not read were made familiar with all of the necessary regulations, military statutes, and laws, as well as with all the new orders coming to the regiment from the government.

Others began to build on and extend that model. For instance, Mamonov created his own indoctrination narrative in the *Epistle*. He began by asking the most important question – why do soldiers fight wars? – and immediately providing the answer. First of all, it was not the soldier's job to pontificate on such philosophical matters. Soldiers fought for their fatherland and faith, and they fought to defend their ancestral lands, their homes, their wives and children. "What is more dear than the fatherland to us?," he asked rhetorically.[81] The *Epistle* also taught soldiers how to die. Mamonov related a bloody scene he had witnessed years earlier in the Battle of Zorndorf during the Seven Years' War, when the Russian armies fought Frederick the Great:

> Admirable is the spirit of the Zorndorf battle,
> In which a hero fought alone so many foes,
> All cut, with bloodshed over him, he kills the enemies.

> And liberates himself from them like a hero
> Your brave spirit derived its strength from honour only,
> You, all in blood and wounds, did not surrender alive [...][82]

The lonely hero had decided to die in battle rather than surrender to the hated Prussians. This was the ideal soldier, the true Russian spirit and the scourge of Russian enemies. Now the recruits knew the true meaning of heroism, now each of them could follow in the steps of this hero. A soldier's job was to "go fight, and win," not to "surrender alive." The *Epistle* was a vehicle for indoctrination – it described the ideal of noble death, self-sacrifice, comradship, and patriotism and in general prescribed the mindset for officers and soldiers. With works like Mamonov's, military culture was explaining not only soldiers' responsibilities but also their purpose in life. It was not just instructing soldiers how to behave; it also aimed to condition their mindset.

Indoctrination methods continued to develop in the 1770s and 1780s in at least two ways. Military authors began to create broader personal narratives of belonging for the soldiers and to describe ways for officers to develop stronger bonds between soldiers and themselves through increased interaction. In doing so they began to advance the importance of primary group coherence. Their ideas went beyond passive indoctrination and began to be based increasingly on human psychology. Count Vorontsov wrote that before beginning to indoctrinate soldiers with ideas of honour, service, and loyalty, it was first necessary to exorcise the peasant spirit that remained deeply engrained not just in recruits but even in some of the old soldiers. To remedy this, the young count developed a comprehensive mechanism for eradicating the roots of the civilian past in future soldiers. First, he reminded his officers to read out loud relevant parts of the *Military Articles* to the soldiers twice a day.[83] Second, he followed Suvorov's strategy and recommended that officers interact more often with their soldiers, especially on an individual basis. This taught recruits military jargon and diminished barriers between officers and soldiers. Frequent interaction also alleviated the anxiety and fear soldiers felt when conversing with their superiors. An officer should not be some rare apparition on the parade ground or a distant and impersonal figure, but an everyday sight in the camp.

Third, it was the officers' job to tell their men stories about the exploits of famous Russian field marshals to generate pride in and loyalty to imperial arms. To nurture pride and love for their regiment, recruits were told its history, the battles it had fought since its formation, and all the honours it had won. "This forces each grenadier serving in this regiment to conduct himself honourably and with courage, so that with his behaviour he would not blemish the reputation of the regiment as a whole," concluded Vorontsov.[84] He was convinced that storytelling was the conveyer belt by which ideas about military values and pride of service could be most efficiently delivered to new recruits. Stories about the military exploits of Peter the Great and Field Marshal Rumiantsev and tales of old battles created narratives of belonging to an institution older than the soldiers, and to something that would exist when they were gone. Perhaps one day they too would become a character in a story, very much like the lonely hero of Zorndorf, and inspire the next generation of recruits.

For Viazemskii as well, the point of departure was the Russian soldier. "Everybody knows, of course, that the glory and security of the state rests on its soldiers," he wrote in his *Military Note* in 1774.[85] Reflecting on training and integration of recruits into the military, he proposed that military service be reduced from twenty-five years to fifteen, contingent on good behaviour.[86] That way soldiers returning to their villages would still be in their thirties, capable of restarting their agricultural lives, having families, and joining organs of local administration. Soldiers could continue their "service" in civilian life because in the military they had had a chance to practise many values that were equally important in their villages, such as "frugality, neatness, subordination to authority, cautiousness, and others." Moreover, if returning soldiers had children they could enlighten them with tales of their service, thus preparing and inspiring them for military life. For Viazemskii, military culture clearly had transferable values that transcended the boundaries of the military and that were beneficial for Russia as a whole.

Meiendorf's approach to indoctrination was to engage in small talk with soldiers during drills, guard duty, or at any other opportune moment. He suggested to his readers that they talk kindly to soldiers and "ask them about their service, about their behaviour, their life, their health, their family, and accompany the answer with some degree of encouragement."[87] This was a much more effective way of turning peasants into conscientious servants of the state than the imposition of mechanical drills and brutal discipline, or making them listen to boring excerpts from the *Military Articles*. Meiendorf went further and advised that older soldiers be used as conduits of ideas and instructions. New recruits often looked up first to their older and more seasoned brethren, and listened to them more than to their noble officers.[88] But this should not discourage officers from conducting political and ideological work with their troops. Meiendorf gave an example from his own military experience. In the evenings he invited old soldiers to dine at his table, and during these artificially created interactions he indoctrinated his

dinner guests about military service – he discussed "all of the circumstances of service that they could encounter. These moral teachings began to spread around the regiment, when old soldiers under
the guise of their own thoughts repeated them to all the younger and
unenlightened recruits."[89] Instead of vertical, top-down indoctrination,
Meiendorf suggested a more horizontal approach. Over days, weeks,
and months, the drills, picket duty, quartering during winter, various
daily rituals such as swearing the military oath, wearing and cleaning
of the uniform, weapons practice, exercises, and indoctrination slowly
challenged and changed the peasant identity of recruits. In the process,
moral and psychological preparedness for military service and military
action was heightened.[90]

Indoctrination reached its apogee in the 1790s. To cultivate the dedication of the Russian peasants to the profession of soldiering was not
an easy task, and Suvorov understood that perhaps better than anyone
else. One of Suvorov's biographers contends that his manual, *Science of
Victory*, is probably the single most recognizable piece of military literature in Russian history. The manual "is the first known written record
on the art of war intended not only for officers but for every serving
man," wrote historian Phillip Longworth.[91] The language Suvorov
used was calculated to be accessible not only to officers but also to
regular soldiers, whom Suvorov placed in the centre of the military
culture, famously calling them "wonder heroes." To indoctrinate his
troops, Suvorov used familiar folk idioms to drive home his messages,
such as "Ignorance is darkness – knowledge is light!," and compared
the craft of war to the toil of peasants in their fields.[92] For the peasant recruits this metaphor was effective and relatable. He went further,
reminding the recruits of their new identity: "Do not harm civilians:
they provide us with food and water. A soldier is not a bandit."[93] From
the first day that recruits were torn away from their families, they were
subjected to a constant bombardment of slogans, aphorisms, and catch-
phrases. The best description of Suvorov's indoctrination work was left
by an old soldier, a veteran of Suvorov's campaigns. If the source is to
be believed, many years after Suvorov's death he still remembered the
sayings of his old commander. The retired soldier related how, during
training, Suvorov would ride through the ranks and say:

"Good job, boys! Good job!" We usually yell back at him: "Hurrah! Happy
to please you, your excellency!" "Good job, boys!" continues Suvorov,
"they give us two for a trained soldier – but we refuse it, they give us
three – but we refuse, they give us four – we will take them, go and smash
all the others! The musket ball is crazy, but the bayonet is a fine chap, you

can miss with a musket ball, but never with a bayonet. Keep the musket ball in the barrel for two or three days, for the whole campaign; shoot rarely but deadly, but with the bayonnet stab firmly ..."

   This is what he said while he rode around the front on a horse ... It would happen that he would pace back and forth and wave his arms around and talk without a break, repeating the same thing: shoot rarely, he would say, but with a bayonnet strike firmly! That is the kind of a person he was; never missed a chance to tell us these truisms.[94]

By the time his army was about to enter Italy in 1799, Suvorov had largely achieved his indoctrination aim. Suvorov's maxims had become "truisms" to his soldiers. Even many decades after Suvorov's death in 1800, soldiers had internalized the main tenets of his teachings.

   Suvorov and his instructions, of course, were not without their critics, and other officers wanted to test their own ideas and approaches to leadership and indoctrination instead of adopting his methods. Sergei Mosolov, for example, related in his memoirs how he did not want to use Suvorov's manual despite being in his army. Mosolov refused to cram and rote-learn *Science of Victory* "by heart" and then parrot it back to his soldiers. He wanted to be his own man, and he felt confident that he could interpret military rules and statutes on his own terms. Mosolov felt that he knew how to talk to soldiers in their tongue without Suvorov's help. "I reasoned it was inappropriate for a colonel to simply recite the words of others, and that instead I could expound the essence of useful rules myself." It is unclear whether Mosolov ever wrote a military instruction for his own regiment. He would later claim that his attitude was not appreciated by Suvorov and resulted in a poor assignment for him and his regiment.[95]

   Toward the end of his life, Suvorov decided to break with written convention and produce a unique visual military manual, perhaps taking inspiration from seventeenth-century European engravings explaining to soldiers the steps necessary to reload a musket. Stephen Norris recently analysed the popular Russian woodcuts called *lubki* for representations of war and the "visual language of nationhood."[96] The political and propagandistic power of the *lubok* imagery was obvious to Norris, yet it was only one part of the larger narrative. In the military, Suvorov was developing a visual language for his soldiers. The shift in the focus of military writing from officers to soldiers was part of the Enlightenment influence on the military. Writers attempted to understand soldiers better as human beings, and to relate to them even if only superficially at first. Officers attempted to explain to them why they needed to perform drills instead of just ordering them to do so.

Officers explained why following instructions was beneficial for soldiers' health and for the military service, and they wanted to introduce soldiers to the values of military culture and not just to musket exercises and marches. Suvorov's drawings were an extension of the ideas of the Military Enlightenment about the training and indoctrination of soldiers. It is not clear when he drew the manual but it must have been sometime after the French Revolution, since one of the sketches makes an explicit reference to 1789.[97]

The drawings were highly metaphorical, but because they often depicted scenes of peasant life or used elements familiar to rural dwellers, they were immediately comprehensible to new recruits. As if that was not enough, Suvorov labelled his art with rhymes and popular sayings, which he clearly had a knack for. Suvorov used this combination of art and rhymes to reinforce the main tenets of military culture. According to historian A. Golubev, Suvorov "asserted in the memory of the illiterate, notions about ... the character of the relations superiors should have with their subordinates, about service duties" and about religion, discipline, and education.[98] In other words, the visual subtext of the images offered an excellent means to indoctrinate soldiers and officers with the values of military culture in the context of the Russian Enlightenment. Unfortunately, the originals have not survived or have yet to be found, and the images are early twentieth-century copies of the original hand-drawings by Suvorov.[99]

Suvorov used a drawing of *flugers*, or weathervanes, popular in peasant culture, to convey a moral teaching about the relationship between subordinates and superiors. The drawing bore the title "Sycophant Service," and underneath it read "Try to please superiors with honest service, instead of dishonest friendship, or unlike the popular saying: 'where the wind blows the vane turns; where the weather vane turns the horsey follows'"[100] (figure 2). Russian soldiers were not weathervanes, and their beliefs and behaviour were not determined by arbitrary winds, but defined by carefully cultivated military values. Returning to the theme of leadership by example and cohesion, Suvorov illustrated the importance of inspiring the troops using a small group of first-rate soldiers. To convey the message about the role of primary group coherence visually, he drew a fire raging above a log, with the caption under it (another popular Russian saying) that read, "With dry splinters you can set fire to wet wood" (figure 3). That is, a few well-trained, motivated, and disciplined soldiers could inspire their less experienced and hesitant comrades, whereas "wet" or unmotivated soldiers could undermine the whole army.[101] Russian soldiers could relate to the image of weathervanes and the difficulty of starting a fire in the rain.

2 (top) & 3 (bottom) K. Nonnenman, ed., *Science of Victory* (1913) (Moscow: Ankil-Voin, 1996), 24–5, 34

One of the most complex of Suvorov's drawings was the "Wall of Protection" (figure 4). The caption read, "A loyal superior – a solid wall which will always defend with honour an honest man from the winds of slander." The slander was represented by flying arrows. On the other side of the wall were human figures ranging from a man lying on the ground to one levitating in the air. The wall was composed of labelled bricks: elder, corporal, officer, captain, colonel, brigadier, general, leader, and finally the tsar. The height of the wall was different for each rank.[102] An officer had the power and indeed the duty to protect his soldiers, "the wonder heroes," and a general was responsible for his entire army, while the tsar used his power to make sure his entire military was fairly treated. The "wall of protection" was not to be taken literally – it represented a wide range of responsibilities that soldiers could expect one another and their superiors to uphold. Here "protection" meant giving an honest *atestat* to deserving soldiers, fair recommendation for promotion, awards for distinguished officers, and above all mutual interdependence and respect within the military community. Everyone was integrated into Suvorov's visual military hierarchy, and soldiers could clearly see where they stood in the larger picture of the army. No doubt taking inspiration from Peter the Great's Table of Ranks, the military culture, by the end of the eighteenth century, had begun to create its own conventions and understandings of it members' duties and responsibilities toward one another.

One of the most interesting of Suvorov's sketches was a combination of four interrelated drawings: a brush, a tongue, a blade, and an Orthodox cross set on what seemed to be a church dome or an orb (figure 5). Suvorov labelled the drawings with a jagged mixture of quips, popular sayings, and biblical quotations. The brush symbolized the Russian army and bore this caption: "The threads are thin, but together they cannot be broken: likewise together the soldiers provided peace, strength, and glory for fatherland." Quoting a passage from the Bible, Suvorov exclaimed, "God is with us!" He then used another popular Russian saying, "One leg helps the other, one arm makes the second strong!" He finished with yet another Bible quotation, this one from Psalm 116, "O praise the Lord, all ye nations!" Written on the tongue was "iazytsy" or nations, relating to the caption underneath, which stated, "In the peoples lies the eternal glory to Russian arms." Then, using the extended metaphor of sharpening the blade, Suvorov explained: "Strengthen and preserve the health of the wonder-heroes, especially from debauchery. Fortify the soul with the Orthodox faith of the fatherland: to train a heathen army is the same as trying to sharpen a damaged sword."[103] The Russian military culture called for not only physical and mental but

4 (top) & 5 (bottom) K. Nonnenman, ed., *Science of Victory* (1913) (Moscow: Ankil-Voin, 1996), 36–7, 39–40.

also spiritual strength. Soldiers should not forget to praise the heavens for their victories. The Holy Church helped overcome even the most unconquerable obstacles: "praising secular powers without praising the Lord is like a tree without its roots."[104] Strength through cohesion, placing soldiers at the centre of the glory of the Russian Empire, promoting health, training, and religiosity as guiding principles for personal well-being – these were the values Suvorov was inculcating in his soldiers. With drawings such as these, Suvorov was attempting to create a visual narrative of military culture for the Russian soldier. He was laying bare the complicated values outlined at length in military manuals, instructions, and essays and making them accessible through crude and simple sketches that all could understand and emulate. Writing about the French Military Enlightenment, Christy Pichichero noted that French officers no longer saw their soldiers as Foucauldian "docile bodies" and instead had begun to appreciate the importance of satisfying their emotional, physical, and psychological needs both on and off the battlefield.[105] It seems that Russian military writers were also beginning to appreciate their recruits as complex human beings with the potential for personal growth and enlightenment.

To achieve the metamorphosis from unwilling recruit to committed soldier required a change in consciousness. Recruits had to be made to feel like soldiers: this meant clothing them in the military uniform, teaching them military jargon, and instructing them in how to act like soldiers. This was a negotiated process within the boundaries of clearly defined values, beliefs, and ideas. Upon entering the military, the Russian soldier was completely enveloped by its culture. He learned about his new vocation as officers regularly and publicly read out official regulations and regimental manuals. His drills were turned into games to alleviate stress and boredom. Religious services kept him awake when the drumbeat of marching did not. He listened to tales about famous field marshals, and his officers related to him stories about his regiment. Old warriors, the mouthpieces of senior officers, told him how to walk, talk, and act like a soldier. Russian military writers had begun to appreciate that stories had the power to shape peoples' identities and that it was an officer's job to be not only a drill instructor but also a father-figure. Having thus been welcomed into the family of warriors, each soldier was individually responsible for subscribing to the larger value system of military culture. Throughout this process, the Russian military culture systematically, unhurriedly but steadily, drained the peasant recruits of their previous identity, way of life, and civilian customs and poured in a mixture of the military values of obedience, hierarchy, order, and professionalism. In all this, many military instructions spoke to the Enlightenment agenda regarding "how to redefine and rationalize the social order, how to change man in heart and mind."[106]

Throughout Catherine's reign, military culture threw its penetrating gaze on the soldier and placed him firmly at the centre of its attention. The Russian Enlightenment did not necessarily reject the religious interpretation of humanity, but it did emphasize the importance of secular, rational, and materialistic aspects of the world, as well as the need for social reform.[107] The Russian military culture closely reflected these larger intellectual trends. In the spirit of the Enlightenment, Russian military writers wanted to transform officers from flesh-biting masters of the cane into the enlightened managers of the human body and soul, and even official military manuals began to develop strategies for integrating peasant recruits into the new world of war and order. Various official and private instructions encouraged officers to interact and socialize with soldiers, during inspections or Meiendorf-style dinners, which means that the conventional image of eighteenth-century Russian aristocratic officers being a world apart from the Russian soldier requires qualification. Officers were clearly aware of the habits, way of life, and in some cases even the mentality of the Russian peasant recruit.[108] Such a recruit was simultaneously burdened with military service and liberated by it. His mind was not a *tabula rasa*, a blank slate that simply needed to be filled with new ideas and traditions. He was the object of officers' transformative efforts to replace his peasant identity with a military one. He was to become the defender of the Russian state, a hero if he survived, a martyr if he perished. Russian peasants were transfigured into soldiers through fun drills, humane treatment, religious rituals, and indoctrination. The success of Catherine's military culture meant that by the nineteenth century, Russian soldiers were difficult to reintegrate back into civilian society, and it seems that the break that eighteenth-century writers wanted to achieve between the two worlds had succeeded.[109] Through practices influenced by the Enlightenment, the psychological and cultural bonds produced by military culture in the twilight of Catherine's reign had left deep and vivid mark on those who were part of it. As the next chapter will show, the above processes were accompanied and reinforced by semiotic performances and displays by the most senior members of the Russian military to further advance the ideals and aspirations of their culture, as well as bind others to it.

Chapter Five

"Fantastic forms of folly": Individualism and the Performance of Military Culture

As we saw in previous chapters, military values were not abstract notions but were products of careful cultivation and reinforcement in the context of the Enlightenment. This chapter shows how sometimes they spilled over into performance and spectacle. The reader of memoirs and diaries from Catherine's Russia is often struck by episodes of eccentric behaviour within the military. These episodes pose both a challenge and an opportunity to interpret the Enlightenment influence on Russian military culture. The influential cultural historian Robert Darnton once wrote that "when we cannot get a proverb, or a joke, or a ritual, or a poem, we know we are on to something."[1] I have taken inspiration from Darton's counsel to focus on explaining, contextualizing, and interpreting the symbolic behaviour of three individuals – Petr Rumiantsev, Grigorii Potemkin, and Aleksandr Suvorov – in the context of the Military Enlightenment. I have chosen these particular historical figures partly because there are enough sources about them to raise questions and draw conclusions about the meaning of their behaviour, and partly because they embody *par excellence* the interaction between the military and the Enlightenment in Catherine's Russia.

What force encouraged and shaped this behaviour in the military, and what gave it consent and approval? Here again the long reach of Enlightenment influence, this time its emphasis on individualism, played an important and powerful role. According to one of the greatest authorities on Russian literature and history, Iuri Lotman, "what is characteristically unique for Russians in the eighteenth century is that the noble world leads a life of games, feeling itself to be forever on stage."[2] This tendency to be an actor was linked to the strong sense of individualism that had begun to possess the Russian nobility during Catherine's reign. In the final third of the eighteenth century, Russian nobles wanted to be unique in their behaviour and expression, and they refused to conform to a specific style or mould. This reflected their desire to be the masters of their own destiny, to assert themselves as independent actors, to be the rulers of their own fate, which produced some very original behaviour.[3]

Faith in science and reason gave rise to a belief in individuals' capacity to make sense of the world around them, and this opened apparently boundless opportunities. The *philosophes* "proclaimed the individual as sovereign over himself."[4] Autonomous individuals had the power to effect change, to make a difference, to leave a mark. Moreover, individualism conformed "to the rational, universal, and uniform standards of the Enlightenment."[5] The military culture marshalled this Enlightenment celebration of individualism for its own use and sanctified the power of individuals to put on performances to emphasize a set of ideas and to assert authority. Individualism was intrinsically linked to practices of power to reinforce the values of military culture and to strengthen personal control and authority. Russian military commanders demonstrated and reaffirmed their power, maintained their positions, and subordinated others through carefully constructed semiotic episodes and behaviours. The military elite, their officers, foreign observers, and even regular soldiers were all involved in this "deep play" that surrounded the individual in military culture.[6]

Spectacles by military commanders conveyed messages and performed cultural functions so as to inspire solidarity and reinforce discipline. The odd behaviour of the Russian military elite was more than just random episodes of eccentricity; it was part of a powerful dialogue that helped define eighteenth-century Russian military culture in the context of the Enlightenment. Collectively, these episodes describe signs, symbols, and complex systems of messages that served as tools for criticism and control, for enforcing professionalism, for asserting authority and independence, for communicating displeasure and satisfaction, and for observing, punishing, and rewarding subordinates and rivals.[7] Symbols and spectacles rooted in individual performances reinforced the values, customs, and aspirations of the Military Enlightenment in Russia.

Rumiantsev

One of the most famous practitioners of symbolic individualism in Catherine's military was Count Petr Rumiantsev, who turned to semiotics to reinforce many of the values and customs he himself wrote about in his military works. On being given command of the Russian forces in southern Ukraine at the start of the First Russo-Turkish War

6   Petr Rumiantsev, unknown artist, 1780s.
Art Collection 2 / Alamy Stock Photo.

(1768–74), Rumiantsev immediately set to work constructing an image
of himself as a benevolent leader, a simple man, and a good Christian,
and as epitomizing the values of the Russian Enlightenment. He understood the significance of spectacle and played his role well. "A general
must be easy and affable to his troops, without descending to meanness,
or being often seen by them, which must render him less respected,"
Rumiantsev once said. And as one contemporary added, "he himself
had learned so much affability by practice, and so rigidly observed his
own rules, that he constantly took off his hat to the very children of his
own peasants when they bowed to him."[8] Rumiantsev was a master
at this symbolic reciprocity. For him, it was important to maintain the
image of humble simplicity for reasons of respect and subordination,
but also power. When he rode through the ranks he always greeted the

soldiers with an amicable "Hello boys!," and the ranks would thunder back greetings to their commander. When one heavily decorated warrior said to Rumiantsev in a familiar fashion, "Well little-father [*batiushka*], this is the third war that I am fighting with you [with familiar *s toboiu*]," the general replied, "Well, my friend, we shall not war together a fourth time."[9] The field marshal was a peacemaker, and with polite wit he reassured the gathered soldiers that the upcoming military enterprise would result in a victory that would end the conflict. They would not have to fight a fourth time.

Rumiantsev used every chance to show his humility and religiosity and never missed an opportunity to thank the heavens for his numerous victories. When a successful attack on the Ottoman army at Riaboia Mogila in 1770 forced the Turks to retreat, Rumiantsev turned his eyes to the skies and began triumphantly to thank God.[10] A few weeks later, after a bloody victory at Kagul, Rumiantsev again hurried to praise Providence – he was quick to offer a prayer in the main bivouac of the defeated Crimean khan. He then constructed a church in its place, consecrating it with a plaque: "We thank you, God."[11] Reason may have informed Rumiantsev's military thought, but God was the true guiding spirit of the Russian armies, never leaving them to misfortune; the victories of Rumiantsev clearly belonged to Him. Rumiantsev knew the importance of emphasizing the religious aspect of war in an army that was constantly instilling Orthodox piety in its soldiers. On the battlefield he reaffirmed this aspect of training with a practical flair.

When after the victory at Kagul, the Russian army arrived near the Romanian town of Jassy, the Turks panicked.[12] Still stinging from their defeat, they quickly evacuated the town, leaving behind their sick and wounded. When Rumiantsev found out about this "inhuman callousness" of the Turks toward their comrades, he declared that "we shall show humility towards our enemy."[13] The Russians were better than the Turks, they were compassionate and civilized, and their commander knew how to show it. Humanity toward the enemy has been a characteristic of all great military leaders since antiquity, and in Russia this trait has been appropriated by narratives of military culture at least since the time of Peter the Great.[14] Humility, compassion, and religion were important to the value system of Russian military culture during the Enlightenment, and Rumiantsev strove to uphold them through his symbolic behaviour.

Rumiantsev never hesitated to play the role of the fair but omnipresent commander and father figure (*batiushka-general*). As one witness wrote, it was a role his troops had already assigned to Rumiantsev in their marching songs, and whenever he rode past, soldiers would start singing one of those songs, such as "Oh our little father, General Count Rumiantsev."[15] For his part, the count never missed an opportunity to reward lowly soldiers, which made a good spectacle for the rest of the army, as he wrote to Catherine in 1769.[16] One of many examples occurred when a Cossack soldier fought off numerous Turkish attackers and managed to capture one of them. Rumiantsev immediately sought him out and requested that the monarch reward the hero of the day with an officer rank.[17] Here, Rumiantsev was skilfully employing a powerful tool used by many military and political administrators of the eighteenth century. His lightning-quick power to observe, interfere, and reward was clearly displayed not only to the object of his attention, but more importantly to the army as a whole, especially to the humble men who populated its ranks. That merit would be recognized, and that just rewards for hard work would be noticed, had to be emphasized. Rumiantsev and many in the military elite reinforced the Napoleonic adage that all soldiers carried a marshal's baton in their backpack.

Rumiantsev was careful to cultivate his image not only among his soldiers but also among his officers, foreign emissaries, and the powerful nobles who often found their way into his headquarters and his suite. Rumiantsev resorted to powerful spectacle as a mechanism for enforcing the values of professionalism that were at the core of the Military Enlightenment. One early morning he went for an inspection of his military camp and encountered one of his officers wearing nothing but a nightshirt, loafers, and a nightcap. An officer should know better than to walk around a military camp without his uniform. Rumiantsev approached the unsuspecting officer and, without making any comment about the latter's attire, kindly took him by the arm and began to talk in a familiar manner. Eventually, Rumiantsev took his companion to his tent, where all the senior officers and generals of the army had gathered for the morning's briefing. One can imagine how surprised everyone there was to see the officer's strange attire, and the embarrassment felt by the man in the nightcap. In this case the feeling of shame had more effect on this poor creature than any other punishment.[18] The episode was an opportunity for the commander to assert himself and to emphasize the importance of professionalism in Russian military culture. Without resorting to formal methods of punishment, Rumiantsev once again demonstrated his personal control of the military and his ability to drive home a message through symbolic display. Just as he had rewarded the brave Cossack who had had to fight his way through a horde of Turkish soldiers, *batiushka* Rumiantsev never missed an opportunity for reprimand and was quick to mete out his creative kind of justice. It was not just the shabbily dressed officer, but also the men already there in the headquarters, the witnesses, who were the students of this lesson in professionalism.

Of course the nightcap and unmilitary attire of the officer had little in themselves to cause the commander of a Russian army, a man with vast power and responsibility, to put so much effort and time into a seemingly mild symbolic lesson in military etiquette. A court marshal would have been a more common alternative. The episode was an opportunity for Rumiantsev to show what it meant to be a professional soldier, and to show the camp and the officers that his eyes saw everything – that while early in the morning some were going about their personal business, he was already dressed and ready to assume his official duties, and that the uniform was an important part of military culture that distinguished its members from the rest of society. In other words, military officers had to dress according to their calling and always be ready for service.

The episode in the camp illustrated a deep-seated problem in the Russian army – a dearth of professionalism. Indeed, finding reliable, professional officers for the army was as difficult as staffing government posts with educated and committed civil servants. This was a chronic problem in eighteenth-century Russia. In the army, senior generals such as Rumiantsev had developed their own strategies for separating the wheat from the chaff. In many instances these episodes were as much spectacles of power as job interviews for the men subjected to them. Lev Engelgardt supplied one such example about Rumiantsev. During the campaign against the Ottoman armies in 1770, Rumiantsev was displeased with the service of one of his colonels, a man by the name of Philippi, and decided to put him to the test. Was Philippi, if the occasion called for it, capable of executing an important assignment? Could he be a reliable and precise tool of the field marshal's will? Rumiantsev gave Philippi a 100 Cossacks and ordered him to reconnoitre the right bank of the river Prut, the same river that was the site of a famous defeat of Peter the Great's army at the hands of the Turks in 1711. Would it be possible, Rumiantsev wanted to know, to directly bombard the enemy camp by placing Russian artillery in Riabaia Mogila, near a major Turkish camp? What Philippi did not know was that Rumiantsev had so little confidence in his abilities that he had already secretly ordered another officer to ride ahead of Philippi with light cavalry to cover him. Rumiantsev had also arranged for a letter to be immediately delivered in a sealed envelope that contained a signed order by Rumiantsev to return at once without completing the reconnaissance mission if there was any danger to Philippi or any of his men.

Without knowing any of this, Philippi felt that he was being sent to his death. After riding out of the Russian camp he asked some Moldovans nearby if there were any Turks on the far bank of the river. The river was so shallow, Engelgardt wrote, that it was knee deep for a horse. It should have been an easy crossing. But since the Moldovans answered in the affirmative – there were indeed many enemy soldiers on the other side – Philippi decided to turn back. He arrived at Rumiantsev's head-quarters later in the day while a meeting was taking place with Austrian officers. As soon as he saw Philippi enter, Rumiantsev approached him and whispered in his ear in German: "Sind Sie da gewesen? So did you go there?" Philippi replied: "Nein, Ihre Erlaucht. No, your highness.""Warum? Why so?" Philippi confessed: "Ich furchtete. I was scared." Then Rumiantsev suddenly cried out in Russian: "You [he used informal *ty*] are lucky you said that in their [Austrians'] language otherwise I would have had you executed by a firing squad." After this incident Philippi was never employed for anything again. Rumiantsev had made his point clear. He had demonstrated the importance of merit and professionalism to all Russian officers present, exercised his power to strike down and discredit an incompetent officer, and made a slighting remark about his Austrian allies by implicating them in sim-ilar behaviour. The discourse that was constructed through symbolic performances by Catherine's top-ranking officers underscored a set of values and messages that they were trying to communicate and relate to a broader audience. The nature of the eighteenth-century army was such that to enforce any kind of control and supervision, senior officers had to continuously resort to symbolic displays, re-enacting their per-formances and staging new ones.

After his disappointment with Philippi, the field marshal decided to try out another officer, this time the divisional quartermaster Fedor Len, who in the end proved to be more reliable. Earlier in the cam-paign season the Russian army had successfully besieged the fortress of Hotin, but the garrison was spared. When the garrison arrived safely at the Turkish camp, the Turkish commander sent an emissary to Rumiantsev formally thanking him for observing leniency in the rules of capitulation. Rumiantsev decided to use this opportunity, and sent Len with an empty compliment back to the Turkish general. Before Len left, Rumiantsev ordered him to use any means available to get the plans of the position of the enemy camp. As soon as he reached the advanced posts of the Turkish army he allowed the Ottoman soldiers to blindfold him, as was the custom. Len listened carefully; when he sensed from the sounds around him that the escort had brought him to the middle of the Turkish camp, he suddenly tore off the blindfold. Some of the Turkish soldiers charged him, but Len grabbed his pistol and warned that he was prepared to defend himself. He was led to a tent surrounded by a wall to prevent him from seeing anything more, but by that time he had already memorized the whole layout of the Turkish camp. When the brave quartermaster returned to the Russian army he was able to sketch the plan of the enemy positions and present it to Rumiantsev. The field marshal wanted to know how he had found this out, and when Len related his story, Rumiantsev embraced him and vowed personal friendship. Rumiantsev's headquarters was a place known for spectacle and symbolic displays, for punishment and friendship. One had to be blind not to notice the difference in symbolic treatment meted out to Philippi and to Len; everyone could see that bravery, intelligence, and initiative were all part of the value system of Russian military culture. Engelgardt certainly took enough note of this to record it in his memoirs.[19]

In his book *Command in War*, Martin van Creveld develops the idea of the "directed telescope," which he uses to describe the system applied by Napoleon "to cut through the regular command hierarchy and take a look, at will, at any part of the army or obtain any kind of information that might be required at the moment."[20] Rumiantsev's morning sojourns and tests of personal character worked like a telescope with which he could zoom in on any part of the sociocultural structure of his army; they allowed him to see, discipline, punish, reward, and command the great mass of men entrusted to him by the Russian government. His pupil, Aleksandr Suvorov, would perfect even further this mechanism of power, observation, and management. Contemporaries realized that Rumiantsev's conduct was more than just a random collection of strange and facetious behaviours. The time and place for prayer was precisely chosen, each individual Cossack was singled out and rewarded for a specific symbolic purpose, and each officer was punished or praised through a symbolic performance in the presence of his peers. All of this was done not only for reasons of discipline but also to reaffirm the values and customs of military culture along with the status of Rumiantsev, and his power to command and control the army as a whole. One Russian officer contrasted Rumiantsev's symbolic actions with the more formal conduct of another Russian general:

It is interesting that even though Count Panin was much more considerate with the soldier than Count Rumiantsev, he was loved much less than the latter, one could say he was not loved at all; and all this is simply because he [Panin] never talked to the lower ranks. He conducted himself so because of his sombre and reserved character; he tried to win the love of his soldiers, and people in general, only through just and honourable conduct, considering any other means useless and even ignoble.[21]

It seems that Panin was kinder, that he was just as attentive to the needs of his troops, but that he refused to participate in symbolic behaviour. He did not take his hat off to his peasants, he did not seek out and reward individual soldiers, he did not talk to junior officers, and in general he rejected the idea of exercising power through anything but conventional channels. Panin's authority in the army and his leadership abilities as an officer were evidently judged as inferior to those of Rumiantsev, who, as Lanzheron wrote, "enjoyed a great trust within his army, and even though he is a stern admirer of brutal discipline, soldiers, especially those who served with him, love him and have boundless respect for him."[22] Through performance, commanders became objects of awe and in the process developed attachments to themselves and the values they embodied. This was an intrinsic part of Russian military culture, especially during Catherine's reign, when individualism had such high currency.

The ambitious and praise-loving Rumiantsev was removed from active command in 1789. The command of the Russian forces now fell into the hands of his great rival, Prince Grigorii Potemkin. Rumiantsev was offended by the clear show of favouritism by Catherine to her consort, and he left the army to live out the remainder of his days in a village on one of his estates.[23] His symbolic displays had made him a popular and powerful commander and continued to reinforce the Enlightenment values that were so dear to him: merit, professionalism, loyalty, humility, and hard work.

Potemkin

Grigorii Potemkin (1739–91) was another famous product of Catherinian military culture. When the Second Russo-Turkish War began in 1787, Potemkin being the president of the War College found himself at the head of the Russian army and navy.[24] Yet despite his political influence, wealth, and authority, or perhaps because of it, he had to resort to the same displays of power as Rumiantsev. Being a favourite was not enough to win the confidence, trust, and respect of officers, foreigners, and soldiers. Traditional methods had to be supplemented with spectacular displays of power, forgiveness, punishment, and religiosity; through these, Potemkin reasserted himself and the values of the Russian military culture in the context of the Enlightenment.

Potemkin's headquarters were the principal theatre where scenarios of magnanimity, humility, and reprimand were played out. The line to see him was a long one, and many officers waited months for an audience with the great prince. Some of them spent all their money

7 Grigorii Potemkin by Johann Baptist von Lampi the Younger, early 1790s. M.Ob.783 MNW, National Museum in Warsaw.

while living in the town where he was staying in the hope of seeing him, and wrote him desperate letters.[25] As Adrian Denisov, the future Cossack general, related in his memoirs, he too had a chance to sit in the waiting room of Potemkin's office, to which he had to return several times. "Everybody saw me, but nobody bothered me with questions," wrote Denisov, "though I bowed to anyone who entered. Vasilii Popov [the head of Potemkin's chancellery] often strolled through the waiting room, and even I saw that he sometimes threw a catechizing look at me."[26] Yet the young man understood his role in the prince's scripted performance: Potemkin wanted to demonstrate his power to all in his headquarters, and Denisov's role was to experience it. Eventually Denisov's patience and quiet deference paid off with the command of a regiment. His experience can be contrasted with another example, when a general came to Potemkin's headquarters at Jassy just to show himself off to the commander-in-chief. For some time he appeared repeatedly in the waiting room to see Potemkin and kept asking the adjutant to inform the prince of his arrival; but every time his request was ignored because Potemkin was busy with some important affair. The general, disappointed with his bad luck, complained to one of the adjutants that he was offended by the continuous refusal of Potemkin to grant him audience. After all, he was not a mere corporal.

These words were duly related back to Potemkin. The next morning when the general routinely arrived back at headquarters and asked to see the prince, he was finally let in. The adjutant said that a special order had been given to the effect that the general could always enter Potemkin's office without asking permission to see him. The amazed general hurried to use such an unusual privilege. He had barely walked through the door of the office when Potemkin informed him that he felt like taking a nap. Having been interrupted in such an unexpected way, the meeting was never resumed.[27] It is likely that Potemkin napped well, because he had just made an effective demonstration of his power, carefully prepared and executed with perfect timing. The story of this encounter left Potemkin's headquarters along with the general and became a warning to superfluous officers. The prince had rid himself of an annoying parasite, re-established the image of absolute command, and defended the boundaries of his time and office.

Outside the headquarters Potemkin was just as ready to resort to symbolic display to dominate his surroundings and show everyone his virtue, his virility, and his power, but also to demonstrate his adherence to a broader set of military values. During the siege of the Turkish fortress of Ochakov in 1788, Prince Charles de Ligne, one of the numerous foreign observers, praised the courage of the Austrian Emperor Joseph II.[28] Ligne called attention to Joseph's personal bravery during the Austrian campaigns against the Ottomans, especially during the siege of Sabach. He said all this in the presence of Potemkin. It must have been difficult for the prince to remain silent, but he said nothing. The next day, however, donning a parade uniform with all of his decorations, and surrounded by his glittering staff, Potemkin went to inspect a newly built redoubt on the coast of the Black Sea, almost under the very walls of the Ochakov fortress. Cannonballs and musket balls were raining down from all directions. Several members of Potemkin's suite, Major-General Senilnikov and a Cossack, were mortally wounded.[29] "Ask Prince de Ligne," said Potemkin haughtily, "if Emperor Joseph was standing any closer to the enemy. Because if he was we can always move a little forward."[30] This episode reflected deeper historical patterns among military commanders, who had to show personal bravery in front of their armies, in part to motivate the troops and in part to reaffirm their authority.

Some historians have dismissed such episodes as empty shows of vanity. Philip Longworth described this scene simply as Potemkin "congratulating himself whenever, in venturing out of his tent, an enemy cannon-shot missed him."[31] But a closer reading of such episodes reveals that the behaviour they describe was part of a semiotic language of military culture by means of which messages and ideas were communicated back and forth. Potemkin certainly made his point, and theatrical bravery was not lost on his contemporaries. Even Ligne admitted that "one could see nothing more noble and cheerfully courageous than the Prince. I loved him to madness that day."[32] Potemkin's visit to the siege was more than a customary display of chivalry so common among the eighteenth-century nobility. Ligne had challenged Potemkin to a metaphorical duel with Joseph, in front of Potemkin's whole suite. Potemkin had to accept the challenge; he had to re-establish his authority among his men; he had to show himself to be on a par with the emperor. Facing the danger was more than mere gallantry. Through an instantaneous symbolic display Potemkin was communicating a message to his captive audience – he was showing himself equal to the Holy Roman Emperor and reaffirming his bravery in the eyes of his subordinates and followers.

When underscoring the importance of merit or punishing subordinates, Potemkin resorted to a mechanism that allowed him to turn these into occasions for demonstrating his power in full view of an audience. One example of this involved a general who had earned his rank through connections at court rather than through merit. He had been given the command of a detachment in Potemkin's army. When another officer, who had distinguished himself in combat, was promoted to divisional commander, the general felt himself unfairly passed over for promotion by Potemkin.

He met Potemkin at a dinner and began to talk to the prince about how pride always belittles a man. Potemkin immediately recognized the basic thrust of the conversation and asked what the latter thought about the following: "Whose pride is more dangerous to society and government, that of him who bases it on his achievements and his distinction, or that of he who, lacking any of the above, ascends to the top by nature of chance, but holds the same pride as the former?" The general had to agree that the pride of the second was more dangerous. "Good," continued Potemkin. "I, for my part, do not pay attention to which one of my generals is more or less incapable than the other in carrying out his duties; but the government and those who have distinguished themselves by their merit cannot be indifferent to such people who, without any distinction, try not only to be equal with them but also to get ahead of them." The general's words had given Potemkin an opportunity to show everyone how he always matched awards to merit. At the end of the dinner Potemkin sent the general away from the army with the following statement: "Your place I will try to give to someone who has as much cause to be proud of his merit, as you have in achieving your rank without it."[33]

Like Rumiantsev before him, Potemkin resorted to clever strategies to reinforce the principles of professionalism. Rumiantsev had discredited Philippi at a staff meeting with the latter's own words; Potemkin had done the same with one of his generals at a dinner party. In both cases the situation was exploited for symbolic display with maximum effect. It was not only the troublesome general who was the student of Potemkin's lesson; more important, it was the people gathered around the dinner table.

Finally, religion provided another important platform for symbolic display. In 1788 Potemkin was in Novogeroisk when he received a message about the first naval victory of the Prince of Nassau, one of many famous foreigners serving in the Russian navy during the Turkish wars. "This was God's will," said Potemkin to the surrounding suite. "Look at this church, I built it in the name of my benefactor St. George, and the battle of Kinburn happened on the next day."[34] He was forging a clear link between praising the heavens and Russian military success. Soon another message arrived regarding two more victories by Nassau over the Turks. "Did I not say," cried Potemkin in excitement, "that the Almighty does not leave me? Here is one more indication that I am a blessed child of the heavens!"[35] Potemkin refused to attribute a Russian victory to a foreigner's skills. Instead he credited it to himself through God's will. This was yet another spectacle, yet another opportunity to reaffirm his leadership and the importance of religion in Russian military culture.

The favours from above continued. During the siege of Bender, a city in modern-day Moldova, Potemkin went to the front lines to personally supervise the placement of the siege artillery. The Turks noted the presence of the prince in the ranks and intensified their fire. One of the cannonballs fell so close to Potemkin that he was splattered with flying earth. "The Turks are taking aim at me," serenely noted the prince, "but God is my protector. He deflected that cannonball!" After standing for some time in that same spot and looking around, he slowly rode along the line, paying no attention to the increasing volleys of enemy fire.[36] The power of the enemy arms was discredited on the spot. Potemkin had demonstrated that God was clearly on the side of the Russians; he had claimed Him for the Russian army. It must have been a magnificent spectacle for the troops and surrounding officers – everyone could see their cool-headed and seemingly invulnerable commander-in-chief.

Once, during the siege of the Ochakov fortress, Potemkin asked the Prince de Ligne if he would like to accompany him to the trials of new mortars. "I have ordered that a boat pick me up and deliver me to the ship where the mortars will be tested," explained Potemkin. Ligne accepted the invitation and together they rode off to Leman; but to their surprise there was no boat waiting for them – for some reason Potemkin's order to send one had not been carried out. The two had no choice but to observe the demonstration of the mortars from the shore. The trials were a complete success, but suddenly several Turkish ships appeared nearby. The sailors on the Russian vessel hurried to prepare for naval combat, but evidently forgot about the gunpowder that remained on the ship's deck. During the first cannonade the gunpowder caught fire and ignited, blowing the ship and its crew into the skies in a great explosion in full view of Potemkin and his guest. "That would have been our fate," said Potemkin to Ligne with humble assurance and a great sense of religiosity, "if the heavens had not bestowed upon me their favour, and did not bother day and night with my preservation."[37] To the excitable Ligne and others who heard this story, it appeared is if Potemkin was indeed truly blessed, and that inevitably, so was his whole military enterprise, notwithstanding the unfortunate sailors who died that night.

To maintain his position of power against the envious coterie of nobles, to humble insubordinates into submission, to prove himself in the eyes of the foreigners, and to reiterate the values of military culture, Potemkin resorted to symbolic displays. These were especially important for his command of the military and the management of the many daily challenges to his authority. Once Potemkin received the command of the army and the fleet, he had to maintain it. He had to work hard and use symbolic language and spectacles of power to help him preserve and continuously reaffirm his position.

Suvorov

Perhaps the most prolific of military symbolists in Catherine's military was Aleksandr Suvorov.[38] While Iuri Lotman provided a fascinating sketch of Suvorov's behaviour within the broader contours of Russian noble culture, it can be further contextualized specifically within Catherine's military culture. Suvorov's impressive martial laurels coexisted with puzzling behaviour and enigmatic social conduct.

Илл. Шмидтъ   Peint par Schmidt

Графъ Александръ Васильевичъ   Le Comte Alexandre Vassiliewitch
Суворовъ-Рымникскій,   Souvoroff-Rymniksky,
1729 — 1800   1729 — 1800

8 Aleksandr Suvorov by J.H. Schmidt, 1800.
Courtesy of Wikimedia.

Suvorov is an excellent subject for the analysis of spectacles of power and individualism because there are so many memoirs and diaries that document his behaviour, his actions, and his sayings at various points in his career. Furthermore, his voluminous correspondence reflects the same irregularity as his behaviour – his letters were just as full of hidden meanings.[39]

Some aspects of Suvorov's lifestyle are now legendary: his bed usually consisted of a pile of hay covered by a sheet; he eschewed formal military dress and preferred to wear simple white shirts; he hated mirrors, and everywhere he went, from balls to army headquarters, they were respectfully covered or altogether removed; and he was religious to the point of superstition.[40] In the army he began his day by pouring cold water over himself and rolling naked on the grass to dry off. He was rumoured to crow like a rooster at dawn to wake up his sleeping soldiers. "You can't oversuvorov Suvorov," joked Potemkin.[41] Stories of Suvorov's eccentricities spread across Europe on the back of his victories and even reached the British Isles, where Lord Byron described him as a "buffoon," "Momus," and "Harlequin in uniform."[42] As Suvorov's secretary, and a spy for the Russian government, Egor Fuks, concluded, "he remains a hieroglyph even in posterity."[43]

Suvorov used the veneer of bizarre behaviour to conceal his real intentions. His behaviour was nothing less than a spectacle of power that was intrinsic to the very real power he gained from such performances. Indeed, spectacle was inherent to Suvorov's military success; it was a tool of leadership and administration inspired by the individualism unleashed by the Enlightenment. Yet some contemporaries refused to believe it. As Engelgardt put it, "generals and people gifted with military acumen have all maintained that it was all luck."[44] In the words of one foreign observer, Suvorov's "gross and ridiculous manners have inspired his soldiers with the blind confidence, which serves him instead of his military talents, and has been the real cause of all his successes."[45] However, the consistency with which Suvorov managed the Russian military machine betrays something deeper than simple good fortune. One reason why he was successful across the entire range of campaigns, from the deep forests of Poland to the steep Swiss Alps, was that he was able to exercise power through symbolic display, which he used to impress and reinforce the main tenets of military culture. In the process he asserted his leadership, reinforced subordination, maintained control, and won the trust of his followers.

Some suspected that his odd behaviour coincided with episodes of binge-drinking.[46] Others thought that he was mentally unstable, and his own secretary, Fuks, confessed that he himself at one time thought so.[47] "What would you have thought," he wrote, "if during an audience with the field marshal, he first runs towards you, then runs away from you, in one corner he would start to make comparisons between ancient Greeks and Romans; suddenly you hear about the past dances in the province of Borovintsk; from there he moves on to the battle of Rymnik, the narrative of which you cannot even understand." But "when Suvorov enters his office," continued Fuks, "all of what you have just seen stops." Perhaps Suvorov was not mentally unstable after all. In his office a new act began. "There he dictates the disposition for the upcoming battle, contemplates the strength of the enemy, directs his troops to new positions, assigns them new battle directives, sketches battle plans, or corrects the mistakes of his quartermasters."[48] Suvorov's office was the reverse of Potemkin's; spectacles were left at the door and secluded work began. Fuks marvelled at how such a cultured and well-educated man turned into a clown and a fool every time he left his office. "One time," remembered Fuks, "I lost my temper and asked him what is the meaning of this?" Confronted in this way, Suvorov dodged, and answered that it meant nothing – "This is my style." He quickly changed the subject and sent Fuks out to do chores.[49] Clearly the field marshal refused to be classified, analysed, or deciphered; he wanted to remain a hieroglyph.

The accounts of British diplomats support this duality in Suvorov's behaviour. The founder of the British Foreign Intelligence Service, William Wickham, after meeting Suvorov in his office, commented that he was of "a vigorous mind and of a clear and sound understanding as little impaired as it could have been in the prime of life."[50] Sir Gilbert Elliott, Envoy-Extraordinary to Austria, saw Suvorov outside the confines of his office in January 1800, and writing to his wife from Prague, called Suvorov "the most perfect Bedlamite that ever was allowed to be at large."[51] As soon as Suvorov stepped outside his office, as Fuks faithfully wrote down, he changed from a "vigorously-minded" diplomat to a "perfect Bedlamite." The wild incongruity of Suvorov's behaviour reflects both the semiotic nature of military culture and Lotman's point about the influences of Enlightenment individualism on the nobility in Catherine's Russia, who felt themselves to be on the stage of life.

This begs the question of when and why this Russian aristocrat turned himself into the god of mockery and satire. After the Seven Years' War, the young Suvorov became the commander of the Suzdal Regiment in the Ladoga region of northern Russia. As Fuks learned from old soldiers, Suvorov's strange conduct began during that time.[52] He first attracted attention when he laid siege to an ancient Orthodox monastery. As part of the routine drill, Suvorov wanted to teach his men how to conduct a proper storm of a fortress, foreshadowing the bloody sieges he would become famous for in the 1790s. One day, during an exercise, the regiment came across a monastery, and letting his imagination get the best of him, Suvorov immediately ordered his men to storm it. Christopher Duffy weighed in with a military analysis of this episode and wrote that "this was a good exercise, since the monasteries constituted some of the very rare stone-walled buildings in Russia."[53] The sight of soldiers wildly pouring over the stone walls must have made an unsettling impression on the monks inside. The whole enterprise was a harmless affair, but the incident reached the ears of the empress. Catherine must have been curious, for she asked to meet the man behind the venture. This first recorded episode of unusual military behaviour had brought Suvorov to the attention of the Russian court.[54] The affair was hushed up.

It is important to place Suvorov's symbolic displays in the context of Russian military culture. Lotman believed that Suvorov's performances were a combination of deliberate actions and improvisations, inspired by the Enlightenment, and that he started out with a specific plan in mind and then got lost in his own act and overplayed his hand.[55] The spectacle usually began at the very first meeting, which was often a traumatic experience for at least one of the parties. The account left by Count Roger de Damas, one of the French officers in the Russian army in 1788, is one of the best and deserves to be quoted in full:

> I had not seen General Souvarow [*sic*] ... and did not know him. The prospect of presenting myself to him made me feel a little agitated, and I was entirely absorbed in the thought of it when my tent was unceremoniously entered by a man dressed in his shirt only, who asked me who I was ... Seeing that I was embarrassed by the fantastic apparition he said "Pray be calm, and do not let me disturb you. To whom were you writing when I came in?" I came to the conclusion that one might be fairly at one's ease with a general in his shirt, so I answered frankly that I was writing to my sister, in the hope that Prince of Nassau might be able to send my letter on the following day ... "It is not the Prince of Nassau who will send it," he said. "It is I; but I want to write her a letter too." He seized some paper and a pen, sat down on a stool, and wrote my sister a letter of four pages, the contents of which I never knew. She received it safely with mine, but has since told me that quite half of it was unintelligible ... He warned me his invariable dinner-hour was at six o'clock, and that he did not wish me to dine anywhere but with him ... On that same evening I arrived at his headquarters for dinner. "You surely made a mistake, monsieur," said his senior adjutant; "it is at six in the morning that his Excellency dines, and he is now in bed." ... These two incidents, following one another so rapidly, made me believe, I confess, that I had to deal with a lunatic ... At precisely six o'clock on the following morning I was at the general's door. He received me with a series of leaps and embraces that disquieted me a good deal; made me swallow a glass of liqueur that set fire to my throat and stomach; and drank some of the same liquid himself with grimaces that were enough to make a *vivandiere* miscarry on the spot.[56]

Contemporaries never underestimated the role of individualism in shaping ideas and messages during these meetings. Suvorov was famous for such spectacles during first introduction.[57] This "fantastic apparition" not only helped to break the ice – Damas admitted Suvorov somehow made him feel at ease – but also helped establish a rapport with new and often foreign officers. The meeting happened outside the officially prescribed ceremonies and rules, it was casual and informal. The meeting was also a baptism, a ritual by which the guest was welcomed into the army under Suvorov's command and became a member of an extended family of warriors.

As with Rumiantsev and Potemkin, Suvorov's symbolic displays and slapstick at court and in the army can be broken down into discernible patterns, designed to convey or enforce the ideals of the Enlightenment within the Russian military culture. Of these, the ideals of professionalism and merit were especially important for Suvorov. Fuks observed that his sudden, strange behaviour, his jumping around, his sharp jokes, and his humorous stories about irrelevant subjects often put out the fires of discontent, rivalry, and jealousy before they could flare up.[58] Simultaneously, they served to drive home the norms of military culture. For example, in 1799, during the Italian campaign, Suvorov generously praised and raised a glass to the successes of the Austrian General Paul Kray, who had taken the city of Turin. Somebody asked Suvorov, "Did you know that Kray comes from the most common stock and worked his way up from the lowest rank of soldier to that of general?" Echoing the Enlightenment ridicule of social status, Suvorov replied that even though Kray did not have the privilege of birth, "after today's deed I would be especially honoured to have him, at least, as a cousin."[59] Similar to the scenes at Potemkin's dinners and Rumiantsev's headquarters, Suvorov publicly undermined some of the deeply engrained traditions of old-regime armies by insisting on rewards based on merit. The message to the audience at the table was very clear.

Suvorov also used and refined the techniques of observation employed by Rumiantsev. His "directed telescope" was even more powerful, penetrating deep into the fabric of the military; and he deployed it everywhere he was sent. For instance, he liked to walk around the camp incognito, wearing a soldier's jacket or an old, torn coat, and was always pleased with himself when he passed unnoticed. This behaviour was by then a well-established trope in military history, and Suvorov probably saw himself following in the footsteps of a long tradition of commanders, from Richard the Lionheart to Peter the Great, who walked among the ranks to see if the living conditions of their troops were adequate.[60] Of course, such methods of observation were much easier to conduct at a time when printed images were rare and some soldiers probably did not know what their commanders looked like. The only opportunity for face-to-face encounters was the parade, during which the ranks and officers were usually separated by a great distance. Suvorov must have known this and relished his ability to examine his men in the shadow of anonymity.

Suvorov did just that when he was named the inspector of the Kuban frontier, in southern Russia. He decided to go walking along the military lines to inspect them in person. Word of this began to spread, and every commander eagerly expected his arrival.[61] But Suvorov disliked pomp and preferred to appear always suddenly, unexpectedly, just as he had done in Damas's tent. One night, travelling by sleigh, he arrived at a station where the captain was an old soldier who did not know what Suvorov looked like. Suvorov explained that he had been sent by Suvorov to prepare horses in advance of the inspection. The old captain received the night traveller in a comradely fashion: he took his guest to his room, offered him a glass of vodka, and invited him to supper; he made jokes, judged various generals, and gossiped. Eventually Suvorov left to continue his journey. In the morning the captain received the following note: "Suvorov has passed through here, thanks captain N. for supper and asks for his continuing friendship."[62] He clearly wanted the captain to know who his late-night guest had been, no doubt so that the gossipy officer would perpetuate the image of Suvorov's omnipresence. Suvorov used his incognito visits as a means to observe everything with his own eyes, undiluted by official reports, as well as to collect information through non-conventional channels. By shedding his epaulets, Suvorov became very well-informed indeed. Suvorov had apparently internalized the strategies, ruses, and symbolic behaviour of Peter the Great, among other military commanders all the way back to antiquity, including Hannibal and Alexander the Great. Having long embraced the Enlightenment obsession with the ancient world, Suvorov had no doubt read and reread histories of ancient wars and campaigns and biographies of great political and military leaders. His personal hero was Julius Caesar, who was famous for talking to his soldiers in comradely fashion and for fighting in their midst.[63]

Suvorov continued these practices throughout his career. Even as he approached the age of seventy, during the Italian campaign in 1799, he continued to make his incognito rounds around the camp. By then he was disguising himself as an old soldier, which was another famous trope, another classic pattern, connected to famous commanders of ancient times. On one occasion he heard a sergeant call him over. The man was trying to deliver some papers from an Austrian general to Suvorov, and asked if he knew where the field marshal was staying. Suvorov had a reply ready: "Hell knows where he is. Don't give him the papers; he is now either dead drunk or crowing like a rooster." The sergeant was about to beat Suvorov for such a demeaning reply, but the field marshal was an agile runner and quickly fled. About an hour later, Suvorov was back at his headquarters, and the sergeant quickly realized that he had almost assaulted the great Russian hero.[64] For the people around Suvorov's headquarters such spectacles were disquieting – the field marshal seemed omnipresent.

In addition to wearing disguises, Suvorov liked to ask sudden and random questions. It appears that Fuks understood why he did this, and he wrote down several examples of these sporadic interrogations. The most important thing was not to panic. Suvorov's war on the *nemoguznaika* (don't-knower) was well known. It was better to lie or make up a ridiculous answer than to say "I don't know ..." or "I can't tell you ..." On such occasions, Suvorov would turn verbally abusive. Engelgardt wrote that if Suvorov asked, "'Is it far from here to Warsaw?' answer '250 verst, 13 sazhen, and 1 arshin' and he would be happy." It did not matter where exactly "here" was.[65] One time, Suvorov asked a soldier, "How far is it from here to the sky?" The answer he got was, "Two campaigns for Suvorov." Another time he asked a night-guardsman on duty, "How many stars are there in the sky?" The soldier did not panic at being so suddenly confronted by his field marshal, and calmly began to count "One, two, three ..."[66] Delagardi, the Swedish ambassador, wrote that Suvorov "was very happy when to his question of how many fish there are in the Danube he received an answer of 42.5 million."[67] It was not necessarily the correct answers that Suvorov wanted; rather, he was testing at random the ability of his soldiers and officers to think on the spot.[68] Sometimes, however, Suvorov lost himself in the performance and this barrage of questioning backfired. As the Spanish general Francisco De Miranda wrote in 1786, when he met Suvorov, "the general plied me with stupid questions until the Prince [Potemkin] told him to shut up."[69]

This sort of behaviour was intended to make a point and reinforce an idea or a set of values that were important to military culture as Suvorov saw it. In other words, he employed extremely symbolic behaviour to impress important points on his audience. Most often, Suvorov's spectacles were triggered by his unquenchable desire to professionalize the Russian army, and he made this clear with his punishments, especially when it came to the nobility, who were exempt from any corporal penalty. How do you inflict physical punishment on a body that is legally immune from it? When Suvorov was still in the Kuban, a lieutenant-colonel by the name of N. arrived at his headquarters. He had brought with him several letters of recommendation and went to see the general well dressed, perfumed, and wearing heeled shoes. Suvorov, after reading the letters, welcomed him quite affectionately. "I am very glad! You seem to know all of my close friends.

Good! My goodness, good. Let us try to get to know each other." He immediately invited the new arrival to go for a ride. Thrilled by such a sign of friendliness from his new commander, N. asked permission to quickly change. "No need, no need!" replied Suvorov. N. was forced to mount a Cossack horse and gallop merrily behind his new chief. The lieutenant-colonel was soon mortified to realize that the casual ride was turning into a two-day inspection of front-line fortifications on horseback. The coarse saddle ruined N.'s attire, and by the end of the trip his legs were raw and bloody.[70] Punishment came together with a lesson: a military man should not wear civilian clothes in the army because he always needs to be ready for action, and the lieutenant-colonel clearly was not. Suvorov was able to inflict pain, humiliation, and punishment in creative ways. In this he was following in the steps of Rumiantsev, Potemkin, and various military writers who were trying to create a class of professional officers out of young noble dandies.

Years later, in 1799, Suvorov was sent to Italy to command the allied forces against the armies of revolutionary France. Before he left Vienna, the Military Council (*Hofkriegsrath*) wanted to see his campaign plan for the upcoming war. Suvorov arrived as promised at a big general meeting where the campaign was to be discussed. Count Johann Thugut, the powerful chancellor of the Habsburg Empire, turned to Suvorov and asked whether he had brought his plans with him to share with the council. Suvorov stood up, reached into his coat to take out a large piece of paper, unfolded it, and put it on the table. Everyone was surprised to see it was blank. "I have never made any other plans for my campaigns," explained the old field marshal in his usual declarative manner. For the council this must have seemed an ominous start.[71] An officer of the Moscow regiment, Captain Griazev, left a similar account. The *Hofkriegsrath* sent several officers to Suvorov to show him the council's plans for the upcoming campaign around the Adda River, in the northernmost part of Italy. The officers asked Suvorov to comment on the plan and to make any corrections he saw fit. The field marshal crossed out the whole plan and wrote instead: "I shall start by crossing the Adda, and finish the campaign where God pleases."[72] Despite the difference in form, the message remained the same, and obvious: in an impressive symbolic display, Suvorov was asserting his independence. It was not that he did not plan his campaigns – he did so meticulously – but rather that he wanted to conduct them *his* way.[73] With his reference to providence, Suvorov was refusing to be tied down by directives or to recognize the *Hofkriegsrath* as having any authority over him. This was a general trend in Russian military culture, which by the end of the eighteenth century was seeking political autonomy.

Behind the performances lurked a calculated cunning and an ability to harness the power of individualism in the context of the Enlightenment. Sudden questionings bordering on interrogation, the ability to observe without being seen, and a knack for punishing officers through unconventional methods were powerful tools that Suvorov used to control and discipline his armies and assert his authority among the troops, but also to reaffirm the values and customs of military culture. Episodes of Suvorov walking among the ranks became legendary in the Russian army. The control he was able to exercise over the troops must have been quite unprecedented: they always had to be on guard because unless they knew exactly what Suvorov looked like and where he was, every soldier with a dirty old coat could be a disguised field marshal.

After an analysis of Suvorov's semiotic eccentricity there is little doubt as to what end such episodes were performed, but the last word should be left to Fuks, Suvorov's secretary, who came to know the field marshal exceedingly well and was one of the few people at his bedside when he died a hero-in-exile in 1800. Fuks remembered a rare occasion when old Suvorov talked about himself with frankness. "Would you like to know me?" he began. "I will tell you: I was praised by the tsars, I was loved by soldiers, friends wondered at me, enemies cursed me, the court laughed at me. I was at court, but I was not a courtier, like Aesop and La Fontaine: with jokes and beastly language I spoke the truth."[74] Aesop was a popular writer of fables in ancient Greece, and Jean de La Fontaine was a renowned fabulist in seventeenth-century France. Both writers used myth and parables in their stories to convey a moral message. Both had informed the Enlightenment culture. Suvorov could hardly have put himself in better company.

The question at this point is whether the audience registered the value of Suvorov's symbolic performances and understood their meaning. There is much evidence that indeed the people who recorded these episodes understood their deeper meaning and the messages they were conveying. For example, after meeting Suvorov, de Segur wrote that Suvorov "formed the strange design of concealing his transcendent merit under fantastic forms of folly."[75] Aleksandr Lanzheron, a Frenchman in Russian service, wrote that Suvorov "is so masterful at playing a mentally disturbed that it became his second nature." He added that while Suvorov played the madman, "in reality he is quite far from being one."[76] And after experiencing some of Suvorov's peculiarities first-hand, Lev Engelgardt thought that Suvorov was a "subtle politician" (tonkii politik). To the untrained eye Suvorov's behaviour appeared odd and whimsical, but Engelgardt thought he acted this way "so as not to attract jealousies."[77] Another testament comes from within the inner circle of the exiled king of France. The Duc de Doudeauville was a close aide to Louis XVIII while the French court was hiding in Russia from the ravages of the French Revolution. The field marshal paid his respects to the French monarch while he was travelling to take up his command in Italy in 1799 and spent more than an hour at his court. As Doudeauville recounted,

> this half-wicked hero has coincided within him such antics, that could have easily been ascribed to a mentally disturbed, if they had not proceeded from the calculations of a subtle and farsighted mind. For this was a man of small height, thin, frail, poorly-built, with an ape-like physiognomy, with lively, crafty eyes, and with manners so strange and hilariously-funny, that one could not observe him without simultaneous laughter and pity; but underneath this original shell, there hid the gifts of a great military genius.[78]

One gathers a clear sense that the observers of Suvorov understood the purpose of his symbolic behaviour; it is also clear that it made a lasting impression on those who witnessed it. The eccentricities of Catherine's military culture seemed to diminish as the nineteenth century progressed; however, several of Suvorov's associates continued the rich tradition of "fantastic follies" into Alexander's reign (r. 1801–25). According to contemporaries, Prince Grigorii Volkonskii, who served under Suvorov in the 1790s, adopted some of his signature traits and habits later in life.[79] Field Marshal Mikhail Kutuzov and General Mikhail Miloradovich, both of whom served under Suvorov in the 1790s, seem to have donned Suvorov's mantle as well, and liked to occasionally display their individual styles of leadership and command through symbolic performances for their officers and soldiers during the Napoleonic Wars.[80]

As historian John Keep observed, "It is curious that Suvorov enjoyed greater popularity in the ranks than Potemkin, although the latter was more humane and sparing of the lives of his men."[81] Suvorov knew the power of his displays, and he must have known that people wrote down what he said and did and that stories about him were widely circulated. This only reinforced his commitment to eccentricity and produced more spectacles. Indeed, symbolic displays were a mechanism of individualism that allowed the performer to criticize without being punished; they also allowed for a dialogue that otherwise would not have taken place; and they allowed for the power of the military elite to be exercised and for values and customs of military culture to be reinforced.

The Enlightenment propelled the importance of individualism and embedded the powers of reason and action and capacity in individual human beings.[82] It made space for individuality, and in the military culture this enabled commanders to distinguish themselves from all others and to put their own stamp on leadership and command. The military culture marshalled individualism for its own purposes. Recent works about ceremonies and spectacles in eighteenth-century Russia show how fundamental such performances were to the power and functioning of the Russian autocracy.[83] Just like the court, Russian military culture created "mini-scenarios of power" to legitimize itself.[84] Spectacle was essential to the power and functioning of the military culture, and Catherine clearly permitted its use for that purpose. Flamboyant performances and semiotic displays were not necessarily a function of individual character but rather parts of a deliberate strategy of control and communication. Like actors changing their costumes, senior officers played different roles and used symbolic displays to maintain their influence, assert their authority, and exercise their power over the vast and nebulous structure of the army. By staging performances, commanders conveyed their ideas and punished, rewarded, disciplined, and reinforced the Enlightenment military culture.

This theatrical dimension of military culture was not exclusive to Russia – a point that calls into question Russian scholarship that maintains that Russian military culture was significantly different from that of Western Europe.[85] Writing about military spectacle in the British army in the nineteenth century, Scott Myerly observed that "the spectacle's trappings exerted a strong psychological and emotional influence on the soldiers, and thus were a vital tool in maintaining the dependability of the military instrument."[86] Moreover, the performances of Catherine's field marshals corresponded to well-established tropes from early military history, tropes that Rumiantsev, Potemkin, and Suvorov had all read about and now internalized.

Spectacles, be they for punishment or praise, were directed not just at the person who would be on the receiving end, but also at a captive audience. Without an audience, the performances would have had no meaning for they would not have been retold or circulated within the military. This explains why most of the documented episodes were performed before a large group of spectators and often at a carefully chosen time and place, such as a council of war or an inspection. Those gathered around became participants in the spectacle by hearing, talking, or writing about the most recent show staged by their commanders. And the meanings of performances and their coded messages were clearly not lost on the audience, as the memoirs of Fuks, Segur, Lanzheron, Engelgardt, Doudeauville, and many others testify. Even years later, as one nineteenth-century author recalled, "while living in Kiev, during long winter evenings I had the chance to listen to stories about the past; most often the subject of conversation was the century of Catherine II and her contemporaries – Rumiantsev and Suvorov; besides oral tales, many anecdotes and stories have been recorded about them in journals and memoirs by their comrades-in-arms and contemporaries."[87] Military commanders became pieces of military culture whose individualism, expressed through semiotic performances, circulated deep within Russian society. In the process they gave meaning to the values of the Military Enlightenment during Catherine's reign and simultaneously helped form and define it.

Chapter Six

"The gutters of the town were dyed with blood": The Siege of Izmail, the Russian Military Culture, and the Limits of the Enlightenment at War

By 1787 Russia was engaged in another war with Turkey over control of the Black Sea and the Crimea. The turning point in the conflict was the grisly capture of Izmail, a Turkish fortress that refused to capitulate and that had to be taken by a desperate onslaught that lasted eleven hours and sent shockwaves throughout Russia and Europe.[1] General Mikhail Kutuzov was one of the commanders leading the attack, and on the following day he wrote a short letter to his wife:

> My dear friend, Katerina ... I, thank God, am well ... and only God knows how I am not wounded. I will not see such an affair for a century. My hair stands on its end. Until yesterday evening I was jovial, because I am alive and this terrible city is in our hands, but when I arrived home at night it was like coming to a wasteland. Ivan St. and Glebov, who lived with me, are dead; whoever I enquire about ... is either dead or dying ... I spent the whole night alone; and there are so many things to do that I cannot even take care of the wounded; I need to restore order in the city, but there are more than 15 thousand dead Turkish bodies alone ... Among your friends, Fedor Vasil'evich Ku. is wounded the worst. I think he has a musket ball in his lung. He is coughing blood ... Burmeister was killed, as was Major Karpov. I can't even collect my corps together, there are almost no officers left alive.[2]

Kutuzov's letter to his wife conveyed the carnage of the assault, which shook the Ottoman Empire. However, the battle at Izmail also represented something larger, something beyond the contest of arms between the Turks and the Russians. Tensions between merit and seniority, professionalism and favouritism, insecurities and confidence, as well as cultural practices of religion, honour, and identity, came together around the besieged fortress. Izmail was a "cultural site," to borrow William Sewell's phrase,[3] one that serves to crystallize the themes of the previous chapters. Izmail showed how military experience informed military writing, how acts worthy of reward were performed, and how events like Izmail promoted and solidified military culture. It was a cultural arena, a social space where anxieties, ambitions, and identities came into focus and manifested themselves and where the ideals and values of the Enlightenment clashed with the realities of war. While the siege at Izmail illuminated only one corner of the larger canvas of military culture during Catherine's reign, it is seminal because of its raw power and impact and because of the availability of Russian and foreign sources. Finally, unlike many other military events, Izmail has not yet been the subject of a detailed cultural analysis in the context of eighteenth-century warfare. The siege and the ensuing battle served as a macabre stage on which Russian military culture played out its spectacle and the Military Enlightenment was tested and reached its limit.

Before the Storm

When Russian forces finally arrived at the gates of Izmail, the war had been raging for three years under the command of Prince Grigorii Potemkin. Izmail stood in a natural amphitheatre on a bank of the Danube. The fortress was protected by seven bastions and by massive fortifications that stretched around the city for 12 kilometres. As Roger de Damas, one of many foreigners in Russian service, wrote: "the surface of the fortifications being of earth it was impossible to make a breach; the guns merely crumbled the earth; the damage was repaired during the night; and so no progress was made."[4] Around the walls ran a deep moat filled with water from the river. The four entrance gates were brimming with artillery. Its southern side was open to the Danube but was protected by a fleet of ships and ten gun batteries. Even if the Russians managed to break through this ring of defences, inside Izmail was the old citadel, which itself would have to be besieged. As the Russians continued to advance from the north, the retreating Turkish troops began to trickle into Izmail, along with provisions and military supplies.[5] Izmail soon turned from a fortress with a garrison into an army with a fortress.

In October 1790 the Russians began to collect reports from spies and defectors to gauge the strength of the forces concealed by the walls of Izmail.[6] Among the volunteers searching for glory and rewards around Izmail was the twenty-eight-year-old Count Grigorii Chernyshev. Writing to his brother, Prince Sergei Golitsyn, in late November 1790, he described the situation in the army in grim terms. "My dear brother," wrote Chernyshev, "the start of the campaign has been most

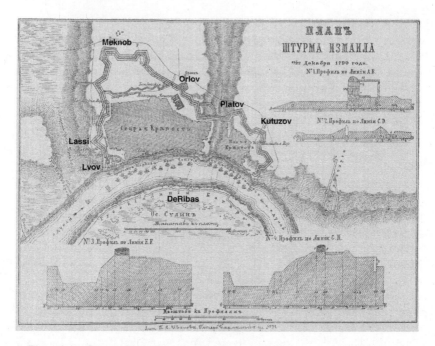

9 Plan of the Siege of Izmail by Suvorov

10 Storming of Izmail from the side of the Danube

unfortunate; everyone is feeling down, nobody knows what to do, and the Turks are celebrating."[7] Potemkin did not dare bypass such a massive city harbouring a large portion of the Turkish army before entering deeper into the Ottoman territories; he was afraid of being attacked from the rear. Izmail had to be conquered, and Chernyshev already realized that the whole affair would have to end in an assault: "otherwise, we, of course, will never take Izmail."[8]

Unfortunately, Potemkin had fallen into one of his bouts of hypochondria, apathy, and lethargy. The same Potemkin who was capable of immense physical and administrative activity succumbed to the comforts of his office. One account stated that "surrounded by courtiers and females, occupied with entertainments, games, and plays, more than with warlike projects, he lived in his camp like one of the Satraps of old, and set a disgraceful example to his soldiers."[9] Instead of regular military meetings in headquarters, Potemkin had daily dinners in the open air, even in the pouring rain. By becoming a "Satrap of Old" and by staging unmilitary spectacles that clashed with the ideals of the professional military nurtured by the Enlightenment, the prince did indeed "set a disgraceful example," one that did not go unnoticed by perceptive Russian officers. By the end of November, Chernyshev was damning himself for volunteering to come to Izmail.[10] Officers who had been raised on the diet of the Military Enlightenment felt ashamed of their commander's conduct, and young men like Chernyshev felt demoralized, underemployed, and superfluous. "Because of all this, I think that tomorrow or the day after, Gudovich and I, will leave this corps and join Kutuzov, where there are more things to do, especially for a volunteer," he wrote to his brother.[11] Chernyshev was prepared to go hungry, live a camp life, and even die in battle, but he was not prepared to be useless.

In the meantime, while the army was bivouacking outside the city gates, old tensions between seniority and ability were bubbling to the surface and undermining the military effort. The Russian forces surrounding Izmail were divided among three commanders. Iosif de Ribas was in charge of the Russian fleet blocking the fortress from the Danube, and Pavel Potemkin, the prince's nephew, and Mikhail Kutuzov were deployed in a semicircle around the fortress, preventing resupply by land. As Chernyshev wrote, "Our misfortune lies in the fact that all three generals, Potemkin, Kutuzov, and Ribas, not only are independent of each other, but do not act in cohesion and do not even want to assist each other, while Lvov [another general] is laughing at them all, and not without a reason."[12] By late November the situation at Izmail had reached a critical impasse. The Turks clearly were not going to be dislodged by the siege or intimidated by Russian manoeuvres or the Russian navy. Yet the three Russian commanders did not have the confidence to do what they all knew was the only way to take the fortress, which was to storm it. The picture that emerges from Chernyshev's letters is one of discord, arrogance, and jealousies. Pavel Potemkin was on bad terms with Ribas, but since both were favourites of the prince they secretly feared each other and consequently did not dare get in each other's way. Other generals, such as Ivan Gudovich, were jealous of Pavel Potemkin, and subordination and cooperation between them was breaking down. According to Chernyshev, it was not the Turks but "personal intrigues [that] are the main cause of all the evil."[13] To solve the crisis that was festering under the walls of Izmail and to extricate themselves from a politically vulnerable situation, the three commanders decided to call a military council.

The institution of the military council had been established by Peter the Great in the *Military Statute* and was an important part of Russian military culture in the eighteenth century. At Izmail, the military council played a crucial role twice, both as a military decision-making body and as a forum for political and military leadership. On this occasion, the council sent its decision to Prince Potemkin on 26 November. In it, the generals argued that it would be futile to undertake any further actions.[14] They wrote that a deserter from Izmail had confirmed that the garrison was large and had more than enough guns to defend itself, as well as plenty of ammunition. They wrote that the Russian forces lacked the necessary siege artillery to reduce the mighty Turkish fortifications. They also pointed out that winter was fast approaching and that the army needed time to reach its winter quarters, which were far away. They warned that even if the bombardment and assault was immediately launched, it was unlikely to succeed and would cost thousands of lives. Finally, citing military principles of siege warfare, the council concluded that a storming of the fortress was out of the question and that the siege should be replaced with a blockade. The Turkish garrison had only six weeks' provisions left, and the army of Her Imperial Majesty need only wait for the infidels inside to succumb to hunger, cold, and dysentery. The military council therefore advised that the army be withdrawn to winter quarters, leaving only enough forces behind to conduct the blockade. The generals asked Prince Potemkin to consider their plan, and in the meantime, citing the relevant chapter of the *Military Statute*, put it into action. While the letter was travelling to Potemkin, before he had a chance to read it and write a reply, a full retreat had begun. The whole affair was a direct challenge to Potemkin's authority as commander-in-chief and demonstrated that his senior officers were losing confidence in his military leadership, which might disastrously undercut his political power.[15]

According to one story, it was one of Potemkin's mistresses who finally drove him into action. Using a pack of cards for fortune telling, "Madame de Witte foretold that he would take Izmail within three weeks."[16] Most likely it was the resolve and insistence of Catherine, rather than the fortune-telling de Witte, that spurred the prince to make one last effort to take Izmail.[17] Potemkin was under pressure to bring the Turks to the negotiating table, but at the same time he probably realized that the technical challenge of storming Izmail was beyond his military skill, so he sent for the one man who could make his fortune come true.

On 25 November, Potemkin personally wrote two letters to Suvorov. In the first, he informed Suvorov that all the forces around the city, including the navy, had been placed under his command, and that he was to depart immediately for Izmail. He then encouraged Suvorov to look for the weakest places in the defences, writing that "I personally think that the side of the city that is open to the Danube is the weakest." At the same time, Potemkin had doubts that even the renowned Suvorov could take the fortress, and he instructed him to make sure he could retreat, in case, "God forbid," his assault failed. In the second letter, written later that day, Potemkin warned Suvorov about the discord among the commanding generals, which had led to inactivity and retreat, and singled out two officers whom Suvorov could depend on. Setting aside patronage networks and family ties, the prince wrote frankly that Suvorov should rely on Kutuzov and Ribas instead of his relatives Aleksandr Samoilov and Pavel Potemkin. As if to lift Suvorov's spirits, he reiterated that the fortress was not impregnable – "there are [weak] places, as long as there is good leadership."[18] Finally, Potemkin hastened to inform Suvorov about the coup d'état by his generals and the decision by the military council to retreat:

> Before my orders had reached General Gudovich, Lieutenant-General Potemkin and Major-General de Ribas about your appointment as the commander of the Danube forces and about conducting the storm of Izmail, they decided to retreat. I, having just now received their report, propose your Excellency to act here according to your best judgment, continuing the Izmail enterprise or dropping it. Your Excellency, being there and having your hands untied, should not, of course, miss any opportunity that will be beneficial for us and that will add to the glory of our arms. Only please hasten to update me about what measures you are taking and inform the above-mentioned generals about your orders.[19]

Potemkin's letters reflected the best aspects of the Military Enlightenment. There were clear recommendations of aptitude based on merit – Ribas and Kutuzov were singled out as especially formidable. There was also a clear emphasis on personal initiative – "act here according to your best judgment" – which underscored professionalism and trust between superiors and subordinates. Potemkin "untied" Suvorov's hands and gave him the opportunity to assess the situation on the spot. He was free to attack or retreat as long as he kept Potemkin informed. At the same time, the siege exposed a certain helplessness of Potemkin as the commander-in-chief, as well as the limits of his power and authority.

The news of Suvorov's imminent arrival began to spread around the camp like wildfire. "We are waiting the arrival of Suvorov every minute," wrote Chernyshev in excitement. Everyone in the army was now certain that as soon as Suvorov arrived, the siege of Izmail would turn into an immediate, if desperate, assault.[20] If military culture had tensions, it also had mechanisms for resolving them. As soon as he did arrive, a whirlwind of furious activity began.

The situation looked unfavourable, however. Suvorov had 30,000 troops, almost half of them Cossack irregulars, to capture a fortress with a garrison of 35,000, while the basic principles of siege warfare dictate that the attacker needs at least three-to-one superiority over the besieged. Even before the first storming ladder touched the walls of Izmail, the new commander had to address the falling morale among the soldiers and prepare them for a terrifying undertaking. He had to address the acrimonious tensions of rank and seniority among the commanders. He had to formally reverse the decision of the military council, which had undermined the confidence of senior officers by concluding that the assault was impossible and that retreat was inevitable. The task before Suvorov was so monumental that he wrote as much to Potemkin a week before the assault, confessing to the prince that he "could not promise anything" and that despite Potemkin's earlier assurances, to Suvorov's eye the fortress "had no weaknesses."[21]

Suvurov began the preparations by personally designing and supervising drills for the assault. He called for the construction of ramparts and moats identical to those of the fortress and ordered soldiers and officers to climb them with ladders.[22] He built dummy enemy soldiers and ordered his troops to attack them with bayonets drawn. These preparations, carried out at a feverish pace, were accompanied by Suvorov's eccentric behaviour and performances. As was common, not everyone understood the value and purpose of these semiotic spectacles. Thus Chernyshev wrote with some annoyance to his brother that as the hour of the assault drew nearer "the count continues to fool around [*durachitsia*]."[23] Unfortunately, the sources do not give any detailed descriptions of what exactly took place, but it is safe to assume that the symbolic displays were part of Suvorov's larger preparatory work. Lord Byron immortalized the scene in several stanzas of Don Juan:

> Also he dressed up, for nonce, fascines
> Like men with turbans, scimitars, and dirks,
> And made them charge with bayonets these machines,
> By way of lesson against actual Turks;
> And when well practised in these mimic scenes,
> He judged them proper to assail the works [...][24]

> Suwarrow [*sic*], who was standing in his shirt
> Before a company of Calmucks, drilling,
> Exclaiming, fooling, swearing at the inert,
> And lecturing on the noble art of killing [...]

The whole affair was a carefully orchestrated spectacle in its own right, one that demonstrated Suvorov's power to turn inertness into motion and humiliating retreat into military victory. As Chernyshev wrote approvingly, Suvorov put on "exercises for the rehearsal of the upcoming storm."[25] By personally demonstrating the drills, the general set an example for the officers, animated the soldiers, and lent the whole affair a new sense of urgency and confidence. Soldiers had no time to think about the December cold and the dangers of the assault – they were too busy building mock fortifications and practising drills. The morale of the troops was not neglected either, nor was their spiritual preparation. As Meiendorf and Vorontsov suggested in their essays, old soldiers were ordered to tell stories about their previous victories to encourage younger recruits. Some spoke about the recent fall of Ochakov to the Russian army, while others reminisced about the brilliant Russian victories at Fokshani and Rymnik.[26] As Damas observed in his memoir, on the evening before the assault, "the troops received the general benediction, and had the whole night at their disposal for rest, or, if they wished it, for the exercise of their various religious observances."[27] Thus religious and psychological preparation went hand in hand with the drills.

While the soldiers were jumping over mock ramparts, receiving spiritual guidance, and listening to stories of past glory, Suvorov turned to the officers. At Izmail, Potemkin could muster only around 30,000 troops, which meant there were not enough units for all the officers to command. This situation resulted in many supernumeraries waiting in the wings, searching for posts, awards, and battle glory, which in turn exposed the perennial tensions between rank and seniority that Suvorov had to resolve. The case of Chernyshev offers insight into the delicate management of the situation and how ranks were matched to responsibilities. Chernyshev had come to Izmail as a volunteer, did not have a single soldier under his command, and was waiting to be assigned to a unit. Being related to the Golitsyns, one of the most powerful families in Russia, certainly helped, for Suvorov allowed the young man to choose the regiment in which he would serve. Most volunteers could only dream of such an arrangement, yet Chernyshev felt this put him in "a difficult position." He explained his dilemma to his brother: "I am senior to all the regimental commanders except for Kutuzov, but even Kutuzov has only five battalions, and he already has Prince Volkonskii and Ribopiere, who is a brigadier general, under his command." In these circumstances Chernyshev would be lucky to command a battalion, and as he confessed, "I am afraid that I will be embarrassed by this vis-à-vis Volkonskii," his junior. The implication was that by agreeing to serve in someone else's regiment, Chernyshev would be forfeiting his seniority. Assuming a position below one's rank could be dangerous for promotion, damaging to one's honour, and injurious to one's self-respect.

On the one hand, officers such as Chernyshev – noble, young, and well-connected – could always refuse assignments below their rank, but on the other, the conventions of the military culture placed them under considerable pressure. In another letter about Suvarov's offer, he wrote: "What will others say about me? It is as if I can already hear people talking around me: there he is, that volunteer who partici-pated in two campaigns, not once seeing the enemy, and who is not even taking part in the storm when he has an opportunity to do so."[28] Considerations of honour, the idea of belonging to something greater than themselves, and fear of the judgment of one's peers were power-ful sources of the military culture that had made the Russian army so successful and that explained the extraordinarily high casualty rates among its officers. Articulation of honour was another example of Western influence on the Russian military, especially in the context of the Enlightenment. Chernyshev confessed to his brother how much personal honour motivated him: "I swear I come to despair, like a child. I have never thought that prejudices of honour are so strong."[29] He was deeply reluctant to participate in an assault in a position below his rank, but even more, he was afraid to be branded a coward by not participating at all. Honour was clearly an important part of Russian military culture and its accompanying world view, at least among Russian officers. Yet some scholars of eighteenth-century Russia have not contextualized the Russian experience in the broader Military Enlightenment of Europe. Christopher Duffy, for example, has called attention to how Russians of that time had radically different concepts of honour than Westerners. "In fact," he writes, "the Russian officer was almost entirely void of those ideals of corporate pride and knightly values which were an attribute of aristocracy as it was known elsewhere in Europe."[30] Others recognize the power of the Military Enlightenment but exclude Russia from it. For instance, writing about the culture of honour in eighteenth-century Europe, Armstrong Starkey maintains that "the rules of this culture were uniquely western European in character."[31] In the context of the Military Enlightenment, honour worked to establish standards that officers should follow off and on the battlefield. Honour underpinned rationalism and humanity during the conduct of battle, when bravery and clemency should go hand in hand. The writers of the Military Enlightenment saw honour as a driver of professional service and self-sacrifice. By the end of the century, Russian noble officers were just as preoccupied as their European counterparts with the question of what it meant to be an honourable soldier at war. As Chernyshev concluded, "life is worth little compared to honour."[32]

How did Suvorov solve Chernyshev's conundrum and balance his seniority with his assignment? Chernyshev wrote to his brother four days before the assault, telling him that "the count has created a special position for me that is considered very important but which, unfortunately, prevents me from the honour of partaking in the siege." Suvorov created the position of "general inspector," tasked with overseeing all of the attacking columns and with feeding Suvorov and his staff necessary information as the battle unfolded. The old general knew the importance of walking the fine line between dismissing parasites and placating powerful noble families, like the one Chernyshev belonged to. Suvorov found a way to make use of the youthful energies of an intelligent officer, while extending his command and observation instruments with another pair of keen eyes. Chernyshev finally had his chance to be useful and to participate in military culture beyond writing gossipy letters from his tent. He now worked "like a horse" and was happy he had been assigned a post that he thought was commensurate with this rank. Yet he still must have heard those murmuring voices around him. Chernyshev promised his brother that despite his duties that kept him from the action, he would "discreetly join one of the attacking columns to be one of the first to enter the city."[33] It is with these inspired methods that Suvorov began to bring his army into a state of readiness for the assault.

Next Suvorov had to summon all his skills of leadership and performance to reverse the mood in headquarters, and to convince the people gathered there, who only two weeks earlier had been ready to drop everything and retreat, to stay and attack. To that end, two days before the storm, Suvorov called a military council of his own. For some people this looked like another sign of indecisiveness.[34] Military councils were often called by irresolute commanders looking for advice and for ways to escape the responsibilities of their office. But on the contrary, Suvorov was not doing any of this. Instead, he wanted the military council to help him impose his will on the army; he wanted to make *his* view the view of his subordinates; he wanted his decision to storm the fortress to become the decision of his commanders.[35]

Surrounded by his officers, young and old, Suvorov delivered a motivating speech with his typical dramatic flair: "Twice have the Russians approached Izmail, and twice have they retreated; now, the third time, all we can do is either take the city, or perish ... Retreat from Izmail could weaken the resolve of our troops and encourage the Turks and their allies. But if we conquer Izmail, who will dare to stand in our way? I have decided to take this fortress, or die under its walls."[36]

Brigadier Matvei Platov, the most junior commander in the military council, who therefore had the first say, cried "Storm!," and other generals immediately joined him. According to the new decision of the military council, retreat would bring shame on the armies of Her Imperial Majesty, and the assault was to begin as soon as possible, so as not to give the garrison an opportunity to further fortify the city.[37] Suvorov had lifted the spirits of his staff, reversed the decision of the previous council, and, as it turned out, sealed the fate of Izmail.

The Storm

On 7 December, Suvorov wrote an eight-page instruction for his army, outlining the disposition of forces, describing his tactics, and providing general rules of engagement. He divided his forces into three corps. Major-General Iosif de Ribas was placed in charge of the navy and was to oversee the landing at what Potemkin called the "weakest place" in the fortress. The two wings of the army were to be commanded by General Pavel Potemkin and General Aleksandr Samoilov. Each of the three commanders had his forces further subdivided into three columns. Suvorov wanted Izmail to be attacked from nine directions simultaneously. If the element of surprise was somewhat lost due to deserters who had informed the Turks of the impending assault, Suvorov still could confuse the defenders as to where the main blow would fall.[38]

In the end Suvorov agreed with Potemkin's initial observation that the Danube side of the fortress presented the fewest obstacles and that it would be Ribas who made the most progress. The other Russian columns needed to prevent the Turks from concentrating their forces in one spot, and force them to spread themsleves around the entire perimeter of the fortress.[39] This way, the enemy would not know where to focus his forces for counter-attacks and Ribas and his men would have the best chance of success. Suvorov concluded his instruction with a brief note reflecting the wider Enlightenment concern with humanity and rules in war. The instruction read: "Christians and unarmed are to be spared, and of course the same applies to women and children."[40] Despite Suvorov's preparations and plans, one foreign observer in Russian service noted how each of the three corps was in a rather lax state of readiness "and would have been defeated if the enemy showed more initiative." There were many shortcomings to how the assault had been organized; indeed, it could be described as a "very frantic affair."[41]

The storm began at half past five in the morning, two hours before sunrise. The accounts of what happened are as fragmented and confusing as for any other battle, and replete with macabre scenes and human error. For example, Suvorov had miscalculated the width of the moat and the height of the walls in his drills. The ladders that had been prepared for scaling the walls were too short, and the soldiers had to tie them together under a hail of musket balls. Columns got lost along the way to their staging positions, and during the fighting many soldiers died from friendly fire. In addition to official reports and correspondence, Andrei Denisov, the future leader of Cossack armies, Sergei Mosolov, the future major-general, and several Frenchman in Russian service, Roger de Damas, Aleksandr Lanzheron, and Armand de Richelieu, left accounts of what took place on that day. Together they depicted not only the brutality of the fighting that ringed Izmail on 11 December 1790, but also the tensions, values, ideals, and limits of the Enlightenment as it influenced Russian military culture.

Andrei Denisov was under the command of Cossack Brigadier Vasilii Orlov, who led a column against the Bender gates, one of the four main entrances to the fortress, and one of the best fortified.[42] The column began to gather around midnight, and when the rockets signalled the start of the attack, Denisov and his men rushed toward the moat in front of the gates, where many of them were killed or wounded. Denisov and his men began to climb the steep ladders they had brought with them and reached the top of the gun battery, but could not take it. They were thrown back, "beaten and injured." Denisov was deafened by a grenade that landed between his shoulders, twice stabbed by enemy bayonets, and struck on the head with an artillery ramrod, causing a concussion. Under this pressure, he and others were forced down from the walls.

Wounded and confused, Denisov retreated behind the moat and wandered around with musket balls whizzing past him, until he encountered another band of Cossacks, where he found his commander Orlov.[43] Here he received the news that his brother and his two cousins had already been killed. Brigadier Orlov confessed that he was shaken by the failure of the Don Cossacks to take the walls of Izmail and asked Denisov to help him regroup. As General Aleksandr Samoilov, the commander of the left flank, wrote to Suvorov, Orlov's entire column had been thrown back by a sudden Turkish counter-attack that poured out of the Bender gates.[44] Orlov and his officers gathered the remaining Cossacks, and with sabre in hand, Denisov once again advanced on the Bender gates, which turned out to be a dangerous mistake. Caught in the passion of the moment, he led his men head-on against entrenched enemy fire that immediately felled many of his comrades. "A Cossack from my own regiment, Kiselev, arrived just in time, grabbed me by the hand and with the help of others, took me to the side and showed me my error," wrote Denisov. After regrouping yet again, Orlov's column once more attacked the battery they had previously been repulsed from, which now had fewer defenders. As Denisov concluded, "the Cossacks climbed over with heroic valour, and finally overpowered however many Turks they found there."[45]

While Denisov was fighting his way through the Bender gates, on the opposite side of the fortress, Sergei Mosolov, in a column commanded by General Fedor Meknob, was trying to climb the western ramparts.[46] Mosolov recounted a specific episode during the siege that highlighted tensions between favouritism and the conceptions of professionalism and merit in Russian military culture. The officer who was supposed to lead Mosolov's battalion was Major Abram Marchenko, who had been sent from the suite of Pavel Potemkin. Marchenko led his battalion in the wrong direction and then disappeared, which compelled General Meknob to ask Mosolov to take over and lead the men forward. "I reasoned that it is better to heed his request than wait for a former order," wrote Mosolov. But he also hinted to his commander that if he agreed to make this extra effort he should merit extra recognition. If Mosolov is to be believed, General Meknob replied that "if we take the fortress and remain alive, you will be doubly-rewarded."[47]

Mosolov's force crossed the deep moat and assaulted an enemy bastion. He lost 312 men in the process and was himself wounded with a musket ball through the brow and temple, leaving him temporarily blind in his right eye. "If a trumpeter had not grabbed me from the cannon bastion," wrote Mosolov, "the Turks would have chopped off my head there." As soon as he regained consciousness from his wound, he realized that only three soldiers around him were still standing; the rest were dead or wounded. Like Denisov, Mosolov regrouped for another attack, and to encourage his officers he shouted that the Turks had abandoned the bastion, which was a lie. But the lie served its purpose, and soon he had enough officers and soldiers under his command for another desperate charge. Despite losing more men, and with blood "streaming" from his temple, Mosolov pressed on until "we shouted Hurrah, burst into the bastion and took it." He was weakened from blood loss and had to lie down, but in the meantime the battalion commander, Marchenko, who had mysteriously disappeared before the attack, and was nowhere to be seen during the storm, reappeared at the bastion. One by one, Russian columns managed to scale the fortress walls, but the enemy did not surrender, and fighting continued for four more hours.[48]

Given the importance the Russian military culture attached to religion, Orthodox priests played an important role during the assault. There is at least one record of a regimental priest not just inspiring but leading a regiment of Russian soldiers during the assault. When an attacking column on the western wall of the fortress got bogged down after its commander was mortally wounded, a regimental priest raised a big cross with Jesus the Saviour over his head and threw himself at the Turks.[49] Several sources related how this episode inspired the soldiers to secure a foothold on the walls. According to Engelgardt, the priest, waving the cross, had called out to the vacillating soldiers, "Steady, brothers! Here is our commander!"[50]

The surviving Russian accounts reveal how deeply embedded the values of military culture had become by the end of Catherine's reign. By leading through example, and by being prepared to sacrifice themselves for the sake of honour, the Russian officers and soldiers showed that they embraced the ideals and principles they first encountered in childhood in cadet corps and military schools, and then in various manuals and instructions. The military essayists would have been proud to see their ideas manifested in the actions of their countrymen. Denisov set a personal example of leadership at the Bender gates, even if it was sometimes misguided by his enthusiasm, and Mosolov accepted responsibility beyond his rank at a moment's notice without a formal order. The soldiers too played a vital part in both narratives – an anonymous trumpeter saved Mosolov, and the Cossack Kiselev pulled Denisov away from danger. This suggested that good officers won the respect and attachment of their men, no doubt in part because they practised the ideas promoted in various military writings.[51] Finally, as official regulations and various authors had stressed for close to thirty years, God was indeed a Russian general and faith could inspire where human leadership floundered.

In addition to the Russian accounts, there are several by foreigners, who left their impressions of the siege in their memoirs. Armand de Richelieu, a French soldier of fortune in Potemkin's army, left one of the most personal and thoughtful reflections on the assault. Like many other foreigners, he was under the command of Ribas, and he was placed in charge of several battalions of infantry that had been ordered to land on the Danube side of the fortress. Richelieu's observations about the Russian officers and soldiers during the assault reveal the extent to which the success of whole affair hung by a thread. At times, generals and officers had to plead with and threaten their soldiers to get them to advance on the enemy instead of just firing their muskets; they did so only after they had used up all their ammunition. Every battery, every tower, every gate, was taken only after heavy losses. Confusion was general, and some Russian soldiers panicked and "lost their heads," fleeing back to their own lines "with faces marked by horror and desperation." In one instance, Richelieu wrote, his soldiers retreated no less than fifty times. Only the fact that the Turks did not attempt a pursuit turned the Russian soldiers around. After Richelieu's men succeeded in taking a Turkish battery, he took out his wallet, which he had carried with him into battle, and distributed its entire contents to the soldiers on the spot.[52] Once in the city, not a minute passed that he did not see somebody's throat being slashed by the Russian troops.[53]

Richelieu did not differentiate the Russians' conduct or their military culture from the wider European practices of the time. Given the atrocities the British had committed in America and the torrent of violence in post-revolutionary France, Europeans could not call "barbarity a peculiarly Russian character[istic]." He wrote how he witnessed the growing rage of the soldiers and officers at the tenacious resistance offered by the besieged, and how this rage spilled over onto civilians and the remaining garrison once the walls of Izmail were finally breached. Richelieu concluded that neither the strict hierarchy within the Russian army nor even Potemkin himself could have saved even a single Turkish life that day. But despite what he saw, the Frenchman made a startling statement on the nature of the Military Enlightenment. "We of course should still maintain our belief," he wrote, "in that the lowest human urges will be suppressed not by discipline and hierarchy but by enlightenment and reason."[54] Russian military writers would have applauded Richelieu's commitment to rationality and objectivity in wartime, but Izmail showed the limits of "Enlightenment and reason" in times of passionate struggle.

Another detailed account of the assault was left by Roger de Damas. Along with Prince Charles de Ligne, Armand de Richelieu, Aleksandr Lanzheron, and many other French and Austrian officers, Damas was under the command of General de Ribas, approaching Izmail from the Danube side, with the Russian navy.[55] Damas was in charge of a regiment of 2,000 Livonian light infantry. His account offers a view of the "weakest part" of the fortress from the perspective of a bewildered Westerner. Eight minutes after the signal for attack was given, Damas with his men crossed the river in boats to attack the underbelly of the fortress. In those eight minutes he lost close to sixty officers and soldiers. Upon disembarking, he and his column made it to the top of the rampart, overpowered the defenders, and turned captured cannons "upon the Turks in the fortress."[56] He related what he saw unfolding around the city walls while he stood on the rampart:

> I was joined by the aide-de-camp of General Ribas, who begged me to hold firm as long as was possible, because none of General Souvarow's [sic] columns had as yet been able to descend from the ramparts, though several had succeeded in reaching the summit, after losing half their men and climbing from corpse to corpse. They could not, however, beat back the Turks, who defended themselves from the inner base of the parapet, without losing ground.[57]

The siege was bitterly contested, with the fortunes of both sides hanging in the balance. Only after the Russian troops succeeded in descending from the ramparts and opening one of the gates from the inside did Suvorov's cavalry rush into the city and secure a Russian victory.

The siege of Izmail concluded with a sudden massacre. What precisely started it is unclear, but it appears that during the surrender of the Seraskier, the Turkish commander, with 4,000 troops, one of his bodyguards cut down a Russian soldier who was probably reaching to take the Seraskier's weapons as trophy.[58] Westerners would be the only participants who described the ensuing butchery. As Damas wrote,

> the most horrible carnage followed – the most unequalled butchery. Two hours were employed in a hand-to-hand fight ... Every armed man was killed, defending himself to the last; and it is no exaggeration when I say that the gutters of the town were dyed with blood. Even women and children fell victims to the rage and revenge of the troops. No authority was strong enough to prevent it.[59]

Finding himself surrounded by dead and dying soldiers and having narrowly escaped death from stray musket fire, Damas was at the point of mental and physical exhaustion. He found a cot in one of the few houses still standing in Izmail "and slept upon it for nineteen consecutive hours without once awakening."[60] Disorder and teamwork, merit and incompetence, brutal fighting and leadership by example were all powerful markers of Russian military culture in the accounts of the assault. The participants attempted to impose a clear narrative on the chaos that had engulfed them and their enemies. Denisov and Mosolov produced sharply distinct characters. Mosolov was professional and brave; Major Marchenko was a coward. The Cossack Kiselev saved Denisov's life. The available accounts make it clear that training, indoctrination, and drills drawn from military essays, manuals, and instructions had had a powerful effect. While Russian units retreated on many occasions, none of the sources report a mutiny. As General Matvei Platov, the commander of one of the columns, wrote to General Samoilov, he saw with his own eyes how "the example of bravery by commanders who were always in front, inspired soldiers."[61] At least some of the participants reflected the ideal of the Enlightenment officer that the military proto-intelligentsia had developed in various writings. All of the accounts documented officers' firm and capable leadership, which was motivated by honour though also no doubt by the prospect of reward. However, humanity in war had a long way to go before taking root, and the Enlightenment influence on the Russian military culture – discipline, the use of reason, psychology, adherence to professional values – was difficult to achieve. As Pichichero conceded, the Military Enlightenment's "notions of humanity and sensibilité had devastating limits."[62] Clearly, some of the Enlightenment influences on Russian military culture could not yet be fully enforced, such as prohibiting massacres of civilians and unarmed combatants. That said, the attitude was changing from normalizing such practices to making them distasteful for a professional military.

Aftermath

On 3 January 1791, Catherine wrote Potemkin to express her amazed congratulations on his successful campaign. "The scaling of Izmail city and its fortress with a corps half the size of the Turkish garrison within the city," she wrote, "is something that has rarely been attempted in history." The empress ordered a special church service in Saint Petersburg as well as an artillery salvo, which invited the people of the capital to celebrate the extraordinary feat of their military.[63] The church service offered the opportunity to mourn the fallen Russian heroes; the thunder of guns connected the people to the martial spirit of the empire.

Meanwhile, 1,200 miles away within Izmail's walls, the carnage and pillaging were unrelenting. The records left by the foreigners, though probably biased, expose the limits of Enlightenment humanitarianism in Russian military culture. "There could not be any talk of saving the wounded [enemies], almost all of them were mercilessly finished off. There were prisoners, who after seeing such terrible slaughter, died of fear," wrote Aleksandr Lanzheron.[64] According to Mosolov, "after the siege the count [Suvorov] permitted the lower ranks to take in the fortress whatever they found for three days." So much loot was available that soldiers were filling their hats and caps full of coins.[65] Even so, Richelieu would later marvel that "despite the strongest indiscretion that reigned in the Russian forces that day, that evening everything was brought to order" under Kutuzov's leadership.[66]

Damas provided one of the first assessments – a surprisingly accurate one – of what the assault had cost the Russians: "Nine thousand Russians were killed and wounded, including several generals."[67] The actual number was close to 10,000, with 400 out of 650 officers dead or wounded.[68] Lanzheron, who had fought his way into the city from Danube side, noted that "almost all of the columns lost a third of their soldiers."[69] For example, Suvorov's Fanagoriiskii Regiment alone suffered more than 400 killed.[70] Almost all of the officers leading the nine attacking columns were killed or wounded. The Russian death toll in senior officers was unprecedented: eleven major-generals, one brigadier-general, six colonels, and more than forty lieutenant-colonels laid down their lives during the assault.[71] Military culture drove its members to extraordinary exertions, and Russian actions during the siege conformed to the ideals of bravery, initiative, and self-sacrifice found in the military literature of the period. Major-General Boris Lassi was wounded in the hand but continued to fight until victory was declared. Major-General Meknob suffered a severe leg wound and had to release his command to one of his subordinates. He died a few days later. Major-General Sergei Lvov was also forced to give up his command after being wounded. Major-General Count Ilia Bezborodko similarly gave up his command, but only just before he fainted from his wound. Colonel Prince Dmitrii Lobanov-Rostovskii, who volunteered to participate in the assault and led 150 musketeers, was seriously wounded. Major Prince Sokolinskii died while climbing the siegeworks and was replaced by Major Prince Trubetskoi.[72] Dead princes, generals, and common soldiers, along with grand viziers, pashas, and janissaries, littered the walls, the trenches, and the streets of Izmail.

The Russians gave their own dead proper burial in accordance with Orthodox custom, but they did not have the manpower, or the will, to provide similar for their fallen enemies. The surviving 10,000 prisoners were employed to clear Izmail of dead Turkish soldiers, civilians, and horses. It took six days to collect more than 25,000 corpses, and because the earth was by then frozen, they were all thrown into the Danube.[73] The atmosphere in the Russian camp was equally grim, with the surviving soldiers and officers anxiously searching for their friends and relatives. Among the officers looking for information about fallen relatives was Andrei Denisov. While he was capturing the bastion he had learned that his brother and his cousin were not dead after all, but instead severely wounded. "I found my brother half-dead," he wrote, "the bone in his arm above the elbow was entirely shattered, a musket ball has ripped through his entire foot, lodging itself in the big toe, that was extracted in my presence ... In the same tent lay General Meknab, my cousin, who was heavily wounded by two musket balls, and several of our regimental commanders and officers."[74]

The day after the assault, while the exhausted soldiers and officers were recovering from the brutal fighting, the Russian army held a large prayer service under the thunder of cannons, again mixing religious with military ceremony. The service was led by the same priest who had heroically led a group of Russian soldiers during the assault.[75] As Suvorov informed Potemkin, the service was held next to a mosque that had been converted into the new Church of St Spiridion, the patron saint of miracles, since the capture of Izmail had taken place on his day.[76] This symbolic gesture, so similar to the one Rumiantsev had made in 1770 after his bloody victory at Kagul, legitimatized the role of providence in Russian military culture, as well as the faith of its soldiers and officers in the divine saviour.

Ten days after the assault, Suvorov finished a forty-three-page report with the details of the battle and a long list of recommendations, which he sent to Potemkin. However, the report contained no details of the massacre. What reward awaited the brave priest who had spurred on the Russian soldiers at the moment of crisis? Had Count Chernyshev been among the first to enter the city, as he had promised his brother? Did General Meknab keep his promise to Mosolov? And what of the many soldiers and officers like Denisov and Damas who had survived the horrors of the walls and streets of Izmail? Finally, would Suvorov receive a field marshal's baton for this incredible feat?

Suvorov's report, which he based on letters sent to him by the commanders of the nine attacking columns, showed how even during the chaotic and confusing circumstances of a siege, Russian military culture strived to document the merit of all those involved. Junior officers had their eyes on their subordinates, while senior officers keenly observed their juniors for evidence of bravery, intelligence, or initiative that could earn them an award or a promotion. For his bravery, the priest received a gold ring in the shape of a cross, on a sash of St George.[77] Despite being dishevelled and depressed, Kutuzov "was the first to enter the city." So boasted his wife, Katerina, in a letter to a relative. He received the Order of St George, Third Class, and was named the commandant of the fortress.[78]

The young Count Chernyshev did not quite manage to out-race Kutuzov to be the first to enter Izmail, but he had seen real action and had plenty to tell his brother about his contribution to the assault. As Suvorov's report stated, Chernyshev had played an important role and especially distinguished himself:

I cannot leave behind, and not justly attest and recommend to your serenity ... her Imperial Majesty's Chamberlain Count Chernyshev, who was appointed by me due to his abilities and knowledge, to observe the actions of all the columns, who threw himself in all the dangers, fearlessly taking notes for the composition of this report, and who was employed by me on numerous occasions in many parts of the army with different assignments and is worthy of my special attention and request for rewarding him for courage and skill.[79]

Chernyshev had sustained Suvorov's "directed telescope" and provided the commander-in-chief and his staff with information the latter required in the moment. He reported back to headquarters about the progress of the attack and about the conduct of individual officers and soldiers. It was in part due to people like Chernyshev that commanders could cross-reference the accounts of the participants and letters of recommendation from field commanders and compose accurate reports.

Sergei Mosolov received even more praise:

Major General Meknob attested to the brave spirit of those in his column during the storm: 4th-lieutenant-colonel and cavalier Fedor Meller and 3rd-premier major Sergei Mosolov; these two climbed the bastion, Meller from the left and Mosolov from the right, and courageously drawing others to follow them, were wounded from the embrasures, the first in the neck, and the second in the head; and Mosolov, overcoming the heavy wound, turned to his men and served as an example to his subordinates in routing the Turks, who he took prisoner, and then continued to fight on, eliminating the enemy with superb valour, but also taking measures to protect the wounded.[80]

Though he would die the following day, General Meknob faithfully noted Mosolov's persistence during the assault, as he had promised. Mosolov's sacrifice had been documented, his leadership had been praised, and the outcome of his initiative – the defeat of the enemy soldiers in the bastion and the assistance he provided to wounded comrades – had been extolled. But despite the strong recommendation he received from his dying general, Mosolov would write bitterly about his experience at Izmail. "All of my extra efforts for the fatherland," he complained, "were for naught; for general Meknob died, and I received only the cross of St. George, 4th class, along with another major, Shekhovskoi ... who lost his arm." What Mosolov really wanted was a promotion. Noting that Potemkin had promoted all the majors after the assault on Ochakov fortress two years earlier, he concluded that his only misfortune was that the prince had not been present during the assault.[81]

Adrian Denisov, along with other majors, "acted with courage" and set "examples for others." Moreover, the report continued, "premier-major Golin, Denisov, Colonel Petr Denisov, and second-major Ivan Grekov and captain Ivan Karpov, overcame stiff resistance and hand-to-hand combat, and were examples for others to ascend the parapet."[82] In conclusion, "the volunteers and regiment of Denisov climbed the curtain wall using ladders with haste and courage, the valour of which is commendable."[83] For his efforts during the assault, Denisov received the coveted Order of St George, Fourth Class. The events at Izmail reflected the vestiges of favouritism, and existing jealousies and bitterness, but also the honest and professional recognition of merit and ability. Chernyshev and his team of staff officers diligently recorded everyone's conduct; Mosolov and Denisov fought on despite being pushed back; many senior commanders fought until they passed out from their wounds or sheer exhaustion; Meknob did his duty of attesting to the conduct of his officers and soldiers before dying. Izmail also reflected how deeply honour figured in the personal consciousness of the military leadership.

The French émigrés, who had exchanged the ravages of the revolution in France for the slightly more comfortable surroundings of Potemkin's army under the walls of Izmail, were rewarded as generously as the Russian officers, and no distinction was made between foreign and Russian participants in the siege. The actions of Damas were carefully documented and reported to the commander-in-chief, Prince Potemkin. After landing with his surviving soldiers, he demonstrated "such courage and zeal that despite the heavy enemy resistance, he passed through the line of fire, cleared the shoreline, pushed back the enemy, and continued to hold his position."[84] Colonel Prince Charles de Ligne supervised the construction of Russian batteries under enemy fire and during the assault was wounded in the leg.[85] Catherine wrote a personal letter to Ligne, rewarding him with the Order of St George. The prince was among those who "shared the dangers of mounting, without an open trench, without a battered breach, the formidable fortress of Izmail, where a whole army of enemies to Christian men were awaiting you," wrote the empress. "The Order of Saint-George," she continued, "having for the basis of its statutes the laws of honour and valour, – precious synonyms to heroic ears – is always by its institution eager to count among its valiant knights whoever gives proof of those military virtues."[86] The case of General de Ribas presents another clear example of how merit was documented, decided, and awarded. On 16 November, when Potemkin was updating the empress on the situation around Izmail, he wrote of Ribas's success in eliminating the Turkish fleet and clearing the Danube of the enemy navy. "Mentioning him I cannot pass over in silence his unparalleled zeal," concluded the prince. A few days before the siege, on 3 December, Potemkin again wrote that "Major-General Ribas deserves a lot, and even more good progress can be expected from him in the future." On 20 December, Catherine wrote back to Potemkin that "for Major-General Ribas on the first occasion I am sending the Order of St. George, 2nd class, which he has rightly earned, and then I leave it up to you how to continue to reward him."[87] Finally, the humble soldiers, the true conquerers of Izmail, were ostensibly given permission to plunder the city as a reward for their tenacity and sacrifice. In addition to a huge amount of loot, all soldiers who participated in the siege received silver medals.[88]

The question of how to reward Suvorov was much more complicated. In a letter to Catherine, Potemkin expressed his thoughts about how to recognize the mastermind of the victory at Izmail. First, he recommended minting a special medal in Suvorov's honour in recognition of his service in taking the fortress. Second, he noted that among all the senior generals, Suvorov was the only one who has seen real action. Suvorov, labouring with his usual zeal, not only had captured Izmail but in doing so had saved the Russian allies, the Austrians, from almost certain defeat at the hands of the Turks. With all of this in mind, wrote the prince, "will it not please you to distinguish him with a rank of a lieutenant-colonel in the guards or as an adjutant-general."[89] As usual, the rewards to the most senior officers were negotiated between the empress and her advisers. As Potemkin had suggested, the hero of the day was rewarded with a special medal and the rank of lieutenant-colonel in the Semenovskii Guards – two highly symbolic, personal, and visibly distinguishing gestures.

The fact that there was no discussion of promoting Suvorov to field marshal, and that he was sent to Finland even while his victory was still being celebrated, is an important part of the story of military culture of Catherine's Russia. The gossip around Saint Petersburg was that the jealous Potemkin had sent him away to remove him from the celebrations in the capital and to prevent him from presenting the prisoners to the empress. Was Suvurov's personal achievement being overshadowed by a jealous favourite? According to Aleksandr Petrushevkii, Suvorov's most famous biographer, and many other historians since, Potemkin was happy to have Suvorov under his command: he valued him highly as a professional and did not hesitate to shower him with awards and honours. Potemkin generously rewarded the successes of his subordinates because their success advanced him in the graces of the empress. But Potemkin was not prepared to promote one of them to the same rank he held.[90] Petrushevskii's analysis has continued to shape the view that obvious merit yielded to crude favouritism during Catherine's reign. A re-evaluation of that notion is long overdue. To begin with, a month after the assault, in his report to Catherine, Potemkin had heaped praise on Suvorov, calling him "the chief organizer of the whole military effort" around Izmail.[91] In February the newspaper *Saint Petersburg Vedomosti* had reprinted his report for the Russian public. With his praise of Suvorov, Potemkin was clearly singling out his efforts for special reward. Minting a medal in honour of Suvorov's victory was a much more exclusive recognition of the unique significance of the event than any other award would have been. The medal, unlike an award, was a mark of individual merit, and it bore Suvorov's silhouette in the style of ancient heroes, thus conforming to the neoclassical style of the century. The medal carried historical significance and was Potemkin's and Catherine's symbolic way of showing Suvorov, the military, and the Russian public who "owned" the victory at Izmail. The honour of a personalized medal was reserved for a select few. In recent times, only Potemkin had received similar recognition, for his victory at the siege of Ochakov. Making Suvorov a lieutenant-colonel of the Semenovskii Guards, of which the empress was the colonel, was similarly a rare and significant honour. Suvorov shared that honour with only ten other people in the Russian Empire, including Potemkin himself.[92] While Suvorov may have felt that he deserved the rank of field marshal, in the mind of the empress, Suvorov's rewards were appropriate for his accomplishment. Storming a fortress, however difficult a task, did not go beyond the extraordinary, and while Suvorov had crushed the Turkish forces at Izmail, his efforts had not won the war, which would last two more years. By comparison, Rumiantsev had been promoted to field marshal in 1770 after defeating an enemy almost ten times the size of his army twice in one month.[93]

Finally, the rumour that Suvorov had been sent to Finland because of Potemkin's intrigues ignored the political situation in Russia at the time. Besides being at war with the Ottoman Empire, Russia had recently concluded a peace treaty with Sweden, with which it had been at war for two years.[94] The Russian government knew that the Swedish king, Gustav III, was vacillating between maintaining the armistice and restarting the war. It also knew that Gustav was being encouraged by the British, who were shocked by the Russian victories around the Black Sea and wanted Sweden to reopen hostilities to put pressure on Russia in the north. Anticipating a Swedish offensive in Finland in 1791, Potemkin suggested keeping a large number of troops in Finland as a deterrent. Who better to send to Finland to dampen Swedish aggression than Suvorov, the Lion of Izmail and the brightest star in the Russian army? Catherine thought this an excellent idea. "At this critical time," writes Russian historian Viachislav Lopatin, "the presence on the frontier of the famous commander could have cooled down several hot heads."[95] It is doubtful that Potemkin was jealous of Suvorov, or indeed had anything to fear from him. Suvorov was not interested in politics, he avoided the court, and, unlike Potemkin, he was never really Catherine's favourite. Suvorov was an excellent general, but Potemkin was an intellectual and political companion of the empress. Suvorov's assignment to the Finnish frontier did not reflect the favouritism associated with Catherine's Russia, or even Potemkin's jealousy, so much as a calculated choice by the empress and her advisers to deter Sweden from further military actions.

Izmail also demonstrated how military writings and codes for conduct as well as behaviour in battle were informed by the military experiences of their authors in a deeply dialectical relationship. Suvorov's *Science of Victory* was clearly inspired by his observations during the siege, and he repackaged the bloody experience as a means to indoctrinate the troops. For example, here is how he described the storming of a fortress in his famous manual:

Break through the abatis,[96] throw down your hurdles over the wolf traps![97] Run, fast! Hop over the palisades,[98] throw down your fascines,[99] go down into the ditch, put up ladders! Marksmen, cover the columns, aim for the heads! Columns, fly over the walls to the parapets, bayonet! On the parapet form a line! Guard the powder cellars! Open the gates for the cavalry! The enemy runs into the city – turn his cannons against him! Hit him hard, lively bombardment! Don't do it for too long. The order is given – get down into the city, cut down the enemy in the streets! Cavalry, charge! Don't enter the houses, attack the enemy in the streets! Storm where the foe has hidden! Occupy city square, put up guards. Put up pickets immediately, by the gates, cellars and magazines! The enemy has surrendered – give him mercy! The walls are ours – now for the spoils![100]

Following the best practices of the Military Enlightenment, Suvorov wrote *Science of Victory* in a style that enabled him to extract incredible physical and mental efforts from his soldiers. The psychological undertone throughout the text was such that the troops need not concentrate on the difficulties of their tasks, because they were made easy by the author. In Suvorov's terminology, soldiers were "wonder-heroes." The heavy infantry backpack was called "the wind"; regiments did not move out from their camp, but "jumped up, put on their winds, and ran forward"; the trench was never "too deep," and the parapet was never "too high";[101] columns "flew" over walls, and soldiers "hopped" over parapets. These clever linguistic formulations blew a cool breeze of simplicity and excitement over the dangers of battle. The passivity of a typical military manual was replaced by an active present tense, and Suvorov's short sentences reflected the fast pace of battle. Suvorov cleverly detached his text from the hardships of military life.[102] Playing on the imagination of the recruits who listened to officers read his manual to them, Suvorov turned the bloodiest and costliest of his battles – he lost close to one third of his army – into an exciting narrative worth emulating.

Izmail also showed a clear tension between the humanitarianism of the Enlightenment and Russian military culture and the realities of war, as well as the difficulty of enforcing moral codes in wartime. *Science of Victory* reflected the wider humanitarian discourse of Russian military culture and European Enlightenment more generally. Echoing the *Military Articles* that warned against the slaughter of women and children, and his instruction before the storm of Izmail, Suvorov stated in his manual that "it is a sin to kill indiscriminately, they [our enemies] are human beings too."[103] Soldiers were not murderers but protectors of the state, its people, and its religion. Several lines down, he wrote again: "Fair Spoils! Take a camp! – all is yours. Take a fortress! – all is yours. In Izmail we took gold and silver by the handful. And in many other places too. But to go for spoils without permission, is forbidden!"[104] As if trying to atone for the pillage and slaughter at Izmail, Suvorov wanted to maintain the idea of humanity in Russian military culture, which clearly melted away in the heat of battle.

Izmail was a military and cultural milestone. It showed how military instructions were products of their authors' experiences. It showed how the Russian experience contradicted and exposed the limits of Enlightenment values in times of war. In the process, Izmail also perpetuated and promoted the Enlightenment brand of the Russian military culture more generally. Four months after Izmail was taken, on Sunday, 9 March 1791, the trophies and prisoners were delivered to the capital, where the Russian court, headed by Catherine, could gaze upon the procession led by the Guards regiments.[105] On 25 March 1791 an official ceremony for the dispensation of rewards took place in the Winter Palace, where Catherine "bestowed royal favour on the commander of the Russian forces in the south, Prince Grigorii Aleksandrovich Potemkin-Tavricheskii, and on the military servicemen of all ranks, recommended by his serenity and individual commanders, for their great feats in the previous campaign and especially in taking by storm the city and fortress of Izmail."[106]

Nothing quite like Izmail had happened since the Battle of Poltava in 1709, where Peter the Great broke the back of the Swedish army, and arguably nothing like it would happen again until the Battle of Borodino in 1812 that precipitated the defeat of Napoleon. The heroic deeds of the Russian army, its military virtues, indeed the achievement of Russian military culture, had to be displayed and amplified beyond the ceremony at court. To further highlight the importance of what had taken place at Izmail, Suvorov's report was edited for publication in newspapers in Saint Petersburg and Moscow.[107] The public at large was invited to participate in the siege of Izmail by reading and imagining the horrors of the battle and by celebrating the fallen heroes. Izmail not only confirmed the ideals of the military culture of merit and bravery in the public imagination, but also linked the military more closely to the national consciousness through hymns, poetry, and other artistic productions. In 1791 Catherine commissioned two paintings of the assault based on accurate sketches by an artist in Potemkin's suite. The famous peasant theatre of Count Nikolai Sheremetev staged a play based on the storming of Izmail in 1791. Much like Pavel Potemkin, many participants yearned for an emotional outlet for what they had witnessed that day and wanted to share their experiences with the rest of Russian society. Pavel Kutuzov, a distant relative of the general, published a poem about the siege, and the same year, E.I. Kostrov published his epistle dedicated to Suvorov.[108] The most famous and lasting contribution to the victory celebrations of Izmail was made by the famed Russian eighteenth-century poet, Gavrila Derzhavin, who in 1791 wrote the ode *Let the Victory's Sound Thunder*:

Let the victory's sound thunder!
Merry be, courageous Ross!

Adorn the glory you have taken.
You Mohammedians have shaken!
   Refrain:
            Glory be to Catherine!
            Glory be to tender mother!

Rapid waters of the Danube
Are in the hands of Russians now
Let the Ross have all the valor
In Tavr and Caucas' we have power [...][109]

The ode was a reminder of Russian military might, a celebration of Catherine's leadership, and a powerful confirmation of Russian military culture. The same year, the "tender mother" Catherine turned Derzhavin's ode into the first anthem of the Russian Empire, which it remained until 1833.

The siege of Izmail was a snapshot of the Russian military at a particular historical moment. It was as much a product of the intellectual and cultural project of the Military Enlightenment as of military strategy and tactics. The siege, the preparations, and the battle and its aftermath reflected the broader values of the Russian military at the twilight of the eighteenth century. Merit, training, professionalism, indoctrination, and military performance, all came together at the siege of Izmail. Potemkin had given Suvorov the freedom to act independently and constantly informed him of the political situation. Upholding the principles of merit, he identified talent during the preparations for the siege based on distinction and past performance, and he recommended reliable officers to Suvorov. Suvorov, for his part, in the spirit of the Military Enlightenment, drilled both soldiers and officers, put on his performances, and made time for religious ceremonies. Reflecting the larger values and ideals of military culture, the battle that followed displayed many acts of leadership by example, episodes of personal bravery and sacrifice that were contrasted with cowardness, and instances of initiative, and of cooperation between soldiers and officers. Finally, both during the fighting and afterwards when accurate attestations were being crafted, honour played an important part in the world of the Russian army, as a motivating factor and as part of officers' identity, which they had inherited from the West.

The aftermath brought scenes that must have troubled military essayists and the commander-in-chief himself. Climbing over parapets under a hail of musket fire, seeing their comrades torn to pieces by artillery, and then enduring exhausting hand-to-hand combat in the streets of the town made Russian soldiers hateful. Potemkin was clearly ashamed of what had taken place under his leadership, for he made no specific mention of the massacre and preferred to concentrate on rewarding the surviving officers and soldiers. "I have nominated for awards only those about whose merit I am entirely certain," he wrote to Catherine in March 1791. "But if, after a close and detailed examination, there are others who are found to be worthy of rewards, then for them too I then dare ask crosses of St George and St Vladimir."[110] Like Bezborodko twenty years earlier, Potemkin recommended for awards only those in whose ability he was confident and whom he was convinced were worthy of an award. When it came to the controversy around rewarding Suvorov, Potemkin's nephew General Aleksandr Samoilov, who was in charge of the eastern part of the assault, defended the impartiality of his uncle. He argued that Potemkin had borne honest witness to all of Suvorov's accomplishments during the siege in his letters to the empress, which "refutes the claims of some authors, who without blushing charge that Prince Grigorii Aleksandrovich [Potemkin] was jealous of the fame of his victorious comrade." After all, Samoilov reminded the empress, it was the profile of Suvorov, not Potemkin, that had been minted on the commemorative medal.

The siege of Izmail was one of the first military events to locate military success at the intersection of memory, national consciousness, and political power. It reaffirmed military culture and brought its achievements increasingly into the public space. For more than a quarter of a century, in all the corners of the vast Russian Empire, people who sang or heard the new anthem, Derzhavin's ode, would conjure up images of Izmail. They imagined the Russian soldiers climbing the steep fortress walls and the brutal fighting within; they thought of Suvorov's spectacles; of Catherine's successful reign; and of the unbreakable power of the Russian military, influenced in no small part by the larger Enlightenment agenda.

Chapter Seven

"His Majesty recommends to gentlemen-officers to dress better and not to stutter": Paul I and the Military Enlightenment

The same month that Izmail fell to Potemkin's army, another event no less significant for Russian military culture, but now forgotten, took place in Saint Petersburg. In December 1791 the Saint Petersburg garrison witnessed the inaugural meeting of a military circle in Russia.[1] It was the first meeting of its kind, and implicit in its agenda was the development of new knowledge and methods to replace outdated, foreign practices. The meeting was voluntary, and its members were brought together by free association and interest in the military profession. Its organizer gave a welcoming speech, and the guests exchanged ideas and practices.[2] The meeting in Saint Petersburg was the culmination of the cultural and intellectual activity within the military that had begun in the 1760s and reflected a set of traditions and values of the Military Enlightenment. As Andreas Schonle and others have noted, "intriguingly, it is in the army that one ought to search for the early symptoms of a developing public sphere in Russia."[3] By the 1790s, the military was indeed participating in the wider public sphere, and the military circle, which gathered that winter in Saint Petersburg, was one example of this process.

Not much is known about the activities of the circle or its fate, but as Catherine's son, Paul, rose to the Russian throne, he set in motion plans that would clash with the cultural arrangements of the military and attempt to severely curtail its autonomy. What Paul did was not so much attack the Enlightenment influence on Russian military culture as introduce his own vision of military culture, which took the Enlightenment principles to their dangerous extremes. Paul's commitment to reforms was inspired by his experiences as Grand Duke and by the Prussian militarism that had tempered his vision.

While on his two visits to Potsdam and Berlin as a young man, Paul was impressed by the Prussian order and discipline he observed, which he linked to the military successes of Frederick the Great during the

11 Paul I by Vladimir Borovikovsky, 1796.
Courtesy of Wikimedia.

Seven Years' War. On his return home he felt frustrated by inconsistencies within the Russian army, which in his view fostered military weakness. Because Paul was looking at Catherine's army from the sidelines, he could see only its outward imperfections. He saw the army only during parades in the capital; he encountered officers only in court. What he saw and heard appalled him. Regiments were trained according to the private instructions of their commanders, which to him seemed contradictory and confusing. Powerful favourites ruled armies as if they were personal fiefdoms. Regimental uniforms and equipment varied greatly, and officers seemed to have little interest in their profession. In 1778,

Paul wrote to General Petr Panin that in the Russian army "everything goes according to individual whim, which often consists of not wanting to do anything except gratify one's unbridled passions. This is the sorry state which the armed forces have reached."[4] By the time he came to power, instead of viewing individualism as a force for change, a source of strong leadership, and a psychological asset, Paul saw it in the context of the political decadence of the French Revolution, in many ways anticipating the strong anti-individualism of the nineteenth century. "Individualism," wrote the French political philosopher Hugues de Lamennais in the 1820s, "destroys the very idea of obedience and of duty, thereby destroying both power and law; and what then remains but a terrifying confusion of interests, passions, and diverse opinions?"[5] Paul must have been asking a similar question. Had he seen the army at Izmail, he perhaps would not have embraced this view, but Catherine had denied him the opportunity to take a field command or visit the front lines in wartime. This meant that Paul was blinded by the short-comings he glimpsed from afar, and failed to distinguish the values and ideas behind the military machine he was about to inherit.

Contemporaries almost uniformly perpetuated a negative image of Paul, establishing the myth of the mad tsar. However, the most recent biography by Roderick McGrew and even earlier works have been more balanced, and they cast valuable light on many positive, if failed, initiatives of Paul and his reign.[6] Besides preventing her son from participating in military campaigns, lest he gain a political base in the army that could challenge her power, Catherine categorically forbade Paul from assuming any political role in her government.[7] When he reached the age of majority, it became apparent that she would not be relinquishing her powers to him or even sharing them, as Maria Theresa had done with her son Joseph II. With the passage of years this political isolation and de facto exile probably began to take a mental toll on the Grand Duke. As one Russian historian put it, being intelligent and energetic, Paul "fretted over his lack of involvement in affairs of state." He was compelled to retreat to his Gatchina estate about 50 kilometres from the capital, where he diligently prepared plans for reforms he one day would implement.[8]

After his mother's death, Paul burst onto the political, diplomatic, and military scene like a tightly wound spring with ideas for kaleidoscopic change and improvement. During the first year alone he issued 48,000 laws, orders, and decrees.[9] The military was the particular focus of his attention. More than 40 per cent of his edicts during his first year of rule dealt with military subjects.[10] The sad irony of Paul's reign was that the emperor and his followers were actually attempting to address the concerns and aspirations of the military writers of his mother's time. Paul took to heart many of the shortcomings he had read about and witnessed as a young man, and he tried to align the practical reality of Russian military culture with the military ideal that had formed in his mind over his years in exile. More thoroughly than Catherine, he developed a doctrine for the Russian military.[11] The major difference was that unlike his mother, the new emperor wanted to take personal charge of military culture. He wanted to centralize and subordinate it to his personal vision, and this led to changes in everything from uniforms and military manuals to the workings of merit and licence to individualism. It also created strong opposition to his rule. Paul saw a Prussian dose of discipline, goose-stepping, and order as an antidote to the deficiencies, inconsistencies, and laxness of the military culture that had emerged during Catherine's reign.[12] His reforms produced a powerful clash between the ideas, values, and priorities of the new emperor and his image of the Enlightenment militarism, and the military culture he had inherited from his mother. Under Paul the military was to radiate the supreme state of organization, centralization, and order; it was to be "stern, ascetic, controlled."[13] In this clash, the emperor wanted not so much to erase Enlightenment influences on the military culture of Catherine's era as take Enlightenment rationalism and amplify its influence further, to what he saw as its logical conclusion. In the process, he reaffirmed the Military Enlightenment in Russia and strengthened its adherents' commitment to it.

Paul's Reform

Catherine's death signalled the most sweeping transformation of the Russian army in more than a generation. Almost immediately there was a sense that the winds of change were about to engulf the Russian military and its culture. Countess Varvara Golovina, a maid of honour at the court of Catherine II, wrote down her first impressions of the sudden new order after the empress's death. "The *Gatchinese* ... ran about and knocked up against the courtiers who asked each in amazement who these Ostrogoths could be ... A new uniform had already been ordered, that of the battalions of the Grand Duke Paul, which became the models after which the whole army was reorganized."[14] Prince Adam Czartoryski, a friend of the future emperor Alexander I, added: "Never was there any change of scene at theatre so sudden and so complete as the change of affairs at the accession of Paul I. In less than a day costumes, manners, occupations, all were altered ... The military parade became the chief occupation of the day."[15] Charles Whitworth, the British ambassador in Saint Petersburg, made a similar observation during the first day of Paul's reign when he wrote that "the Court and the town is entirely military, and we can scarcely persuade ourselves that instead of Petersburg we are not at Potsdam."[16] Contemporary views were unanimous – some strange military force was transforming the landscape of Russian cultural life.

Paul's transformation of Catherine's military order began with the Guards regiments. His black-booted soldiers overnight ascended to the same level of traditional importance and prestige as the century-old Guards, which for all intents and purposes they absorbed and replaced. As one anonymous diarist wrote: "On the 10th [December 1796], the sovereign himself led the regiment of his black-booted soldiers and congratulated them as guardsmen."[17] To Paul's rational mind, since the Guards had ceased to be battle worthy and were now ceremonial troops with no military purpose, they could be eliminated altogether.[18] Unsurprisingly, a month after Paul's accession "half the officers in the guards [had] already voluntarily resigned," wrote the Habsburg ambassador to Saint Petersburg, Ludwig von Cobenzl.[19] Besides fulfilling a rational military policy of eliminating wastage, the plan to disband the Guards was part of a political strategy. By inserting his own people, many of them foreigners, into the heart of the Russian military, Paul hoped to encourage change in the military and create a counterweight to the reaction from the established elites.[20]

After humiliating the privileged Guards, he turned to the regular officers. Paul made every effort to abolish the special privileges enjoyed by officers and to undermine patronage networks, which had been prevalent during Catherine's years. Paul wanted officers "to make their military duties their primary concern," which meant strengthening corporate, diagonal ties at the expense of vertical ties to benefactors and family networks. Echoing the writings of Rumiantsev, Mamonov, and others, Paul wanted officers to wear their uniforms at all times. Paul also cancelled the indefinite leaves that were so popular among young nobles. Now officers had a choice of either spending their time with the regiment or leaving the military altogether. One week a month of service was no longer tolerated. Furthermore, nobles could no longer enrol their sons in the Guards regiments at a young age for the sake of gaining rank without performing military service. In these ways, Paul actually strengthened the values of professionalism and merit that were so important to the Military Enlightenment. What Catherine could not achieve during her long reign, Paul wanted to implement in a few years through brutal coercion. Also, he limited the number of aides-de-camp to one per general (Catherine's lover Count Zubov alone had more than 200), and junior officers had to be used solely for military-related tasks. Finally, Paul set out to reform methods of provisioning, and he approached this in ways that cut into the illegal incomes of many officers and that attempted to ensure that the soldiers received the food and equipment allotted to them. This must have impressed writers such as Kutuzov, who lamented the present situation.[21] The emperor also tried to reform the system of high military orders. For example, the Order of St George, the most prestigious award that Catherine had established, would have been abolished if not for the timely intervention of Paul's close associates. The Order of St Vladimir, however, *was* abolished, and would be restored only after Paul's death.[22]

After shaking the world of Russian officers, the emperor turned to the soldiers. In his 1796 regulations, once again echoing many of the military writers of Catherine's time, the emperor wrote that "the soldier must always be regarded as a human being, for almost anything can be attained through friendly dealings. Soldiers will do more for an officer who treats them well, and receives their trust, then for one who they merely fear."[23] His humanistic Enlightenment impulses, however, were undermined by the introduction of new uniforms that were unanimously hated: they were tight, impractical, and bulky. The uniforms of his mother's reign reflected the historical roots of the army, which could be traced back to the times of Peter the Great, and thus were an important part of military culture.[24] Setting aside minor variations between regiments, commanders like Potemkin had given soldiers uniforms that fostered pride and a sense of identity, while at the same time making their daily routine easier. Paul did away with Potemkin's uniforms and replaced them with attire that at times was so tight that it constricted movement. Paul also changed the names of all the regiments in the army. The new system of renaming regiments was another attack on the established military culture and further confused the often illiterate soldiers. The regiments were no longer named after geographical regions but instead bore the names of their commanding officers. Semen Vorontsov related that when he went to visit some of the wounded Russian soldiers during Paul's reign and asked what regiment they belonged to, the men could not answer him. They explained that the emperor had given their regiment over to a German general.[25] New uniforms, new codes of service, and new names for old regiments all signalled a cultural and symbolic departure from customs that had been carefully nurtured during the previous reign. To make sure his orders were implemented and followed, Paul instituted inspectors for cavalry, artillery, and infantry. They were drawn from the black-booted Gatchinese troops and were regarded as spies by other Russian soldiers.[26] Thus, the autonomy in the military that had emerged during the Enlightenment was now being policed.

Table 2 Breakdown of general officers by rank, 1799[27]

Rank	#	%
Generalissimus	1	0.2
Field marshals	4	0.9
Generals	33	7.9
Lieutenant-generals	92	22.0
Major-generals	284	68.0
Brigadiers	2	0.4
Total	416	100.0

On top of all these changes, there was a sense that the system of rank and merit was being altered as well. Petr Volkonskii noted the renaming of the ranks in the Guards regiments, and Princess Dashkova recorded in her memoirs an instance when a young colonel told her that after Paul became emperor, "soldier, general, and colonel are now all equals ... and in the current times it is useless to pride oneself on one's rank."[28] This may have had something to do with the sudden explosion in the number of generals during Paul's reign. The number of major-generals and lieutenant-generals, for instance, doubled from Catherine's time.

That being said, the proportions within the pyramid of high-ranking officers remained almost unchanged after Catherine's death. Field marshals comprised about 1 per cent of officers, while lieutenant-generals and major-generals dominated the senior officer corps. These proportions remained relatively stable even during the turbulent reign of Paul. However, in the popular imagination this may have been seen as an assault on the balance between merit and seniority.

In addition to all this, the rich tradition of military writing was withering under Paul. In 1796, military printing presses were closed down by imperial decree.[29] Any spontaneous intellectual initiative from the bottom was discouraged in an attempt to standardize and distil some sort of unified doctrine, one that would accommodate the army as a whole, at all levels. Naturally, in such an environment, home-cooked military texts were unwelcome. They were seen as challenges to central authority rather than as useful additions to government regulations. They were viewed as disruptions in the larger narrative rather than voices participating in shaping it. During Paul's reign, private manuals like Suvorov's *Suzdal Regulations* were banned. To create a new culture, the previous culture would have to be eviscerated and old texts – the bearers of traditions and values – would have to be replaced.[30]

Paul's challenge to Catherine's military culture was thorough and complete. The emperor was a child of the Enlightenment and took its rationalizing tendencies to the extreme. Laws, traditions, orders and awards, uniforms, regiment names, and manuals were all changed. Paul succeeded in bringing the army under his personal control and in checking the tyranny of senior officers and colonels, but he was replacing that tyranny with a new one of his own.[31] He came close to accomplishing his agenda, but he paid a heavy price in cultural capital: the military was overwhelmed with reprimands, threats, and surveillance, which bred resentment and opposition.

On the way to his objectives, Paul departed from the traditions of the Military Enlightenment but at the same time continued some of its practices. Unlike his mother, Paul inserted himself at the top of the military, yet he did so by following in the footsteps of her military pantheon. Paul used drills and parades to stage his own semiotic performances as a means to introduce and reinforce his ideas of military culture. The parade was key to Paul's self-realization as a conquering monarch: it was a place where he demonstrated his mastery and his commitment to reform, a place where he set out to transform the Russian military culture in full view of the army, the government, and the Russian people. The parade became a symbolic space where awards, punishments, and decisions were made in full transparency.[32] The military kept notebooks in which Paul's daily orders during his morning inspections were written down by an adjutant. The entries show an autocrat grappling with the imperfections he saw in the legacy of Catherine's military culture and illustrate how he tried to correct them. They show how, in descending to the parade ground from the throne, Paul wanted to be in the midst of soldiers and officers, just like the popular military commanders of his mother's reign.

A sample of orders from the notebooks from the year 1799 reveals the scope of Paul's attack:

"3 January, Expel from the military Engineering Corps Lieutenant Gorbunov for drunken behaviour and indifference to service";[33] "15 January, His Imperial Majesty recommends to the gentlemen officers not to be late for the inspection and always to arrive at half past eight";[34] "29 January, His Majesty makes a reprimand to Junior-Lieutenant Savelev because he took a vacation and came back from it, without going to see Major-General Nedobroi and Colonel Sukin, and recommends that he become better acquainted with the customs of military service";[35] "9 February, for pretending to be severely ill and for laziness in service, Lieutenant Ardabdev of the Zigodev Garrison Regiment is expelled from it";[36] "19 February, His Imperial Majesty recommends to Lieutenant Alsuf'ev, Junior-Lieutenant Malyshev and Ensign Roslavlev of Izmailov Leib Guard Regiment, to not disgrace themselves and show more diligence";[37] "21 February, His

Majesty recommends to Lieutenant Tolstoi to be tidier in appearance";[38] "27 February, Leib-Guards Grenadier Regiment is reprimanded for brawling and unbecoming behaviour (the junior-lieutenant of the above regiment is to be court-marshaled, and the regiment's colonel put under arrest)";[39] "4 March, His Majesty reprimands Preobrazhenskii Regiment Major-General Fedorov's battalion about today's exercises and recommends staff-and-ober officers not to be lazy. Otherwise they will be sent to army regiments";[40] "5 March, His Imperial Majesty reprimands Preobrazhenskii Regiment ... and recommends not to let its standards slide. Lieutenant Iakhotov and Count Tolstoi of the same regiment are transferred to the Viazmitinov Garrison Regiment";[41] "His Imperial Majesty makes a reprimand to gentlemen-officers because they once again begin to be late for the exercises and recommends everyone to arrive at their posts in such a way so as not to bring upon themselves the shame that befell today the Preobrazhenskiis'";[42] "22 April, His Majesty recommends to gentlemen-officers to dress better and not to stutter."[43]

By April, some gentlemen-officers were apparently so stressed by daily drills that they began to stutter in the presence of the overbearing new emperor and his entourage. The avalanche of reprimands, threats, and dismissals was unprecedented. During long mornings, the emperor transferred officers from the ceremonial Guards regiments to obscure army regiments and garrisons. He reprimanded officers for not following military protocol. He expelled them from the military for poor behaviour. Paul wanted to Westernize the Russian army, to centralize and streamline its decision-making, to serialize and standardize its uniforms and equipment; he wanted officers to be familiar with military regulations that demanded professional behaviour. Paul's reprimands about laziness, diligence, tidiness, standards, and knowledge of military customs all conformed to the larger agenda of the Military Enlightenment, but unlike Rumiantsev, who would single out one officer to make a larger symbolic point, Paul used his power coercively. Paul's petty outbursts of displeasure flowed from his inability to suppress his obsessive commitment to his version of military culture, and his intellectual failure to recognize the need for a compromise with reality.

It was not only soldiers and low-ranking officers who earned reprimands and were expelled from service. Generals and princes were also the objects of Paul's wrath:

"7 January, His Imperial Majesty reprimands General of the Cavalry von der Phalen and Lieutenant-General Prince Golitsyn for faults in Guard Cavalry";[44] "24 January, Engineer Lieutenant-General Churnasov and

Ogovsk's commandant Major-General Demidov, for lack of diligence in service and for not evacuating from the run-down barracks that collapsed on volunteers along with the guards who were there with them, are expelled from the military";[45] "7 March, Stavropol'sk commandant Major-General Knyshev, for asking for retirement at an inappropriate time, is expelled from service";[46] "8 March, His Majesty makes a reprimand to Prince Shcherbatov for not correcting his mistakes";[47] "21 March, Lieutenant-General Shiz is reprimanded for not knowing military service and the numbers of the squadrons";[48] "22 March, Major-General and chief of the Jager regiment Baron Gil'delshold has been reprimanded because the officers of his regiment carried sabres";[49] "11 April, a reprimand is made to the Colonel Rakhmanov of the Guard Preobrazhenskii regiment for not knowing customs of military service";[50] "24 August, the chief of the dragoon regiment Major-General DeUviz is expelled from service for not knowing the customs of military service."[51]

The above storm of reprimands, arrests, and expulsions represented only eight months of the five-year reign.[52] There were praises, awards, and words of encouragement to be sure, but the Sword of Damocles hung over everyone without exception.

In addition to performances on parade grounds, less than a week after being crowned emperor, Paul began a campaign of political repression aimed at dismantling the military leadership. The first victim of the emperor's displeasure was Lieutenant-General Mikhail Izmailov, who on 22 November 1796 was forbidden to be in either Moscow or Saint Petersburg while Paul was there.[53] On the same day, Colonel Aleksandr Elagin was "forever" incarcerated in the Peter and Paul Fortress for his "daring conversations."[54] On 13 December, Paul ordered the exile of Unter-Officer Ivan Zass, of the politically untouchable Seminovskii Guards, for writing "daring letters."[55] The following year, an Izmail veteran, the future hero of the Napoleonic Wars, and an officer close to Suvorov, Major-General Matvei Platov, was exiled to Kostroma, where he remained under surveillance for two years. Eventually Paul allowed him to return to Saint Petersburg and charges against him were dropped, but he came back shattered.[56] In August 1798, Lieutenant-General Maslov was exiled to his village of Shekhotov, where he was kept under surveillance by the local authorities.[57] In December, Lieutenant-Colonel Aleksei Ermolov, another future hero of the Napoleonic Wars, the conqueror of the Caucasus, and the founder of Groznyi, came under the searchlight of Paul's suspicions. In 1797 the young Ermolov had written a letter to his brother, full of "daring expression," that had subsequently been discovered. The investigators found only one such letter, and it was unrelated to Ermolov's service, yet Paul still ordered Ermelov's exile to Kostroma and demanded that the local governor "establish close surveillance of his behaviour."[58] The discovery of letters circulating deep within the military sphere shows how, in the spirit of the Enlightenment, officers had become active critics of policy, government, and their profession.

The year 1799 brought even more exile and surveillance. In January, Lieutenant-Colonel Sukhotin was exiled to his villages and put under surveillance for "crimes known to His Majesty."[59] Vice-Admiral Litt was another prominent exile, sent to his villages with the by now familiar order that his behaviour be monitored and his visitors be reported.[60] Lieutenant-General Zorich, an old favourite of Catherine, the founder of a military school where many of her officers received their education, was put under secret surveillance. Paul had heard that in the town where Zorich was residing there had gathered many retired and expelled officers, which naturally raised the eyebrows of the emperor. A trusted servant of the Secret Expedition, the eighteenth-century precursor to the Russian secret police, was instructed to find out how many officers lived there and who they were.[61] The same year, Pavel Chichagov, son of the famous Catherinian admiral, Vasilii Chichagov, was imprisoned in the Peter and Paul Fortress, on false suspicion of wanting to join the British navy and for his violent protests during his interview on this matter with the emperor.[62] In 1800, the ranks of exiled officers continued to swell.[63] Those who did not follow Paul's instructions, or who had taken pity on or sympathized with exiles, prisoners, or the expelled, were themselves persecuted.[64]

All of this is to say that dissent, challenges to the new military order, and suspicious behaviour were all immediately suppressed. The above officers were only a few of the more than 2,000 who suffered some form of repression during Paul's short reign. The purges have to be seen against the backdrop of the French Revolution, given that many of the exiled were of foreign extraction; however, most of the officers were Russian nobles whose behaviour offended not so much Paul's political sensibilities as his military priorities.[65] Paul's attack was aimed above all at protégés of the giants of Catherine's military culture – Potemkin, Rumiantsev, and Suvorov. The new emperor held them responsible for the state of the military, its conduct, its values, and its performance. His parades, military regulations, reprimands, and mass exiles were intended to fix what he thought was broken.[66] Paul wanted to remove the troublemakers, to purify the military culture, and to mould it according to his own design. By 1799, forty-four generals had resigned, retired, or been expelled – about 11 per cent of the senior military staff. By 1801,

Paul had purged more than 20 per cent of the officer corps.[67] This systematic poicy of exile worked to break apart networks, to compartmentalize officers in watertight, faraway places, to dissolve the filaments of military culture, and to prevent any concentrated resistance to change. The officers of Catherine's reign had embodied the military culture of that era and were perpetuating and defending both its values and its vices. Paul wanted to be the final arbiter of military culture, and for that it was necessary to destroy the influence of its individual members.

Nor was Paul afraid to challenge and undermine the paragons of the established order. By 1796 the old stalwarts of Catherine's army, Potemkin and Rumiantsev, were dead and only Suvorov remained. At first Paul tried to win the old warrior over, seeing him as an ally as well as a representative of the Military Enlightenment in the army. On 15 December 1796, Paul sent a short conciliatory letter to the field marshal, calling him an old friend and addressing him with the familiar "ty." "Comencons denouveau [sic. Let us begin afresh]," wrote the emperor. "Dwell on the past and you'll lose an eye, though, others had only one eye to begin with. Happy New Year and I invite you to come to Moscow for the coronation, if you can. Take care and do not forget old friends." But the letter ended with this ominous line: "Please bring yours into my customs."[68] Suvorov had to implement Paul's reforms in his armies without delay.

Suvorov was insulted by the sea change brought by Paul's coronation. The old field marshal expressed his confusion and frustration over the Prussian-style military reforms, which he interpreted as an attack on the Russian military culture instead of an attempt to improve it. In a note he wrote in 1797, Suvorov was especially vehement regarding the use of Paul's manual, *Experience in the Field of Military Art*:

A captain from the Prussian service in Pavlovsk (I now recall) demonstrated Prussian exercises that I had not seen, or even heard about. Thus in 20 odd years there has emerged "experience of military art" and, apparently, with it a hare will defeat Alexander. Merit is no longer necessary, neither is experience, and so, field marshals are equal with junior generals. Advantage is out the window here, completely absent ... The commander enjoys privileges from the tsar; it is insufferable! I will be six feet under before I do that. What experience from military art terms *point de vue*, in Russian is called an objective. The Russians have always beaten the Prussians, why follow them now?[69]

Suvorov's note yields an array of masked but subtle messages. The author probably wrote down on paper what he really wanted to tell

Paul in person, but to do so was impossible.[70] The note expressed many of the intellectual and cultural anxieties and insecurities that beset the late eighteenth-century Russian military. Paul's aggressive dismissal of Russian achievements was counterproductive in Suvorov's eyes. Despite borrowing much from Prussia in his youth, Suvorov now recoiled at what he saw as an intrusion of foreign culture into the Russia military. He did not think about the possible benefits of introducing of new European ideas. He wrote out *point de vue* in Cyrillic to underscore the alien nature of the French language. Why use foreign terms if there are words for them in the native tongue? He felt offended by favouritism, implying that the values of professionalism and meritocracy that had been developed in the Russian army were being weakened. By referencing Paul's new military manual, which was derived almost entirely from a 1767 Russian text mimicking Prussian military regulations, Suvorov was mocking Paul's attempt to graft Western ideas and methods onto the Russian army.[71] With the reference to Alexander the Great he was contrasting the brainless hare with the wisdom of the ancient Greeks. He sarcastically noted that nowadays to become a military genius, all one had to do was read Paul's manual. Suvorov did not capitalize the title of the manual but treated it with an ironic twist, putting its name in quotations. Finally, by referencing Prussia with a distinct streak of national disdain, he reflected how Russia had developed an autochthonous military culture. The old field marshal concluded that according to the recent "experience from military art" – implying the recent successes against the Prussians, Turks, Poles, and Swedes in the last "20-odd years" – Russia had no need for unconditional advice from the West or changes to its military practices.

Paul's curbing of manual writing and his introduction of Prussian texts were part of a much larger project to promote the Military Enlightenment on *his* terms, not the military's. The problem was that Paul was attempting to achieve this goal by borrowing from the West, in the same way his great-grandfather, Peter the Great, had done a hundred years earlier. But Paul's Russia was no longer the Russia of Peter the Great, when borrowing from the West was often the only path to reform. By the end of the eighteenth century, a corpus of Russian military literature, experts, and experience was available for Paul to mobilize. To borrow from abroad was humiliating for the Russian military, especially after the string of victories during Catherine's reign. Paul underestimated, or perhaps lacked the tact to accommodate, the national consciousness and the intellectual initiative in the military community that had begun to emerge by the time he came to power.

Suvorov made his objections to Paul's reforms clear in his notes and in letters to friends, but if written language got him nowhere, Suvorov was prepared to use symbolic performance. And he soon got the opportunity to do just that. Paul eventually invited Suvorov to one of his parades as a guest of honour. This was another attempt to win the old hero to his side and to show Suvorov his vision for the Russian military. The parade, with its massive audience, was too tempting an opportunity to miss. Resorting to the semiotic behaviour that had been so prevalent in Catherine's military culture, Suvorov offered his critique of the new rules, uniforms, and equipment, even in the presence of the emperor.[72] On the parade ground, Suvorov appeared to get confused about his hat, trying to adjust it first with one hand, then with both, and finally dropping it on the ground, to the great consternation of Paul. As the columns marched past, Suvorov jumped up and ran among them. Clearly, Suvorov was trying to introduce chaos into the well-ordered machine that Paul wanted to create out of the Russian army. When getting into the carriage, Suvorov wedged his sword into the door, which prevented him from getting in. He tried opening the door on the other side, but to no avail – the sword was still in the way. All these performances were carefully watched by the emperor, his court, the officers, and thousands of soldiers. Paul angrily demanded an explanation of this behaviour from his entourage, but either no one knew what Suvorov was doing or they dared not tell the emperor.[73]

Suvorov understood that Paul wanted to win him over and that he thus had the political capital to make his point.[74] He was using his performance to open a dialogue, but for some reason Paul refused to engage him. It is possible, though doubtful, that the sovereign did not understand what Suvorov was signalling.[75] After all, Paul was an accomplished symbolist himself, who reaffirmed and entrenched his vision of military culture every morning at half past eight.[76] Furthermore, the message Paul was communicating to the military at his morning parades clashed with the message Suvorov was trying to convey with his performance. Paul was creating a new culture even while Suvorov was trying to take it apart. There is also evidence that even before becoming emperor, Paul had refused to engage with Suvorov's performances. As Prince Ivan Ukhtomskii related, when during an audience with the heir Suvorov wanted to start his usual tricks and pranks, Paul interrupted him and said "We understand each other without this." Coming out of the meeting, the courtiers heard Suvorov sing a simple rhyme in French: "Prince Adorable, despote implacable," and this was duly related to the future emperor.[77] Most likely, Paul knew what Suvorov wanted – more power for himself at the expense of the tsar – and that was not something he was prepared to give him. Suvorov wanted the privileges he had enjoyed under Catherine to be restored, specifically the authority to promote, demote, and decorate officers. Paul thought such prerogatives belonged to the sovereign, not his field marshals.[78] Catherine's military culture was clearly being challenged and reformed.

The emperor had no patience for Suvorov and responded to his challenges in a heavy-handed way. Suvorov had to disband his staff and send them off to different regiments. He could no longer use adjutants for personal matters, such as delivering letters – his adjutants now had to attend to military business only, not to the errands of their commanders. Finally, Suvorov was warned that he could no longer allow his officers leaves of absence, as the whole process was now reviewed by the emperor himself.[79] Fed up with this government intrusion into what he felt was his personal sphere of competence, the field marshal wrote a daring note to Paul, stating that since there was no war, there was nothing for him to do in the army, for which he was promptly dismissed in February 1797.[80]

Soon after, Suvorov was sent to one of his estates in the village of Borovichi in the Novgorod province, where he was kept effectively under house arrest.[81] Suvorov's file in the papers of the Secret Expedition contains some 150 pages of surveillance reports, including a unique instruction on how to conduct clandestine surveillance.[82] Suvorov knew he was being watched. Furthermore, he was forbidden to see visitors, he could not leave his village, and his mail was monitored. By September 1797 he was finally breaking down, and wrote to Paul, pleading: "Today Collegiate Counselor Nikolev has arrived. Great Monarch! Have mercy: take pity on the old man, forgive me, if I have done something wrong."[83] Nikolev was an agent of the secret police, and Paul made no reply. Suvorov, the most powerful field marshal in the Russian army, who had held so much sway over military affairs, and who had been until recently the thunder of the Russian armies, had been humbled into submission. It was not only the field marshal himself who had been exiled, but the military tradition, ideas, and practices he stood for. Paul had made an example out of Suvorov for everyone else in the military.

Despite the exile of Suvorov and many other generals, military opposition persisted, and at least some officers continued to reject the new military culture. The secret investigation of officers in the Saint Petersburg Dragoon Regiment in the summer of 1798 serves as a window onto that world of resistance. The report submitted to the Secret Expedition was indeed disturbing. The regiment, it claimed, was composed of "young and thoughtless men." Its commander, Colonel Kindiakov, refused to enforce discipline, and the colonel's younger brother, who had been expelled from military service, still daringly wore his Catherinian-era uniform, despite Paul's decree forbidding it. Even more shocking was that the younger Kindiakov continuously encouraged other people in the regiment to do the same.

At the regiment's headquarters the situation was even more alarming. Some of these "thoughtless, young men" wore nothing but dressing gowns and showed no respect for the staff who gathered there for work. Eventually Junior-Lieutenant Dogonovskii grew so impetuous that he dared to offend one of his superiors. The colonel refused to do anything about it, and Dogonovskii's mockery finally drove one of the officers to assault him with a knout. Paul's first response after learning of this incident was an immediate order that officers should "not dare express their thoughts on the new uniform, or pass judgment about the new customs of service." This clashed with a major influence of the Enlightenment, which permitted discussion and expression of thought among the military.[84] Paul's second order was to dispatch Nikolev, who had barely finished with his surveillance of Suvorov, to Saint Petersburg.

It is difficult to understand what officers like Kindiakov and Dogonovskii were trying to achieve. Did they think they would get away with challenging the new military culture, or was it just a public display of their disapproval of the reforms? It could be that the actions of the young officers of the Saint Petersburg Dragoons were not unique. Apparently in some circles appearing in irregular and untidy dress was a means to express displeasure with the new military customs, and dismissal was seen a mark of honour.[85] As Carrie Hertz reminds us, "clothing is a silent but visual marker of social identities and relationships."[86] Catherine's military culture was individualistic; each commander had a slightly different uniform to distinguish himself and his regiment from all the others. This striving for uniqueness, to define oneself against the larger mass of people, reflected the values of Enlightenment society more generally. Paul's military reforms were diametrically opposed to the principle of individuality. He wanted uniformity, conformity, cohesion, and regularity in his military machine. For Paul, the uniform was not a mechanism for defining individuality but a way to suppress it. If anything, the episode underscored the tension between two military cultures, between those used to Catherine's decentralization and independence and those tasked with implementing the emperor's regulations. The frustration with the new rules eventually boiled over into a physical confrontation.

When Nikolev arrived to investigate the regiment, he began by interrogating the officers and found a willing person in none other than

Lieutenant-Colonel Lev Engelgardt. After completing his investigation, Nikolev produced the following report for the Secret Expedition:

> In February of this year at the headquarters of Colonel Kindiakov he [Engelgardt] found the latter showing something secretly to Major Balk, Colonel Sterlingov, Colonel Kakhvoskii and other officers who after looking at it, passed it from hand to hand, exploding with laughter and commenting "Oh what a likeness!." To the question of Major Potemkin – "who drew this" – Colonel Kindiakov answered – "one discontented captain living in Kakhvoskii's village" ... Then Kindiakov showed him a small portrait in which Engelgardt did not even discover any human resemblance, but Colonel Kindiakov said with surprise: "can you really not guess who this looks like, take a better look ..." Engelgardt still could not make the connection, but the colonel exclaimed that this was a portrait of the sovereign in caricature. The colonel had big grudges, and had nightly gatherings for drinks, during which the criticism of the current government, military customs, dress, the groaning of the people, and the fact that there was not a single person who did not slight the sovereign, were expressed; and especially when his brother, Pavel Kindiakov, arrived, burning with the spirit of liberty, he perverted everyone from their path, often praising the French government and discussing numerous times books by Montesquieu and other vile French authors. On top of this, he expressed his view that there was nothing more base than to be slaves, for we do not belong to ourselves and what we own is also not ours, but the time would change everything, because today people are not stupid, and with similar daring words, Engelgardt thinks, many staff and ober-officers in the regiment are perverted, for more then once he found them in this outrage, from which he was forced to flee.[87]

The secret report is a rare window onto military participation in the public sphere. The influence of the Enlightenment on the military culture continued, and soon, another chilling piece of evidence came to light. As Nikolev described in his report, Major Potemkin once visited Colonel Kakhovskii on his estate while the latter was reading Voltaire's tragedy the *Death of Caesar* out loud, translating it into Russian as he went, for a group of officers. As soon as he finished the part about the assassination of the Roman emperor, he put his book down, took some snuff tobacco, and said "and what about ours." To which Major Potemkin jokingly replied that he would do it right away for 10,000 roubles.[88] The grudges that originated in changes to military culture had turned into personal grievances, which then grew into threats and eventually into a conspiracy that would result in the emperor's assassination.

The investigation also discovered that Colonel Kakhovskii had approached Suvorov himself with the request that he raise the army under his control against Paul, because "the sovereign wants everything to be Prussian-like in Russia and even change the laws." Kakhovskii urged Suvorov to rally his troops and "march them on St. Petersburg." The field marshal refused to be involved in any sort of coup, which would probably have failed anyway. What is illuminating, however, is the conversation Suvorov supposedly had with the bellicose colonel. It was related by Kakhovskii's brother, Aleksei Ermolov, in the last years of his life:

> One time while talking about emperor Paul, he [Kakhovskii] said to Suvorov: "I am surprised, Count, that you, idolized by the army, having such influence on the minds of Russians, while at the same time having such forces at your disposal, agree to subordinate yourself to Paul." Suvorov jumped up and made the sign of a cross over Kakhovskii's mouth. "Be quiet, be quiet," he said, "I cannot. It will be fellow-citizens' blood!"[89]

Ermolov's implication was that the field marshal had chosen exile over launching a civil war. It is difficult to verify this story, yet it is not impossible to imagine that a conversation of this sort took place at some point during Paul's reign.[90] In the end, Paul showed magnanimity toward the outrages happening under his nose, and none of the guilty officers were executed.[91] But the entire affair must have only aggravated the already irritated and insecure emperor and driven him to accelerate reform of the military culture he had inherited from his mother, a culture he viewed as rife with insubordination, indiscipline, and conspiracies.

Notwithstanding Paul's order forbidding discussion or criticism of the new military regulations, it seems that those conversations continued unabated. By the end of his reign Paul was systematically monitoring his military, conducting internal espionage, and compiling notes about the mood of his officers and soldiers. One report he received accurately summarized the grievances of officers against his military reforms. Many of them were waiting impatiently for an opportunity to resign. Officers complained about their poor salaries and that they lacked the resources to undertake the new responsibilities Paul has assigned them. They protested that according to the new law, officers had to pay a fine for every soldier that deserted, which was bankrupting them. Yet the new rules the government introduced were so strict they almost guaranteed desertion. "What shall we do?" officers asked. "Shall we avoid punishing a soldier when he is at fault, in order for him to refrain from deserting? But if you do not punish them, you will be demoted to a soldier yourself."[92] The report clearly summarized the impact of Paul's reforms on officers and soldiers in the Russian army. The dilemma the officers faced was that if they did not punish runaway soldiers, they themselves could get demoted to the ranks, yet if they did punish runaway soldiers, it only increased the likelihood of desertion, which could get the officers demoted all the same. The severity of the system instituted by Paul's regime was backfiring. Uncomfortable uniforms, resignations, desertion, lack of pay, surveillance, and diminished power and prestige, as well as increased responsibilities, prevented Russian officers from embracing the new military order Paul wanted to create.

Ironically, many of Paul's ambitions were aligned with the ideals of the Military Enlightenment of Catherine's reign. What Paul had in common with many writers and reformers – even with the unorthodox and outspoken Suvorov – was a desire to instil a military professionalism that could serve as the sword and shield of the growing Russian empire. The difference was that Paul was demanding that his officers pursue this goal in very different ways than Catherine would have wanted. Paul's overcommitment to rules was an expression of the Enlightenment emphasis on legal process – the belief that laws can clarify daily experience and bring an end to arbitrariness and ambiguities. But soon, the emperor's obsession with following rules and laws became suffocating rather than liberating. Paul's attack on individualism did not lead to harmonious social order within the military, as he had expected, but instead further atomized it. And there is no evidence that his application of Enlightenment rationalism improved the military's performance; most likely, it worked against his goals. Catherine's reformers had carved out an independent cultural and intellectual sphere for military culture to develop; now Paul wanted to suffocate the military's spirit of independence and bring it under the autocrat's absolute personal control. By trying to fit the Military Enlightenment into a straightjacket, Paul was distorting its influence on the Russian military culture; what he saw as an attempt at improvement others interpreted as an attack. In the process he made the ideal the enemy of tradition, and his approach to enforcing his ideal was a principal cause of his downfall. It is little wonder that the opposition to Paul walked the streets in uniform.[93]

The Legacy of the Enlightenment in Russian Military Culture

Both intellectual and cultural narratives of the Enlightenment are well-established in Russian history. In this book I have sought to build upon this and to ask a new set of questions about the intersection of the Enlightenment and military culture in late eighteenth-century Russia. How did members of the military reconcile the ideas of the Enlightenment with their profession? Were Russian military writings a part of the wider Enlightenment discourse? What ideas did they express? Did the Russian military participate in the wider public sphere? And finally, was Russia part of the larger European Military Enlightenment? All of these questions lead to several broader questions: How do we evaluate the successes and failures of the Enlightenment in the military context? To what extent has the Russian cultural experience been the product of *samobytnost'* or European practices and traditions? And what is the legacy of the Enlightenment influence on Russian military culture?

It is misleading to measure eighteenth-century Russia and its intellectuals and reformers, their behaviour, their values, and their thoughts by the standards of the European, particularly French, Enlightenment. Mid-eighteenth century Russia had no bourgeoisie class that was struggling against the monarchy for political or economic freedoms. The most articulate members of Russian society had no major grievances against the Russian state, its structure, or its policies. The Orthodox Church was less powerful than in the West and did not have oppressive power. Also, the variety of social grievances had been largely addressed by the emancipation of the nobility before Catherine's reign.[1] Thus, the Russian military culture needs to be contextualized in this wider world of the Russian Enlightenment. Nobles were emancipated from compulsory state service in 1762, and this put the military in a unique position. Despite their new freedom, for many nobles the military remained an important source of income and identity. That is to say that emancipation of the nobility and the relaxation of censorship, among various other legal and cultural initiatives of Catherine's reign, helped give military culture a degree of autonomy from the government. The nobility as an estate was no longer forced to serve in the military, and those who remained had to rethink the nature of their service, why they should continue to serve, what the values of the military should be, and what it meant to be an officer in this new age in which military service was optional. Military authors took the initiative to share their ideas and thoughts on all of these questions, hoping to shape the military according to their views, which were influenced by the prevailing cultural and intellectual movement of the time. Individualism, rationalism, humanism, self-respect, the challenging of authority, the importance of merit and ability over seniority, the emphasis on education – all of these were part of the system of ideas and values that found its way into military works during Catherine's reign and that were simultaneously part of Russia's Enlightenment. While the educated elites, as moral teachers, grappled with how to spread the Enlightenment throughout Russian society, Russian officers faced a similar challenge in the military.[2] Writings from Catherine's era show how contemporaries thought that the condition in the military needed to change, that the military as it existed was different from what it had to be. This attitude reflected the broader Enlightenment conscience, a frame of mind that saw "the world to be profoundly other that it should be."[3] In Catherine's military we begin to meet people who had faith in the power of human reason and human action to change the world they lived in.

The Enlightenment influence on the military started in the Cadet Corps and in various other educational encounters, where attempts were made to mould the future officers "into something more closely resembling Rousseau's natural man."[4] Catherine and many members of the military proto-intelligentsia wanted to heighten the prestige of officers and their profession as a whole, and one way to do this was through formal training and by increasing their authority by accumulating specialized knowledge. Catherine's government was not alone in this. In Habsburg Austria, Maria Theresa wanted to heighten officers' prestige through education, but it seems that the Habsburg nobility was lukewarm to this endeavour.[5] Count Ivan Betskoi, Catherine's education reformer, provided the empress and the government with a sustained critique of the Russian military officer and offered a plan to remedy his deficiencies. Beginning in the 1760s, officers were expected to engage an amorphous field of knowledge. But Betskoi left it up to the students how to practise the Military Enlightenment. In the meantime, the idea that professional military knowledge was necessary for a successful career was slowly setting in among the Russian nobility. Uncles helped with education and made arrangements to improve their nephews' integration into the military culture. Retired soldiers tutored them, foreigners prepared them for military examinations, and family friends shared their experiences and formal knowledge. In this way, the Enlightenment informed the growth of what I call the military proto-intelligentsia, which coincided with the larger Russian Enlightenment project to create "a new type of people," who would play an important cultural, military, and political role in the nineteenth century.

The Enlightenment's influence seeped into military essays, manuals, and instructions. Far from being static, the military developed a cultural and intellectual space in which private views were openly expressed and ideas were exchanged. In the process the military participated in the budding public sphere. As in France, Russian writers and reformers increasingly recognized the need to relate military practice to its social, cultural, and political background, and to that end they submitted the military profession to systematic and rational analysis. Russian military writers in the late eighteenth century wanted to form a new generation of military professionals who would appreciate their role in the military and who could contribute to the creative process of the culture of which they were now members. Their goal was to train a new type of officer – one who thought about more than how to protect the autocracy as a political institution. He was to be someone with a strong moral and spiritual compass who would not abuse the power he held over thousands of soldiers. He would use rational means to maximize the effectiveness of the Russian military, improve the living conditions of his soldiers, and participate in discussions about the importance of his profession. The Enlightenment rejected the notion of soldiers as automatons, embraced the notion that regular soldiers and conscripts were capable of patriotic feeling long before the Patriotic War of 1812, and saw war and politics as closely related long before Clausewitz wrote about it in his *Vom Krieg* in 1832. Military texts also served as a platform for an incipient national consciousness, in that they expressed cultural anxiety about Western Europe. In this sense, the military was another stage on which discussion about the Westernization of Russia played out, which anticipated the debates between Slavophiles and Westernizers in the nineteenth century. Finally, it was during the Enlightenment that Russian military authors actively sought to distinguish the military from the civilian sphere.

The Enlightenment also mounted a serious challenge to undeserved privilege and called for commitment to the idea of merit, which was another powerful influence on the military culture. Meritocratic and egalitarian ideas of heroism came on the back of the larger European Military Enlightenment, which promoted a "rational, ordered, and rule-bound" approach to promotion, even if this was not always achieved.[6] Debates about merit were one way the military operationalized the Enlightenment. Letters of recommendation and internal debates show how Catherine's military embraced this crucial tenet of the Enlightenment and contributed to the larger discourse of professionalism.

Equally important, the military allowed a high degree of individualism, sanctifying what the *philosophes* declared as autonomous individuals' power to effect change, to leave a mark. Enlightenment individualism was celebrated and visible, at the performative level of military culture, in the panoply of various regimental dress styles, and in the military essays that provided diverse training models for various units. Russian military culture marshalled this celebration of individualism for its own use, and the semantic performance of military culture emphasized a set of values congruent with the larger European Military Enlightenment.

Unravelling the influences of the Enlightenment on military culture challenges the assumption that the military was a strict and vertical institution. In fact, the military was a world of constant negotiations, between the government and officers, between officers and soldiers, between traditions and innovations. The military allowed room for independent and critical thought, a forum where ideas and values of the Enlightenment could be tested and take root, where traditions could be questioned and practices exposed to experiment. After Catherine's death, in some respects the emperor Paul picked up where the military proto-intelligentsia had left off, and what he set out to do was perhaps not so different from what other reformers were doing in Western Europe. The French minister of war, Louis Philippe de Segur, for example, also aimed to create a professional military caste in France, united by a sense of duty and high standards of education.[7] The influence of the Enlightenment on Russian military culture was undeniable, but it was also a work-in-progress. The work of Potemkin, Rzhevskii, Rumiantsev, and other reformers was incomplete. Russian soldiers still suffered at the hands of their officers, and officers, in turn, were far from the ideal to be found in manuals and essays. Military education proceeded slowly. Merit had to fight for its survival, patronage networks persisted, and talented people were often overlooked and underappreciated.[8] The Seige of Izmail showed the contradiction of the Military Enlightenment. The calls for humanity, efficiency, education, and discipline did not bracket destruction but instead produced increasingly violent warfare. The Enlightenment, however gradual and incomplete its influence, nevertheless was an evident and powerful force that shaped Russian military culture in the eighteenth century.

Beyond its impact on the military, the story of the Military Enlightenment sheds light on larger questions in Russian history more broadly, such as militarization and Western influences. By the end of the eighteenth century, military culture began to see itself as a separate entity from the civilian world, and this separation was an important part in the emergence of the modern form of militarism in the century that followed. In addition to that, as Abeed Khalid suggested, the idea of Russian uniqueness, *samobytnost'*, has worked as a lore, often self-serving, that imposed limitations on Russian historiography.[9] Here, the story of the influence of the Enlightenment on the Russian military can help challenge the exaggerated national claims of the Russian exceptionalism.

Did the influence of the Enlightenment on the Russian military wither and die after Catherine's reign? Was it strangled along with Paul, who died at the hands of his officers in 1801? In Paul's successor, Alexander I, the military found a figure who reflected many of the qualities of the Age of the Enlightenment.[10] As a consequence, the Enlightenment's intellectual influence maintained a deep and lasting hold on the Russian military culture, radiating throughout the military and permeating its thought and practices, with very real consequences for the Russian Empire in the nineteenth century. The participation of the military in the public sphere continued unabated and indeed grew stronger. The Saint Petersburg military circle, incipient and small in the 1790s, had morphed into a fully fledged Military Society by the 1810s with the help of a relative of Fedor Dmitriev-Mamonov. In 1819, the Military Society helped publish the first Russian military encyclopaedia, edited by Sergei Tuchkov, who was by then a major-general. The meetings of the society took place around various General Staff headquarters, where officers spent long hours reading about, discussing, and debating the military arts and sciences. These gatherings, organized by the officers of Catherine's era, had a significant impact on the younger generation of military men. The attendees discussed works ranging from Caesar's *Commentaries* on the Gallic War and on the Civil War to those by Enlightenment authors such as Chevalier de Foulard's *Seven Years' War*.[11] By 1816 there was a permanent military circle comprised of both naval and military officers that held regular meetings and even published its own journal, whose editor was Sergei Glinka's younger brother.[12] In this atmosphere of military circles and the Military Society, officers became better acquainted and made new connections. Eventually their military discussions began to touch on political topics, especially after many of the participants returned from France after defeating Napoleon. This was how the Decembrist movement of the early nineteenth century could trace its cultural and intellectual origins to a handful of Enlightenment military professionals gathering in Saint Petersburg at the sunset of Catherine's reign.[13]

The home-cooked manuals that Paul had suppressed during his reign reappeared soon after his death, and the vision of the familiar figures of Catherine's era, their values, ideas, and aspirations, lived again. In 1802, Semen Vorontsov wrote his fascinating critique of the military in his *Note about the Russian Army*, and the same year Colonel de Romano published a tract about military leadership that built on the work of Catherine's commanders.[14] In 1808, Ivan Sabanev wrote his *General Rules*, and fused religion with military duty in his *Soldier's Catechism*.[15] In 1810, at the request of Alexander I, the famous military essay by le comte de Guibert, the ubiquitous figure of the French Military Enlightenment, was translated into Russian. Some historians have pointed out that the translation "exuded a critical spirit hitherto unusual in Russia."[16] These are just a few examples of the ongoing influence of the Enlightenment on the Russian military culture, and as the century wore on, military literature continued to expand into a flood of important works.[17] Building on the experience of Catherine's era, Russian officers began to delve deeper into how to mobilize the resources of the state, how to harmonize military with political considerations in times of war, and how to extract more energy from both officers and soldiers. They also began to ask what were the necessary qualities of modern military leadership. The nineteenth-century Russian writers were indeed standing on the shoulders of the Military Enlightenment.

By the 1830s the *militaires philosophes* who comprised the Catherinian military proto-intelligentsia had evolved into a corporate class of military professionals. The idea that Russia needed a formal military academy for the education of its senior officers, especially its General Staff, was introduced by the Swiss military theorist Henri Jomini (1779–1869), who by 1810 had join the Russian army. By 1832 the St Nicholas Military Academy had been founded in Saint Petersburg, and under Jomini's influence it began to expand the Enlightenment influence on Russian military thinking. Soon after, theoreticians such as Baron Nikolai Medem (1798–1870) were elaborating and codifying the ideas, methods, and practices of Russian eighteenth-century military authors.[18]

In the second half of the nineteenth century, the threads of the Military Enlightenment were picked up by a new generation of writers, reformers, and theorists. Among them were Dmitrii Miliutin (1816–1912), the Minister of War for twenty years between 1861 and 1881, Mikhail Dragomirov (1830–1905), the chief Russian tactician of the late nineteenth century and the head of the St Nicholas Military Academy for more than a decade, and Genrikh Leer (1829–1904), the chief Russian military theoretician and Dragomirov's successor as the head of the academy until 1898. It is no exaggeration to say that these three men, as Peter von Wahlde wrote, "formed an intellectual triumvirate which virtually ruled the Russian army and Russian military thought during the last half of the nineteenth century."[19] These men were all influenced by the Enlightenment frame of reference, albeit in very different and contradictory ways. Dragomirov pioneered the back-to-Suvorov movement and was influenced by late eighteenth-century military writings; Leer was influenced by the British representative of the Military Enlightenment, Henry Lloyd, who plunged him into the depths of esoteric positivism; and Miliutin expanded Russian military education even while rejecting the Prussian model for the General Staff.[20]

Miliutin was among the "enlightened bureaucrats" of Nicholas I's reign and would become a reformer during Alexander II's and the founder of a modern Russian army.[21] Born into the impoverished Russian gentry, he won his laurels in the Caucasus, then became a professor at the St Nicholas Military Academy, after which he became Minister of War. As a minister he took up many of the crusades of his Enlightenment predecessors, openly embracing the ideas of eighteenth-century military intellectuals such as Rumiantsev and Suvorov in his writings.[22] He fought for an army built on merit, not on social status or class privilege,[23] as well as for the modernization and professionalization of the Russian officer corps. And he fought for the advancement of military education throughout the empire, which produced impressive results. In the early 1860s the literacy rate among the recruits stood at about 8 per cent; by the end of the decade it had climbed to 28 per cent.[24] Echoing the *militaires philosophes,* he wrote that "the improvement of the army is based for the most part on the education of individuals, their character, and upon the development of their natural talents, not only physical, but also intellectual."[25] Miliutin did not win all his battles, but his efforts would have earned him the praise of Count Betskoi and of Catherine herself.

General Mikhail Dragomirov likewise built on the eighteenth-century experience. Dragomirov was the star pupil of the St Nicholas Military Academy, participated in several military observation missions to European armies, led a division during the Russo-Turkish War of 1877–78, and eventually became the head of his alma mater. His 1879 textbook on tactics became the bible of the Russian army in the later nineteenth century.[26] In his studies of Suvorov, Dragomirov perverted the teachings of the Enlightenment. He began a sustained intellectual campaign, through books, articles, lectures, and training, to demonstrate that in war human will trumps human reason. Building on the "moral-spiritual" aspects of the Russian military writers of the Enlightenment, of which Suvorov was the chief representative, Dragomirov maintained that technology was secondary to the human element in battle.[27] He took Suvorov's dictum "the musket ball is a fool, the bayonet is a fine chap" to its extreme. Emphasis in war was to be on the human element in battle, on subjective rather than objective factors, on soldiers' will and their mental and psychological state.[28] If technology was reduced to a subordinate element, religion figured prominently in the context of Christian morality and as motivating factor in combat. The Enlightenment emphasis on the intimate, fatherly, even tender relations between officers and soldiers also survived in Dragomirov's thought.[29] In this, he undoubtedly was making an important contribution to the field of military psychology, which stretched back at least to the writing of Saxe in the 1730s; however, Dragomirov's critics argued that if Suvorov and Saxe were alive, they would have berated their disciple. Dragomirov's final contribution to the Russian military was his supervision of the development of field regulations in 1900. The Russian tactical failures during the Russo-Japanese war of 1905 were in no small part rooted in Dragomirov's teachings, outlook, and training doctrine.[30]

General Genrikh Leer's outlook was also affected by the Enlightenment, but in a different way. Leer had been educated as an engineer and after several stints as a General Staff officer, he became Professor of Strategy and then the head of the St Nicholas Academy. His *Notes on Strategy*, among other theoretical volumes, went through several editions and played an important role in forming military thought in *fin de siècle* Russia.[31] Leer took his inspiration from the writings of the British military writer Henry Lloyd (1718–1783). He had discovered Lloyd's writings as a student and was impressed by the latter's call to "formulate the concept of strategy as a science."[32] In this respect Lloyd was a child of the Enlightenment and the intellectual founder of the early-modern school of scientific military theory. According to Lloyd, mathematics was visible in many branches of military art. Engineering, marches, artillery, battle formations, logistics, all could be expressed with precise algebraic calculations. This scientific understanding of the constituent parts of the military was further projected onto analysis of the process of war as a whole. Through Lloyd the profound influence of the European Enlightenment and rationalism on the Russian military culture accelerated. Leer swung in the opposite direction from Dragomirov. Instead of the human will, he focused on the adoption of scientific, critical, logical analysis of military action and on methods and procedures for the study of war. His tools became classification, isolation, induction, deduction, and analogy.[33] Leer never truly succeeded in turning the subjective elements in war into objective, analysable factors; even so, through him the major influences of the eighteenth-century Enlightenment reached the nineteenth-century Russian army. Bruce Menning concluded that, along with Dragomirov, Leer's ideas and theories informed the generation of Russian officers who encountered the spectre of modern conflict during the Russo-Japanese war of 1904–5.[34]

The realism and scientific inquiry that the Enlightenment stood for joined the modernizing forces of the late nineteenth century that challenged traditions of Russian military culture.[35] In the process, the imperial army gained a criterion for rational analysis of military problems rooted in critical and methodological analysis. It gained clear definitions, explanations of principles, and clear historical examples that provided further insight into the conduct of war. The imperial army was making strides in military psychology and soldier training, continuing the production of Russian "wonder-heroes." That said, Miliutin and his contemporaries were still struggling to solve the problems faced by their eighteenth-century predecessors. How to organize and train the Russian peasant soldiers for modern warfare? How to turn the officers away from paradomania and unproductive uniformity? How to improve discipline and professionalism? Along with Miliutin and Dragomirov, Leer worked to create a new type of officer with a broader world view and the education to match the ever-changing landscape of modern conflict. Their efforts showed that the influence of the Enlightenment on the Russian military culture did not solve all of its problems. Tensions remained, and even by the nineteenth century the Enlightenment influence was a work in progress, never complete, but never ceasing.

The influence of the Enlightenment on the Russian military lived on, in contradictory yet powerful ways. William Fuller introduced a useful paradigm to help us fully grasp the extent of this long-lasting influence. To understand the divergent approaches to warfare in late nineteenth-century Russia, Fuller proposed that we view the clash of ideas in terms of two competing schools: "the technologists" and "the magicians." The technologists, who emerged after the disastrous Russian performance during the Crimean War in the mid-1850s, insisted that "technological mastery was, increasingly, a precondition for victory."[36] This meant modern and technical education for officers and soldiers, emphasis on firepower and modern rifles, the use of telegraphs for communication, and the construction of railways for mobilization. The magicians, by contrast, placed their faith in the subjective qualities of the Russian soldier and held moral, physical, and spiritual qualities supreme over advances in technology. The magicians used the eighteenth-century writers to identify these qualities. Faith, persistence, obedience to commanders, fervent love of the holy Russian motherland, all ensured that even with inferior equipment Russian armies would triumph. The magical properties of the Russian soldiers bestowed on them the ability to outsuffer, outperform, outlast, and outfight any other Western army. Fuller wisely cautioned against pressing the distinction between the technologists and the magicians too far, given that there was a lot of cross-pollination of ideas between the two camps. Leer and Miliutin belonged largely in the technologist camp, while Dragomirov and his followers were the magicians. But the larger intellectual battle lines remained visible, and both drank deeply from the Russian military culture of late eighteenth century and its representatives. Both schools took the Military Enlightenment to its extreme. The technologists came close to substituting technology and science for strategy, and the magicians concentrated on tactics and performance in battle at the expense of larger questions of modern warfare.[37] This was in large part the inheritence of the Enlightenment for Russian military culture, and its legacy.

This legacy was consolidated in the nineteenth century and continued in one form or another, for good or bad, into the twentieth century, when it reached a genuinely new type of people. The Soviet magicians and technologists would fuse the eighteenth-century soldier qualities with "the motivational power of the Communist ideology" and with the weapons of industrialized warfare.[38] The faint echoes of the *militaires philosophes* were heard in 1918 when Lenin included parts of Suvorov's *Science of Victory* in the training manual for the Red Army, and when during the Second World War some Soviet generals attempted to use Suvorov's language in their orders.[39]

Notes

Introduction: The Enlightenment, the Army and the State

1 Anon., *Zelmira i Smelon*, 46.
2 Ibid., 47.
3 Ibid., 52.
4 Wirtschafter, *The Play of Ideas*, 126.
5 David D. Bien, "The Army in the French Enlightenment," 97. Adding to the intersection of the Enlightenment and the military, Janis Langins, in a narrower study, examined French military engineering during the Enlightenment and showed how it served as a template for modern engineering practices. Langins, *Conserving the Enlightenment*, 429.
6 Duffy, *The Military Experience*, 5, 154, 313; Strachan, *European Armies and the Conduct of War*, 37.
7 Starkey, *War in the Age of Enlightenment*, 8.
8 Gat, *The Origins of Military Thought*, 26.
9 Krimmer and Simpson, eds., *Enlightened War*, 9.
10 Dobie, "The Enlightenment at War," 1852.
11 I thank one of my anonymous reviewers for this insight.
12 Pichichero, *The Military Enlightenment*, 2–6.
13 Starkey, *War in the Age of Enlightenment*, 9.
14 The history of eighteenth-century Russia and the Russian Enlightenment has advanced significantly since the collapse of the Soviet Union, both conceptually and in terms of imparting new knowledge and challenging old assumptions. See, for example, Barran, *Russia Reads Rousseau, 1762–1825* (2002); Whittaker, *Russian Monarchy: Eighteenth-Century Rulers and Writers in Political Dialogue* (2003); Jones, *Nikolay Novikov, Enlightener of Russia* (2009); Levitt, *The Visual Dominant in Eighteenth-Century Russia* (2011); Kuxhausen, *From the Womb to the Body Politic: Raising the Nation in Enlightenment Russia* (2014); Wirtschafter, *Religion and Enlightenment in*

Catherinian Russia: The teachings of Metropolitan Platon (2014); Waegemens, Koningsbrugge, and Levitt, eds., *A Century Mad and Wise: Russia in the Age of the Enlightenment* (2015); Hamburg, *Russia's Path toward Enlightenment: Faith, Politics, and Reason, 1500–1801* (2016). In Russian, see Marasinova, *Psikhologiia elity rossiiskogo dvorianstva poslednei treti XVIII veka. Po materialam perepiski* (1999); Rogulin, *"Polkovoe uchrezhdenie" A.V. Suvorova i pekhotnye instruktsii ekaterininskogo vremeni* (2005); Aurova, *Ot kadeta do generala. Povsednevnaia zhizn' russkogo ofitsera v kontse XVIII – pervoi polovine XIX veka* (2010); Marasinova, "Zakon i grazhdanin. K istorii politicheskogo soznaniia v Rossii vtoroj poloviny XVIII v.," in N.M. Rogozhin, ed., *Issledovaniia po istochnikovedeniiu istrorii Rossii (do 1917 g.)* (2012).

15 Best, *War and Society in Revolutionary Europe, 1770–1870*, 44; Fuller, *Strategy and Power in Russia 1600–1914*, xvii.

16 Here my inspiration has been Siegelbaum, *Cars for Comrades*, x.

17 To clarify, this study concentrates exclusively on the Russian army, at the expense of the navy, whose military culture remains to be examined in detail.

18 V.I. Bazhukov, "Poniatie voennoi kultury. Problemy stanovleniia," *Sotsial'no-gumanitarnye znaniia*, vol. 1 (2009): 284–96.

19 V.N. Greben'kov, "Metodologicheskii potentsial kontsepta 'viennaia kul'tura obshchestva' v istoricheskikh i poleticheskikh isledovaniiakh." *Vestnik Rossiiskogo gosudarstvennogo universiteta im. I. Kanta* 12 (2009): 83–9; Anatolii Grigoriev, "Chto Takeo 'voennaia kultura?,'" *Zhurnal voennyi i literaturnyi*, http://wv2.vrazvedka.ru/index.php?option=com_content&view=article&id=138:—q–q&catid=88888906&Itemid=88888919; A.V. Korotenko, "Poniatie voennoi kultury. Sushchnostnye kharakteristiki i itogovaia definitsiia," *Vestnik Povolzhskogo Instituta* (2013): 15–20; Viacheslav Kruglov, "Fenomen voennoi kultury," *Nezavisimoe Voennoe Obozrenie*, http://nvo.ng.ru/forces/2015–03–13/10_fenomen.html; E.N. Romanova, "Voennaia kultura i ee osnovnye kharakteristiki," *Vestnik Samarskogo Gosuniversiteta* 1 (2008): 213–18.

20 Hull, *Absolute Destruction*, 94–8.

21 Cole, *Military Culture and Popular Patriotism*, 15.

22 Darnton, *The Great Cat Massacre*; Geertz, *The Interpretation of Cultures*.

23 Raeff, *Understanding Imperial Russia*.

24 Lotman, *Besedy o russkoi kul'ture*, 18.

25 Wortman, *Scenarios of Power*.

26 Blaufarb, *The French Army, 1750–1820*; Bell, *The First Total War*.

27 Black, *Rethinking Military History*; Gat, *The Origins of Military Thought*.

28 Jones, "Opposition to War and Expansion," 36, 46.

29 Porter and and Teich, eds., *The Enlightenment in National Context*, vii.

30 Walicki, *A History of Russian Thought*, 1.
31 Marc Raeff, "The Enlightenment in Russia and Russian Thought in the Enlightenment," in Garrard, ed., *The Eighteenth Century in Russia*, 29.
32 Ibid., 35.
33 Isabel de Madariaga, "Catherine the Great," in Scott, ed., *Enlightened Absolutism*, 306.
34 Isabel de Madariaga, "The Russian Nobility, 1600–1800," in Scott, ed., *The European Nobilities*, 270; Scott, "Introduction: The Problem of Enlightened Absolutism," in Scott, ed., *Enlightened Absolutism:*, 15; Paul Dukes, "The Russian Enlightenment," in Porterand and Teich, eds., *The Enlightenment in National Context*, 180.
35 Madariaga, *Politics and Culture in the Eighteenth-Century Russia*, 262, 267.
36 Hamburg, *Russia's Path toward Enlightenment*, 728.
37 Ibid., 742.
38 Wirtschafter, *The Play of Ideas*, x.
39 Outram, *The Enlightenment*, 2–3.
40 Pichichero, *The Military Enlightenment*, 4.
41 Wortman, *Scenarios of Power*, 122.
42 Ibid.
43 Hamburg, *Russia's Path toward Enlightenment*, 406.
44 In his famous decree, Peter III abolished obligatory state and military service for Russian nobility. *Polnoe Sobranie Zakonov Rossiiskoi Imperii*, vol. 15, no. 11444 (herafter PSZ) See also Raeff, *Origins of the Russian Intelligentsia*, 109–10. Raeff argued that instead of conceding to the demands of the nobility, the state actually made itself independent from it; see also Raeff, "The Eighteenth-Century Nobility." Robert Jones disagrees that Catherine embraced the emancipation out of weakness, contending instead that she did so because it aligned with her domestic policy goals. Jones, *The Emancipation of the Russian Nobility*, 279, 295.
45 Madariaga, in Scott, ed., *The European Nobilities*, 252; Corvisier, *Armies and Societies in Europe*, 183.
46 Madariaga, *Russia in the Age of Catherine the Great*, 281–2.
47 Madariaga, *Politics and Culture in the Eighteenth-Century Russia*, 267.
48 Madariaga, *Russia in the Age of Catherine the Great*, 296; Dixon, *Catherine the Great*, 271.
49 Ibid., 301.
50 Jones, *The Emancipation of the Russian Nobility*, 298–9.
51 Keep, *Soldiers of the Tsar*, 2.
52 Dixon, *Catherine the Great*, 157. Riasanovksy, *A History of Russia*, 258–9. See also Paul Dukes, *Catherine the Great and the Russian Nobility: A Study Based on the Materials of the Legislative Commission of 1767* (London: Cambridge University Press, 1967).

53 Madariaga, *Politics and Culture in the Eighteenth-Century Russia*, 276.

54 Hamburg, *Russia's Path toward Enlightenment*, 391.

55 Ibid., 386.

56 Anderson, *War and Society*, 190.

57 Hamburg, *Russia's Path toward Enlightenment*, 20.

58 Krasnobaev, *Ocherkii Istorii Russkoi Kultury xviii veka*, 74.

59 Raeff, in Garrard, ed., *The Eighteenth Century in Russia*, 37. The regulations of the corps were co-authored by Catherine herself, *Ustav Imperatorskogo Shchiakhetnogo Sukhoputnogo Kadetskogo Korpusa* (St Petersburg, 1766).

60 Robert Jones (1973), 40–1.

61 Dubina, "The 'Distinction,'" 84.

62 Barran, *Russia Reads Rousseau, 1762–1825*, 74–81; Madariaga, *Politics and Culture in the Eighteenth-Century Russia*, 268.

63 Zoltan Kramar, "The Military Ethos of the Hungarian Nobility, 1700–1848," in *War and Society in East Central Europe: Special Topics and Generalizations on the 18th and 19th Centuries*, ed. Kiraly K. Bela and Gunther E. Rothenberg (New York: Brooklyn College Press, 1979), 73.

64 Madariaga, in Scott, ed., *The European Nobilities*, 270.

65 Ibid., 262, 264.

66 Kamenskii, *The Russian Empire in the Eighteenth Century*, 241; Raeff, in Garrard, ed., *The Eighteenth Century in Russia*, 45.

67 To paraphrase Madariaga, *Politics and Culture in the Eighteenth-Century Russia*, 266.

68 Bradley, *Voluntary Associations in Tsarist Russia*, 3, 8, 38–49; Prescott, "The Russian Free Economic Society"; Leckey, "Patronage and Public Culture."

69 Papmehl, *Freedom of Expression in Eighteenth-Century Russia*, 90–2.

70 Hamburg, *Russia's Path toward Enlightenment*, 402–3.

71 Madariaga, *Politics and Culture in the Eighteenth-Century Russia*, 278.

72 "De Ligne to Comte de Segur, 10 August 1788," in De Ligne, *His memoirs, letters, and miscellaneous Papers*, 79.

73 Dixon, *The Modernisation of Russia*, 34.

74 Stevens, *Russia's Wars of Emergence*, 296–301; Stone, *A Military History of Russia*, 89.

75 Hartley, *Russia, 1762–1825*, 214.

76 Janet M. Hartley, "Russia as a Fiscal Military State, 1689–1825," in Storrs, ed., *The Fiscal-Military State*, 137.

77 Brian L. Davies, "The Development of Russian Military Power, 1453–1815," in Black, ed., *European Warfare, 1453–1815*, 176.

78 Ibid., 282.

79 LeDonne, *The Grand Strategy of the Russian Empire*, 163, 205.

80 Hamish Scott, "Russia as a Great European Power," in Bartlett and Hartley, eds., *Russia in the Age of the Enlightenment*, 9.

81 Davies, *Empire and Military Revolution in Eastern Europe*, 243.

82 Duffy, *Russia's Military Way to the West*, 233–8; Black, *European Warfare, 1660–1815*, 113–18.

83 Bruce Menning, "The Russian Imperial Army, 1725–1796," in Kagan and Higham, eds., *The Military History of Tsarist Russia*, 74.

84 Beskrovnyi, *Russkaia armiia i flot v vosemnadtsatom veke*, 633, 636, 642.

85 V. Goncharov, "Ot izdatelia," in Goncharov, ed., *Russkaia voennaia mysl': VIII vek*, 5; Tatarnikov, ed., Stroevye Ustavy, vol. 1, 5–7.

86 Fuller, *Strategy and Power in Russia*, 175.

87 Glinoetskii, *Istoriia Russkogo general'nogo shtaba*, vol. 1, 7.

88 Pinter, "The Burden of Defense in Imperial Russia," 246; Hartley, *Russia, 1762–1825*, 8.

89 Pinter, "The Burden of Defense in Imperial Russia," 253.

90 Best, *War and Society in Revolutionary Europe*, 36, 41.

91 Hochedlinger, *Austria's Wars of Emergence*, 298; Wilson, "The Politics of Military Recruitment," 558; Scott, "Russia as a Great European Power," in Bartlett and Hartley, eds., *Russia in the Age of Enlightenment*, 16.

92 Hartley, *Russia, 1762–1825*, 16; LeDonne, *The Grand Strategy of the Russian Empire*, 422. For comparative army sizes across the eighteenth century see Browning, *The Changing Nature of Warfare*, 12.

93 Duffy, *Russia's Military Way to the West*, 126–7.

94 Black, *European Warfare, 1660–1815*, 220; Houlding, *Fit for Service: Training of the British Army, 1715–1795*, 118.

95 Wilson, "The Politics of Military Recruitment," 542. Duffy, *The Military Experience in the Age of Reason*, 92–93. Archer, Ferris, and Herwig, *World History of Warfare*, 356–7.

96 Beskrovnyi, *Russkaia armiia i flot v vosemnadtsatom veke*, 633; Duffy, *Russia's Military Way to the West*, 234, 238; Fuller, *Strategy and Power in Russia*, 171.

97 Keep, "Catherine's Veterans," 390.

98 Leonov and Ul'ianov, *Reguliarnaia Pekhota*, 126–7; Duffy, *Russia's Military Way to the West*, 128; Elise Wirtschafter, "Social Misfits: Veterans and Soldiers' Families in Servile Russia," *Journal of Military History* 59, no. 2 (1995): 215–36.

99 Hartley, "The Russian Recruit," in *Reflections on Russia in the Eighteenth Century*, ed. Joachim Klein, Simon M. Dixon, and Maarten Fraanje (Cologne: Böhlau Verlag, 2001), 34.

100 Bohac, "The Mir and the Military Draft," 655–6.

101 Hartley, *Russia, 1762–1825*, 15; Elise Wirtschafter, "Soldiers' Children, 1719–1856: A Study of Social Engineering in Imperial Russia," *Forschungen zur osteuropaischen Geschichte* 30 (1982): 61–136.

102 Meiendorf, *Opyt nekotorykh razsuzhdenii o voinstve voobshche*, 20; Keep, *Soldiers of the Tsar*, 117.

103 RGVIA f. 53, op. 1/194, d. 3, l. 60, 60ob. I have been able to find several variants of the oath, though there was a standard prescribed model both in *Artikul Voinskii* and in general edicts. For example see, PSZ vol. 16, no. 11722. All of them were signed by the swearing new officer, and always by several witnesses, who included a senior officer and a priest. For example, RGVIA f. 53, op. 1/194, d. 3, l. 1066, and RGVIA f. 53, op. 1/194, d. 3, l. 418. For an example of a Catholic officer taking a military oath, see RGVIA, f. 52, op. 1/194, d. 301a, l. 160.

104 For example, the case of soldier Mikhailov, who renounced his military oath and was sent to Siberia in 1797. RGADA, f. 7, op. 2, d. 3034, l. 1.

105 *Artikul Voinskii* (1777), 3–4. A sample of a military oath is presented on page 4.

106 Hartley, *Russia, 1762–1825*, 13.

107 Kohut, *Russian Centralism and Ukrainian Autonomy*, 115.

108 Longworth, "Transformation in Cossackdom: Technological and Organization Aspects of Military Change, 1650–1850," in Rothenberg, Király, and Sugar, eds. *East Central European Society and War*, 460.

109 Kohut, *Russian Centralism and Ukrainian Autonomy*, 116.

110 Ibid, 162–3.

111 Montefiore, *Prince of Princes*, 394.

112 Hartley, *Russia: 1762–1825*, 162.

113 Ibid., 163.

114 Ibid., 30; Keep, *Soldiers of the Tsar*, 148.

115 Münnich had to turn back because most of the oxen and horses died from heat or lack of forage. Fuller, *Strategy and Power in Russia*, 111.

116 Duffy, *Russia's Military Way to the West*, 94; Szabo, *The Seven Years War in Europe*, 82, 90, 170, 188.

117 Ibid., 371, 426.

118 Fuller, *Strategy and Power in Russia*, 160.

119 Goncharov, ed., *Russkaia voennaia mysl'*, 325.

120 Longworth, *The Art of Victory*, 158. Longworth provides no reference for this statement, so I was unable to verify its validity. Probably it is an over-statement, since the troops were moving in bad weather, across some of the most difficult terrain in Europe, carrying heavy equipment.

121 Fuller, *Strategy and Power in Russia*, 160; Duffy, *Russia's Military Way to the West*, 51.

122 *Artikul voinskii s kratkim tolkovaniem*, 27.

123 "Suvorov to Bibikov, 8 January 1772," in Meshcheriakov, ed., *A.V. Suvorov*, vol. 1, 478.

124 Petr Rumiantsev, "Mysl', May 1777", in Goncharov, ed., 38.

125 Marshal Maurice de Saxe, "My Reveries Upon the Art of War," in Phillips, ed., *The Roots of Strategy*, 198.

126 Davies, *Empire and Military Revolution in Eastern Europe*, 254.

127 *Artikul voinskii s kratkim tolkovaniem*, 1777, 27.

128 Leonov and Ul'ianov, *Reguliarnaia Pekhota*, 167.

129 Dixon, *The Modernisation of Russia*, 92.

130 Leonov and Ul'ianov, *Reguliarnaia Pekhota*, 173; Keep, *Soldiers of the Tsar*, 157.

131 Fuller, *Strategy and Power in Russia*, 173.

132 Ibid., 161.

133 Leonov and Ul'ianov, *Reguliarnaia Pekhota*, 136–7.

134 Pinter, "The Burden of Defense in Imperial Russia," 253, 256.

135 Anderson, *War and Society in Europe of the Old Regime*, 197.

136 RGADA, f. 20, op. 1. d. 219, ch. 1, l. 46 and 57–71.

137 Mikaberidze, *The Russian Officer Corps*, xxxvii.

138 Hartley, *Russia, 1762–1825*, 53.

139 Keep, *Soldiers of the Tsar*, 233. Hartley, *Russia, 1762–1825*, 49.

140 Ibid., 51; Keep, *Soldiers of the Tsar*, 246.

141 Anderson, *War and Society in Europe of the Old Regime*, 204.

142 Mikaberidze, *The Russian Officer Corps*, xxvii.

143 Marasinova, *Psikhologiia elity rossiiskogo dvorianstva poslednei treti XVIII veka*, 63.

144 Hartley, "Russia as a Fiscal Military State, 1689–1825," in Storrs, ed., *The Fiscal-Military State*, 141.

145 Hartley, *Russia, 1762–1825*, 249.

146 Keep, *Soldiers of the Tsar*, 122; PSZ vol. 22, no. 16163.

147 Lotman, *Besedy o russkoi kul'ture*, 42.

148 Taylor, *Politics and the Russian Army*, 41. See also N.A. Salbukov, "Zapiski N.A. Salbukova," in *Tsareubiistvo 11 marta 1801 goda. Zapiski uchastnikov i sovremennkov*, Izd. 2e (St Petersburg, 1908), 9.

149 Duffy, *Russia's Military Way to the West*, 140–1.

150 Davies, *Empire and Military Revolution*, 97.

151 Ibid., 63–4;

152 Beskrovnyi, *Russkaia armiia i flot v vosemnadtsatom veke*, 634; LeDonne, *Absolutism and Ruling Class*, 100.

153 Lanzheron, "Russkaia armia v god smerti Ekatiriny II," no. 5, 165.

154 Glinoetskii, *Istoriia Russkogo general'nogo shtaba*, 99. See also N.P. Glinoetskii, "Russkii General'nyi shtab v tsarstvovanie Imperatritsy Ekateriny II," *Voennyi Sbornik* 1 (January 1872): 5–64. For the history of the War College during Catherine's reign, see D.A. Skalon, ed., *Stoletie Voennogo Ministerstva, 1802–1902*, vol. 3 (St Peterburg, 1902–1911), 163–258.

155 "4: Officers off the Battlefield: Managers and Thinkers," in Schönle, Zorin, and Evstratov, eds., *The Europeanized Elite in Russia*, 156.

156 Janet M. Hartley, "The Russian Empire: Military Encounters and National Identity," in *War, Empire and Slavery, 1770–1830*, ed. Richard Bessel, Nicholas Guyatt, and Jane Rendall (New York: Palgrave, 2010), 218–34.
157 Pichichero, *The Military Enlightenment*, 36.
158 Sewell, *Logics of History*, 169.
159 Duffy, *The Military Experience in the Age of Reason*, 313.

1 Between Patronage and Education

1   Mikhail Petrov, "Rasskazy sluzhivshago v 1-m egerskom polku polkovnika Mikhaila Petrova o voennoi sluzhbe i zhizne svoei i trekh rodnykh bratiev ego, zachavsheisia s 1789 goda," in Petrov et al., eds., 1812: *Vospominaniia voinov russkoi armii*, 118.
2   Volkov, *Russkii ofitserskii korpus*, 49.
3   Popov, "K probleme tsennostnogo soderzhaniia poniatiia 'Voennaia Intelligetsiia,'" 59–60; Popov, *Voennaia intelligentsia Rossii*, 192.
4   Emelianova, "Memuary o domashnem obuchenii detei v Rossii XVIII v, 4.
5   Ermolov, "Zapiski," 367.
6   Protasev, "S Stranitsy iz starago dnevnika," 408; Gudovich, "Zapiski o sluzhbe," 609.
7   Sanglen, "Rasskazy Iakova Ivanovicha de Sanglena," 137.
8   Darnton, *The Great Cat Massacre*, 99–100.
9   Kettering, "Patronage and Kinship in Early Modern France," 408. Patronage networks and the nature of political power have largely been ignored in historiography of Imperial Russia. LeDonne, "The Eighteenth-Century Russian Nobility," 145. Patronage in the military has received even less attention; LeDonne, "Outlines of Russian Military Administration," *Jahrbucher fur Geschichte Osteuropas*, 33 (1985): 183–8.
10 Burke, *History and Social Theory*, 72; David L. Ransell, "Character and Style of Patron-Client Relations in Russia," in Maczak and Mueler-Leuckner, eds., *Klientelsysteme im Europa der Fruhen Neuzeit*, 214–24; Valerie Kivelson, "Kinship politics/autocratic politics: a reconsideration of early eighteenth-century political culture," in Burbank and Ransel, eds., *Imperial Russia*, 5–31. A good example of a formation of a patronage network, between Potemkin and Jean le Bon, a French émigré who would stay in Russia after 1789 and become one of Potemkin's suite, is described by his nephew Aleksei Imberg, "Iz zapisnoi knizhki Alekseia Osipovicha Imberga," 373–4.
11 RGADA, f. 20, op. 1. d. 232, l. 1.
12 RGADA, f. 20, op. 1, d. 228, l. 16–17.
13 RGADA, f. 20, op. 1, d. 276, l. 13.
14 Bell,*The First Total War*, 26. As he added, "the army was delighted to see them go," because the French army was suffering from extreme excess of

officers. In 1789 it provided "full time employment for less than a third of its 35,000 active officers."

15 Hochedlinger, *Austria's Wars of Emergence*, 116; Rothenberg, "Nobility and Military Careers."
16 Smith, *The Culture of Merit*, 228.
17 Bruce, *The Purchase System in the British Army*, 35.
18 Volkonskii, "Rasskazy P. M. Volkonskago," 176.
19 Ibid.
20 Ibid.
21 Ibid., 177.
22 Tregubov, "Dela davno minuvshikh let," no. 11 (1908), 314.
23 Zagriazhskii, "Zapiski (1770–1836)," 98–100.
24 Pecherin, "Zapiski Fedora Panteleimonovicha Pecherina," 599.
25 Engelgardt, *Zapiski Lva Nikolaevicha Engelgardta*, 1.
26 Ibid., 37.
27 Glukhov, "Zhizn'," 203.
28 Hosking, "Patronage and the Russian State"; Wortman, *The Development of a Russian Legal Consciousness*, chapter 1; LeDonne, Ruling Russia, 20.
29 Vinskii, *Moe vremia, zapiski*, 29.
30 Denisov, *Zapiski donskogo atamana*, 31.
31 Ibid., 35.
32 Ibid., 40. The extensive bibliography appended to the memoir lists all of the archival documents associated with Adrian Denisov and his campaigns, but there is no reference to his regimental instruction. I looked for this document in the RGVIA but was unable to find it. After consulting with the RGVIA archivist specializing in eighteenth-century documents, Kiril Tatarnikov, we concluded that the document has either been lost or is yet to be discovered.
33 Ibid., 41.
34 Ibid., 42–3.
35 Dashkov, *Zapiski*, 191.
36 Ibid., 205. The famous poet Gavril Derzhavin related a similar story about his mother's role in him becoming an officer. Derzhavin, *Zapiski Gavrila Romanovicha Derzhavina*, 6–16.
37 Mosolov, "Zapiski," 124.
38 Ibid.
39 Ibid., 125.
40 Ibid., 126.
41 Pishchevich, "Zhizn' Pishchevicha," 1 (1885), 8.
42 Presumably Pishchevich meant Count Fedor Grigorievich (1741–1796). Ibid., 22.
43 Ibid., 23.
44 Ibid., 24–32.

45 Migrin, "Pokhozhdeniia ili istoria Ivan Migrina chernomorskogo kazaka," 1.

46 Ibid., 2–3.

47 Ibid., 5–9.

48 Aleksandrova, "Spetsifika vospitaniia i obrazovaniia rossiiskogo," 26.

49 Raeff, *Origins of the Russian Intelligentsia*, 126.

50 Aleksandrova, "Spetsifika vospitaniia i obrazovaniia rossiiskogo," 26.

51 Tuchkov, *Zapiski Sergeia Alekseevicha Tuchkova*, 4.

52 Ibid., 5.

53 Ibid.

54 Ibid., 6.

55 Kamenev, *Istoriia podgotovki ofitserskih kadrov v Rossii*, 29–30. See also M.S. Lalaev, *Istoricheskii ocherk voenno-uchebnykh zavedenii, podvedomstvennykh Glavnomu ikh upravleniiu*, vol. 1 (St Petersburg, 1880), 54–61.

56 Tuchkov, *Zapiski Sergeia Alekseevicha Tuchkova*, 7.

57 Ibid., 8–11.

58 Ibid., 21.

59 Engelgardt, *Zapiski Lva Nikolaevicha Engelgardta*, 3.

60 Ibid., 5.

61 Ibid., 6–8.

62 Ibid., 7.

63 Ibid., 9.

64 Ibid., 59.

65 Ibid., 95.

66 Ibid., 60.

67 Ibid., 33.

68 Ibid., 34.

69 Harold James Perkin, *The Rise of Professional Society: England Since 1880* (London: Routledge, 1989), 2–3.

70 Tregubov, "Dela davno minuvshykh let," 315.

71 Denisov, *Zapiski*, 29.

72 Ibid., 30–1.

73 Ibid., 30.

74 Aurova, *Ot kadeta do generala*, 86.

75 Glinka, *Zapiski Sergeia Nikolaevicha Glinki*, 31.

76 For many future officers, the average age at which formal education stopped was quite early indeed. On the other hand, those who entered a cadet school were commissioned at the age of eighteen or older. See Vasilii Khvostov, "Zapiski Vasiliia Semena Khvostova,"*Russkii Arkhiv* 1, no. 3 (1870): 553–4. Gudovich, who was born in 1741, also entered service as an engineer-*praporshchik* at the age of eighteen. Gudovich, 607. The statistical data compiled for the officers who fought in 1812 by Mikaberidze,

even though it belongs to a later period, still shows that the average age of officers joining the army was between seventeen and nineteen. Mikaberidze, xviii.

77 PSZ vol. 16, no. 12741, 963.
78 Starobudtsev, "Sukhoputnyi Shchiakhetnuy Kadetskii Korpus," 225.
79 Hochedlinger, "Mars Ennobled," 159.
80 Glinka, *Zapiski Sergeia Nikolaevicha Glinki*, 53.
81 Starobudtsev, "Sukhoputnyi Shchiakhetnuy Kadetskii Korpus," 224.
82 Glinka, *Zapiski Sergeia Nikolaevicha Glinki*, 72.
83 Ibid., 76.
84 Ibid., 68.
85 Ibid., 44.
86 Okenfuss, "From School Class to Social Caste," 341.
87 Starobudtsev, "Sukhoputnyi Shchiakhetnuy Kadetskii Korpus," 226.
88 Betskoi was inspired by many idea form Rousseau's educational work, Emile, when he drafted his statute. Glinka, *Zapiski Sergeia Nikolaevicha Glinki*, 34.
89 PSZ vol. 16, no. 12741, 971.
90 Ibid., 970.
91 Ibid., 973.
92 Ibid., 972.
93 Ibid., 969.
94 Ibid., 970.
95 Ibid., 973–4.
96 Ibid., 988.
97 Ibid., 975.
98 Ibid., 975.
99 Ibid., 975.
100 Ibid., 977.
101 Ibid., 982.
102 Ibid., 978.
103 Ibid., 974.
104 Ibid., 980.
105 Ibid., 987.
106 Ibid., 988.
107 Ibid., 981.
108 Ibid., 986.
109 Ibid., 988.
110 Ibid., 985.
111 Ibid., 976.
112 Ibid., 987.
113 Glinka, *Zapiski Sergeia Nikolaevicha Glinki*, 65.

114 Ibid., 46.
115 Ibid., 70.
116 Ibid., 35.
117 Somov, "Nikolia-Gabriel Leklerk," 205–6.
118 Glinka, *Zapiski Sergeia Nikolaevicha Glinki,* 67.
119 Ibid., 51.
120 Poletika, "Moi Vospominania," 306–7.
121 Glinka, *Zapiski Sergeia Nikolaevicha Glinki,* 54–5.
122 Ibid., 308.
123 Ibid., 309; V. Selivanov, "Iz davnykh vospominanii," 162–3.
124 White, *The Enlightened Soldier: Scharnhorst and the Militärische Gesellschaft in Berlin, 1801–1805,* 4–5
125 Glinka, *Zapiski Sergeia Nikolaevicha Glinki,* 72–3.
126 Glinka, "Vospominania," 46; Pyl'nev, "Rekreatsionnyi," 244.
127 Poletika, "Moi Vospominania," 310. Actually, there were two books published, one based on the writings on the cadet wall and the other based on the writings in the recreation hall. *La Murraille Parlante* (1790) and *La Salle de recreation* [...] (1791).
128 Poletika, "Moi Vospominania," 310.
129 Zhilin, *Mikhail Illarionovich Kutuzov,* 54–6. For Kutuzov's tenure as the director see Beskrovnyi, ed., *M.I. Kutuzov. Dokumenty,* vol. 1 (Moscow: Voen. izd-vo, 1950), 345–74.
130 Poletika described a sad episode: one of his close friends at the cadet school, who was repeatedly denied graduation due to his poor marks, finally committed suicide by shooting himself in the head. Poletika, "Moi Vospominania," 310–15. Selivanov wrote that when Mikhail Kutuzov became the new director of the cadet school there was a revolution of sorts and the relaxed atmosphere of the Anhalt years gave way to strict discipline and severe punishments. Selivanov was told that two cadets had killed themselves by jumping out of a window. Selivanov, "Iz davnykh vospominanii," 165. Not everybody had the same gloomy experience at the cadet corps. For example, for a contrast with Poletika's sombre tone, see the diary of the illegitimate son of Catherine the Great and Count Orlov, Aleksei Bobrinskii, who it seemed spent more time dining outside the walls of the cadet corps than studying within them. Aleksei Bobrinskii, "Dnevnik grafa Bobrinskago vedennyi v kadetskom korpuse i vo vremia puteshestviia po Rossii i za granitseiu," *Russkii Arkhiv* 3, no. 10 (1877): 116–31.
131 Poletika, "Moi Vospominania," 313.
132 Glukhov, "Zhizn'," 203.
133 Ibid., 204.
134 Pishchevich, "Zhizn' Pishchevicha," 11.

135 Ibid., 14.
136 *Zapiski Seregeia Nikolaevicha Glinki*, 64.
137 Glinka, "Vospominania," 46.
138 Aurova, *Ot kadeta do generala*, 144.
139 Benda, "Garnizonnye voennye shkoly v XVIII v.," 35; Beskrovyi, *Russkaia armiia i flot v vosemnadtsatom veke*, 457.
140 Safronova and Kravchenko, "Zakonodatelnye i normativnye akty," 175.
141 The subject of home libraries is explored in Nadezhda Aurova, "Pomeshchichi biblioteki v kontse xviii-nachale xx vv.," 53. There has not yet been a comprehensive study to ascertain which were the most important military books that were read by this generation of Russian officers and how they influenced their readers. A groundbreaking study by Ira Gruber attempted to do just that for the British army. Gruber, *Books and the British Army*. Gruber based his work on case studies of forty-two officers. For Russia during the same period, identifying the same number of detailed memoirs is a challenge.
142 Mosolov, "Zapiski," 124.
143 Ibid., 126.
144 Ibid., 127. For a brief description of another regimental schooling, see Ivan Andreev, "Domovaia letopis' Andreeva, po rody ikh, pisannaia kapitanom Ivanom Andreevym v 1789 dogu," *Chtenia v Imperatorskom Obshchestve Istorii i Drevnostei Rossiiskikh* 5, no. 5 (1870): 74.
145 Vinskii, 27.
146 Duffy, *Russia's Military Way to the West*, 144.
147 Aurova, *Ot kadeta do generala*, 365.
148 Starkey, *War in the Age of Enlightenment*, 87.
149 Fedyukin, "Learning to Be Nobles," argued that during Anna's reign the government undertook a systematic policy to fashion a modern, Westernized nobility out of the Petrine elite. Even after Peter's reign the majority of nobles were not interested in opportunities for education offered by the government, especially in the Noble Cadet Corps, founded by Anna in 1731. However, by the time of Catherine II this situation has changed. As memoirs show, parents began to actively push their children to acquire wide and specialized knowledge.
150 Raeff, *Origins of the Russian Intelligentsia*, 131; Aurova, *Ot kadeta do generala*, 237.
151 Ibid., 203.
152 For example see Dennis E. Showalter, ""No Officer Rather Than a Bad Officer': Officer Selection and Education in the Prussian/German Army, 1715–1945," in Kennedy and Neilson, eds., *Military Education Past, Present, and Future*, 35–61.
153 Leonov and Ulianov, *Reguliarnaia Pekhota*, 132.

2 Favourites and Professionals

1 Not everyone agrees. Jay Smith, for example, criticizes "the long-established tendency to regard merit and meritocracy as direct products of the Enlightenment." He sees origins of merit in France in the noble culture of the seventeenth century. Smith, *The Culture of Merit*, 263.

2 Duffy, *The Military Experience*, 65. See, for instance, Ligne, *Mélanges militaires*, 127.

3 Blaufarb, *The French Army*, 196.

4 Pichichero, *The Military Enlightenment*, 10–11.

5 David D. Bien, "The Army in the French Enlightenment," 97.

6 Hochedlinger, "Mars Ennobled," 162.

7 Houlding, *Fit for Service: Training of the British Army, 1715–1795*, 106.

8 Bakunina, "Persidskii pokhod v 1796 godu," 357.

9 Lanzheron, "Russkaia armiia v god smerti Ekateriny II," 186.

10 Levin, "Chinoproizvodstvo v Rossii XV-nachala XX vv," esp. chapter 2.2. For the military perspective see, N. Glinoetzkii, "Istoricheskii ocherk razvitiia ofitserskih chinov i sistema chinoproizvodstva v Russkoi armii," in Efermov, ed., *Offitserskii Korpus Russkoi Armii*, 13–20.

11 *Ustav Voinskii* (1716).

12 James Hassel argues that the Table of Ranks, the goal of which was to establish merit rather than birth for the award of positions, had failed because commoners were still largely excluded from important posts. However, this argument ignores the role of merit within the noble estate as whole. Hassel, "Implementation of the Russian Table of Ranks," 294. For the evolution of the concept, see Bennet, "Evolution of the Meaning of Chin."

13 Hughes, *Russia in the Age of Peter the Great*, 184; Keep, *Soldiers of the Tsar*, 124; Glinoetzkii in Efermov, ed., *Offitserskii Korpus Russkoi Armii*, 14.

14 The data for the table have been collected from RGADA, f. 20, op. 1. d. 219, ch. 1, l. 46 and 57–71; and ch. 11, l. 1. The percentages have been rounded.

15 RGADA, f. 20, op. 1, d. 219, ch. 11, l. 1.

16 RGVIA, f. 52, op. 1/194, d. 59, ch. I, l. 116.

17 RGVIA, f. 52, op. 1/194, d. 250, l. 114–16.

18 RGVIA, f. 53, op. 1/194, d. 15, l. 455. The stamp was used to verify the validity of the documents. PSZ vol. 13, no. 9690; vol. 15, no. 10952; and vol. 23, no. 17355. An example of a complete document package is the one submitted by the Hussar Lieutenant-Colonel Leshievich in 1771. His package consisted of a petition letter asking for a promotion, a brief summary of his service record based on his *formuliarnyi spisok*, and three short *atestaty*: the first letter was written by Quartermaster-General

Vokhovskii, the second by Major-General Zorich, and the third by Major-General Shcherbinin. All three attested to Leshievich's bravery, good leadership skills, and unwavering service to the empire. RGVIA, f. 52, op. 1/194, d. 59. ch. 1, l. 7–9. The high military ranks of the referees were impressive and should have helped Leshievich receive his promotion. Zorich was Catherine's favourite, which suggests that Leshievich may have been a member of his patronage network.

19 Dixon, *The Modernization of Russia*, 12.
20 *Ustav Voinskii* (1776) and *Artikul Voinskii* (1777). For the Instructions, see PSZ, vol. 16, no. 12289, vol. 22, no. 16586, and vol. 17, no. 12543, as well as *Instruktsiia Polkovichiia* (1764). Its authors included Count Razumovskii, Prince Alexander Golitsyn, Count Zakhar Chernyshev, Petr Panin, Kirill Volkonskii, Vasilii Suvorov, the father of the famous Aleksandr Suvorov, and Baron Thomas von Diz. Many of them were veterans of the Seven Years' War.
21 Floyd, "State Service," 65. Floyd covered the eighteenth century only as a background; however, his dissertation traces venues of ennoblement and examines the dilemma faced by successive rulers trying to keep ennoblement open to talented commoners. Ennoblement was a great incentive for hard work and was in the interests of state; but the old nobility pressured the government to close these channels. Floyd argues that it was only during the reign of Nicholas I that the assault on ennoblement began.
22 Floyd, "State Service," 64. See also Volkov, *Russkii ofitserskii korpus*, 53.
23 Petro, *Russkaia Voennaia Sila*, 157.
24 Volkov, *Russkii ofitserskii korpus*, 56.
25 Glinoetskii, *Istoriia Russkogo general'nogo shtaba*, 275; Menning Bruce, "Paul I and Catherine II's Military Legacy," in Kagan and Higham, eds., *The Military History of Tsarist Russia*, 80. By 1764 the War College was actively recruiting foreigners to plug holes in the officer corps and, by 1784, due to an ongoing shortage of officers, the War College was resorting to recruiting merchants and low-ranking civilians to serve as officers.
26 Catherine II, *Sochineniia Ekateriny II*, vol. 12, 617.
27 Münnich, "Zapiska."
28 RGADA, f. 16, op. 1, d. 246, l. 60–60ob.
29 RGADA, f. 16, op. 1, d. 249, l. 306.
30 Ibid., l. 319.
31 Anon., *Istoricheskie rasskazy i ankedoty*, 362–3.
32 "Rumiantsev to Catherine, 20 June, 1770," in Fortunatov, ed. *P.A. Rumiantsev*, vol. 2, 315.
33 RGVIA, f. 24, op. 1, d. 249, l. 39.
34 Petr Rumiantsev, "Obriad Sluzhby," in Goncharov, ed., 113.
35 Aleksandr Mikhailovich Turgenev, "Zapiski," RGB OR, f. 261, k. 19, l. 4.

36 Engelgardt, *Zapiski L'va Nikolaevicha Engelgardta*, 93.
37 "Rumiantsev to Catherine, 12 July, 1770," in Fortunatov, ed. *P.A. Rumiantsev*, vol. 2, 336. In addition to those recommended by Rumiantsev, nineteen other people received the Order of St George of various classes, including Rumiantsev himself. "War College to Rumiantsev, 30 July 1770," in Fortunatov, vol. II, 348 and "List of bestowed military order ...," ibid., 349.
38 "Rumiantsev to Catherine, 12 July, 1770," ibid., 338.
39 "Rumiantsev to Catherine, 10 June 1774," ibid., 748. For example, General Mikhail Kaminski wrote to Rumiantsev that in recognition of their special efforts (*viashchim trudam*), Colonels Ilovaiskii and Ustinov were worthy of "a golden medal for their zealous service."
40 "Rumiantsev to Catherine, 23 August, 1769," ibid., 130.
41 Madariaga, *Russia in the Age of Catherine the Great*, 344.
42 RGVIA, f. 52, op. 2, d. 16, l. 39.
43 Ibid., l. 43.
44 "Potemkin to Catherine, 24 June 1791," in Lopatin, ed., *Ekaterina II i G.A. Potemkin*, 458.
45 RGVIA, f. 52, op. 1/194, d. 59, ch. I, l. 49.
46 RGVIA, f. 52, op. 1/194, d. 59, ch. I, l. 34.
47 Ibid., l. 115. The signature is unintelligible, so it is difficult to ascertain who the referee was in this case.
48 For example, Brigadier Demedem's *atestat* for one of his lieutenants was very short, just stating the dates the man was under his command. Clearly, the lieutenant was not well-known to the brigadier. Ibid., l. 91. In another instance, Major Ivan Vriukov wrote a very short *atestat* to one of his relatively low-ranking Cossacks on 21 May 1774. Ibid., l. 1.
49 For example RGVIA, f. 52, op. 1/194, d. 571. ch. II, l. 49 (17 December 1788).
50 For instance RGVIA, f. 52, op. 1/194, d. 250, l. 98ob. Fedor Denisov, a Cossack chieftain, who had already received the Order of St George, was recommended again for another award, this time the Order of St Vladimir. The recommendation was based on the fact that Denisov had brought his Cossack regiments serving in the Tauride region under discipline. The methods by which Denisov had done so were left to Potemkin's imagination. Whatever the Cossack did, "the local population has been so content that they did not have any complaint about his command." The document did not have a date, but was most likely written between 1777 and 1785.
51 RGVIA, f. 52, op. 1/194, d. 571.ch. II, l. 9.
52 "Almost all of the people in my volunteer cohort received promotions except the following: Lieutenant Ivan Batyst-Bozhika; Ensign Pantelei Iakov Frandzha, and Bairaktar Kostia Fila, who from the beginning of the current war with the Turks worked for me and were part of the Ochakov campaign and participated in all the battles." Ibid.

53 RGVIA, f. 52, op. 1/194, d. 130, l. 9–9ob.

54 Ibid., l. 93–7ob. The seven recommendation letters, four of them quite short, were written by Lieutenant-General Demedem, Major-General Aleksei Stupishyn, Major-General Nikolai Potatov, Major-General Fedor Faritsanz, Colonel Fedor Parners, Colonel Ivan Shtenberg, and a local chief (*voevoda*) by the name of Khamzin. An impressive list of referees for a humble translator.

55 RGADA, f. 16, op. 1, d. 246, l. 521–2ob.

56 Daniel Roche, *France in the Enlightenment* (Cambridge, MA: Harvard University Press, 1998), 306.

57 Many laws governed the process of petitioning in general, and the monarch in particular. All Russian nobles had the right to petition. Catherine had created a legal framework for the process of petitioning her directly. See PSZ, vol. 16, no. 11590, no. 11868.

58 RGADA, f. 16, op. 1, d. 249, l. 193.

59 RGVIA, f. 52, op. 1/194, d. 59, ch. I, l. 168.

60 RGVIA, f. 52, op. 1/194, d. 59, ch. I, l. 68–8ob (18 November 1774) The left margin of the document has crumbled away, and parts of the letter are unintelligible.

61 Prozorovskii, *Zapiski General-Feldmarshala*, 89.

62 Glinoetzkii, in Efermov, ed., *Offitserskii Korpus Russkoi Armii*, 15.

63 RGVIA, f. 52, op. 1/194, d. 59, ch.I, l. 3. I was unable to find the law Leontiev was referring to in PSZ.

64 Ibid., l. 46.

65 RGADA, f. 16, op. 1, d. 246, l. 528–528ob (14 December 1792).

66 RGVIA, f. 52, op. 1/194, d. 59, ch. I, l. 50.

67 Blaufarb, *The French Army*, 67; Hochedlinger, "Mars Ennobled," 149.

68 Hughes, *Russia in the Age of Peter the Great*, 182–3; Keep, *Soldiers of the Tsar*, 96–7.

69 Ibid., 119.

70 Volkov, *Russkii ofitserskii korpus*, 74.

71 RGVIA, f. 53, op. 1/194, d. 1, l. 411. The year is unclear/undated but most likely it was written in 1762, as it is in the same *sviazka* as other documents from that year.

72 PSZ, vol. 16, no. 12289, 672.

73 Ibid., 673.

74 RGVIA f. 52, op. 1/194, d. 59. ch. 1, l. 7–9.

75 RGADA f. 20, op. 1, d. 2771, l. 369.

76 RGVIA, f. 52, op. 1/194, d. 250, l. 231–231ob.

77 Ibid., l. 86.

78 RGVIA, f. 52, op. 2, d. 16, l. 9. 23 January 1790. Actual Privy Councillor was a civil service rank equivalent to full general in army.

79 Suvorov participated in six wars: the Seven Years' War (1756–63), the Polish Civil War (1768–76), the First Turkish War (1768–74), the Second

Turkish War (1787–92), the Second Polish War (1793–94), and the War of the Second Coalition (1798–1800).

80 Some have argued that Suvurov's promotion was slow due to machinations at court. His was not the only slow one, though it is perhaps the best known. For another example, see the note attached to the biography of Petr Panin, "Zapiska o ne shchastlivom prodolzhenii sluzhby generala Grafa Panina v sravnenii ego sverstnikov," which also sheds light on the "unfairness" of the seniority system. Geisman and Dubovskoi, *Graf Petr Ivanovich Panin*, 115–19.

81 "Potemkin to Catherine, 16 September 1787," in Lopatin, ed., *Ekaterina II i G.A. Potemkin*, 230.

82 "Potemkin to Catherine, 6 October 1787," in ibid., 239. For more detailed correspondence about the Battle of Kinburn, see Maslovskii, *Pis'ma i bumagi A. V. Suvorova*. For Suvorov's battle report with recommendations of officers to Potemkin, see page 51.

83 "Catherine to Potemkin, 16 October 1787," in Lopatin, ed., *Ekaterina II i G.A. Potemkin*, 342.

84 PSZ, vol. 18, no. 13387.

85 In 2000 the Russian president Vladimir Putin resurrected the order by a special decree.

86 "Catherine to Suvorov, 30 July 1773," in Meshcheriakov, ed., *A.V. Suvorov*, vol. 1, 677.

87 "Potemkin to Catherine, 1 November 1787," in Lopatin, ed., *Ekaterina II i G.A. Potemkin*, 246–7.

88 Longworth, *The Art of Victory*, 144; "Suvorov to Potemkin, 1 October 1787," Meshcheriakov, ed., *A.V. Suvorov*, vol. 2, 339; and "Suvorov to Tekelli, 1 February 1788," in Korobkov, ed., *Feldmarshal Rumiantsev*, 157.

89 Glinka, *Russkie anekdoty*, vol. 3, 104–5.

90 RGVIA, f. 196, op. 1, d. 1, l. 1.

91 RGVIA, f. 196, op. 1, d. 2, l. 1–1ob.

92 "War College to Rumiantsev, 2 August, 1770," in Fortunatov, ed. *P.A. Rumiantsev*, vol. 2, 359.

93 "Catherine to Rumiantsev, 27 August 1770," ibid., 377.

94 RGADA, f. 16, op. 1, d. 249, l. 430–1ob.

95 For Panin's efforts during the Pugachev rebellion, see Geisman and Dubovskoi, *Count Peter Ivanovich Panin*, 58–87.

96 RGADA, f. 16, op. 1, d. 249, l. 432ob.

97 "Catherine to Potemkin, 9 November 1787," in Lopatin, ed., *Ekaterina II i G.A. Potemkin* 252.

98 In an attempt to remove Rumiantsev from the seat of military power, and from his independent military command in Ukraine, Potemkin cleverly proceeded to undermine the former's supply system. As Jeanne de

Cerenville explained, Potemkin "kept the army of the Ukraine in want of the most necessary articles; and yet, having as president of the council of war the direction of all operations, he expected of the Marshal the performance of movements which required a much larger and better equipped army than the one he had command of." Rumiantsev grew "weary of such glaring injustices" and eventually "solicited his recall," which was promptly granted to him from St Petersburg. Cerenville, *Memoirs of the Life of Prince Potemkin*, 205; Aksan, "The One-Eyed Fighting the Blind"; LeDonne, "Geopolitics, Logistics, and Grain."

99 When Potemkin died, General Anshef Mikhail Kakhovskii wrote a detailed report about the state in which he had left the army. There were problems, but interestingly enough, the picture was not as bleak as some contemporaries and secondary sources make it look. See the whole file on this matter in RGADA, f. 20, op. 1, d. 328.

100 "Suvorov to Potemkin, 11 September 1789," in Meshcheriakov, ed., *A.V. Suvorov*, vol. 2, 476–82; Beskrovnyi, *Russkaia armiia i flot v vosemnadtsatom veke*, 544–50; Blease, *Suvorof*, 99–108. Before Suvorov received the title of count, the war title of Rymnikskii, and the Order of St George 1st class, he of course wrote a letter complaining to Potemkin about how disappointed he was that his efforts were never sufficiently rewarded. Using highly allegorical language and comparing himself to half the generals of ancient Rome and Greece, as well as to famous commanders of contemporary Europe, Suvorov concluded: "Open the road to my foolhardiness (*prostodushiiu*), I shall be twice better," meaning that he would serve twice as hard if he felt that his efforts were being commensurately rewarded. "Suvorov to Potemkin, 18 September 1789," in Meshcheriakov, ed., *A.V. Suvorov*, vol. 2, 486. The same day, Catherine sent Suvorov her letter informing him of his new awards. "Catherine to Suvorov, 18 September 1789," ibid., 492.

101 RGADA, f. 16, op. 1, d. 246, l. 467–68ob.

102 For example, *Zhurnal voennykh deistvii armii eia Imperatorskago Velichestva, 1769–1771* (St Petersburg: Gosudarstvennaia Voennaia Kollegiia, 1772), 564–6, 571.

103 *Arkhiv Kniazia Vorontsova*, vol. 12, 144–5.

104 For eyewitness accounts of the siege, which saw massacres on both sides, see Kipinskii, "Osada Varshavy v 1794 Gody,"3, nos. 1 (1909), 2 (1909), 3 (1909), and 4 (1909). See also Bulgarin, *Vospominaniia*, 681–94. For contemporary coverage, see, for example, "Particulars of the Storming Of Praga." For a military analysis, see Orlov, *Shturm Pragi Suvorovym v 1794 godu*.

105 RGVIA, f. 295, op. 1, d. 1, l. 1. Compare this to the letter Catherine wrote to Rumiantsev congratulating him for his victory at the Battle of Larga in 1770 and rewarding him with the Order of St George, 1st Class. "Catherine to Rumiantsev, 27 July 1770," in Fortunatov,

ed., *P.A. Rumiantsev*, vol. 2, 349. In a symbolic gesture in the spirit of Potemkin, she sent Rumiantsev her Star of St George, explaining that ostensibly the gold workers in Moldavia were scarce and therefore they would not be able to produce the award locally.

106 Engelgardt, 121–2. In the end, however, for that particular battle, Engelgardt would go home empty handed.

107 Quoted in Mikhail Velizhev, "The Political Language of the Europeanized Military Elite in the Early Nineteenth Century: The Unpublished Diary and letters of Vasilii Viazemskii," in Schönle, Zorin, and Evstratov, eds., *The Europeanized Elite in Russia*, 181.

108 As Keep points out, for example, in the eighteenth century genealogical seniority still could play a role in promotions. Keep, *Soldiers of the Tsar*, 124–5.

109 Smith, *The Culture of Merit*, 227.

110 Blaufarb, *The French Army*, 5.

111 I gained this insight from Brett D. Steele, "Military 'Progress' and the Newtonian Science in the Age of Enlightenment," in Brett D. Steele and Tamera Dorland, eds., *The Heirs of Archimedes: Science and the Art of War Through the Age of Enlightenment* (Cambridge, MA: MIT Press, 2005), 379.

112 See RGADA, f. 20, op. 1, d. 277, l. 369, for the process of determining the merit of candidates for the Order of St. George by the Orders Committee (*kavalerskoi Dumy*), the importance it attached to letters of recommendation, and how the letters of recommendation were cross-referenced with reports from commanders-in-chief and other documents.

113 Feld, "Middle-Class Society."

114 This seems to support the broader point suggested by John LeDonne in his study of power structures in eighteenth-century Russia. There was regular influx of fresh blood into the army and into the nobility in general, which both rejuvenated the nobility and sustained the political regime. LeDonne, *Absolutism and Ruling Class*, 11–12.

3 "We must distinguish the military establishment ..."

1 Polovtsov, *Russkii biograficheskii slovar'*, vol. 16, 463–72.

2 Dmitriev-Mamonov, *Pravila*, 5.

3 Liutov, *Kniga v Russkoi Armii*, 20.

4 Bradley, "Subjects into Citizens"; Engelstein, "The Dream of Civil Society in Tsarist Russia"; Smith, *Working the Rough Stone*, 61–86.

5 Marker, *Publishing, Printing*, 78.

6 *Pekhotnyi Stroevoi Ustav* (1763); *Ustav Voinskii o Konnoi Ekzertsitsii* (1763); *Instruktsiia Polkovnichia* (1764); *Instruktsiia Pekhotnogo Polka Polkovniku* (1764); *Instruktsiia Konnogo Polka Polkovniku* (1766); *Ob Obuchenii Egerskogo*

Korpusa (1764); *Dopolnitelnye Glavy k Generalnomu Ustavu o Polevoi Sluzhbe* (1765); *Garnizonyi Ustav* (1766).

7 Oelsnitz, *Ofitserskie Uprazhneniia* (1777); Anglesi, Sovety voennago cheloveka synu svoemu; Fredrick II, *Tainoe nastavlenie*.

8 *Ustav ratnykh, pushechnykh i drugikh del* (1777).

9 Pichichero, *The Military Enlightenment*, 2.

10 Fuks, Anekdoty Kniazia Italianskogo, 41; Rastopchin, "Anekdoty grafa," 249.

11 Rogulin, *"Polkovoe uchrezhdenie,"* 171.

12 Suvorov, "Polkovoe Ucherezhdenie," in Goncharov, ed., 242.

13 Ibid.

14 Keep, *Soldiers of the Tsar*, 123–8; Hughes, *Russia in the Age of Peter the Great*, 74–9.

15 Suvorov, "Polkovoe uchrezhdenie," in Goncharov, ed., 246.

16 "Every officer and every lower commander will realize," he wrote, "that when he holds his entire command in a strict, correct and decent way, what glory he will earn for himself and for the regiment in general." Conversely, any laxness in executing his duty brought the ignobility of demotion to the officer and shame to his regiment. Ibid., 209–10.

17 Ibid., 285. Interestingly, Suvorov's analogy was not that different, at least in literary terms, from the one written down by his future oppressor Emperor Paul, who sketched out his own observations in 1774 about the military and the state. RGADA, f. 20, op. 1, d. 276, l. 2ob. See also David Ransel, "An Ambivalent Legacy: The Education of Grand Duke Paul," in Ragsdale, ed., *Paul I*, 7–9.

18 Shitkov, *Blagodarstvo v general'skom mundire*, 5–8.

19 Kiril Tatarnikov suggests that the manual was once part of a collection of at least six documents, because the top of the manuscript contains the letter F. This suggests it was once part of a series, of which manuscripts A, B, C, D, and E have been lost. Tatarnikov, ed., *Stroevye Ustavy*, vol. 1, 18.

20 Timofei Tutolmin, "Obriad Sluzhbi Sumskogo gusarskogo polku," in ibid., vol. 2, 174–5.

21 Rogulin, *Polkovoe uchrezhdenie,"* 97–105.

22 "A vot nachto eshche est' nizhnii Ofitser, / Chtob chesti zavsegda dovat' on vsem primer. / Kak bratu starshemu est' stydno byt negodnym, / Tak unter -officer byt' dolzhen est' dostoinym." Dmitriev-Mamonov, *Epistola*, 5.

23 "Voina est' dvukh rodov, odin rod nastupat', / Drugoi est' vid voiny, sebia oboroniat'. / Odna strana vsegda imeet spravedlivost', / Drugai ail' koryst', il' vredu gordelivost'." Ibid., 8.

24 "Odnako pritchi te ne voisku rasbirat', / Nam delo lish itti srazhatsia, pobivat'." Ibid.

25 "Veliko rzhanie premnozhestva konei, / Komandy krepkoi glas, ston rannenykh liudei. / Poslednii inogda dushoi vsei umoliaiut, / Chtob zhizn'

im prekratit', v kotoroi stol' stradaiut... Vse pole mertvymi pokryto est' telami, / Krov' s mozgom mezhdu ikh techet vezde rekami." Ibid.

26 Ibid., 19.

27 "V pokoe sidia vam togo ne mozhno zret', / Kakoi velikoi trud soldat dolzhen imet', / Kotoriu est' kak vy s zhivoiu ze dushoiu, / Vy spite, on idet s vsei tiagostiu svoeiu." Ibid., 15.

28 Pichichero, *The Military Enlightenment*, 117–19.

29 Bruce Menning, "G.A. Potemkin and A. I. Chernyshev: Two Dimensions of Reform and Russia's Military Frontier," in Schimmelpennick and Menning, eds., *Reforming the Tsar's Army*, 279–280.

30 "Potemkin to Suvorov, 18 December 1788," in Maslovskii, *Zapiski po Istorii Voennago Iskusstva v Rosii*, 23.

31 Ibid., 24.

32 RGVIA f. 52, op. 1, d. 586, ch. 1, l. 256–66.

33 Dmitriev-Mamonov, *Pravila*, 29.

34 Ibid., 6.

35 Ibid., 20–1.

36 Ibid., 40.

37 Pigarev, *Soldat polkovodets*, 127–8.

38 Suvorov, *Nauka pobezhdat'*, 22.

39 Baiov, *Natsional'nyia cherty russkago voennago iskusstva*, 15; and Fuller, *Strategy and Power in Russia*, 303; Suvorov, *Nauka pobezhdat'* (1980), 13.

40 Ibid., 29.

41 RGVIA f. 7, op. 2, d. 3119, l. 6.

42 Gat, *The Origins of Military Thought*, 71–2.

43 Polovtsov, *Russkii biograficheskii slovar'*, vol. 16, 155–6.

44 Rzhevskii, *Sochinenie*, v.

45 Ibid., vi.

46 Ibid. John Randolph has argued that by the beginning of the nineteenth century an idea was emerging among the Russian nobility that one could continue to serve the fatherland in retirement in the countryside. Randolph, *The House in the Garden*, 272–3.

47 Rzhevskii, *Sochinenie*, i.

48 Ibid., 28. This call for more professional solidarity echoed the one in France. Christy Pichichero, "Le Soldat Sensible: Military Psychology and Social Egalitarianism in the Enlightenment French Army," *French Historical Studies* 31, no. 4 (October 2008): 557.

49 Walicki, *A History of Russian Thought*, 40.

50 Petr Rumiantsev, "Obriad Sluzhby," in Goncharev, ed., 136, 138.

51 "Doklad voennoi kollegii Ekaterine II o tselesoobraznosti primeneniia 'Obriada sluzhby' P.A. Rumiantseva kak obshchearmeiskogo ustava, 29 sentiabria 1776," in Goncharov, ed., 139.

52 Meiendorf, *Opyt nekotorykh rasuzhdenii*, 172.
53 Ibid., 87.
54 Ibid., 5.
55 Ibid., 8.
56 Rzhevskii, *Nastavlenie kakim obrazom*, 6.
57 Ibid., 14.
58 Ibid., 11.
59 Ibid., 9.
60 Ibid., 16–17.
61 Ibid., 71.
62 Ibid., 4.
63 Viazemskii, "Zapiska Voennaia, 1774," 3.
64 Ibid., 5.
65 Ibid.
66 Houlding, *Fit for Service: Training of the British Army, 1715–1795*, 258.
67 Ibid., 6.
68 Ibid., 19.
69 Rzhevskii, "Raznye Zamichaniia."
70 Ibid., 8.
71 Pichichero, "Le Soldat Sensible," 568.
72 Meiendorf, *Opyt nekotorykh rasuzhdenii*, 14.
73 Ibid., 15.
74 Ibid., 89.
75 Vorontsov, "Instruktsiia Rotnym Kommandiram," 33.
76 Rumiantsev, "Mysl'," in Goncharov, ed. 99.
77 Myerly, *British Military Spectacle*, 124.
78 Bolotov, *Zhizn' i Prikliucheniia*, vol. 1, 76–7.
79 Engelgardt, *Zapiski*, 6.
80 Mosolov, "Zapiski," 126.
81 Petrov et al., eds. *1812*, 116.
82 Rumiantsev, "Mysl'," in Goncharov, ed., 116.
83 Dmitriev-Mamonov, *Pravila*, 10.
84 Ibid., 11.
85 Grigorii Potemkin, "Ob odezhde i vooruzhenii voisk," in Tatarnikov, ed.,
    Materialy po istorii russkogo, 241.
86 Ibid. and RGVIA, f. 2, op. 13, d. 86, l. 122–3.
87 Wishon, *German Forces and the British Army: Interactions and Perceptions,
    1742–1815*, 23 and 17.
88 Conway, *War, State, and Society in Mid-Eighteenth-Century Britain and
    Ireland*, 297.
89 Frederick the Great, "The Instruction of Frederick the Great for his
    general, 1747," in Phillips, ed., *The Roots of Strategy*, 314.

90 Cited in Duffy, *Russia's Military Way to the West*, 169.
91 Meiendorf, *Opyt nekotorykh rasuzhdenii*, xi.
92 Dixon, *The Modernization of Russia*, 183.
93 Rumiantsev, "Mysl'," in Goncharov, ed., 116.
94 Menning, "Chapter 4: The Imperial Russian Army, 1725–1796," in Kagan and Higham, eds., *The Military History of Tsarist Russia*, 75. Catherine's management of the military could also have had something to do with her views of governance more broadly, and her conscious construction of discourses of a matriarchy, whose "authority did not undermine traditional social hierarchies." This strategy may have helped Catherine legitimize her authority. Ivleva, "Catherine as Female Ruler," 27.
95 "Catherine to Potemkin, 29 August 1787," in Lopatin, ed., 226; O. I. Eliseeva, ""Liubeznui moi pitomets." Ekaterina II i G. A. Potemkin v gody vtoroi russko-turetskoi voiny," *Otechestvennaia Istoria* 5 (1997): 25–39.
96 "Potemkin to Catherine, 16 September 1787," Lopatin, ed., *Ekaterina II i G.A. Potemkin*, 230; "Catherine to Potemkin, 24 September 1787," ibid., 234.
97 Brian L. Davies, *The Russo-Turkish War, 1768–1774: Catherine II and the Ottoman Empire* (London: Bloomsbury, 2016), 244.
98 Whittaker, *Russian Monarchy*. Whittaker counted about 250 authors who participated in the practice of political dialogue with the Russian autocrats over the span of the entire eighteenth century, publishing more than 500 works. However, military works were largely ignored in this group of texts.
99 Suvorov, "Plan, poddanyi Suvorovym," 163.
100 Jean-Jacques Rousseau, *The Social Contract* (1762) (London: Penguin Books, 2004), 59.
101 Viazemskii, "Zapiska Voennaia, 1774," 4.
102 Volyntsov, *Artilleriiskiia predlozhenii*, v–vi.
103 Rumiantsev, "Mysl'," in Goncharov, ed., 99.
104 Ibid., 114.
105 Ibid., 103–4.
106 RGADA f.1453, op. 1, d.400, 183ob. There is no date on the document, but since Samoilov mentioned Catherine's edict from 1793, I presume it was written either the same year or shortly thereafter.
107 Ibid., 18.
108 Ibid., 28.
109 For example, we know from Adrian Denisov's memoirs that he wrote an instruction for his regiment when he was a young colonel, but it has been lost. Denisov, *Zapiski donskogo atamana*, 40. We also know that Lieutenant-Colonel Dibich was also composing a military manual in his retirement, which was mentioned in private correspondence. RGADA, f. 7, op. 2, d. 3355, l. 4. I did not find this document in Dibich's *delo*, and I was unable

to locate it elsewhere. Looking for a personal *fond* under the name of Dibich likewise produced no results.

110 Liutov, "Russkaia voennaia kniga," 65.
111 Pishchevich, "Zhizn' Pishchevicha," 34; Engelgardt, *Zapiski*, 59.
112 Rogger, *National Consciousness in Eighteenth-Century Russia*, 258.
113 Geoffrey Hosking, *Russia: People and Empire* (Cambridge, MA: Harvard University Press, 1997), 190.
114 Goncharov, ed. *Russkaia voennaia mysl'*, 5; Liutov, *Kniga v Russkoi Armii*, 26. A.V. Kutishchev, *Armiia Petra velikogo. Evropeiskii analog ili otechestvennaia samobytnost'*. (Moscow: Kompaniia Sputnik, 2006), 61–123.
115 Gat, *The Origins of Military Thought*, ch. 2; Starkey, *War in the Age of the Enlightenment*, 69–71; Duffy, *The Military Experience*, 74–84.

4 "Always remember he is not a peasant, but a soldier"

1 Lanzheron, "Russkaia armia v god smerti Ekateriny II," 160; Kamenskii, *Deviatyi vek na sluzhbe Rossii*, 28–56.
2 Officers were almost always nobles, and the nobility were freed from physical punishment, such as flogging. Schrader, *Languages of the Lash*, 12; Keep, "No Gauntlet for Gentlemen"; Vish, "Telesnye nakazaniia," 113–24.
3 Berkovich, *Motivation in War*, 228; Berkovich, "Discipline and Control," 114.
4 Keep, "The Origins of Russian Militarism," 5–15; Pipes, "Militarism and the Soviet State," 1–4.
5 Pinter, "The Burden of Defense in Imperial Russia," 256.
6 Elise Wirtschafter disagrees with this assessment. Wirtschafter, "Military Service and Social Hierarchy: the View from Eighteenth-Century Russian Theatre," in Lohr and Poe, eds., *The Military and Society in Russia*, 223.
7 Hartley, *Russia: 1762–1825*, 209–11. John Keep disagreed. Keep, "The Military Style of the Romanov Rulers," *War and Society* 1, no. 2 (1983): 61–84.
8 Wirtschafter, *From Serf to Russian Soldier*, xiv.
9 Ibid., 150.
10 PSZ, vol. 16, no. 12289, 681–3.
11 "Potemkin to Nashchokin, 18 June 1788," in Dubrovnik, *A.V. Suvorov*, 113.
12 *Artikul Voinskii* (1777), 14, 20, 46; Wirtschafter, *From Serf to Russian Soldier*, 119.
13 PSZ, vol. 16, no. 12289, 681.
14 Suvorov, "Polkovoe Ucherizhdenie," in Goncharov, ed., 209–10.
15 Ibid., 211.
16 Ibid., 273–4.
17 Ibid., 273–4.
18 "Poslushaite druz'ia, poslushaite o deti, / Vam dolzno vsem menia, otsa vmesto imieti, / Mne dolzhno vas liubit kak istinnykh detei," Dmitriev-Mamonov, *Epistola*, 3–4.

19 "Tak vertezh mne vy v tom, luibeznye o deti! / Chto shchiastie v tom
   moe, chtob zdravykh vas imeti. / A chtob vas legkostiu i pishcheiu
   snabdit', / Ia dolzhen zavsegda peshchis o tom i mnit'." Ibid., 3.

20 For example, the Dutch army, which pioneered some of the most
   draconian punishments for soldiers, recognized that soldiers and officers
   were bound by a social contact of sorts. If captains did not "hold to
   their end of the bargain," the soldiers in theory had the right to desert.
   Pepijn Brandon, "'The Privilege of Using Their Legs': Leaving the Dutch
   Army in the Eighteenth Century," in *Desertion in the Early Modern World:
   A Comparative History*, ed. Matthias van Rossum and Jeanette Kamp, 85.

21 Walicki, *A History of Russian Thought*, 39.

22 "Vam dolzhno vse chiny, kotory starei vas, / Toliko pochitat, kak
   oko vashykh glaz. / Oni lish durakam i slabym strakh byvaiut, / No
   chestnykh vsekh oni i sami pochitaiut." Dmitriev-Mamonov, *Epistola*, 4.

23 Meiendorf, *Opyt nekotorykh rasuzhdenii*, 170–1.

24 Keep, *Soldiers of the Tsar*, 238.

25 Blanning, *Culture of Power and the Power of Culture*, 431.

26 Vorontsov, "Instruktsiia Rotnym Kommandiram," 34.

27 Ibid.

28 Keep, *Soldiers of the Tsar*, 206.

29 Melton, "Enlightened Seigniorialism," 679.

30 Writing in 1762, Major Petr Svistunov, from the Cadet Corps, presented
   a rather dry instruction for training. Petr Svistunov, *Stroevoi Ustav
   Pekhotnago Polku*, 22–9. Suvorov clearly wanted to challenge and change
   such practices.

31 Suvorov, "Polkovoe Ucherizhdenie," in Goncharov, ed., 192. See also
   V.V. Kurasov, "Suvorovskie printsipy obucheniia i vospitaniia voisk," in
   A.V. Suvorov. Iz materialov, opublikovannykh v sviazi 150-letiem so dnia smerti
   (Moscow: Voennoe Izdatel'stvo, 1951).

32 Vorontsov, "Instruktsiia Rotnym Kommandiram," 39.

33 Viazemskii, "Zapiska Voennaia," 8.

34 Dmitriev-Mamonov, *Pravila*, 36.

35 "Potemkin to Krechetnikov, 30 June 1790," in Dubrovnik, *A.V. Suvorov*, 113.

36 Keep, *Soldiers of the Tsar*, 155.

37 Kutuzov, *Primechaniia*, 4.

38 Ibid., 41.

39 "Potemkin to Talyzin, 31 December 1782," in Dubrovnik, *A.V. Suvorov*, 111.

40 "Potemkin to Nassau, 12 April 1788," in ibid., 112.

41 "Potemkin to Selevin, 16 June 1788," in ibid., 113.

42 Quoted in Heuser, *Strategy Makers*, 144.

43 Frederick II, "The Instruction of Frederick the Great for his Generals,
   1747," in Phillips, ed., *The Roots of Strategy*, 348.

44 DeLanda, *War in the Age of Intelligent Machines*, 65–6.

45 Duffy, *The Army of Frederick the Great*, 62.

46 "Potemkin to Nashchokin, 18 June 1788," in Dubrovnik, *A.V. Suvorov*, 113.

47 Maurice de Saxe, "My Reveries Upon the Art of War," in Phillips, ed., *The Roots of Strategy*, 201.

48 Wirtschafter, *Religion and Enlightenment*, 130.

49 Werth, *The Tsar's Foreign Faiths*, 3–4. See also Robert Crews, "Empire and the Confessional State: Islam and Religious Politics in Nineteenth-Century Russia," *The American Historical Review* 108, no. 1 (2003): 50–83.

50 *Instruktsiia Polkovichiia* (1764), 117.

51 *Artikul Voinskii* (1777), 5. In addition, Article 9 stated that religious services were to take place every morning and every night. These included singing hymns and saying public prayers in churches and in military camps. The military priest was to be a respected member of the army, and anyone who dared to disrespect him was punished. Ibid., 7.

52 Ibid., 98–9.

53 Ibid., 99.

54 *Instruktsiia Polkovichiia* (1764), 303–5.

55 Ibid., 202.

56 Hamburg, *Russia's Path toward Enlightenment*, 394, 733, 742; Wirtschafter, *Religion and Enlightenment*, 21.

57 Zhukova, Tvoiesm' az, 146, 160; Keep, *Soldiers of the Tsar*, 206.

58 Suvorov, "Polkovoe Ucherezhdenie," in Goncharov, ed., 200–1.

59 Such attention to religion in the regiment was not unique to Russia. Compare, for instance, Suvorov's practices with the experience recorded by an eighteenth-century young Prussian officer. Duffy, *The Army of Frederick the Great*, 58.

60 Ibid., 218.

61 Ibid., 250.

62 Menning, "Train Hard, Fight Easy.

63 Best, *War and Society in Revolutionary Europe*, 44.

64 Suvorov, *Nauka pobezhdat'* (1980), 29.

65 Ibid., 23.

66 I.O. Popadichev, "Vosspominania suvorovskogo soldata," in Semanov, ed., *Aleksandr Vasilevich Suvorov*, 85.

67 Rumiantsev, "Obriad Sluzhby," in Goncharov, ed., 132.

68 This practice continued during the Napoleonic Wars. Ivan Skobelev wrote during the Battle of Reims: "Turning to my companions, I then said "Repeat the oath, my friends! Let's pray fervently to the Lord so he may show his innumerable favours on the loyal subjects of the Russian Tsar; may He infuse our hearts with new strength, and courage, and may He raise our spirit and mind above the perils that surround us! Until now

we have shown how the Russians fight, let's now show how they die!" Skobelev, "Rasskazy Russkogo Invalida," 194.

69 Meiendorf, *Opyt nekotorykh rasuzhdenii*, vii.

70 Ibid., 16.

71 Ibid., 23.

72 "Potemkin to Igelstrom, 4 June 1784," in Dubrovnik, *A.V. Suvorov*, 114.

73 Meiendorf, *Opyt nekotorykh rasuzhdenii*, 19–20.

74 Geisman and Dubovskoi, *Count Petr Ivanovich Panin*, 35.

75 Petr Panin, *Nastavlenie ot predovoditelia vtoroi armii*, 7–8.

76 Ibid., 8.

77 Ibid., 9.

78 Ibid., 15.

79 Hartley, *Russia, 1762–1825*, 184–5.

80 Suvorov, "Polkovoe Ucherezhdenie," in Goncharov, ed., 212.

81 Dmitriev-Mamonov, *Epistola*, 4.

82 "Ia dukhom voskhishchen, gde byl Zorndorfa boi; / Gde bilsia s mnogimi odin togda geroi' / Izrublen i v krovi vragov sam porazhaet, / I sam sebia ot nikh geroiski svobozhdaet... / Odnoi uchestiu tvoi khrabroi dukh pitalsia, / Ves' v ranakh i v krovi, no zhiv vragam ne dalsia." Ibid., 23.

83 Vorontsov, "Instruktsiia Rotnym Kommandiram," 35–6.

84 Ibid., 36.

85 Viazemskii, "Zapiska Voennaia," 4.

86 Ibid., 8.

87 Meiendorf, *Opyt nekotorykh rasuzhdenii*, 84.

88 Ibid., 17.

89 Ibid., 120.

90 Nikitin, "Moral'no-psikhologicheskoe obespechenie," 185.

91 Longworth, *The Art of Victory*, 220.

92 Suvorov, *Nauka pobezhdat'* (1980), 29.

93 Ibid., 23.

94 Popadichev in Semanov, ed., *Aleksandr Vasilevich Suvorov*, 87. As the old soldier added, upon his arrival in the army in 1799, just before the allied campaign in Italy against the French, Suvorov continued his old practices. "Hello, boys! ... I have again came to serve with you! Let's go defeat the enemy! Do not worry! You are trained – they give us two for a trained one, we don't want them, they give us three – we'll take it, they give us four – so be it, we'll beat them all." He loved to repeat these sayings, as I have already once told you, very often, and here, after a long absence from us, he once again repeated them, as if he was afraid we would forget them!" Ibid., 99.

95 Mosolov, "Zapiski," 147.

96 Norris, *War of Images*, 4–7.

97 The drawings were first published in 1913 and subsequently reprinted in 1996. In the introduction, the editor of the collection pointed out that the original documents from which the drawings were copied came from the family archives of K.L. Nonnenman, who provided some interpretations. The drawings were donated by the Nonnenman family to the military publishing house of V. Zhukov. Unfortunately, it appears that the original drawings are not in the RGVIA or the RGADA. Similarly, there are no collections of personal *fonds* in the Russian archives under the names Zhukov or Nonnenman. When I inquired, the RGVIA staff pointed out that pre-revolutionary documents from personal *fonds*, let alone small publishing houses, most likely had been lost due to neglect or relocation. Some archives left the country along with their keepers during the emigration after the revolution; others rotted away in damp conditions. Finally, large troves of RGVIA documents, including those relating to Suvorov, are in Siberia, where they were moved in 1942, and are not accessible to researchers.

98 Golubev, "Suvorov's canons of army and state governance."

99 Nonnenman wrote the commentary and copied the drawings. Nonnenman, ed., *Science of Victory*.

100 "Ugozhai nachal'nikam vernoiu sluzhboiu, a ne krevoiu druzhboiu, ne po poslovitse: kuda veter' tuda i petel'; kuda petelok', tuda i konek'!" Ibid., 24–5.

101 "Pri sukhikh shchepkakh i syroe derevo razgoritsia." Ibid., 34.

102 Ibid., 36–7.

103 Ibid., 39.

104 Ibid., 40.

105 Pichichero, "Le Soldat Sensible: Military Psychology and Social Egalitarianism in the Enlightenment French Army," 557.

106 Quoted in Melton, 679.

107 Speelman, *Henry Lloyd and the Military Enlightenment*, 62. Wirtschafter, *Religion and Enlightenment*, 8–9

108 Keep, *Soldiers of the Tsar*, 238.

109 Wirtschafter, *From Serf to Russian Soldier*, 73.

5 "Fantastic forms of folly"

1 Darnton, *The Great Cat Massacre*, 5.

2 Iuri Lotman, "Kul'tura i programmy povedeniia: Poetika bytovogo povedeniia v russkoi kul'ture xviii veka," in *Izbrannye Statii*, vol. 1, 250.

3 Lotman, *Besedy o russkoi kul'ture*, 254.

4 Steven Lukes, "The Meanings of "Individualism,'" *Journal of the History of Ideas* 32, no. 1 (1971): 47. For critique of Enlightenment individualism see Schmidt, "What Enlightenment Project?," 734–6.

5 Steven Lukes, *Individualism* (Oxford: B. Blackwell, 1973), 17.
6 By "deep play" I mean behaviour that has a meaning in a specific context to insiders. See Geertz, *The Interpretation of Cultures*, ch. 6, and also also his "thick description" in chapter 1.
7 Stollberg-Rilinger, "The Impact of Communication Theory," 315–16.
8 Anon., *General observations*, 36.
9 Engelgardt, *Zapiski*, 76.
10 Lubchenkov and Romanov, *Anekdoty*, 12.
11 Ibid., 10.
12 LeDonne, The Grand Strategy, 94.
13 Lubchenkov and Romanov, *Anekdoty*, 10.
14 Nikanorova, *Istoricheskii anekdot v russkoi literature XVIII veka*, 171.
15 Engelgardt, *Zapiski*, 66. The full song can be found in Alekseeva and Emelianov, *Istoricheskie pesni XVIII veka*, 242.
16 "Rumiantsev to Catherine, 23 August, 1769," in Fortunatov, ed., *P.A. Rumiantsev*. vol. 2, 130.
17 Lubchenkov and Romanov, *Anekdoty*, 6.
18 Ibid., 18.
19 Engelgardt, *Zapiski*, 73.
20 Martin Van Creveld, *Command in War* (Cambridge, MA: Harvard University Press, 1985), 97. For an example of the actual working of the directed telescope system, see 75–8.
21 Shtrandman, "*Zapiski*," vol. 34 (1882), 317.
22 Lanzheron, "Russkaia armia," no. 3 (1895), 153–4.
23 Segur, *Memoirs and Recollections*, vol. 3, 39.
24 Golitsyn, "Zapiski," 1279–80.
25 RGVIA, f. 52, op. 1/194, d. 59. ch. 1, l. 156 (17 July 1775).
26 Denisov, *Zapiski*, 42.
27 Anon., "O privatnoi zhizni kniazia Potemkina," no. 2 (1852), 8–9.
28 R.M. Tsebrikov, "Vokrug Ochakova."
29 Sinelnikov was apparently hit in the groin by a cannonball and died two days later. Montefiore, *Prince of Princes*, 405.
30 "Prince de Ligne to Emperor Joseph II, July, 1788," in Ligne, *Letters and Memoirs*, 64–5; Lubchenkov and Romanov, eds., *Ekaterina II i Grigorii Potemkin*, 89.
31 Longworth, *The Art of Victory*, 148.
32 Cited in Montefiore, *Prince of Princes*, 405.
33 Anon., "O privatnoi zhizni kniazia Potemkina," 7.
34 "Suvorov's report to Potemkin about the battle of Kinburn, 1 October 1787," in Meshcheriakov, *A.V. Suvorov*, vol. 2, 338; Beskrovnyi, *Russkaia armiia i flot v XVII veke*, 524–30; Longworth, *The Art of Victory*, 140–4.
35 Glinka, *Ruskie anekdoty*, vol. 3, 91.

36 Ibid., 87.
37 Lubchenkov and Romanov, *Ekaterina II i Grigorii Potemkin*, 115. Potemkin
    wrote about this incident to Catherine. "Potemkin to Catherine,
    22 August 1788," in Lopatin, ed., *Ekaterina II i G.A. Potemkin*, 308.
38 Lotman, *Besedy o russkoi kul'ture*, 269–86.
39 As Prince Dmitrii Mirskii wrote in the 1920s, Suvorov's "writings are
    as different from the common run of classical prose as his tactics were
    from those of Frederick or Marlborough." Dmitrii Mirskii, *A History of
    Russian Literature*, 5th ed. (New York: A.A. Knopf, 1964), 59. Reading
    some of Suvorov's correspondence, one gets a feeling that the author
    was developing a different language, a military jargon intermingled
    with juxtapositions and references to ancient history. See for example his
    letter to D.I. Khvostov from the winter of 1797. Suvorov, *Pis'ma*, 318–20.
    This was a general trend that culminated in the formation of a language
    particular to the military culture. As Lotman pointed out, by the end of
    the eighteenth and the beginning of the nineteenth there had emerged a
    so-called "guards language" or "gvardeiskii iazyk." Lotman, "K funktsii
    ustnoi rechi v kul'turnom bytu pushkinskoi epokhi," in *Stat'i po semiotike
    kul'tury i iskusstva* (St Petersburg: Akademicheskii proekt, 2002), ed.
    R.G. Grigor'eva 531–2. The role of terminology in the development of
    military culture has not yet received the concentrated attention of a major
    study and promises to be a fruitful avenue for future research.
40 Suvorov's secretary left a fascinating sketch titled "One Day in the Life of
    Suvorov." Fuks, *Sobranie Raznyh Sochinenii*, 92–113.
41 Montefiore, *Prince of Princes*, 390.
42 In Greek mythology, Momus was the god of mockery, satire, and criticism.
    George Gordon Byron, *Don Juan* (Boston: Houghton Mifflin, 1958), 239.
43 Fuks, *Anekdoty Kniazia Italianskogo*, ii.
44 Engelgardt, *Zapiski*, 184.
45 Charles Masson, *Secret Memoirs of the Court of Petersburg* (New York: Arno
    Press, 1970), 177.
46 Engelgardt, *Zapiski*, 185; Lanzheron, "Russkaia armia v god smerti
    Ekatiriny II," no. 3 (1895), 159; "Letter from 25 June 1779," in Tolstoi, ed.,
    Pisma Grafini, 236. There is no convincing evidence of Suvorov being an
    alcoholic. He drank, but no more than his peers.
47 Fuks, *Anekdoty Kniazia Italianskogo*, ii.
48 Ibid., iii.
49 Ibid., 26.
50 Wickham, *The Correspondence*, vol. 2, 274.
51 Elliot, *Life and Letters*, 107–8.
52 Fuks, *Anekdoty Kniazia Italianskogo*, vi.
53 Duffy, *Russia's Military Way to the West*, 191.

54 Ibid., 114–16; Smitt, *Suworow und Polens Untergang*, vol. 1, 215.

55 Lotman, *Besedy o russkoi kul'ture*, 272. As Lotman put it, "Staring to play, he over did it (Nachinaia igrat', on zaigryvalsia)." Ibid., 270.

56 Damas, Memoirs, 28–32. *Vivandiere* in French was a female camp follower, a sutler, a soldier's wife.

57 Some first encounters were more embarrassing. Engelgardt, *Zapiski*, 185–6.

58 Fuks, *Anekdoty Kniazia Italianskogo*, vii.

59 Ibid., 18.

60 Nikanorova, *Istoricheskii anekdot v russkoi literature XVIII veka*, 186.

61 For inspections, see Lanzheron, "Russkaia armia v god smerti Ekatiriny II," no. 5 (1895), 199.

62 Aleksander Suvorov, *Nauka pobezhdat'* (1999), 337–8.

63 For example, Yavetz, *Julius Caesar and His Public Image*, 162–3; and Meier, *Caesar*, 244.

64 Fuks, *Anekdoty Kniazia Italianskogo*,.

65 Engelgardt, *Zapiski*, 183.

66 Fuks, *Anekdoty Kniazia Italianskogo*, 165.

67 Delagardi, "Moe posishchenie russkogo," 833.

68 Duffy, *Russia's Military Way to the West*, 192.

69 Madariaga, *The Travels of General Francisco De Miranda*, 7.

70 Suvorov, *Nauka pobezhdat'* (1999), 367–9.

71 Komarovskii, "Zapiski Grafa E. F. Komarovskago," 360–1; another version of this event is in Suvorov, *Nauka pobezhdat'* (1999), 346.

72 Nikolai Griazev, "Pokhod Suvorova v 1799 g.," in Semanov, ed., *Aleksandr Vasilevich Suvorov*, 161.

73 Duffy, Ea*gles Over the Alps*, 81, 116.

74 Fuks, *Anekdoty Kniazia Italianskogo*, 77–8.

75 Segur, *Memoirs and Recollections*, vol. 2, 54.

76 Langeron, "Russkaia armia v god smerti Ekateriny II," no. 3 (1895), 155.

77 Engelgardt, *Zapiski*, 182–3; Duffy, *Russia's Military Way to the West*, 194.

78 Louis XVIII, "Liudovik XVIII-i v Rossii. Izvlecheno iz ego Zapisok D.D. Riabininym." *Russkii Arkhiv* 9 (1877): 65.

79 Bulgakov, "Iz pisem Aleksandra Yakovlivecha Bulgakova ego bratu," 133; N.I. Zeidel related a similar story about Voklonskii in Orenburg. Zeidel, "Istoricheskie Anekdoty," 238.

80 Specific examples from the battlefield are Anon., *Anekdoty*, 73–4; and Miloradovich, *Anekdoty*, 41–2.

81 Keep, *Soldiers of the Tsar*, 211.

82 Lukes, *Individualism* (1973), 22.

83 Bekasova, "Geroi Zadunaiskii," 660; Proskurina, *Creating the Empress*, 150–1.

84 For the detailed description of an argument, see Wortman, *Scenarios of Power*, 1–10.
85 Bell, *The First Total War*, 34–7.
86 Myerly, *British Military Spectacle*, 10.
87 Anon., "Nekotorye svedeniya," 595; Korsakov, "Rasskazy o bylom"; Custine, *Letters from Russia*, 5.

6 "The gutters of the town were dyed with blood"

1 The European press reported the event in sensational terms, when it described how Izmail "was taken by storm on the 22nd of December [11 December Julian], 1790, and the garrison (whose bravery merited and would have received from a generous Foe, the highest honours) were massacred in cold blood by the merciless Russians, to the amount of upwards of 30,000 men, by their own account; and the place was given up to the unrestrained fury of the brutal soldiery. The most horrid outrages were perpetuated on the defenceless inhabitants; and the conduct of the conquerors was more that of a horde of cannibals than of a civilized people." Anon., "For the Courier." Blease reminds his readers that it was nothing unusual to compensate the troops for their exertions and that during Wellington's expedition on the Peninsula, the British troops enjoyed the same licence as Suvorov's troops did in Izmail. Blease, 120–1n.
2 Mikhail Kutuzov, "Arkhiv Kniazia," 500–1.
3 Sewell, *Logics of History*, 169.
4 Damas, *Memoirs*, 137.
5 Mosolov, "Zapiski," 138; Damas, *Memoirs*, 136.
6 RGADA f.1453, op.1. d. 20, l. 1–2ob.
7 "Chernyshev to Golitsyn, 21 November 1790," in Chernyshev, "Pisma vo vremia," 388.
8 Ibid., 389.
9 Cerenville, *Memoirs of the Life of Prince Potemkin*, 215.
10 "Chernyshev to Golitsyn, 23 November 1790," in Chernyshev, "Pisma vo vremia," 394.
11 "Chernyshev to Golitsyn, 24 November 1790," in ibid., 395.
12 Ibid., 396.
13 "Chernyshev to Golitsyn, 27 November 1790," in ibid., 399.
14 Orlov, *Shturm Izmaila Suvorovym*, 37.
15 "Zapiska Soveta," in Orlov, *Shturm Izmaila Suvorovym*, 130.
16 Jeanne Eleonore de Cerenville, *Memoirs of the Life of Prince Potemkin*, 215.
17 Damas, *Memoirs*, 136.
18 "Potemkin to Suvorov, 25 November 1790," in Orlov, *Shturm Izmaila Suvorovym*, 128–9.

19 "Potemkin to Suvorov, 29 November 1790," in Orlov, *Shturm Izmaila Suvorovym*, 130.

20 "Chernyshev to Golitsyn, 29 November 1790," in Chernyshev, "Pisma vo vremia," 399–400.

21 "Suvorov to Potemkin, 3 December 1790," in Orlov, *Shturm Izmaila Suvorovym*, 131.

22 Petrushevksii, *Generalisimus kniaz Suvorov*, vol. 1, 384.

23 "Chernyshev to Golitsyn, 1 December 1790," in Chernyshev, "Pisma vo vremia," 401–2.

24 Byron, *Don Juan*, 238.

25 "Chernyshev to Golitsyn, 1 December 1790," in Chernyshev, "Pisma vo vremia," 401–2.

26 Bogdanovich, *Pokhody Rumiantseva*, 244.

27 Damas, *Memoirs*, 138–9.

28 "Chernyshev to Golitsyn, 6 December 1790," in Chernyshev, "Pisma vo vremia," 403.

29 Ibid., 404.

30 Duffy, *Russia's Military Way to the West*, 154.

31 Starkey, *War in the Age of Enlightenment*, 76.

32 "Chernyshev to Golitsyn, 6 December 1790," in Chernyshev, "Pisma vo vremia," 403.

33 "Chernyshev to Golitsyn, 7 December 1790," in ibid., 403.

34 Ibid.

35 Orlov, *Shturm Izmaila Suvorovym*, 46–7.

36 Quoted in ibid., 47–8.

37 The document was signed in order of reversed seniority by the thirteen generals under Suvorov's command: Brigadier Matvei Platov, Brigadier Vasilli Orlov, Brigadier Fedor Vestfalen, Major-General Nikolai Arsenev, Major-General Sergei Lvov, Major-General Iosif De Ribas, Major-General Lasii, Major-General Il'ia Bezborodko, Major-General Fedor Meknob, Major-General Petr Tischev, Major-General Mikhail Kutuzov, Lieutenant-General Aleksandr Samoilov, and Lieutenant-General Pavel Potemkin. Orlov, *Shturm Izmaila Suvorovym*, 50–1; Damas, *Memoirs*, 137.

38 Orlov, *Shturm Izmaila Suvorovym*, 60.

39 Osipov, *Alexander Suvorov*, 88.

40 "Dispozitsiia A. V. Suvorova k shturmu Izmaila, December 1790," in Meshcheriakov, ed., *A.V. Suvorov*, vol. 2, 532.

41 Richelieu, "Journal de mon voyage en Allemange," 191.

42 Denisov, *Zapiski*, 49.

43 Ibid., 50.

44 RGADA, f. 1453, op. 1, d. 15, l. 1ob.

45 Denisov, *Zapiski*, 50.

46 Mosolov, "Zapiski," 138.
47 Ibid., 139.
48 Ibid., 138–9.
49 Orlov, *Shturm Izmaila Suvorovym*, 69.
50 Engelgardt, *Zapiski*, 117; Damas, *Memoirs*, 141.
51 I thank Richard Hall for this insight.
52 Richelieu, "Journal de mon voyage en Allemange," 181.
53 Ibid., 184–5.
54 Ibid., 189.
55 Elena Polevshchikova, "Frantsuzkie volontery v Izmaile.
    Neopublikovannaia zapiska grafa Lanzherona," *Deribasovskaia-Reshilevskaia.
    Literaturno-khudozhestvennyi, istoriko-kraevedcheskii illiustrirovannyi almanakh*
    29 (2007): 11.
56 Damas, *Memoirs*, 140.
57 Ibid.
58 Longworth, *The Art of Victory*, 173.
59 Damas, *Memoirs*, 140.
60 Ibid., 141.
61 RGADA, f.1453, op.1, d.16, l. 1.
62 Pichichero, *The Military Enlightenment*, 150.
63 "Catherine to Potemkin, 3 January 1790," in Lopatin, ed., *Ekaterina II i
    G.A. Potemkin*, 446.
64 Polevshchikova, "Frantsuzkie volontery v Izmaile," 11.
65 Mosolov, "Zapiski," 139; Orlov, *Shturm Izmaila Suvorovym*,78–9. I could
    not find this order, which several authors allude to.
66 Ibid., 191.
67 Damas, *Memoirs*, 141.
68 Montefiore, *Prince of Princes*, 580.
69 Polevshchikova, "Frantsuzkie volontery v Izmaile," 10.
70 Shavrov, *Kratkaia istoriia*, 17.
71 Polevshchikova, "Frantsuzkie volontery v Izmaile," 10–11; Orlov, 81.
72 "Suvorov to Potemkin, 21 December 1790," in Meshcheriakov, ed.,
    A.V. Suvorov, vol. 2, 551–61.
73 Petrushevksii, *Generalisimus kniaz Suvorov*, vol. 1, 395.
74 Denisov, *Zapiski*, 51.
75 Orlov, *Shturm Izmaila Suvorovym*, 80.
76 "Suvorov to Potemkin, 13 December 1790," in Meshcheriakov, ed.,
    A.V. Suvorov, vol. 2, 540.
77 Engelgardt, *Zapiski*, 117.
78 "Ekaterina Kutuzova to Aleksei Kutuzov, 6 January, 1791," in Barskov,
    ed., *Perepiska Moskovskikh masonov XVIII veka*, 77; Kutuzov, "Arkhiv
    Kniazia," 2.

79 "Suvorov to Potemkin, 21 December 1790," in Meshcheriakov, ed., *A.V. Suvorov*, vol. 2, 554.

80 Ibid., 559.

81 Mosolov, "Zapiski," 140.

82 "Suvorov to Potemkin, 21 December 1790," in Meshcheriakov, ed., *A.V. Suvorov*, vol. 2, 562–3.

83 Ibid., 564.

84 Ibid., 553.

85 Ibid., 554.

86 "Catherine to Prince De Ligne, January 1790," in Ligne, *The Prince De Ligne*, 194.

87 Quoted in Skritskii, *Georgievskie kavalery pod Andreevskim flagom*, 368.

88 Orlov, *Shturm Izmaila Suvorovym*, 85.

89 "Potemkin to Catherine, 24 March 1791," in Lopatin, ed., *Ekaterina II i G.A. Potemkin*, 454.

90 Petrushevskii, *Generalisimus kniaz Suvorov*, vol. 1, 402.

91 Quoted in Lopatin, *Potemkin i Suvorov*, 204.

92 Ibid., 216–7.

93 Baiov, *Istoriia Russkoi Armii*, 85–9.

94 Brikner, *Voina Rossii so Shvetsiei v 1788–1790 godakh*, 290.

95 Lopatin, ed., *Ekaterina II i G.A. Potemkin*, 944.

96 An abatis was a part of eighteenth-century siege fortifications. It usually took the form of trees laid down in line with branches directed at the enemy. The purpose of an abatis was to slow down the enemy and expose him to the fire of the defenders.

97 A hole with sharp stakes planted in its bottom.

98 A wooden fence or an earthwork.

99 A bundle of wood tied together. It was carried by soldiers for negotiating such obstacles as ditches.

100 Suvorov, *Nauka Pobezhdat*, 24–5.

101 Ibid., 24. Suvorov preferred to avoid long sieges and instead strove for decisiveness, which could be guaranteed by a storming. This approach was clearly in accord with his highly aggressive military thought.

102 Ibid. See also the introduction to the 1980 publication of *Nauka Pobezhdat'* by the Soviet Ministry of Defence, 3–14.

103 Ibid., 23.

104 Ibid.

105 *Kamer-furerskii tseremonialnyi zhurnal 1791 goda* (1890), 187.

106 Ibid., 204–5.

107 "Fevralia 5 Dnia," Sobranie vsekh v vedomostiakh obeikh stolits, s 1787 po 1791 god vkliuchitel'no, reliatsii o voennykh deistviiakh protiv neprii-atelei rossiiskoi impreii. Chast I. (Moscow, 1791), 125–59.

108 Kostrov, *Epistola Ego Siiatelstvu Grafu Aleksandru Vasilevichu Suvorovu-Rymnikskomu.*

109 Quoted in Batishin-Kamenski, Biografii Rossi'skikh Generalissimusov i General-Feildmarshalov, vol. 2, 79. Derzhavin also wrote a lengthy poem specifically about the Izmail battle. Derzhavin, *Stikhotvoreniia*, 73–82.

110 Quoted in Lopatin, *Potemkin i Suvorov*, 222.

7 "His Majesty recommends to gentlemen-officers ..."

1 Kochetkov, "Russkaia voennaia literatura," 112.

2 Baturin, *Rech pri otrkytii sobranii ofitserov.*

3 Andreas Schönle, Andrei Zorin, and Alexei Evstratov, eds., "Officers off the Battlefield: Managers and Thinkers," *The Europeanized Elite in Russia,* 157.

4 Quoted in Lebedev, "Preobrazovateli russkoi armii," 577.

5 Quoted in Lukes, *Individualism* (1973), 22.

6 McGrew, *Paul I of Russia*, 355; Duffy, *Russia's Military Way to the West*, 200–7; Ragsdale, *Paul I*; Iurkevich, *Voennyi Peterburg epokhi Pavla I.* The latter book in general follows the revisionist tradition and sympathizes with Paul's attempted reforms, but does not use any significant archival material.

7 For Paul's relationship with his mother, see McGrew, *Paul I of Russia*, 135–6, 163–4, 178–9, 193–5; and Madariaga, *Russia in the Age of Catherine the Great*, 256–7, 569–70.

8 Kamenskii, *The Russian Empire in the Eighteenth Century*, 266.

9 For Paul's daily routine see Peskov, *Pavel I*, 71–2. Longworth has a rather negative assessment of Paul's reforms. Longworth, *The Art of Victory*, 223–4.

10 McGrew, *Paul I of Russia*, 228.

11 Iurkevich, "Phenomen "poteshnykh" voisk."

12 Bruce Menning, "Paul I and Catherine II's Military Legacy," in Kagan and Higham, eds., *The Military History of Tsarist Russia*, 82.

13 McGrew, *Paul I of Russia*, 229; Duffy, *Russia's Military Way to the West*, 200–7.

14 Golovine, *Memoirs*, 126–7.

15 Czartoryski, *Memoirs*, vol. 1, 140–1. Rostopchin, a close associate of Paul, naturally left a more sympathetic account of the first days of his master's reign. *Arkhiv Kniazia Vorontsova*, vol. 8, 158–74.

16 Cited in McGrew, *Paul I of Russia*, 208.

17 RGB OR, f. 178, no. 8634, anon., "1796, diary," l. 71; Volkonskii, "Rasskazy P.M. Volkonskago," 179.

18 Ibid., 209–10.

19 Cited in ibid., 212.

20 Menning Bruce Menning, "Paul I and Catherine II's Military Legacy," in Kagan and Higham, eds., *The Military History of Tsarist Russia*, 80. See also

Lebedev, *Russkaia armiia v nachale tsarstvovaniia Ekateriny II*, 227–60; and Lebedev, "Preobrazovateli russkoi armii," 577–608.

21 Ibid., 229.
22 McGrew, *Paul I of Russia*, 238.
23 Duffy, *Russia's Military Way to the West*, 207.
24 Roche, *The Culture of Clothing*, esp. ch. 9, "The Discipline of Appearances," 221–56.
25 *Arkhiv Kniazia Vorontsova*, vol. 10, 470.
26 McGrew, *Paul I of Russia*, 227; Menning, "Paul I and Catherine II's Military Legacy, 1762–1801," in Kagan and Higham, eds. *The Military History of Tsarist Russia*, 78–86.
27 *Spisok Generalov po Starshenstu* (1799).
28 Volkonskii, "Rasskazy P.M. Volkonskago," 180; Dashkova, *Zapiski*, 270.
29 Liutov, *Kniga v Russkoi Armii*, 26.
30 For the broader censorship context see Marker, *Publishing, Printing*, ch. 1.
31 Ibid., 231.
32 Wortman, *Scenarios of Power*, vol. 1, 182.
33 RGB, OR, f. 95, k. 7, d. 1, I.N. Durnovo, 1799, l. 6. no. 4.
34 Ibid,. l. 27ob., no. 5.
35 Ibid,. l. 56, no. 10.
36 Ibid,. l. 78ob., no. 6.
37 Ibid,. l. 98ob, no. 8.
38 Ibid,. l. 103ob, no. 9.
39 Ibid,. l. 115, no. 4.
40 Ibid,. l. 125ob, no. 5.
41 Ibid,. l. 127, no. 2.
42 Ibid,. l. 127–127ob, no. 4.
43 Ibid,. l. 224, no. 10.
44 Ibid,. l. 11ob., no. 12.
45 Ibid,. l. 45, no. 3.
46 Ibid,. l. 131ob, no. 6.
47 Ibid,. l. 134, no. 19.
48 Ibid,. l. 159ob., no. 6.
49 Ibid,. l. 161, no. 8.
50 Ibid,. l. 201, no. 2.
51 RGB, OR, f. 95, no. 9467, I.N. Durnovo, "Prikazy po leib-gvardeiskim polkam, 1799," l. 120.
52 This is not to say there were no expulsions from the military during Catherine's reign. Expulsion from military service was a very real danger. See for example Anon., "Nachalo vospominanii neizvestnogo, pisanykh v 1859 godu," in *Sbornik Starinnykh Bumag, Khraniashchikhsia v Muzee P.I. Shchukina*, vol. 8 (Moscow, 1901), 170–1, whose author was enrolled

into the Izmailovskii Regiment as a child in 1784 but then was expelled from military service for absenteeism.

53 RGADA, f. 7, op. 2, d. 2906, l. 1–3.

54 RGADA, f. 7, op. 2, d. 2915, l. 1ob. What the conversations were about the report did not mention.

55 RGADA, f. 7, op. 2, d. 2907, l. 1–2. The file does not describe the contents of the letters written by Zass.

56 See for example the sympathetic description of Platov's mental and physical state by the local governor, RGADA, f. 7, op. 2, d. 3068, l. 15; and Platov's own letter to Prince Petr Lopukhin, the Procurator General, de facto prime minister, and the head of the Secret Expedition, l. 18.

57 RGADA, f. 7, op. 2, d. 2047, l. 43.

58 RGADA, f. 7, op. 2, d. 3246, l. 10–12. Also RGADA, f. 7, op. 2, d. 3246, l. 1.

59 RGADA, f. 7, op. 2, d. 3250, l. 1. The report does not reveal what Sukhotin's crime was.

60 RGADA, f. 7, op. 2, d. 3345, l. 1–1ob.

61 RGADA, f. 7, op. 2, d. 3347, l. 1–4. The agent diligently compiled a register that included four fired generals, fourteen discharged officers, and ten more officers without ranks, along with medical and education staff.

62 Pavel was eventually let go as a result of personal interference by Count von der Phalen, one of Paul's favourites. RGADA, f. 7, op. 2, d. 3398, l. 8.

63 RGADA, f. 7, op. 2, d. 3471, l. 1–2; d. 3550, l. 1; d. 3585, 1.2. Again, there is no information about what this officer did to earn Paul's displeasure.

64 RGADA, f. 7, op. 2, d. 3546, l. 1. Major-General Markolovskii was court-marshalled for allowing one of the prisoners of his fortress to receive correspondence. In another instance, a governor who out of sympathy passed a letter by an exiled officer to the tsar was dismissed. RGADA, f. 7, op. 2, d. 3471, l. 4–5.

65 For example, Colonel Dibich, who had family and relatives in France. While living in exile he wanted to visit them, fearing for their safety. His request was denied. However, he was discharged with full pension, for which he was grateful to Paul. Another exile, Major Shtakelberg, lived nearby and wanted to go to Moscow to get married. His request too was denied. RGADA, f. 7, op. 2, d. 3355, 1.1–7.

66 Keep, "The Russian Army's Response to the French Revolution," 506.

67 Brian D. Taylor, 42. John Keep estimates that Paul's purge amounted to 340 generals and 2,261 officers. Keep, "The Russian Army's Response to the French Revolution," 506.

68 "Paul to Suvorov, 15 December 1796," in Meshcheriakov, ed. *A.V. Suvorov*, vol. 3, 563. The reference to people with one eye was made with regard to Potemkin, who only could see from one eye, and for whom Paul reserved a special loathing.

69 "Suvorov's note about the introduction of Prussian tactics into the Russian army, 3 January 1797," in ibid., 570.

70 Lotman, *Besedy o russkoi kul'ture*, 285.

71 In 1794, Paul produced a military book called *Experience in the Field of Military Art*, which his Gatchina troops used as a manual. This book was derived almost entirely from *Tactics or Discipline according to new Prussian Regulations*, first published in Russia in 1767. When Paul came to power he republished this book as a regulation for the entire Russian army. Ibid., 570n.

72 Petrushevskii, *Generalisimus kniaz Suvorov*, vol. 2, 390.

73 Iurkevich, *Voennyi Peterburg epokhi Pavla I*, 181.

74 Longworth, *The Art of Victory*, 232.

75 McGrew, *Paul I of Russia*, 233.

76 Aleksandr Ribopier, "Zapiski grafa Aleksandra Ivanovicha Ribopiera," *Russkii Arkhiv* 1, no. 4 (1877): 481.

77 Karabanovym, "Istoricheskie rasskazy i anekdoty," 770.

78 Petrushevskii, *Generalisimus kniaz Suvorov*, vol. 2, 389; Lanzheron, "Russkaia armia v god smerti Ekatiriny II," no. 5 (1895), 186.

79 "Paul to Suvorov, 2 January 1797," in Meshcheriakov, ed. *A.V. Suvorov*, vol. 3, 569; "Rostopchin to Suvorov, 14 January 1797," in Meshcheriakov, ed. *A.V. Suvorov*, vol. 2, 577; "Paul to Suvorov, 23 January 1797," in ibid., 580.

80 Suvorov's service record, in ibid., vol. 1, 22.

81 Longworth, *The Art of Victory*, 228–30.

82 RGADA, f. 7, op. 2, d. 3038, l. 49. Here we also learn that Suvorov's annual income was as much as 50,000 roubles, an enormous sum at the time, while his total debts added up to 110,200 roubles, l. 128–128ob.

83 "Suvorov to Paul, 20 September 1797," in Meshcheriakov, ed. *A.V. Suvorov*, vol. 3, 588.

84 RGADA, f. 7, op. 2, d. 3085, l. 1–4.

85 Duffy, *Russia's Military Way to the West*, 205–6.

86 Hertz, "The Uniform," 1.

87 RGADA, f. 7, op. 2, d. 3085, l. 1–5ob.

88 Ibid., l. 85. As the investigation progressed, Colonel Dekhterev was linked to Count Zubov, the last favourite of Catherine. Naturally, Paul ordered that the count and his brother be put under "discreet" surveillance. RGADA, f . 7, op 2, d. 3252, l. 43.

89 Suvorov, *Pis'ma*, 690–1.

90 Lotman took this episode seriously. Lotman, *Besedy o russkoi kul'ture*, 283.

91 RGADA, f. 7, op. 2, d. 3085, l. 208–90. Prince Khovanskii was sent to his estates in Belorussia, to the city of Nevl, where he was under constant surveillance. RGADA f. 7, op. 2, d. 2047, l. 28. Colonel Kakhovskii ended up in the Diunamindsk Fortress, where he was under surveillance, but as

usual there was not much to report, for he, like all the other exiles, led a quiet existence. RGADA, f. 7, op. 2, d. 3268, 1. 1–5.

92 RGADA, f. 7, op. 2, d. 3283, l. 182ob–183.

93 The phrase was originally applied to the reign of Paul's father, Peter III, but holds equally true for Paul's reign as well. Hartley, *Russia, 1762–1825*, 63.

Conclusion: The Legacy of the Enlightenment in Russian Military Culture

1 Jones, *Nikolay Novikov, Enlightener of Russia*, 1.

2 Wirtschafter, *Religion and Enlightenment*, 128.

3 Howard, *War and the Liberal Conscience*, 3.

4 Kuxhausen, *From the Womb to the Body Politic Raising the Nation in Enlightenment Russia*, 153.

5 Hochedlinger, "Mars Ennobled," 153, 155–7.

6 Jackson, "The Eighteenth-Century Antecedents," 1293.

7 Anderson, *War and Society in Europe of the Old Regime*, 199. .

8 Rich, *The Tsar's Colonels: Professionalism, Strategy, and Subversion in Late Imperial Russia*, 151–53.

9 Adeeb Khalid, "Russian History and the Debate over Orientalism," *Kritika: Explorations in Russian and Eurasian History* 1, no. 4 (2000): 692.

10 In his new book, Patrick O'Meara writes that Alexander was committed to merit over social standing, for example, and in some cases even placed military service to the state above that of the nobles. O'Meara, The Russian Nobility in the Age of Alexander I, 18.

11 Wahlde, "Military Thought in Imperial Russia," 22.

12 Glinoetskii, *Istoriia russkogo general'nogo shtaba*, vol. 1, 365–6. The first military journal in Russia, *Artillery Journal*, appeared in 1808, followed by *Military Journal* in 1810. Whalde, "Military Thought in Imperial Russia," 22.

13 Beskrovnyi, *Russkaia armiia i flot v XIX veke*, 216–17.

14 S. R. Vorontsov, "Zapiska grafa S. R. Vorontsova"; Beskrovnyi, *Russkaia armiia i flot v vosemnadtsatom veke*, 259.

15 I. Iu. Fomenko, "I.V. Sabaneev i M. S. Vorontsov," 53–4.

16 Wahlde, "Military Thought in Imperial Russia," 18.

17 Examples included Antonovskii, *Nauka Pobezhdat' po Pravilam Petra Velikogo*, and several other works – Sanglen, *O voennom iskusstve drevnyhk i novykh vremen*, and many others.

18 Dyke, *Russian Imperial Military Doctrine and Education, 1832–1914* (New York: Greenwood Press, 1990), 3–6. Hines, "Russian Military Thought," 10.

19 Wahlde, "Military Thought in Imperial Russia," 117.

20 Miliutin opposed the idea of a strong general staff because he saw it as challenging the powers of the war minister (i.e., himself). Oleg Airapetov, "Miliutin contra Moltke: Russia's Refusal to Adopt a Prussian-Style

General Staff," in Schimmelpenninck and Menning, eds. *Reforming the Tsar's Army*, 297.

21 Hines, "Russian Military Thought," 29.
22 Menning, *Bayonets before Bullets*, 7; Dyke, Dyke, *Russian Imperial Military Doctrine and Education* 20.
23 Hines, "Russian Military Thought," 42.
24 Forrestt A. Miller, *Dmitri Miliutin and the Reform Era in Russia* (Nashville: Vanderbilt University Press, 1968), 90.
25 Quoted in ibid., 96.
26 Dragomirov, *Uchebnik Taktiki*.
27 Dragomirov, *Izbrannye Trudy*, 7.
28 Rich, *The Tsar's Colonels*, 81–3.
29 Wahlde, "Military Thought in Imperial Russia," 131.
30 Ibid., 122.
31 Leer, *Zapiski strategii*.
32 Wahlde, "A Pioneer of Russian Strategic Thought," 149.
33 Wahlde, "Military Thought in Imperial Russia," 136.
34 Menning, *Bayonets before Bullets*, 126
35 Wahlde, "A Pioneer of Russian Strategic Thought," 152.
36 Fuller, *Strategy and Power in Russia*, 303.
37 Ibid., 304.
38 Ibid.
39 Kirill Meretskov, *Na Sluzhbe Narodu*.

Bibliography

Archival Sources

Rossiiskii Gosudarstvennyi Voenno-Istoricheskii Arkhiv (RGVIA)
    fond 2 – Kantseliariia Voennoi Kollegii
    fond 24 – Kabinet I. E. V.
    fond 52 – Kantseliaria G. Potemkina
    fond 53 – Kantseliaria G. Razumovskogo
    fond 196 – Belokopytov, I. P.
    fond 295 – Dashkov, A. A.
    fond 314 – 1ia Petrogradskaia Gimnaziia Voennogo Vedomstva
Rossiiskii Gosudarstvennyi Arkhiv Drevnikh Aktov (RGADA)
    fond 7 – Sekretnaia Ekspeditsiia
    fond 16 – Vnuterennee Upravlenie
    fond 20 – Dela Voennye
    fond 1453 – Samoilovi
Rossiskaia Gosudarstvennaia Biblioteka, Otdel Rukopisei (RGB OR)
    fond 95 – Prikazy Leib-Gvardiiskim Polkam
    fond 178 – Anon. "Dnevnik, 1796."
    fond 261 – Aleksandr Mikhailovich Turgenev, "Zapiski."

Printed Primary Sources

Alekseeva, O.B., and L.N. Emelianov. *Istoricheskie pesni XVIII veka.* Leningrad: Nauka, 1971.
Andreev, Ivan. "Domovaia letopis' Andreeva, po rodu ikh, pisannaia kapitanom Ivanom Andreevym v 1789 dogu." *Chtenia v Imperatorskom obshchestve istorii i drevnostei rossiiskikh* 5, no. 5 (1870): 63–176.
Anglesi, Timofei. *Soviety voennago chelovieka synu svoemu.* St Petersburg, 1787.

Anon. *Anekdoty, ili dostopiamiatnyia skazaniia o ego svetlosti general feldmarshale kniaze Mikhaile Larionoviche Golenshcheve-Kutuzove Smolenskom. Nachinaia s pervykh let ego sluzhby do konchiny, s priobshcheniem nekotorykh pisem, dostopiamiatnykh ego rechei i prikazov.* St Petersburg, 1814.
– "For the Courier." *New Annual Register*, 27 December 27 1794.
– *General observations regarding the present state of the Russian Empire.* London, 1787.
– *Istoricheskie rasskazy i ankedoty.* St Petersburg, 1885.
– "Nachalo vospominanii neizvestnogo, pisanykh v 1859 godu." In *Sbornik starinnykh bumag, khraniashchikhsia v muzee P.I. Shchukina*, vol. 8 (Moscow, 1901): 169–71.
– "Nekotorye svedeniya o grafe Rumiantseve Zadunaiskom, peredannye ego sovremennikami." *Russkii Invalid*, vol. 127 (1854): 585–620.
– "O privatnoi zhizni knazia Potemkina, o nekotorykh chertakh ego kharaktera i anekdotakh (v poslediee vremia)." *Moskvitianin* 1, no. 2 (1852): 4–22; no. 3: 23–30.
– *Zelmira i Smelon ili vziatie Izmaila. Liricheskaia drama.* St Petersburg, 1795.
Antonovskii, M.I. *Nauka Pobezhdat' po Pravilam Petra Velikogo.* St Petersburg, 1808.
Arkhiv Kniaiza Vorontsova. Moscow, 1870–95.
Artikul voinskii s kratkim tolkovaniem. St Petersburg, 1777.
Bakunina, Varvara. "Persidskii pokhod v 1796 godu. Vospominaniia Varvary Ivanovny Bakuninoi." *Russkaia Starina* 53, no. 2 (1887): 343–64.
Barskov, Ia.L., ed. *Perepiska Moskovskikh masonov XVIII veka.* Petrograd, 1915.
Baturin, E. *Rech pri otrkytii sobranii ofitserov inzhenernykh i artilleriiskikh, bombardirskikh, grebnogo flota, uchrezhdennykh dlia dal'neishego issledovaniia teorii, kasaiushcheisia do ikh zvaniia.* St Petersburg, 1792.
Blease, Lyon W. *Suvorof.* London: Constable and Company, 1920.
Bobrinskii, Aleksei. "Dnevnik grafa Bobrinskago vedennyi v kadetskom korpuse i vo vremia puteshestviia po Rossii i za granitseiu." *Russkii Arkhiv* 3, no. 10 (1877): 116–31.
Bolotov, Andrei. *Zhizn' i Prikliucheniia.* St Petersburg, 1870–3.
Brikner, A.G. *Voina Rossii so Shvetsiei v 1788–1790 godakh.* St Petersburg, 1869.
Bulgakov, Aleksandr. "Iz pisem Aleksandra Yakovlivecha Bulgakova ego bratu, 1817–1818 gody." *Russkii Arkhiv* no. 9 (1900): 107–37.
Bulgarin, F.B. *Vospominaniia (1789–1859).* Moscow: Zakharivm, 2001.
George Gordon, Byron. *Don Juan.* Boston: Houghton Mifflin, 1958.
Catherine II. *Sochineniia Ekateriny II.* St Petersburg, 1901–7.
Chernyshev, Grigorii. "Pisma vo vremia osady Izmaila 1790 goda. Ot grafa G.I. Chernysheva k kniaziu G.F. Golitsynu." *Russkii arkhiv* 3 (1871): 386–408.
Custine, Astolphe de. *Lettes from Russia* (1839). New York: New York Review Books, 2002.

Czartoryski, Adam. *Memoirs of Prince Adam Czartoryski*. New York: Arno Press, 1971.

Damas, Roger De. *Memoirs of the Comte Roger De Damas (1787–1806)*. London: Chapman and Hall, 1913.

Dashkova, Ekaterina. *Zapiski*. St Petersburg: Azbuka, 2011.

Delagardi, Ia.G. "Moe posishchenie russkogo fel'dmarshala kniazia Suvorova." *Russkaia Starina* 17, no. 12 (1876): 832–4.

Denisov, A.K. *Zapiski donskogo atamana*. St Petersburg: VIRD, 2000.

Derzhavin, Gavril. *Zapiski Gavrila Romanovicha Derzhavina, 1743–1812*. Moscow, 1860.

Derzhavin, Gavrila. *Stikhotvoreniia*. Moscow: Gosudarstvennoe izdatelstvo khudozhestvennoi literatury, 1958.

Dmitriev-Mamonov, Fedor. *Epistola ot generala k ego podchinennym ili geneal v pole s svoim voiskom, izdannaia sochinitelem allegorii dvorianina filosofa*. Moscow, 1770.

– *Pravila po kotorym vsiakoi offitser sleduia, voennuiu sluzhbu s polnym udovolstviem prodolzhat' mozhet*. Moscow, 1788.

Dopolnitelnye Glavy k Generalnomu Ustavu o Polevoi Sluzhbe. St Petersburg, 1765.

Dubrovnik, N. *A.V. Suvorov sredi preobrazovatelei ekaterininskoi armii*. St Petersburg, 1886.

Elliot, Gilbert. *Life and Letters of Sir Gilbert Elliot, First Earl of Minto, from 1751 to 1806*. London: Longmans, Green and Co., 1874.

Engelgardt, Lev. *Zapiski L'va Nikolaevicha Engelgardta, 1766–1836*. Moscow: Izdanie Russkago Arkhiva, 1868.

Ermolov, A.P. "Zapiski." *Russkii Arhiv*. No. 3 (1867): 366–76.

Fortunatov, P.K., ed. *P.A. Rumiantsev*. 2 vols. Moscow: Voennoye Ministerstvo SSSR, 1953.

Frederick II, *Tainoe nastavlenie*. Moscow, 1791.

Fuks, E. *Anekdoty Kniazia Italianskogo, Grafa Suvorova Rymnikskago*. St Petersburg, 1827.

– *Sobranie Raznykh Sochinenii E. Fuksa*. St Petersburg, 1827.

Garnizonyi Ustav. St Petersburg, 1766.

Gertz, Graf von. "Russkii dvor v 1780 godu." *Drevniia i novaia Rossiia* (October 1879): 85–92.

Glinka, Fedor. "Vospominania." *Moskvitianin* 1 (1846): 35–64.

Glinka, Sergei. *Ruskie anekdoty, voennye, grazhdanskie, ili poviestvovanie o narodnykh dobrodieteliakh Rossiian drevnikh i novykh vremen*. Moscow, 1822.

– *Zapiski Seregeia Nikolaevicha Glinki*. St Petersburg, 1895.

Glukhov, I.A. "Zhizn'." *Shchukinskii Sbornik*, vol. 6 (1907): 202–68.

Golitsyn, Fedor. "Zapiski Fedora Nikolaevicha Golitsyna." *Russkii Arkhiv* 1, no. 5 (1874): 1271–1336.

Golovine, Countess Varvara. *Memoirs of Countess Golovine*. London: David Nutt, 1910.

Goncharov, V., ed. *Russkaia voennaia mysl': VIII vek*. St Petersburg: Terra Fantastica, 2003.

Gudovich, I.V. "Zapiski o sluzhbe." *Russkii Vestnik* 1, no. 3 (1841): 607–81.

Imberg, Aleksei. "Iz zapisnoi knizhki Alekseia Osipovicha Imberga." *Russkii Arkhiv*, no. 7 (1871): 373–404.

Instruktsiia Konnogo Polka Polkovniku. St Petersburg, 1766.

Instruktsiia Pekhotnogo Polka Polkovniku. St Petersburg, 1764.

Instruktsiia Polkovichiia. St Petersburg, 1764.

Kamer-furerskii tseremonialnyi zhurnal 1791 goda. St Petersburg, 1890.

Karabanovym, P.F. "Istoricheskie rasskazy i anekdoty, zapizannye so slov imenitykh liudei P.F. Karabanovym," *Russkaia Starina* 5, no. 5 (1872): 767–72.

Khvostov, Vasilii. "Zapiski Vasiliia Semrna Khvostova." *Russkii Arhiv* 1, no. 3 (1870): 551–610.

Kipinskii, Ia. "Osada Varshavy v 1794 Gody." *Istoricheskii Zhurnal Dlia Vskekh* 3, no. 1 (1909): 77–90; no. 2 (1909): 125–36; no. 3 (1909): 235–43; no. 4 (1909): 303–9 and 425–37.

Komarovskii, E.F. "Zapiski Grafa E.F. Komarovskago." *Istoricheskii Vestnik* 69 (1897): 343–61.

Korobkov, N. M., ed. *Feldmarshal Rumiantsev: Sbornik dokumentov i materialov*. Moscow: OGIZ, 1947.

Korsakov, A.N. "Rasskazy o bylom." *Istoricheskii Vestnik* 15, no. 1 (1884): 133–43.

Kostrov, E.I. *Epistola Ego Siiatelstvu Grafu Aleksandru Vasilevichu Suvorovu-Rymnikskomu*. St Petersburg, 1791.

Kurasov, V.V. "Suvorovskie printsipy obucheniia i vospitaniia voisk," in *A.V. Suvorov: iz materialov, opublikovannykh v sviazi 150-letiem so dnia smerti* (Moscow: Voennoe Izdatel'stvo, 1951), 26–43.

Kutuzov, Mikhail. "Arkhiv Kniazia M. I. Golensheva-Kutuzova-Smolenskogo, 1745–1813." *Russkaia starina* 2 (1870): 498–514.

– *Primechaniia o pekhotnoi sluzhbe voobshche i o egerskoi osobenno* (1786). Moscow: Voennoe Izdatel'stvo, 1955.

La Murraille Parlante. St Petersburg, 1790.

La Salle de récréation, ou La suite et le second volume de la Muraille parlante, ou Tableau de ce qui se trouve dans la salle de récréation du 4 et 5 ages du Corps Impérial des cadets gentilshommes: À l'usage du Corps des cadets. St Petersburg, 1791.

Lanzheron, Aleksandr. "Russkaia armia v god smerti Ekatiriny II." *Russkaia Starina* 83, no. 5 (1895): 83, no. 3: 147–66; no. 4: 145–77; no. 5: 185–202.

Ligne, Charles Joseph. *Mélanges militaires, littéraires et sentimentaires. Préjugés militaires*. Vienna, 1795.

Ligne, Charles Joseph de. *Letters and Memoirs of the Prince De Ligne, With Selections from His Other Works*. London: G. Routledge, 1927.

– *Prince de Ligne: His memoirs, letters, and miscellaneous Papers,* Volume 2. New York: Brentano's Publishers, 1899.

– *The Prince de Ligne: His Memoirs, Letters and Papers.* Boston: Hardy, Pratt & Co, 1899.

Lopatin, Viachislav, ed. *Ekaterina II i G.A. Potemkin: lichnaia perepiska, 1769–1791.* Moscow: Nauka, 1997.

Louis XVIII. "Liudovik XVIII-i v Rossii. Izvlecheno iz ego Zapisok D. D. Riabininym." *Russkii Arkhiv* 9 (1877): 52–95.

Lubchenkov, Iuri, and Vladislav Romanov, eds. *Anekdoty o general-feldmarshalakh P.A. Rumiantseve i A.V. Suvorove.* Moscow: Mezhdunarodnii biznes-tsentr, Obyedinenie Kino-kniga, 1990.

– *Ekaterina II i Grigorii Potemkin: istoricheskie anekdoty.* Moscow: Mezhdunarodnii biznes-tsentr, Ob'edinenie Kino-kniga, 1990.

Maslovskii, D.O. *Pis'ma i bumagi A.V. Suvorova, G.A. Potemkina, i P.A. Rumiantseva, 1787–1789 g.g. Kinburn-Ochakovskaia operatsiia.* St Petersburg, 1893.

– *Zapiski po Istorii Voennago Iskusstva v Rosii. Vypusk II. 1762–1771.* St Petersburg, 1894.

Masson, Charles. *Secret Memoirs of the Court of Petersburg.* New York: Arno Press, 1970.

Meiendorf, Reingold Iogan von. *Opyt nekotorykh rasuzhdenii o voinstve voobsche, i osoblivo o ustroenii ispravnago polku v nastavlenii molodym ofitseram.* St Petersburg, 1777.

Meshcheriakov, G.P., ed. *A.V. Suvorov.* 4 vols. Moscow: Voennoye Ministerstvo SSSR, 1949–53.

Migrin, Ivan. "Pokhozhdeniia ili istoria Ivan Migrina chernomorskogo kazaka." *Russakia Starina* 9 (1878): 1–32.

Miloradovich, Mikhail. *Anekdoty, cherty iz zhizni Grafa Miloradovicha.* Kiev: 1881.

Mosolov, Sergei. "Zapiski." *Russkii Arhiv* 1 (1905): 124–73.

Münnich, Christoph von. "Zapiska, podannaia General-Fel'dmarshalom Grafom Minikom Gosudaryne Imperatritse Anne Ioannovne, 1737 godu Dekabria 22 dnia, o svoistvakh Generalov vo vverennoi iemu armii," *Severnyi Arkhiv* 1, no. 3 (February 1822): 205–13.

Nonnenman, K. ed., *Science of Victory* (1913). Moscow: Ankil-Voin, 1996.

Ob Obuchenii Egerskogo Korpusa. St Petersburg, 1764.

Oelsnitz, Anton Leopold von. *Ofitserskie Uprazheniia.* St Petersburg, 1777.

Panin, Petr. *Nastavlenie ot predovoditelia vtoroi armii, General-Anshefa, Senatora i Kavalera Grafa Panina voisku emu vruchennomu, na predvoditel'stvo v nastupatel'nyia deistviia protivu voiska Turetskogo, sochineno pri vstuplenii v nepriiatel'skuiu zemliu, Iiunia 7 dnia 1770 goda.* Moscow, 1770.

"Particulars of the Storming of Praga." *The Times* (London), 23 December 1794, 4.

Pecherin, Fedor. "Zapiski Fedora Panteleimonovicha Pecherina, 1737–1816." *Russkaia Starina* 72, no. 12 (1891): 587–614.

Pekhotnyi Stroevoi Ustav. St Petersburg, 1768.

Petrov, F.A. et al., eds. *1812: Vospominaniia voinov russkoi armii*. Moscow: Mysl', 1991.

Pigarev, Kiril. *Soldat polkovodets*. Moscow: ORIZ, 1944.

Pishchevich, A.S. "Zhizn' Pishchevicha." *Chteniya v Obshestve Istorii i Drevnostei Rossiiskikh* 1, no. 1 (1885): 1–112; 2, no. 1: 113–273.

Poletika, P.I. "Moi Vospominania." *Russkii Arhiv* 3, no. 11 (1885): 305–36.

Polevshchikova, Elena. "Frantsuzkie volontery v Izmaile: neopublikovannaia zapiska grafa Lanzherona." *Deribasovskaia-Reshilevskaia: Literaturno-khudozhestvennyi, istoriko-kraevedcheskii illiustrirovannyi almanakh* 29 (2007): 6–11.

Polnoe Sobranie Zakonov Rossiiskoi Imperii.

Protasev, N. "S Stranitsy is starago dnevnika." *Istoricheskii Vestnik* 30, no. 11 (1887): 408–24.

Prozorovskii, Aleksandr. *Zapiski General-Feldmarshala Kniazia Aleksandra Aleksandrovicha Prozorovskogo, 1756–1776*. Moscow: Russkii Akhiv, 2004.

Rastopchin, F.B. "Anekdoty grafa F. B. Rastopchina o Suvorov." In Sergei Glinka, ed. *Russkoe chtenie Sergeia Glinki*, vol. 1 (Moscow, 1845).

Ribopier, Aleksandr. "Zapiski grafa Aleksandra Ivanovicha Ribopiera." *Russkii Arkhiv* 1, no. 4 (1877): 460–506.

Richelieu, Armand de. "Journal de mon voyage en Allemange." *Sbornik Imperatorskago Russkago Istoricheskago Obshchestva* 54 (1886): 111–200.

Rousseau, Jean-Jacques. *The Social Contract* (1762). London: Penguin Books, 2004.

Rzhevskii, Grigorii. *Sochinenie podpolkovnika Rzhevskoga*. Moscow, 1793.

Rzhevskii, Stepan. *Nastavlenie kakim obrazom v budushchem lagere proisvodit' uchenie kak v pekhote tak i v kavalerii*. St Petersburg, 1774.

– "Raznye Zamichaniia po zluzhbe armeiskoi." *Russkii Arkhiv* 1, no. 3 (1879): 357–62.

Salbukov, A. "Zapiski N. A. Salbukova." In *Tsareubiistvo 11 marta 1801 goda. Zapiski uchastnikov i sovremennkov*. Izd. 2e. St Petersbrug, 1908: 1–105.

Sanglen, Iakov. *O voennom iskusstve drevnyhk i novykh vremen*. Moscow, 1808.

– "Rasskazy Iakova Ivanovicha de Sanglena, 1776–1796." *Russkaia starina* 40, no. 10 (1883): 137–150.

Segur, Louis-Philippe de. *Memoirs and Recollections of Count Louis Philippe De Segur*. New York: Arno Press, 1970.

Selivanov, V. "Iz davnykh vospominanii." *Russkii Arkhiv* 1 (1869): 153–74.

Semanov, Sergei, ed. *Aleksandr Vasilevich Suvorov: slovo Suvorova, slovo sovremennikov, materialy dlia biografii*. Moscow: Russkii Mir, 2000.

Shtrandman, Gustav von. "Zapiski Gustava fon Shtrandmana, 1742–1803." *Russkaia Starina* 34, no. 5 (1882): 289–318; 43, no. 7 (1884): 55–86; no. 8: 271–88.

Skobelev, Ivan. "Rasskazy Russkogo Invalida." In Alexander Mikaberidze, ed. *Russian Eyewitness Accounts of the Campaign of 1814*, 189–98. London: Frontline Books, 2013.

Sobranie vsekh v vedomostiakh obeikh stolits, s 1787 po 1791 god vkliuchitel'no, reliatsii o voennykh deistviiakh protiv nepriiatelei rossiiskoi impreii. Chast I. Moscow, 1791.

Spisok Generalov po Starshenstu. St Petersburg, 1799.

Svistunov, Petr. *Stroevoi Ustav Pekhotnago Polku dlia Imperatorskoii Armii.* St Petersburg, 1762.

Suvorov, Aleksandr. *Nauka pobezhdat'* (1796). Moscow: Voennoe Izdatel'stvo Ministerstva Oboroni SSSR, 1980.

– *Nauka pobezhdat': mysli, aforizmy, anekdoty.* Moscow: Olma-Press, 1999.

– *Pis'ma.* Moscow: "Nauka," 1986.

– "Plan, poddanyi Suvorovym na utverzhdenie Eia Velichestvu Russkoi Imperatritse v 1795 godu." *Russkii Arhivi* 6–7 (1914): 159–90.

Tatarnikov, K.V., ed. *Materialy po istorii russkogo voennogo mundira, 1730–1801.* Moscow: Russkaia panorama, 2009.

– *Stroevye Ustavy, instruktsii i nastavleniia russkoi armii xviii veka.* 2 vols. Moscow: Russkaia panorama, 2010.

Tolstoi, D.A., ed. *Pisma Grafini E.M. Rumiantsevoi k eia muzhu feldmarshalu grafu P.A. Rumiantsevu-Zadunaiskomu, 1762–1779.* St Petersburg, 1888.

Tregubov, Nikolai. "Dela davno minuvshykh let." *Russkaia Starina* 136, no. 10 (1908): 97–108; no. 11: 311–28.

Tsebrikov, R.M. "Vokrug Ochakova. 1788. (Dnevnik ochevidtsa)." *Russkaia Starina* 9, no. 84 (1895): 147–212.

Tuchkov, Sergei. *Zapiski Sergeia Alekseevicha Tuchkova.* St Petersburg, 1908.

Ustav Imperatorskogo Shchiakhetnogo Sukhoputnogo Kadetskogo Korpusa. St Petersburg, 1766.

Ustav Ratnykh, pushechnykh i drugikh del. St Petersburg, 1777.

Ustav Voinskii o Konnoi Ekzertsitsii. St Petersburg, 1763.

Ustav Voinskii. St Petersburg, 1716.

Ustav Voinskii. St Petersburg, 1776.

Viazemskii, Andrei. "Zapiska Voennaia, 1774." In *Arkhiv kniazia Viazemskogo.* St Petersburg, 1881: 1–20.

Vinskii, Grigorii. *Moe vremia, zapiski.* New York: Oriental Research Partners, 1974.

Volkonskii, M. "Rasskazy P.M. Volkonskago." *Russkaia Starina* 16, no. 5 (1876): 176–90.

Volyntsov, Ivan. *Artilleriiskiia predlozhenii, dlia obucheniia blagorodnogo iunoshestva artilleriiskago i inzhenernago schliakhtnago kadetskago korpusa.* St Petersburg, 1777.

Vorontsov, Semen. "Instruktsiia Rotnym Kommandiram, 1774." *Voennyi Sbornik* 11 (1871): 33–46.

– "Zapiska grafa S.R. Vorontsova o russkom voiske (1802)." *Russkii Arkhiv* 3 (1867): 345–61.

Wickham, William. *The Correspondence of the Right Honourable William Wickham from the Year 1794.* London: R. Bentley, 1870.

Zagriazhskii, Mikhail. "Zapiski (1770–1836)." in A.A. Il'in-Tomich, ed. *Litsa. Biograficheskii al'manakh. Vypusk 2*, 83–102. St Petersburg: Feniks, 1993.
Zeidel, N.I. "Istoricheskie Anekdoty." *Russkii Arkhiv* 2 (1880): 236–40.
Zhurnal voennykh deistvii armii eia Imperatorskago Velichestva, 1769–1771. St Petersburg: Gosudarstvennaia Voennaia Kollegiia, 1772.

Secondary Sources

Aksan, Virginia. "The One-Eyed Fighting the Blind: Mobilization, Supply, and Command in the Russo-Turkish War of 1768–1774." *International History Review* 15, no. 2 (May 1993): 221–38.
Aleksandrova, N.V. "Spetsifika vospitaniia i obrazovaniia rossiiskogo dvorianstva v posledneii chetverti 18 veka." *Vestnik Cheliabinska* 1 (1998): 26–30.
Anderson, M.S. *War and Society in Europe of the Old Regime, 1618–1789.* Montreal and Kingston: McGill–Queen's University Press, 1998.
Archer, Christon I., John Robert Ferris, and Holger H. Herwig. *World History of Warfare*. Lincoln: University of Nebraska Press, 2002.
Aurova, Nadezhda. *Ot kadeta do generala: povsednevnaia zhizn' russkogo ofitsera v kontse XVIII – pervoi polovine XIX veka.* Moscow: Novyi khronograf, 2010.
– "Pomeschich'i biblioteki v kontse xviii-nachale xx vv." In *Sel'skaia Rossiia: proshloe i nastoiashchee. Materialy XII Vserossiiskoi nauchnoi-prakticherskoi konferentsii*, 53–61. Moscow, 2010.
Baiov, A.K. *Istoriia Russkoi Armii. Kursk Voennykh Uchilisch. Epokha Petra Velikogo. Epokha Rumiantseva i Suvorova. Epokha voin s Napoleonom.* St Petersburg, 1912.
– *Natsional'nyia cherty russkago voennago iskusstva v Romanovskii period nashei istorii.* St Petersburg, 1913.
Bartlett, Roger, and Janet Hartley, eds. *Russia in the Age of the Enlightenment.* London: Palgrave Macmillan UK, 1990.
Barran, Thomas. *Russia Reads Rousseau, 1762–1825.* Evasnton: Northwestern University Press, 2002.
Batishin-Kamenski, Dm. *Biografii Rossi'skikh Generalissimusov i General-Feildmarshalov*, vol. 2. (1854) Moscow: Kultura, 1990.
Bazhukov, V.I. "Poniatie voennoi kultury: problemy stanovleniia." *Sotsial'no-gumanitarnye znaniia*, vol. 1 (2009): 284–96.
Bekasova, Aleksandra. "Geroi Zadunaiskii: konchina, pogreblenie i pamiat o nem," *Naukovi zapiski* 1, no. 19 (2009): 655–73.
Bell, David. *The First Total War: Napoleon's Europe and the Birth of Warfare As We Know It.* Boston: Houghton Mifflin, 2007.
Benda, Vladimir. "Garnizonnye voennye shkoly v XVIII v." *Istoricheskie, filosofskie, politicheskie nauki, kulturologiia I iskusstvovedenie. Voprosy teorii i praktiki* 4, no. 18 (2012): 33–6.

Bennet, Helji Aulik. "Evolution of the Meaning of Chin: An Introduction to the Russian Institution of Rank Ordering and Niche Assignment from the Time of Peter the Great's Table of Ranks to the Bolshevik Revolution." *California Slavic Studies* 10 (1977): 1–43.

Berkovich, Ilya. "Discipline and Control in Eighteenth-Century Gibraltar." In Kevin Linch and Matthew McCormack, eds. *Britain's Soldiers: Rethinking War and Society, 1715–1815*, 114–32. Liverpool: Liverpool University Press, 2014.

– *Motivation in War: The Experience of Common Soldiers in Old-Regime Europe.* Cambridge: Cambridge University Press, 2017.

Beskrovnyi, L., ed. *M.I. Kutuzov: dokumenty.* Moscow: Voen. izd-vo, 1950.

– *Russkaia armiia i flot v XIX veke.* Moscow, 1973.

– *Russkaia armiia i flot v vosemnadtsatom veke.* Moscow: Voennoe Izdatelstvo, 1958.

Best, Geoffrey. *War and Society in Revolutionary Europe, 1770–1870.* Leicester: Leicester University Press in association with Fontana Paperbacks, 1982.

Bien, David D. "The Army in the French Enlightenment: Reform, Reaction and Revolution." *Past & Present* 85 (1979): 68–98.

Black, Jeremy, ed. *European Warfare, 1453–1815.* London: Macmillan, 1999.

– *European Warfare, 1660–1815.* London: University College London Press, 1994.

– *Rethinking Military History.* New York: Routledge, 2004.

Blanning, T.C.W. *Culture of Power and the Power of Culture.* Oxford: Oxford University Press, 2002.

Blaufarb, Rafe. *The French Army, 1750–1820: Careers, Talent, Merit.* Manchester: Manchester University Press, 2002.

Bogdanovich, M.N. *Pokhody Rumiantseva, Potemkina i Suvorova v Turtsii.* St Petersburg, 1832.

Bohac, Rodney D. "The Mir and the Military Draft." *Slavic Review* 47, no. 4 (Winter 1988): 652–66.

Bradley, Joseph. "Subjects into Citizens: Societies, Civil Society, and Autocracy in Tsarist Russia." *American Historical Review* 107, no. 4 (November 2002): 1094–23.

– *Voluntary Associations in Tsarist Russia: Science, Patriotism, and Civil Society.* Cambridge, MA: Harvard University Press, 2009.

Brandon, Pepijn. "'The Privilege of Using Their Legs': Leaving the Dutch Army in the Eighteenth Century." in *Desertion in the Early Modern World: A Comparative History*, ed. Matthias van Rossum and Jeanette Kamp, 73–93. London: Bloomsbury, 2016.

Browning, Peter. *The Changing Nature of Warfare: The Development of Land Warfare from 1792 to 1945.* Cambridge: Cambridge University Press, 2006.

Bruce, Anthony. *The Purchase System in the British Army, 1660–1871.* London: Royal Historical Society, 1980.

Burbank, Jane and David L. Ransel, eds. *Imperial Russia: New Histories for the Empire.* Bloomington: Indiana University Press, 1998.

Burke, Peter. *History and Social Theory.* Ithaca: Cornell University Press, 1993.

Cerenville, Jeanne Eleonore de. *Memoirs of the Life of Prince Potemkin: Comprehending Original Anecdotes of Catherine the Second, and of the Russian Court*. London: Printed for H. Colburn, 1812.

Cole, Laurence. *Military Culture and Popular Patriotism in Late Imperial Austria*. Oxford: Oxford University Press, 2014.

Conway, Stephen. *War, State, and Society in Mid-Eighteenth-Century Britain and Ireland*. Oxford: Oxford University Press, 2006.

Corvisier, Andre. *Armies and Societies in Europe, 1494–1789*. Bloomington: Indiana University Press, 1979.

Creveld, Martin Van. *The Culture of War*. New York: Presidio Press/Ballantine Books, 2008.

Crews, Robert. "Empire and the Confessional State: Islam and Religious Politics in Nineteenth–Century Russia." *American Historical Review* 108, no.1 (2003): 50–83.

Darnton, Robert. *The Great Cat Massacre*. New York: Basic Books, 1984.

Davies, Brian L. *Empire and Military Revolution in Eastern Europe: Russia's Turkish Wars in the Eighteenth Century*. London: Continuum, 2011.

– *The Russo-Turkish War, 1768–1774: Catherine II and the Ottoman Empire* London: Bloomsbury, 2016.

DeLanda, Manuel. *War in the Age of Intelligent Machines*. New York: Zone Books, 2003.

Dixon, Simon. *Catherine the Great*. London: Profile Books, 2010.

– *The Modernisation of Russia, 1676–1825*. Cambridge: Cambridge University Press, 1999.

Dobie, Madeliene. "The Enlightenment at War." *PMLA* 124, no. 5 (October 2009): 1851–4.

Dragomirov, M.I. *Izbrannye Trudy*. Moscow, 1956.

– *Uchebnik taktiki*. St Petersburg, 1879.

Dubina, Vera S. "The 'Distinction': Russian Nobility and Russian Elites in the European Context (the 18th–19th Century)." *Social Evolution and History* 7, no. 2 (September 2008): 80–100.

Duffy, Christopher. *The Army of Frederick the Great*. Newton Abbot: David and Charles, 1974.

– *Eagles over the Alps: Suvorov in Italy and Switzerland, 1799*. Chicago: Emperor's Press, 1999.

– *The Military Experience in the Age of Reason*. New York: Atheneum, 1988.

– *Russia's Military Way to the West: Origins and Nature of Russian Military Power, 1700–1800*. London: Routledge and Kegan Paul, 1981.

Dukes, Paul. *Catherine the Great and the Russian Nobility: A Study Based on the Materials of the Legislative Commission of 1767*. London: Cambridge University Press, 1967.

Dyke, Carl Van. *Russian Imperial Military Doctrine and Education, 1832–1914*. New York: Greenwood Press, 1990.

Efermov, I.I. ed. *Offitserskii Korpus Russkoi Armii*. Moscow: Russkii Put', 2000.

Eliseeva, O.I. "'Liubeznui moi pitomets.' Ekaterina II i G.A. Potemkin v gody vtoroi russko–turetskoi voiny." *Otechestvennaia Istoria*. 5 (1997): 25–39.

Emelianova, A.V. "Memuary o domashnem obuchenii detei v Rossii XVIII v.: istoriia publikatsii," *Dokument. Akhiv. Istoriia. Sovremennost* 14 (2015): 90–102.

Engelstein, Laura. "The Dream of Civil Society in Tsarist Russia: Law, State, and Religion." In *Civil Society before Democracy: Lessons from Nineteenth-Century Europe*, ed. Nancy Gina Bermeo and Philip G. Nord. Lanham: Rowman and Littlefield, 2000.

Feld, M.D. "Middle-Class Society and the Rise of Military Professionalism." *Armed Forces and Society* 1, no. 4 (August 1975): 419–42.

Fomenko, I.Iu. "I.V. Sabaneev i M. S. Vorontsov (po materialam RGADA)." In *Otechestvennaia voina 1812 goda: Istochniki. Pamiatniki. Problemy*, ed. V.R. Klimov, 47–56. Borodino: Gosudarstvennyi Borodinskii voenno–istoricheskii muzei–zapovednik 2016.

Fuller, William C. *Strategy and Power in Russia, 1600–1914*. New York: Free Press, 1992.

Garrard, John Gordon, ed. *The Eighteenth Century in Russia*. Oxford: Clarendon Press, 1973.

Gat, Azar. *The Origins of Military Thought: From the Enlightenment to Clausewitz*. Oxford: Clarendon Press, 1989.

Geertz, Clifford. *The Interpretation of Cultures*. New York: Basic Books, 1973.

Geisman, P.A., and A.N. Dubovskoi. *Count Peter Ivanovich Panin (1721–1789)*. St Petersburg, 1897.

Glinoetskii, N.P. *Istoriia Russkogo general'nogo shtaba*. St Petersburg, 1883.

– "Russkii General'nyi shtab v tsarstvovanie Imperatritsy Ekateriny II." *Voennyi Sbornik* 1 (January 1872): 5–64.

Golubev, A.Iu. "Suvorov's canons of army and state governance." *Voennaia Mysl'* 14, no. 2, (April 2005), http://www.highbeam.com/doc/1G1–135818498.html.

Greben'kov, V.N. "Metodologicheskii potentsial kontsepta 'viennaia kul'tura obshchestva' v istoricheskikh i poleticheskikh isledovaniiakh." *Vestnik Rossiiskogo gosudarstvennogo universiteta im. I. Kanta* 12 (2009): 83–9.

Grigoriev, Anatolii. "Chto Takeo 'voennaia kultura?'" *Zhurnal voennyi i literaturnyi*, http://wv2.vrazvedka.ru/index.php?option=com_content&view=article&id=138:—q–q&catid=88888906&Itemid=88888919.

Gruber, Ira. *Books and the British Army in the Age of the American Revolution*. Chapel Hill: University of North Carolina Press, 2010.

Hamburg, Gary. *Russia's Path toward Enlightenment: Faith, Politics, and Reason, 1500–1801*. New Haven: Yale University Press, 2016.

Hartley, Janet M. *Russia: 1762–1825: Military Power, the State, and the People*. Westport: Praeger, 2008.

– "The Russian Empire: Military Encounters and National Identity." In *War, Empire, and Slavery, 1770–1830*, ed. Richard Bessel, Nicholas Guyatt, and Jane Rendall, 218–34. New York: Palgrave, 2010.

– "The Russian Recruit." In *Reflections on Russia in the Eighteenth Century*, ed. Joachim Klein, Simon M. Dixon, and Maarten Fraanje, 34–42. Köln: Böhlau Verlag, 2001.

Hassel, James. "Implementation of the Russian Table of Ranks during the Eighteenth Century." *Slavic Review* 29, no. 2 (June 1970): 283–95.

Heuser, Beatrice. *Strategy Makers: Thoughts on War and Society from Machiavelli to Clausewitz*. New Delhi: Pentagon Press, 2012.

Hochedlinger, Michael. *Austria's Wars of Emergence: War, State, and Society in the Habsburg Monarchy, 1683–1797*. Harlow: Longman, 2003.

– "Mars Ennobled: The Ascent of the Military and the Creation of a Military Nobility in Mid-Eighteenth-Century Austria." *German History* 17, no. 2 (April 1999): 141–76.

Hosking, Geoffrey. "Patronage and the Russian State." *Slavonic and East European Review* 78, no. 2 (April 2000): 301–12.

– *Russia: People and Empire*. Cambridge, MA: Harvard University Press, 1997.

Houlding, J.A. *Fit for Service: Training of the British Army, 1715–1795*. Oxford: Oxford University Press, 1981.

Howard, Michael. *War and the Liberal Conscience*. London: Hurst & Co., 2011.

Hughes, Lindsey. *Russia in the Age of Peter the Great*. New Haven: Yale University Press, 1998.

Hull, Isabel V. *Absolute Destruction: Military Culture and the Practices of War in Imperial Germany*. Ithaca: Cornell University Press, 2005.

Iurkevich, Evgenii. "Phenomen 'poteshnykh' voisk v Rossii vtroroi poloviny xviii veka." In *Voina i oruzhie: Novye issledovaniia i materialy*, vol. 2, 428–30, ed S.V. Efimov. St Petersburg: Voenno–istoricheskii muzei, 2010.

– *Voennyi Peterburg epokhi Pavla I*. Moscow: Tsentrpoligraf, 2007.

Ivleva, Victoria. "Catherine as Female Ruler: The Power of Enlightened Womanhood." *Vivliofika: e--journal of eighteen-century Russian studies* 3 (2015): 20–46.

Jackson, Michael. "The Eighteenth-Century Antecedents of Bureaucracy, the Cameralist." *Management Decision* 43, no. 10 (2003): 1293–303.

Jones, Robert E. "Opposition to War and Expansion in Late Eighteenth Century Russia." *Jahrbücher Für Geschichte Osteuropas* 32, no. 1 (1984): 34–51.

– *The Emancipation of the Russian Nobility, 1762–1785*. Princeton: Princeton University Press, 1973.

Jones, W. Gareth. *Nikolay Novikov, Enlightener of Russia*. Cambridge: Cambridge University Press, 2009.

Kagan, Frederick W., and Robin Higham, eds. *The Military History of Tsarist Russia*. New York: Palgrave, 2002.

Kamenev, A.I. *Istoriia podgotovki ofitserskih kadrov v Rossii*. Moscow: VPA im. Lenina, 1990.

Kamenskii, Aleksandr. *The Russian Empire in the Eighteenth Century: Searching for a Place in the World*. Armonk: M.E. Sharpe, 1997.

Kamenskii, N.N. *Deviatyi vek na sluzhbe Rossii: iz istorii roda grafov Kamenskikh*. Moscow: Izd–vo OOO "Velinor," 2004.

Keep, John. "Catherine's Veterans." *Slavonic and East European Review* 59, no. 3 (1981): 385–96.

– "The Military Style of the Romanov Rulers." *War and Society* 1, no. 2 (1983): 61–84.

– "No Gauntlet for Gentlemen: Officers' Privileges in Russian Military Law, 1716–1855." *Cahiers du Monde russe et sovietique* 34, nos. 1–2 (January–June 1993): 171–92.

– "The Origins of Russian Militarism." *Cahiers du Monde russe et soviétique* 26, no. 26–1 (1985): 5–19.

– "The Russian Army's Response to the French Revolution." *Jahrbücher für Geschichte Osteuropas* 28, no. 4 (1980): 500–23.

– *Soldiers of the Tsar: Army and Society in Russia, 1462–1874*. Oxford: Clarendon Press, 1985.

Kennedy, Greg, and Keith Neilson, eds. *Military Education Past, Present, and Future*. Westport: Praeger, 2002.

Kettering, Sharon. "Patronage and Kinship in Early Modern France." *French Historical Studies* 16, no. 2 (Autumn 1989): 408–35.

Khalid, Adeeb. "Russian History and the Debate over Orientalism." *Kritika: Explorations in Russian and Eurasian History* 1, no. 4 (2000): 691–9.

Kivelson, Valerie. "Kinship Politics/Autocratic Politics: A Reconsideration of Early Eighteenth-Century Political Culture." In *Imperial Russia: New Histories for the Empire*, ed. Jane Burbank and David L. Ransel, 5–31. Bloomington: Indiana University Press, 1998.

Kochetkov, A.N. "Russkaia voennaia literatura i voennaia mysl' vtoroi poloviny XVII–nachala XIX v." In *Voprosy voennoi istorii Rossii: XVIII i pervaia polovina XIX vekov*, ed. V.I. Shunkov. Moscow: Nauka, 1969.

Kohut, Zenon E. *Russian Centralism and Ukrainian Autonomy: Imperial Absorption of the Hetmanate, 1760s–1830s*. Cambridge: Distributed by Harvard University Press for the Harvard Ukrainian Research Institute, 1988.

Korotenko, A.V. "Poniatie voennoi kultury: sushchnostnye kharakteristiki i itogovaia definitsiia." *Vestnik Povolzhskogo Instituta* (2013): 15–20.

Kramar, Zoltan. "The Military Ethos of the Hungarian Nobility, 1700–1848," in *War and Society in East Central Europe: Special Topics and Generalizations on the 18th and 19th Centuries*, ed. Kiraly K. Bela and Gunther E. Rothenberg, 67–79. New York: Brooklyn College Press, 1979.

Krasnobaev, Boris. *Ocherkii Istorii Russkoi Kultury xviii veka*. Moscow: Prosvishchenie, 1972.

Krimmer, Elisabeth, and Patricia Anne Simpson, eds. *Enlightened War: German Theories and Cultures of Warfare from Frederick the Great to Clausewitz*. New York: Boydell and Brewer Group, 2013.

Kruglov, Viacheslav. "Fenomen voennoi kultury." *Nezavisimoe Voennoe Obozrenie*. http://nvo.ng.ru/forces/2015–03–13/10_fenomen.html.

Kutishchev, A.V. *Armiia Petra velikogo: evropeiskii analog ili otechestvennaia samobytnost'*. Moskva: Kompaniia Sputnik, 2006.

Kuxhausen, Anna. *From the Womb to the Body Politic: Raising the Nation in Enlightenment Russia*. Madison: University of Wisconsin Press, 2013.

Langins, Janis. *Conserving the Enlightenment: French Military Engineering from Vauban to the Revolution*. Cambridge, MA: MIT Press, 2004.

Lalaev, M.S. *Istoricheskii ocherk voenno–uchebnykh zavedenii, podvedomstvennykh Glavnomu ikh upravleniiu*, vol. 1. St Petersburg, 1880.

Lebedev, A. *Russkaia armiia v nachale tsarstvovaniia Ekateriny II. Materially dlia russkoi voennoi istorii*. Moscow: Universitetskai Tipografiia, 1899.

Lebedev, P.S. "Preobrazovateli russkoi armii v tsarstvovanie imperatora Pavla Petrovicha, 1796–1801." *Russkaia starina* 18 (1877): 577–608.

Leckey, Colum. "Patronage and Public Culture in the Russian Free Economic Society, 1765–1796." *Slavic Review* 64, no. 2 (Summer, 2005): 355–79.

LeDonne, John. *Absolutism and Ruling Class: The Formation of the Russian Political Order, 1700–1825*. New York: Oxford University Press, 1991.

– "The Eighteenth-Century Russian Nobility: Bureaucracy or Ruling Class?" *Cahiers du Monde russe et sovietique* 34, nos. 1–2 (January–June 1993): 139–47.

– "Geopolitics, Logistics, and Grain: Russia's Ambitions in the Black Sea Basin, 1737–1834." *International History Review* 28, no. 1 (March 2006): 1–41.

– *The Grand Strategy of the Russian Empire, 1650–1831*. Oxford: Oxford University Press, 2004.

– "Outlines of Russian Military Administration 1762–1796." *Jahrbucher fur Geschichte Osteuropas* 31 (1983): 321–47; 33 (1985): 175–204; 24 (1986): 188–213.

– *Ruling Russia: Politics and Administration in the Age of Absolutism, 1762–1796*. Princeton: Princeton University Press, 1984.

Leer, G.A. *Zapiski strategii*. St Petersburg, 1877.

Leonov, O., and I. Ul'ianov. *Reguliarnaia Pekhota, 1898–1801*. Moscow: AST, 1995.

Levitt, Marcus C. *The Visual Dominant in Eighteenth-Century Russia*. DeKalb: Northern Illinois University Press, 2011.

Liutov, S.N. *Kniga v Russkoi Armii. Konets 18–nachalo xx veka*. Novosibirsk: Novosibirskii Voennyi Institut, 2001.

– "Russkaia voennaia kniga vo vtoroi polovine xviii veka." *Voenno Istoricheskii Zhurnal* 10 (2007): 63–6.

Lohr, Eric, and Marshall Poe, eds. *The Military and Society in Russia 1450–1917*. Leiden: Brill, 2002.

Longworth, Philip. *The Art of Victory: The Life and Achievements of Field Marshal Suvorov, 1729–1800*. New York: Holt, Rinehart and Winston, 1966.

Lopatin, Viachislav. *Potemkin i Suvorov*. Moscow: Nauka, 1992.

Lotman, Iuri. *Besedy o russkoi kul'ture, byt i traditsii russkogo dvorianstva*. St Petersburg: Isskustvo-SPB, 1994.

– *Izbrannye Statii*, vol. 1. Tallinn: Aleksandra, 1992.

– "K funktsii ustnoi rechi v kul'turnom bytu pushkinskoi epokhi." In *Stat'i po semiotike kul'tury i iskusstva*, ed. R.G. Grigor'eva, 529–40. St Petersburg: Akademicheskii proekt, 2002.

Lukes, Steven. *Individualism*. Oxford: Basil Blackwell, 1973.

– "The Meanings of "Individualism"." *Journal of the History of Ideas* 32, no. 1 (1971): 45–66.

Maczak, Antoni and Elizabeth Mueler-Leuckner, eds. *Klientelsysteme im Europa der Fruhen Neuzeit*. Munich: R. Oldenbourg, 1988.

Madariaga, Isabel de. *Politics and Culture in Eighteenth-Century Russia: Collected Essays by Isabel De Madariaga*. London: Routledge, 2016.

– *Russia in the Age of Catherine the Great*. London: Phoenix Press, 2003.

– *The Travels of General Francisco De Miranda in Russia*. London: Kitchen and Barratt, 1950.

Marasinova, Elena. *Psikhologiia elity rossiiskogo dvorianstva poslednei treti XVIII veka: po materialam perepiski*. Moscow: ROSSPEN, 1999.

– "Zakon i grazhdanin: K istorii politicheskogo soznaniia v Rossii vtoroj poloviny XVIII v.." In *Issledovaniia po istochnikovedeniiu istrorii Rossii (do 1917 g.)*, ed. N.M. Rogozhin, 290–311. Moscow: ROSSPEN, 2012.

Marker, Gary. *Publishing, Printing, and the Origins of Intellectual Life in Russia, 1700–1800*. Princeton: Princeton University Press, 1985.

McGrew, Roderick E. *Paul I of Russia, 1754–1801*. Oxford: Clarendon Press, 1992.

Meier, Christian. *Caesar*, trans. David McLintock. New York: Basic Books, 1995.

Melton, Edgar. "Enlightened Seigniorialism and Its Dilemmas in Serf Russia, 1750–1830." *Journal of Modern History* 62, no. 4 (December 1990): 675–708.

Menning, Bruce. *Bayonets before Bullets: The Imperial Russian Army, 1861–1914*. Bloomington: Indiana University Press, 1992.

– "Train Hard, Fight Easy: the Legacy of A.V. and His 'Art of Victory.'" *Air and Space Power Chronicles* (1986). http://www.airpower.maxwell.af.mil /airchronicles/aureview/1986/nov-dec/menning.html.

Meretskov, Kirill. *Na sluzhbe narodu*. Moscow: Politezdat, 1968. http://militera .lib.ru/memo/russian/meretskov/21.html.

Mikaberidze, Alexander. *The Russian Officer Corps in the Revolutionary and Napoleonic Wars, 1792–1815*. New York: Savas Beatie, 2005.

Miller, Forrest A. *Dmitri Miliutin and the Reform Era in Russia*. Nashville: Vanderbilt University Press, 1968.

Mirskii, Dmitrii. *A History of Russian Literature*, 5th ed. New York: A.A. Knopf, 1964.

Montefiore, Simon Sebag. *Prince of Princes: The Life of Potemkin*. London: Weidenfeld and Nicolson, 2000.

Myerly, Scott Hughes. *British Military Spectacle: From the Napoleonic Wars through the Crimea*. Cambridge, MA: Harvard University Press, 1996.

Nikanorova, Elena K. *Istoricheskii anekdot v russkoi literature XVIII veka: anekdoty o Petre Velikom*. Novosibirsk: Sibirskii Khronograf, 2001.

Norris, Stephen. *War of Images: Russian Popular Prints, Wartime Culture, and National Identity, 1812–1945*. DeKalb: Northern Illinois University Press, 2006.

Okenfuss, Max J. "From School Class to Social Caste: The Divisiveness of Early-Modern Russian Education," *Jahrbücher Für Geschichte Osteuropas* 33, no. 3 (1985): 321–44.

O'Meara, Patrick. *The Russian Nobility in the Age of Alexander I*. London: Bloomsbury Academic, 2019.

Orlov, N.A. *Shturm Izmaila Suvorovym v 1790 godu*. St Petersburg, 1890.

– *Shturm Pragi Suvorovym v 1794 godu*. St Petersburg, 1894.

Osipov, K. *Alexander Suvorov*. New York: Hutchinson and Co., 1944.

Outram, Dorinda. *The Enlightenment*. Cambridge: Cambridge University Press, 1995.

Papmehl, K.A. *Freedom of Expression in Eighteenth-Century Russia*. The Hague: Nijhoff, 1971.

Perkin, Harold James. *The Rise of Professional Society: England Since 1880*. London: Routledge, 1989.

Peskov, A.M. *Pavel I*. Moscow: Molodaia gvardiia, 1999.

Petro, Andrei. *Russkaia Voennaia Sila*. St Petersburg, 1892.

Petrushevskii, Aleksandr. *Generalisimus kniaz Suvorov*. St Petersburg, 1884.

Phillips, Thomas R., ed. *The Roots of Strategy*. Harrisburg: Stackpole Books, 1985.

Pichichero, Christy. *The Military Enlightenment: War and Culture in the French Empire from Louis XIV to Napoleon*. Ithaca: Cornell University Press, 2017.

– "Le Soldat Sensible: Military Psychology and Social Egalitarianism in the Enlightenment French Army." *French Historical Studies* 31, no. 4 (October 2008): 553–80.

Pinter, Walter. "The Burden of Defense in Imperial Russia, 1725–1914." *Russian Review* 43, no. 3 (July 1984): 231–59.

Pipes, Richard. "Militarism and the Soviet State." *Daedalus* 109, no. 4 (Fall 1980): 1–12.

Polovtsov, A.A. *Russkii biograficheskii slovar'*. St Petersburg, 1913.

Popov, Aleksandr. "K probleme tsennostnogo soderzhaniia poniatiia 'Voennaia Intelligetsiia.'" *Vestnik Severnogo Arkticheskogo federalnogo universiteta* (2008): 59–67.

– *Voennaia intelligentsia Rossii: ginezis, formirovanie i razvitie ee dukhovno-nravstvennyh tsennostei (x – nachalo xix v.)*. Ivanovo: Ivanovskii gosudarstvcennyi universitet, 2007.

Porterand, Roy, and Mikulas Teich, eds. *The Enlightenment in National Context*. Cambridge: Cambridge University Press, 1981.

Prescott, James Arthur. "The Russian Free Economic Society: Foundation Years." *Agricultural History* 51, no. 3 (July 1977): 503–12.

Proskurina, Vera. *Creating the Empress: Politics and Poetry in the Age of Catherine II*. Brighton: Academic Studies Press, 2011.

Pyl'nev, A.A. "Rekreatsionnyi zal Impertorskogo Sukhoputnogo Schliakhetnogo korpusa v iskhode proshlogo stoletiia." *Pedagogocheskii sbornik* 4 (1883).

Raeff, Marc. "The Eighteenth-Century Nobility and the Search for a New Political Culture in Russia." *Kritika* 1, no. 4 (Fall 2000): 769–82.

– *Origins of the Russian Intelligentsia: The Eighteenth-Century Nobility*. New York: Harcourt, Brace and World, 1966.

– *Understanding Imperial Russia: State and Society in the Old Regime*. New York: Columbia University Press, 1984.

Ragsdale, Hugh, ed. *Paul I: A Reassessment of His Life and Reign*. Pittsburgh: University Center for International Studies, University of Pittsburgh, 1979.

Randolph, John. *The House in the Garden: The Bakunin Family and the Romance of Russian Idealism*. Ithaca: Cornell University Press, 2007.

Riasanovksy, Nicholas. *A History of Russia*, 6th ed. New York: Oxford University Press, 2000.

Rich, David Alan. *The Tsar's Colonels: Professionalism, Strategy, and Subversion in Late Imperial Russia*. Cambridge, MA: Harvard University Press, 1998.

Roche, Daniel. *The Culture of Clothing: Dress and Fashion in the Ancien Régime*. Cambridge: Cambridge University Press, 1994.

– *France in the Enlightenment*. Cambridge, MA: Harvard University Press, 1998.

Rogger, Hans. *National Consciousness in Eighteenth-Century Russia*. Cambridge, MA: Harvard University Press, 1960.

Rogulin, N.G. *"Polkovoe uchrezhdenie" A.V. Suvorova i pekhotnye instruktsii ekaterininskogo vremeni*. St Petersburg: D. Bulanin, 2005.

Romanova, E.N. "Voennaia kultura i ee osnovnye kharakteristiki." *Vestnik Samarskogo Gosuniversiteta* 1 (2008): 213–18.

Rothenberg, Gunther E. "Nobility and Military Careers: The Habsburg Officer Corps, 1740–1914." *Military Affairs* 40, no. 4 (1976): 182–86.

Safronova, A.M., and O.S. Kravchenko, "Zakonodatelnye i normativnye akty o garnizonnykh shkolakh Rossii XVIII v." *Dokument. Arkhiv. Istoriia. Sovremennost* 14 (2014): 173–97.

Schimmelpenninck, David van der Oye, and Bruce Menning, eds. *Reforming the Tsar's Army: Military Innovation in Imperial Russia from Peter the Great to the Revolution.* Washington, D.C.: Woodrow Wilson Center Press, 2004.

Schmidt, James. "What Enlightenment Project?" *Political Theory* 28, no. 6 (December 2000): 734–57.

Schönle, Andreas, Andrei Zorin, and Alexei Evstratov, eds. *The Europeanized Elite in Russia, 1762–1825: Public Role and Subjective Self.* DeKalb: Northern Illinois University Press, 2017.

Schrader, Abby M. *Languages of the Lash: Corporal Punishment and Identity in Imperial Russia.* DeKalb: Northern Illinois University Press, 2002.

Scott, Hamish M., ed. *Enlightened Absolutism: Reform and Reformers in Later Eighteenth-Century Europe.* Basingstoke: Macmillan, 1996.

– *The European Nobilities in the Seventeenth and Eighteenth Centuries*, vol 2. London: Longman, 1995.

Sewell, William. *Logics of History: Social Theory and Social Transformation.* Chicago: University of Chicago Press, 2005.

Shavrov, K. *Kratkaia istoriia 11-go grenaderskago Fanagoriiskago generalissimusa kniazia Suvorova polka.* Moscow, 1890.

Shitkov, A.V. *Blagodarstvo v general'skom mundire. Timofei i Aleksei Tutolminy.* Staritsa: Starits tip., 2008.

Siegelbaum, Lewis H. *Cars for Comrades: The Life of the Soviet Automobile.* Ithaca: Cornell University Press, 2011.

Skalon, D.A., ed. *Stoletie Voennogo Ministerstva, 1802–1902.* St Petersburg, 1902–11.

Skritskii, Nikolai. *Georgievskie kavalery pod Andreevskim flagom. Russkie admiraly – kavalery ordena Sviatogo Georgiia I i II stepenei.* Moscow: ZAO Tsentrpoligraf.

Smith, Douglas. *Working the Rough Stone: Freemasonry and Society in Eighteenth-Century Russia.* DeKalb: Northern Illinois University Press, 1999.

Smith, Jay. *The Culture of Merit: Nobility, Royal Service, and the Making of Absolute Monarchy in France, 1600–1789.* Ann Arbor: University of Michigan Press, 1996.

Smitt, Friedrich von. *Suworow und Polens Untergang.* Leipzig, 1858.

Somov, Vladimir. "Nikolia-Gabriel Leklerk – uchastnik i propagandist pedagogicheskikh reform Ekateriny II." *Frantsuzskii Ezhegodnik* (2011): 200–17.

Speelman, Patrick J. *Henry Lloyd and the Military Enlightenment of Eighteenth-Century Europe.* Westport: Greenwood Press, 2002.

Starkey, Armstrong. *War in the Age of Enlightenment, 1700–1789.* Westport: Praeger, 2003.

Starobudtsev, Mikhail. "Sukhoputnyi Shchiakhetnuy Kadetskii Korpus kak universal'noe uchebnoe zavedenie xviii veka." *Uchenye zapiski universiteta imeni P. F. Lesgafta* 1, no. 131 (2016): 223–8.

Steele, Brett D. "Military 'Progress' and the Newtonian Science in the Age of Enlightenment," in *The Heirs of Archimedes: Science and the Art of War through the Age of Enlightenment*, ed. Brett D. Steele and Tamera Dorland, 361–90. Cambridge, MA: MIT Press, 2005.

Stevens, Carol Belkin. *Russia's Wars of Emergence, 1460–1730*. Harlow: Pearson Longman, 2007.

Stollberg-Rilinger, Barbara. "The Impact of Communication Theory on the Analysis of the Early Modern Statebuilding Processes." In *Empowering Interactions: Political Cultures and the Emergence of the State in Europe, 1300–1900*, ed. Willem Pieter Blockmans, André Holenstein, and Jon Mathieu, 313–18. Farnham: Ashgate, 2009.

Stone, David. *A Military History of Russia: From Ivan the Terrible to the War in Chechnya*. Westport: Praeger Security International, 2006.

Storrs, Christopher, ed. *The Fiscal–Military State in Eighteenth-Century Europe*. London: Ashgate, 2009.

Strachan, Hew. *European Armies and the Conduct of War*. London: Hyman, 1983.

Szabo, Franz A.J. *The Seven Years War in Europe, 1756–1763*. Harlow: Pearson/ Longman, 2008.

Taylor, Brian D. *Politics and the Russian Army: Civil–Military Relations, 1689–2000*. Cambridge: Cambridge University Press, 2003.

Van Creveld, Martin. *Command in War*. Cambridge, MA: Harvard University Press, 1985.

Vish, N. "Telesnye nakazaniia v voiskakh i ikh otmena." *Voennyi Sbornik* 279, no. 10 (1904): 133–42; no. 11 (1904): 113–24; no. 12 (1904): 113–48.

Volkov, S.V. *Russkii ofitserskii korpus*. Moscow: Voen. izd-vo, 1993.

Waegemens, Emmanuel, Hans van Koningsbrugge, and Marcus Levitt. *A Century Mad and Wise: Russia in the Age of the Enlightenment*. Groningen: Instituut voor Noord- en Oost-, 2015.

Wahlde, Peter von. "A Pioneer of Russian Strategic Thought: G.A. Leer, 1829–1904." *Military Affairs* 35, no. 4 (December 1971): 148–53.

Walicki, Andrzej. *A History of Russian Thought: From the Enlightenment to Marxism*. Stanford: Stanford University Press, 2000.

Werth, Paul W. *The Tsar's Foreign Faiths: Toleration and the Fate of Religious Freedom in Imperial Russia*. Oxford: Oxford University Press, 2014.

White, Charles Edward. *The Enlightened Soldier: Scharnhorst and the Militärische Gesellschaft in Berlin, 1801–1805*. New York: Praeger, 1989.

Whittaker, Cynthia. *Russian Monarchy: Eighteenth-Century Rulers and Writers in Political Dialogue*. DeKalb: Northern Illinois University Press, 2003.

Wilson, Peter H. "The Politics of Military Recruitment in Eighteenth-Century Germany." *English Historical Review* 117, no. 472 (June 2002): 536–68.

Wirtschafter, Elise. *The Play of Ideas in Russian Enlightenment Theater*. DeKalb: Northern Illinois University Press, 2003.

– *Religion and Enlightenment in Catherinian Russia: The Teachings of Metropolitan Platon*. DeKalb: NIU Press, 2013.

– *From Serf to Russian Soldier*. Princeton: Princeton University Press, 1990.

– "Social Misfits: Veterans and Soldiers' Families in Servile Russia." *Journal of Military History* 59, no. 2 (1995): 215–36.

– "Soldiers' Children, 1719–1856: A Study of Social Engineering in Imperial Russia." *Forschungen zur osteuropaischen Geschichte* 30 (1982): 61–136.

Wishon, Mark. *German Forces and the British Army: Interactions and Perceptions, 1742–1815*.

Basingstoke : Palgrave Macmillan, 2013. Bottom of Form

Wortman, Richard. *The Development of a Russian Legal Consciousness*. Chicago: University of Chicago Press, 1976.

– *Scenarios of Power: Myth and Ceremony in Russian Monarchy: From Peter the Great to the Death of Nicholas I*. Princeton: Princeton University Press, 1995.

Yavetz, Zvi. *Julius Caesar and His Public Image*. Ithaca: Cornell University Press, 1983.

Zhilin, Pavel. *Mikhail Illarionovich Kutuzov: zhizn' i polkovodcheskaia deiatel'nost'*. Moscow: Voenizdat, 1978.

Zhukova, Maria G. *Tvoi esm' az: Suvorov*. Moscow: Izdanie Sretenskogo monastyrya, 2006.

Unpublished Sources

Fedyukin, Igor. "Learning to Be Nobles: The Elite and Education in Post-Petrine Russia." PhD diss., University of North Carolina at Chapel Hill, 2009.

Floyd, Jerry Lee. "State Service, Social Mobility, and the Imperial Russian Nobility, 1801–1856." PhD diss., Yale University, 1981.

Hertz, Carrie. "The Uniform: As Material, as Symbol, as Negotiated Object." 2007. Unpublished paper.

Hines, Kerry Lee. "Russian Military Thought: Its Evolution through War and Revolution, 1860–1918." PhD diss., George Washington University, 1998.

Levin, Lev. "Chinoproizvodstvo v Rossii XV-nachala XX vv: Istoriko-pravovoi aspect." PhD diss., Sankt-Peterburgskii Universitet, 2004.

Nikitin, Oleg. "Moralno-psikhologicheskoe obespechenie deiatelnosti russkoi armii v XVIII v.: istoricheskii opyt, uroki." PhD diss., Voennyi Universitet, Moscow, 2016.

Wahlde, Peter Von. "Military Thought in Imperial Russia." PhD diss., Indiana University, 1966.

Index